THE MOST DANGEROUS BOOK

KEVIN BIRMINGHAM is a literary historian living in Cambridge, Massachusetts, where he teaches on the History & Literature program at Harvard. He earned his Bachelor's degree in English at Yale and his Ph.D. in English at Harvard. He was a bartender in a Dublin pub featured in *Ulysses* for one day before being unceremoniously fired. This is his first book.

THE MOST DANGEROUS BOOK

THE BATTLE FOR
JAMES JOYCE'S *ULYSSES*

KEVIN BIRMINGHAM

HEAD
of ZEUS

First published in the United States of America in 2014 by The Penguin Press,
a member of Penguin Group (USA) LLC

First published in the United Kingdom in 2014 by Head of Zeus Ltd

9 7 5 3 1 2 4 6 8

A catalogue record for this book is available from the British Library.

ISBN (HB) 9781784080723
ISBN (E) 9781784080716

Page 419 constitutes an extension of this copyright page.

Designed by Gretchen Achilles

Printed and bound in Germany by CPI Books GmbH, Leck

Head of Zeus Ltd
Clerkenwell House
45–47 Clerkenwell Green
London EC1R 0HT

WWW.HEADOFZEUS.COM

For Dad, who taught me about free expression

A NOTE ON THE TEXT

Much of the source material for this book derives from personal letters. I have made small changes to punctuation and capitalization where necessary. The occasional typo has been corrected from original documents, and abbreviations are spelled out. For example, Ezra Pound's references to "L.R." or "M.C.A." in various letters are changed to "*The Little Review*" and "Margaret Anderson." All italics are in the original sources unless otherwise noted in the endnotes. On the rare occasions where I speculate based on available documents, I indicate that in the endnotes. Please see my website for more extensive endnotes and a complete bibliography.

CONTENTS

THE MOST DANGEROUS BOOK

INTRODUCTION

W hen you open a book, you are already at the end of a long journey. It began with an author whose first challenge was to imagine the readers who would turn the unwritten pages. The author wanted to meet the audience's expectations and draw the reader in. The book would have a voice, a perspective and a consistent style. It would be accessible. If the book has characters—be they simple or complex, sympathetic or repugnant—the author would make them believable. They would stay in character and speak in a consistent idiom. The spoken words would be in quotation marks. The characters' thoughts and the story's action would be clearly distinguishable, and when the author began writing, the story's elements were sharpened. Clear boundaries staked out the pathways for the journey.

A publisher signed a contract with the author. The publisher researched the marketplace and weighed costs and risks against potential profits and demand. The publisher knew the trade. The publisher had published books before. The book had an editor who pruned and revised, who offered perspective and who sometimes said no. The book was probably advertised in various markets. The first copies were printed and bound months before publication day, and they were delivered without incident by the post office or private carriers. They were displayed openly in stores.

Whether the book is careless or thoughtful, disposable or durable, chances are the sales will dwindle. The printers will stop printing it, and the remaining copies will be sold off at a steep discount and left to languish in used bookstores. It will not change the way books are written, nor will it change the way you see yourself or the world around you. It will be swept up by the rising tide of culture and washed away. It will probably be forgotten.

If it is not forgotten—if it does change the way people see the world—reviewers and critics will be able to quote from its pages freely. Radio hosts will be able to mention the title on the air. Students will be able to check the book out of a library. Professors will be able to assign the book and deliver lectures on it without the fear of being demoted or dismissed. If you purchase the book, you will not be afraid to travel with it. No one will be arrested for printing it. No one will be monitored for distributing it. No one will go to prison for selling it. Wherever you live, your government probably protects this book against piracy. Your government has never issued a warrant for this book. Your government has never confiscated this book. Your government has never burned this book.

When you open James Joyce's *Ulysses*, none of these things are true.

So much has been written about what's exceptional within the pages of Joyce's epic that we have lost sight of what happened to *Ulysses* itself. Scholars have examined the novel's dense network of allusions, its museum of styles and its insight into the human mind so thoroughly that the scholarship buries what made *Ulysses* so scandalous: nothing, in *Ulysses*, is unspeakable. The book that many regard as the greatest novel in the English language—and possibly any language—was banned as obscene, officially or unofficially, throughout most of the English-speaking world for over a decade. Being forbidden is part of what made Joyce's novel so transformative. *Ulysses* changed not only the course of literature in the century that followed, but the very definition of literature in the eyes of the law.

This is the biography of a book. It charts the development of *Ulysses* from the first tug of inspiration in 1906, when it was just an idea for a short story—a Homeric name appended to someone Joyce met in Dublin one drunken night—to the novel's astounding growth during and after World War I as Joyce wrote out its 732 pages in notebooks, on loose-leaf sheets and on scraps of paper in more than a dozen apartments in Trieste, Zurich and Paris. And yet the years that Joyce spent writing his novel are just a portion of its story. *Ulysses* was serialized in a New York magazine, monitored as it passed through the mails and censored even by its most vocal advocate, modernism's unstinting ringleader, Ezra Pound.

The transgressions of *Ulysses* were the first thing most people knew about it. A portion was burned in Paris while it was still only a manuscript draft, and it was convicted of obscenity in New York before it was even a book. Joyce's woes inspired Sylvia Beach, an American expatriate running a small bookstore in Paris, to publish *Ulysses* when everyone else (including Virginia Woolf) refused. When it appeared in 1922, dozens of critics praised and vilified Joyce's long-anticipated novel in unambiguous terms. Government authorities on both sides of the Atlantic confiscated and burned more than a thousand copies of *Ulysses* (the exact number will never be known) because Joyce's big blue book was banned on British and American shores almost immediately. Other countries soon followed. Over the course of a decade, *Ulysses* became an underground sensation. It was literary contraband, a novel you could read only if you found a copy counterfeited by literary pirates or if you smuggled it past customs agents. Most copies came from Shakespeare and Company, Sylvia Beach's Paris bookstore, where, as one writer remembered, "*Ulysses* lay stacked like dynamite in a revolutionary cellar." It was the archetype of a modernist revolution—it is, in fact, the primary reason why we think of modernism as revolutionary at all.

Modernism's discordant, contrarian and sometimes violent aspects weren't entirely new. What was new was that this cultural discord became a sustained movement, and it was Joyce who had taken modernism's assorted experiments and turned them into a masterpiece. After *Ulysses*, modernist experimentation was no longer marginal. It was essential. Turmoil became the substance of beauty rather than the seed of chaos, and this peculiar aesthetic emerging from a more versatile sense of order seemed to usher in a new era. For what modernism rebelled against was entrenched empiricism, a century of all-too-confident belief in perpetual technocratic progress, in the ever-expanding limits of power and commerce, and in the order of things as tidy, sanitized and always available for public examination.

The enemy of the empirical is not the illogical. The enemy of the empirical is the secretive. All of the things empirical culture couldn't utilize, didn't want or refused to acknowledge were sequestered from the public sphere and classified as hazardous categories: the hidden, the uselessly subjective, the unspoken and the unspeakable. The apex of the secretive is the obscene. Obscenity is deeply, uselessly private—a category of thoughts, words and images so private, in fact, that to make it public is illegal. To claim that obscenity had some empirical, public value would have been absurd. It would have violated the confidence that supposedly built civilization. *Ulysses* was dangerous because it accepted no hierarchy between the empirical and the obscene, between our exterior and interior lives. It was dangerous because it demonstrated how a book could abolish secrecy's power. It showed us that secrecy is the tool of doomed regimes and that secrets themselves are, as Joyce wrote, "tyrants, willing to be dethroned." *Ulysses* dethroned them all.

For modernist writers, literature was a battle against an obsolete civilization, and nothing illustrated the stakes of modernism's battle more clearly than the fact that its masterpiece was being burned. Censorship was the tyranny of established cultural standards. In the United States and Britain, the censorship regime was a diffuse enforcement network empowered by mid-nineteenth-century moral statutes. Laws against vices like obscenity were designed to control urban populations, and the primary enforcers of those laws were quasi-official vigilante organizations that flourished because urban centers were growing faster than governments could handle. Cities like London and New York maintained their tenuous order largely through societies for the "suppression" of various blights: beggars, prostitutes, vagrants, opium and cruelty to children and animals.

One of the most successful organizations was the London Society for the Suppression of Vice, which helped write the anti-obscenity laws it enforced. The problem with volunteer-based censorship regimes, however, was that their power would ebb and flow with moral fads. Fluctuations in vice-society membership and finances ensured that they were never as effective as they wanted to be—pornographers simply adapted to a boom-and-bust business cycle. British vice societies were spearheaded by aristocrats who funded legal proceedings and publicity campaigns that were orchestrated by a revolving door of volunteers who weren't willing to do the unseemly work that stopping an illicit business required. They weren't on the streets nabbing pornographers. They didn't entrap suspects. They didn't carry guns. They didn't threaten or hound or rough anyone up.

Things were different in the United States, where the fight against obscenity could be brutal. From 1872 until his death in 1915, the single most important arbiter of what was and was not obscene was a man named Anthony Comstock. His forty-year dominance over artistic standards made him an icon, the personification of a cultural order that rejected the base impulses threatening both our salvation and our civilization. And lust, as Comstock explained, was the most destructive impulse.

> Lust defiles the body, debauches the imagination, corrupts the mind, deadens the will, destroys the memory, sears the conscience, hardens the heart, and damns the soul. It unnerves the arm, and steals away the elastic step. It robs the soul of manly virtues and imprints upon the mind of the youth visions that throughout life curse the man or woman.

Comstock saw human nature as a withering thing, a form of purity corrupted by the fallen world. His mechanism for rolling back the tide of lust was the United States Post Office, and his authority over the content of the letters, newspapers and magazines sent through the mail derived from a law that bears his name.

The 1873 Comstock Act made the distribution or advertisement of any "obscene, lewd, or lascivious book, pamphlet, picture, paper, print or other publication of an indecent character" through the U.S. mail punishable by up to ten years in prison and a ten-thousand-dollar fine, and state laws throughout the country—"little Comstock Acts"—extended the ban to obscenity's publication and sale. Armed with the power of the law, sworn in as a special agent of the Post Office and named the head of the New York Society for the

Suppression of Vice (NYSSV), Comstock destroyed books by the ton and imprisoned thousands of pornographers. By the 1910s, his bushy muttonchops served a dual purpose: they hearkened back to the values of an older era, and they concealed the scar left by a pornographer's knife. "You must hunt these men as you hunt rats," Comstock said, "without mercy."

Comstock was an instrument of God and the State, a guardian protecting vulnerable citizens from exotic influences, a defender of rigid principles over base impulses, of resolve over experimentation. He and his Society, in other words, represented much of what modernism opposed. By the time Comstock's successor, John Sumner, took over the NYSSV in 1915, publishers big and small were voluntarily submitting manuscripts for the Society's approval. Its power was so well established by World War I that Sumner was compelled to file criminal charges only in exceptional cases. *Ulysses* was one of them.

Joyce and his literary allies had to wage a battle against vigilantes, moralists, literary pirates, protective fathers, outraged husbands and a host of law enforcement officials—postal inspectors, customs agents, district attorneys, detectives, constables and crown prosecutors. The fight against charges of obscenity (which is still a crime) was about more than the right to publish sexually explicit material. It was a dimension of the larger struggle between state power and individual freedom that intensified in the early twentieth century, when more people began to challenge governmental control over whatever speech the state considered harmful. State control and moral control reinforced each other. Comstock's era of moral surveillance contributed to the rise of the federal government (the Post Office was its cornerstone), and the government's crackdown on subversive speech during and after World War I in turn helped the NYSSV expand its campaign against obscenity in the 1920s. Joyce, whether he liked it or not, was affiliated with anarchists, highbrows and the Irish—all suspect populations after 1917.

For the outspoken writers of the era, the battle lines were not drawn on the margins of art. They were central to it. When Joyce's unseemly candor left him unable to find anyone willing to publish or print his first novel, *A Portrait of the Artist as a Young Man*, Ezra Pound ranted in *The Egoist*, "If we can't write plays, novels, poems or any other conceivable form of literature with the scientist's freedom and privilege, with at least the chance of at least the scientist's verity, then where in the world have we got to, and what is the use of anything, *anything?*"

Pound was still railing against the Comstock Act in the late 1920s, when he wrote to Supreme Court Chief Justice Taft to ask for help overturning a statute enacted, he insisted, by "an assembly of baboons and imbeciles." Part of what made the Comstock Act so loathsome was that it underscored the fact that renegades and iconoclasts like Pound depended on the Post Office for their survival. For while modernism drew upon the turbulence surrounding World War I, when empires crumbled and millions moved across borders to exchange new ideas and radical styles, it was precisely its iconoclastic nature that made modernism beholden to the largest, most mundane government bureaucracy there was.

Modernists used mass cultural resources and marketing strategies even as they shunned the large audiences that inhibited controversy and experimentation. Rather than writing a novel for a million readers, Joyce said, he preferred to write novels that one person would read a million times. Modernists courted small numbers of avid, idiosyncratic readers scattered across countries and time zones, and one way to foster such a dedicated community was through boisterous magazines that could generate an ongoing creative exchange among far-flung readers and writers. But because modernist magazine readerships were too small for most bookshops and newsstands to carry, artists like Joyce needed an extensive, government-subsidized distribution system to bring subscribers together. It was the Post Office that made it possible for avant-garde texts to circulate cheaply and openly to wherever their kindred readers lived. The Post Office was also the institution that could inspect, seize and burn those texts.

THE DISPUTES OVER the astonishing content of Joyce's writing began years before *Ulysses* was published. We think of *Ulysses* as a mighty tome, but its public life began as a series of installments in a New York modernist magazine called *The Little Review*, the unlikely product of Wall Street money and

Greenwich Village bohemia. *The Little Review* was the brainchild of an extravagant Chicagoan named Margaret Anderson who moved with her partner, Jane Heap, to Greenwich Village and cultivated a magazine devoted to art and anarchism, ecstasy and rebellion. Their taste for conflict and publicity, however, infuriated their principal patron, Ezra Pound's friend John Quinn. Quinn was an irascible Wall Street lawyer, a resolute bachelor and probably the most important American collector of modern art during the 1910s and early twenties. He bankrolled *The Little Review* and became its overworked legal counsel despite his misgivings about the magazine's "editrixes." Quinn initially pegged Anderson and Heap as "willful women" before deciding that they were, even worse, typical Washington Squareites ("stupid charlatans and silly fakers"), and his opinion only deteriorated from there.

While this uneasy partnership of money and willfulness lasted, *The Little Review* managed to serialize about half of *Ulysses* from the spring of 1918 to the end of 1920. Installments of Joyce's book (sometimes less than ten pages) appeared alongside Sherwood Anderson stories, squabbles with other magazines, drawings and woodcuts of varying skill, Dadaist poetry ("skoom / vi so boo / rlez") and advertisements for chocolates and typewriters. Serialization exposed Joyce to strident responses from the magazine's readers. One subscriber praised him as "beyond doubt the most sensitive stylist writing in English" while another claimed he was helping to turn *The Little Review* into a "freak magazine" by "throwing chunks of filth into the midst of incoherent maunderings." Some readers found the filth powerful. The way Joyce "slings 'obscenities'" at readers inspired one Dadaist poet's rapturous praise ("vulgar!"), which probably didn't help when that particular issue of the magazine landed in court. The most ominous and influential reactions to *Ulysses* came from U.S. state and federal governments. The Post Office repeatedly banned *The Little Review* from mail circulation because of its chunks of Joycean filth, and in 1920 the New York district attorney—spurred by John Sumner and the NYSSV—brought obscenity charges against Margaret Anderson and Jane Heap.

"There is hell in New York about 'Nausikaa,'" Joyce wrote to a friend after hearing about the trial against his indicted episode. And yet in the aftermath of the New York troubles, he decided to make the episode filthier—and two subsequent episodes were filthier still. To casual readers, the long evolution of *Ulysses* made Joyce seem like either an uncompromising artist or a petulant provocateur stoking outrage by freighting his work with difficulty and offensiveness. "Each month he's worse than the last," one *Little Review* reader complained, to which Jane Heap aptly replied: Joyce "has no concern with audiences and their demands."

It was Joyce's independence from everyone's demands but his own that drew many people to *Ulysses*. Simone de Beauvoir remembered not only her "utter amazement" when she read the novel but also the auspicious moment when she actually saw James Joyce, "the most remote and inaccessible" of writers, "materialize before me in flesh and blood" at a bookshop in Paris. Since 1918, when *Ulysses* began to appear, Joyce had become an icon of individuality for the new century. He was a stateless wanderer living in self-imposed exile from Ireland. He had spent over a decade writing in obscurity and near poverty. He refused to yield to the demands of burgeoning governments and markets, to the laws that restricted the circulation of literature and to the readers that made literature a professional option in the first place.

And yet he was also an icon of individuality because he was so palpably a man of "flesh and blood." The body was central to Joyce's work because he was a captive of both its erotic pleasures and its intense pains. From as early as 1907 and into the 1930s, Joyce suffered from an illness that caused bouts of iritis (a swelling of his iris), which in turn brought about episodes of acute glaucoma and other complications that withered his eyesight almost to the point of blindness. He collapsed on city streets and rolled on the floor in pain during years of recurrent "eye attacks," and the agony of his illness was as traumatizing as the eye surgeries he underwent to save his vision—all of them performed without general anesthetic. When Joyce was not bracing himself before having his eye "slit open," as he described it, he endured a battery of injections, narcotics, disinfectants and dental extractions (seventeen, in fact, just in case his teeth were the cause) as well as applications of tonics, electrodes and leeches. From 1917 onward, Joyce had to wonder if the next attack—or the next surgery—would end his career.

Joyce's grievous health and feeble eyesight made him heroic and pitiable, inaccessible and deeply human. The images of Joyce wearing eye patches and postsurgical bandages or reading with thick spectacles and a magnifying glass gave him the aura of a blind seer, a twentieth-century Homer or Milton. Illness was taking away the visible world only to give him an experience whose intensity was too deep for others to fathom. Ernest Hemingway once wrote to Joyce after his son's fingernail lightly scratched his eye. It "hurt like hell," Hemingway said. "For ten days I had a very little taste of how things might be with you."

Joyce's life would become every bit as ravaged as Anthony Comstock would have expected, and yet Joyce's resilience encouraged even those unfamiliar with his work to see modern individuality as a sort of durable ruin persevering against uncontrollable forces. *Ulysses* turned that resilience into art. It reads like a desperate, beloved labor, a work of uncanny insight behind thick spectacles, a procession of desires and memories interspersed with spells of suffering and boredom. It is a work of ardor and arduousness, something fragile and yet indomitable. It is the book of a man who, even in a hospital bed— even with both eyes bandaged—would reach for a notebook under his pillow and trace phrases blindly with his pencil so that he could insert them into his manuscript when he could see again. It's no wonder that Joyce's fiction explored the interior world. Beyond his family, it was all he had.

Over time, Joyce's unstinting devotion to his craft established him as modernism's consummate artist rather than a mere provocateur—one does not write through so much suffering only to provoke. But the provocations were inevitable. Something about James Joyce and *Ulysses* inspired irrational hostility. Just before *Ulysses* was published, a man brushed past him as he was walking in Paris and muttered—in Latin no less—"You are an abominable writer!" The bile did not subside. In 1931, the French ambassador to the United States, the poet Paul Claudel, refused to help stop the piracy of *Ulysses* and declared Joyce's novel "full of the filthiest blasphemies where one senses all the hatred of an apostate—also afflicted with a truly diabolical lack of talent." Rebecca West complained that "the excrementitious and sexual passages

have a non-aesthetic gusto about them," and the surest sign of their inadequacy was the "spurt of satisfaction" one got while reading them. Yet Joyce's
writing wreaked havoc on the opinions of careful readers. West was "overcome by fury at Mr. James Joyce's extraordinary incompetence" though she
was nevertheless convinced that he was "a writer of majestic genius."

The fury *Ulysses* provoked was a part of Joyce's majesty. His fight against
censorship shaped the novel's public reception and enhanced the devotion
of kindred spirits (especially those who thought of themselves as besieged
individualists), but it did much more than that. The legal battles surrounding *Ulysses*—in a New York City Police Court in 1921, in a U.S. District Court
in 1933 and in a U.S. Circuit Court of Appeals in 1934—effectively turned
the standard bearer of an avant-garde movement into a representative of art
as a whole, a symbol of creativity fighting against the authority that would
constrain it. *Ulysses* removed all of the barriers to art. It demanded unfettered freedom of artistic form, style and content—literary freedoms that were
as political as any speech protected by the First Amendment. Freedom, after
all, can have no real meaning if it is taken away as soon as we tell the stories
about who we are. If we can't publish and read *Ulysses*, then what is the use of
anything?

Joyce's demand for absolute freedom gave him a special place in the arts
community, even among those who had torn opinions about his work. When
Sylvia Beach launched an official protest against the piracy of *Ulysses* in 1927,
167 writers from around the world signed it. W. B. Yeats helped Joyce obtain
grants during the war. T. S. Eliot promoted him throughout literary London.
Hemingway helped Sylvia Beach smuggle copies of *Ulysses* into the United
States. Samuel Beckett took dictation from Joyce when he couldn't see, and
F. Scott Fitzgerald offered to fling himself out of a window for him (the offer,
thankfully, was declined).

Several donors, including a Rockefeller, helped Joyce when times were
bleak. John Quinn purchased Joyce's manuscripts, and his devotion tethered
him to *The Little Review* and its legal misadventures long after he swore to
abandon its Washington Squareite editors. Joyce's most important patron was

a prim London spinster named Harriet Shaw Weaver, whose dedication to Joyce puzzled Londoners as well as her devout family. Miss Weaver, as she was known to everyone, subsidized Joyce during the years he wrote *Ulysses* and continued to support him until he died. And Sylvia Beach, as Joyce belatedly acknowledged, devoted the best years of her life to Joyce and his novel. One of the ironies of *Ulysses* is that while it was banned to protect the delicate sensibilities of female readers, the book owes its existence to several women. It was inspired, in part, by one woman, funded by another, serialized by two more and published by yet another.

Sylvia Beach's eleven printings of *Ulysses* throughout the 1920s helped make Shakespeare and Company a nexus for Lost Generation expatriates, and it was only a matter of time before the book's enduring appeal enticed larger U.S. publishers to mount a legal battle. In 1931, an ambitious New York publisher named Bennett Cerf became eager to acquire a risky, high-profile book that could jump-start his young company, Random House. Cerf teamed up with an idealistic lawyer named Morris Ernst, a founder of the ACLU, to defend *Ulysses* in front of patrician federal judges like Learned Hand, who reshaped modern law, and John Woolsey, who reshaped obscenity law.

It took a transformation of all of this—artists, readers, patrons, the publishing industry and the law—to make modernism mainstream. Publishers like Random House marketed modernism as a collection of treasures accessible to everyone, regardless of educational background—affordable books were supposed to be a democratic form of acculturation. But the marketing strategy for *Ulysses* was a federal court case. Its accessibility became secondary to its legality, and that was the impression of modernism that stuck: Joyce's novel represented not a finished monument of high culture but an ongoing fight for freedom. When the *Ulysses* case came before Judge Woolsey in the fall of 1933, Nazi book burnings had taken place only four months earlier, which is why owning *Ulysses* without ever reading it was not an idle gesture. In the ominous climate of the 1930s, Woolsey's decision did more than legalize a book. It turned a cultural insurgency into a civic virtue of a free and open society. The renovation of *Ulysses* from literary dynamite to a "modern classic" is a microhistory of the way modernism was Americanized.

———

THE PUBLICATION HISTORY of *Ulysses* reminds us that what makes Joyce's book difficult is a facet of what makes it liberating. *Ulysses* declared its ascendancy over stylistic conventions and government censors alike—the freedom of form was the counterpart to the freedom of content. The way people actually spoke and what people actually thought and did during a typical day became the stuff of art. This seems unremarkable until we remember that a full account of our lives had been illegal to put on paper for distribution. Novelists before Joyce took it for granted that a veil of decorum separated the fictional world from the actual world. To write was to accept that entire categories of human experience were unspeakable. Joyce left nothing unspoken, and by the time *Ulysses* was legalized and published in the United States in 1934, it seemed as if art had no limitations. It seemed as if the dynamite stacked in Shakespeare and Company exploded unspeakability itself.

The story of the fight to publish *Ulysses* has never been told in its entirety, though several scholars (including Jackson Bryer, Rachel Potter, David Weir, Carmelo Casado and Marisa Anne Pagnattaro) have examined some of the more infamous moments, and I am indebted to their important work. Joseph Kelly, for example, includes an illuminating chapter on the *Ulysses* trials in *Our Joyce*. Paul Vanderham's *James Joyce and Censorship* is the only full-length study of the subject, though Vanderham's book is an argument rather than a history—the events surrounding *Ulysses*, and the people shaping those events, are secondary to Vanderham's theory about Joyce's late revisions of the text and the critical strategies that followed. Several scholarly articles and book chapters examine the role of the *Ulysses* censorship within Joyce's career, the history of obscenity and the development of modernism, but the remarkable story about the book itself has always come to us in sidelong glances.

Four important biographies cover portions of Joyce's censorship saga from differing perspectives. Jane Lidderdale and Mary Nicholson wrote the definitive biography of Harriet Weaver, *Dear Miss Weaver*, which chronicles Weaver's involvement in Joyce's censorship troubles in London. Noël Riley Fitch's *Sylvia Beach and the Lost Generation* recounts Beach's arduous task of publishing *Ulysses* and her efforts to deal with its exacting author. B. L. Reid's biography of John Quinn, *The Man from New York*, documents Joyce's legal troubles in New York as well as Quinn's struggle to find a publisher for Joyce's book. Detailed as these biographies are, they necessarily offer limited insight into the story of Joyce's book. Quinn and Beach, for example, had little or nothing to do with the second trial, and Weaver had little to do with the first. The elaborate publication history gets lost even in Richard Ellmann's celebrated biography, *James Joyce*, which discusses the trials only in passing— Ellmann devotes two pages to the New York trial and only one page to the federal trial.

The disputes surrounding *Ulysses* encapsulated the dual rise of print culture and modern governmental power. They involved the history of censorship law, the pervasive fears of radicals, and the turbulent mixture of the smugglers, the vice societies, the artists and the cultures of some remarkable modern cities: Dublin, Trieste, London, Paris, Zurich and New York. If we want to see how a culture changes, we must examine how localities reimagine themselves through the creation and reception of their most enduring works. The biography of *Ulysses* gives us insight into the lives of all books, into the roots of our contemporary culture, into modernism and its most talked-about novelist.

There are at least eight Joyce biographies of varying seriousness. The first was published in 1924, when Joyce was only forty-two years old, and the most recent in 2012. One of the hallmarks of Joyce's genius was his ability to fold his hardships into elaborate designs, and yet nine decades of biographies have failed to capture the degree to which adversity (and persecution) inspired Joyce—it was probably not a coincidence that the idea for *Ulysses* came to him immediately after he received Grant Richards's rejection letter for *Dubliners*. Joyce wrote *Ulysses* through a world war, financial uncertainty, the threat of censorship and a serious, recurrent illness. A life in pain shaped the novel that Joyce called "the epic of the human body," and the nature of that pain has never been fully explored.

This book is the result of years of research involving hundreds of books, articles and newspaper accounts. It incorporates unpublished material in twenty-five archives housed in seventeen different institutions from London to New York to Milwaukee. The archives contain troves of manuscripts, legal documents, unpublished memoirs, official reports and countless letters. Several Woolsey family documents, photographs and home movies reveal a portrait of Judge Woolsey that we have never before seen, and his library in Petersham, Massachusetts, remains nearly unchanged since 1933.

The biography of *Ulysses* is more than the story of a defiant genius. Joyce's persistence and sacrifice, his talent and painstaking work, inspired the devotion of those around him, and he needed that devotion desperately—even the most individualist endeavor requires a community. Of all the people who made *Ulysses* possible, the most important is Nora Barnacle, the woman who fled Ireland with Joyce when he decided to become an artist, the woman whose letters inspired some of his most beautiful and obscene writing and the woman whose first evening with Joyce in 1904 hovers over everything that happens in *Ulysses*. The story surrounding the novel shows us how high modernism emerged from the low regions of the body and the mind. It shows us how artworks containing the extremities of experience—rapture and pain—went from being contraband to being canonical. It's a snapshot of a cultural revolution.

The battles over *Ulysses* didn't end literary censorship. They didn't usher in an era of untrammeled freedom or pervasive avant-garde aesthetics. But they did force us to recognize that beauty is deeper than pleasure and that art is larger than beauty. The biography of *Ulysses* revisits a time when novelists tested the limits of the law and when novels were dangerous enough to be burned. You do not worry about your words being banned partly because of what happened to *Ulysses*. The freedom it won shapes more than our idea of art. It shapes the way we make it.

PART I

Now, my darling Nora, I want you to read over and over all I have written to you. Some of it is ugly, obscene and bestial, some of it is pure and holy and spiritual: all of it is myself.

—JAMES JOYCE

1.

NIGHTTOWN

Dublin wasn't always like this. In the eighteenth century, aristocrats walked the paths of St. Stephen's Green and the spacious new avenues on the city's north side. Mansions and town houses with terrace gardens lined Rutland and Mountjoy Squares, and the clubhouses and ballrooms radiating out from the squares hosted salons and masquerades. Dublin had its share of elegance. It was, after all, a seat of power—the second city of the British Empire and the fifth largest city in all of Europe. Four hundred members of the Irish Parliament and their families supported fashionable shops, a professional class and a proud enclave of civilization.

But the Irish Parliament had become a nuisance, and after thousands of rebels and British soldiers died in the Irish Rebellion of 1798, a new law from London simply dissolved the Irish assembly to create the United Kingdom of Great Britain and Ireland. On January 1, 1801, the aristocrats and power brokers departed, followed by the professionals and the shops and the masquerades. Dublin's Georgian grandeur evaporated from all but a few streets lining the squares, and even there the remaining wealthy families seemed more like stubborn survivors with roots too deep to be removed. The larger properties became hotels, offices and almshouses, and the rest were divided up into tenements that were left to molder and decay. By 1828, a third of Dublin's houses were worth less than £20.

The city's population swelled in the nineteenth century as people from around the country came looking for jobs. Then the famine struck, and the refugees who escaped mass starvation in the countryside found themselves crammed in a squalid city and still hungry. Slaughterhouses were scattered among tenements sheltering dozens of people in airless rooms that bred dysentery, typhoid and cholera. The sewers, where they existed, emptied directly into the River Liffey, and the tides washed the waste back through the city so that the stench blended with the rich smells from brewery chimneys, streetside manure and waste heaped in tiny backyards. In some neighborhoods, children were more likely to die than see their fifth birthday, and still-rotting bodies were dug up from graveyards to make more room for the dead. Ireland's industries—shipbuilding, ironworks and textiles—were channeled northward to Anglo-Irish Belfast while Catholic Dublin remained stagnant longer than anyone could remember. By 1901, as Europe crossed the threshold of the twentieth century, Dublin stood as the overflowing wreckage of a bygone era.

In 1901, James Joyce was nineteen years old and ready to declare his antipathy toward his country. He wrote an essay for the Royal University's literary magazine attacking the Irish Literary Theatre for refusing to stage the best European drama. The Theatre was the primary institution of the Irish Renaissance, which had emerged in the 1880s as an expression of nostalgia for the days before the famine, when agrarian life dominated Irish culture. After the famine, one in four people were either dead or gone, and for Ireland's reeling survivors, the revival of Celtic folklore, countryside life and the Irish language became a form of nationalism without bloodshed. And yet Joyce considered Irish nationalism a provincial fantasy. The writers of the Irish Renaissance themselves (Lady Gregory, William Butler Yeats, John Synge, Sean O'Casey, George Russell, George Moore) were all wealthy Anglo-Irish Protestants mining Irish peasant themes.

Joyce's essay "The Day of the Rabblement" insisted that a century of decline made Ireland hostile to artists, so instead of Tolstoy and Strindberg, the Theatre produced mediocre plays that flattered the Irish public—it was, as Joyce put it, a "surrender to the trolls." For Joyce, being an artist meant storming the barricades of an entire society built on lies—no one had the courage to write what life in Dublin was actually like—but attacking the Irish Literary

Theatre was possibly the most ill-advised thing an aspiring Dublin writer could do. The Theatre dominated Ireland's small literary ecosystem, and alienating it meant alienating the people who could help him the most.

The university banned Joyce's essay, which should not have been surprising. In the place of Irish writers, Joyce celebrated apostates, including a heretic burned at the stake for insisting that God could be found in an atom. Joyce gravitated toward writers who turned art into an embattled faith, writers like Henrik Ibsen, the provocative Norwegian playwright who thrived on contempt. "To live," Ibsen said, "is to war with trolls." Joyce's essay was, in fact, partly inspired by Ibsen—he learned Dano-Norwegian to read the playwright in his native tongue and to write to him as he was dying. To carry Ibsen's spirit onward, Joyce and a friend printed eighty-five copies of the censored essay (the most they could afford) and distributed them around Dublin themselves.

Joyce's contempt for the trolls was a nineteen-year-old's preemptive defense against literary society's rejection: instead of evading that rejection, he courted it. One night in 1902, Joyce knocked on the poet George Russell's door uninvited. They began talking about literature, and Joyce expounded on the shortcomings of the Irish Renaissance into the early morning hours. William Butler Yeats, Joyce insisted, was pandering to the Irish, and Russell himself was not a very good poet at all. Joyce read some of his own verse and recited Ibsen in Dano-Norwegian. Russell was impressed, and he wanted Joyce to meet Yeats, Ireland's most important writer. "He is an extremely clever boy," Russell wrote to Yeats, "who belongs to your clan more than to mine and still more to himself."

Like most of Ireland's writers, Yeats was living elsewhere, but he returned to Ireland to stage a play just as Joyce was graduating from the Royal University in 1902. After Russell arranged a meeting, the two writers sat in the smoking room of a restaurant on O'Connell Street, Dublin's main thoroughfare. Yeats thought the young man had a disarming vitality. He was intense and soft-spoken, almost timid. But when Yeats asked Joyce to read some of his poems, the younger man replied, "I do so since you ask me, but I attach no more importance to your opinion than to anybody one meets in the street."

Yeats listened to Joyce's lyrics and prose sketches and decided he had "a very delicate talent," though he wasn't quite sure what the talent was for. Yeats explained that he himself was shifting from poems of beauty to experiments in Irish folklore. "That," the younger writer said, "shows how rapidly you are deteriorating." When Yeats protested that he had written his plays rather easily, Joyce said that made his deterioration quite certain. He stood up to leave, but turned back to Yeats. "I am twenty. How old are you?" Yeats said he was thirty-six, one year younger than the truth.

"We have met too late. You are too old for me to have any effect on you."

JOYCE LEFT DUBLIN for Paris a month after his graduation ceremony. He planned to enroll in the Ecole de Médecine, support himself by giving English lessons to Left Bank professionals and earn the medical degree his grandfather once held but his father failed to complete. He would be both a doctor and an artist, and with his first paycheck he would buy his mother a new set of teeth. A medical career was the least he could do for the family. The meager income his father earned when he had a job was siphoned away from the younger children and given to his promising eldest son for his education.

But Joyce was unprepared for Paris. The medical school demanded his enrollment fees up front and rejected his university degree before granting him, reluctantly, a provisional pass to attend chemistry lectures. He went for one day and quit. Living in Paris without friends, a career or a decent coat, Joyce fell into a rhythm of reading, writing and walking. He barely sustained himself by the fees he earned teaching English to his two students, desperate money orders from home and small payments for writing the occasional book review for London or Dublin papers.

Joyce measured the winter of 1903 by the hours he spent without food. Twenty hours today. Forty-two hours last week. Once, when the food finally came, he vomited. He developed a cruel toothache that made chewing painful. He would pass by the cafés near l'Odéon before giving his three *sous* to one of the women in wooden clogs selling steaming bowls of chocolate on the sidewalks. He used his tie to conceal the stains on the shirt he couldn't afford to launder. His mother sent nine shillings when she wrote to him in March. "How are yr clothes and boots wearing? and does the food you eat nourish you?"

It was in Paris that Joyce's life as an artist began in earnest. He threw himself into Aristotle, Aquinas and Ben Jonson at the Bibliothèque Nationale. When the library closed, he worked in his room at the Hotel Corneille by the flickering light of candles burned down to nubs. Joyce was working out the fundamentals of his craft. He wrote sweeping definitions of comedy and tragedy next to budgets and calendars in his penny notebooks.

The notebooks were also filled with small scenes he called "epiphanies," flashes of intensity that focused on a moment or an object. They were his first tentative steps from poetry to prose. One of his epiphanies was about the prostitutes of Paris walking along the boulevards. He described them as "chattering, crushing little fabrics of pastry, or seated silently at tables by the cafe door, or descending from carriages with a busy stir of garments, soft as the voice of the adulterer." An epiphany was not a miraculous dispensation from above but, as Joyce defined it, an insight into "the soul of the commonest object." Epiphanies were everywhere. Illuminations came out of small things, like God from an atom.

The challenge Joyce confronted was combining the ever-diminishing scope of his prose with his ever-increasing artistic ambition. Joyce wanted to distill an order out of history's chaos. He wanted to write a book that would usher in a new era. He wanted, as he later put it, "to pierce to the significant heart of everything."

On Good Friday, Joyce received a disturbing letter about his mother's health. In the early evening he crossed the Seine, stood in the back of Notre Dame Cathedral and observed his favorite mass of the calendar. The priest snuffed out the candles one by one, a shiver of awe swept across the darkening nave, and in complete darkness, the priest slammed his Bible shut to symbolize the Lord's death. When the evening service was over, Joyce walked for hours along the vacant boulevards before returning to his room on rue Corneille, where he found a telegram slipped under his door. He tore the seal open and folded back the sides.

MOTHER DYING COME HOME FATHER

JOYCE BORROWED MONEY from one of his students and returned to Dublin to be at his mother's deathbed. Mary Joyce lay in the front room of a two-story brick rowhouse on the north side of Dublin. A doctor diagnosed her with cirrhosis, though it was probably liver cancer—she was vomiting green bile. For Easter, she asked her oldest son to go to confession and take communion in her final attempt to coax him back to his faith. Joyce's objections to the Church had multiplied over the years, and her impending death did not dissolve them. Joyce stood next to his Aunt Josephine in the darkened room, with the acrid smell of his mother's sickness around them, and refused her request.

His mother's death throes went on for months, and her mind deteriorated through the summer of 1903. His father, John Joyce, hadn't held a steady job in years, and he returned drunk at unpredictable hours to a home of ten children. Four had already died. Nevertheless, Joyce's return from Paris provided comfort. Every now and then the children were cleared out of the front room so he could read sketches of his writing to their mother. Once while he was reading to her, he found his sister May, the quiet one, hiding under the sofa so that she could listen to the stories. Joyce told her she could stay.

The Joyces were a family in decline. John Joyce squandered a respectable inheritance by the time Joyce finished primary school, but they had reason to be hopeful that their oldest son was destined for success. Joyce devoured books and won school prizes. It was his honor to carry the family portraits under his arms from one house to the next whenever they were evicted. Their father would agree to move when the current landlord gave him a false receipt for rent paid in order to satisfy the next landlord. The family would pile their dwindling belongings onto a cart pulled up the street by a sullen horse, and Pappie, as his children called him, would sing defiantly cheerful songs while the neighbors and their children gathered to look at the Joyces outside. They migrated to eleven addresses in ten years. That was how Joyce learned about Dublin.

On a Tuesday in August 1903, Mary Joyce fell into a coma. The family gathered at the house and knelt down at her bedside. At some point, their uncle John turned around, saw Joyce standing in the middle of the room and gruffly gestured to his nephew to kneel. Joyce remained standing. While the other children prayed aloud, their mother's eyes suddenly opened, darted about and briefly made contact with her intractable son. Then it was over.

Her body was washed and clothed in a brown habit, and the mirror was draped with a sheet to keep her spirit from being trapped inside its reflection. Just before midnight, Joyce woke up his sister Margaret to see if they could catch a glimpse of their mother's departing ghost. They couldn't. He waited until everyone in the house was asleep, and then James Joyce, motherless, cried alone.

Mary Joyce's death stripped away the last vestiges of the family's middle-class stability, and Joyce sensed that doors were being closed on him. He wore his debonair tie and felt hat from the Left Bank, and he ambled through the streets of Dublin with a thin ashplant cane, but neither his attire nor his obvious literary talent could eclipse his circumstances. Joyce never drank during his university days, but after his mother's death the floodgates opened. First it was sack, then Guinness and then whatever was at hand. He usually drank with Vincent Cosgrave, one of his more listless former classmates, and Oliver St. John Gogarty, who belonged to one of Dublin's esteemed families. Three generations of Gogartys were physicians, and Oliver would be the fourth in a country where Catholic doctors were rare. The family had two Dublin homes, and Oliver wasn't bashful about his circumstances—he regularly sported a yellow vest with gold buttons. Gogarty and Joyce bridged their social differences with poetry, alcohol and irreverence. They spent long nights reciting Blake and Dante, holding forth on Ibsen and the Irish Theatre and singing French songs through the streets while most Dubliners tried to sleep.

Once, Joyce's drinking got him into a one-sided fight in St. Stephen's Green. He approached a woman who he did not realize was accompanied, and Cosgrave simply walked away while the man beat the would-be writer senseless. As Joyce lay bleeding in the dirt, a stranger, a reputedly Jewish Dubliner named Alfred H. Hunter, lifted him up and brushed him off. He steadied Joyce by the shoulders, asked the young man if he was all right and proceeded to walk him home just as a father would have done. Joyce never forgot it.

Joyce and his friends often ventured into Dublin's redlight district. Nighttown was a collection of shabby eighteenth-century houses crumbling into tenements near the Great Northern Railway terminus and the fetid horse stables on Dublin's north side. Painted facades with motley lamps in the windows were scattered among the tenements. There were dozens of brothels in Nighttown—more here than in Paris, actually. It was one of the worst slums of Europe, and the police had given up trying to enforce the law. Gogarty and Joyce would drink until they were "arse over tip," as Gogarty put it, and proceed to the more economical houses on the far end of Tyrone Street.

The walls of the brothels displayed pictures of the saints and the Blessed Virgin. In secret alcoves behind the sacred images the prostitutes hid hefty pieces of lead pipe in case someone started trouble, but Joyce was not a troublemaker. He paid with the money he earned writing book reviews, and his good humor made him popular in Nighttown. One of the women, Nellie, quite liked him. "He has the fuckin'est best voice I ever heard," she said. She even offered to loan him money—his poverty made him all the more endearing.

Nighttown was an escape from the miserable Joyce household on St. Peter's Terrace, where the family managed to stay for more than a year. Their father's gravelly voice bullied the children relentlessly. "Ye dirty pissabed, ye bloody-looking crooked-eyed son of a bitch. Ye ugly bloody corner-boy . . ." John Joyce would reach for the nearest threatening object—a tin cup if they were lucky, a pot stick if they were not—and launch it blindly at whoever happened to be nearest. After their mother died, Joyce, Stannie and Charlie took turns guarding their sisters. "I'll break your heart! I'll break your bloody heart!" John Joyce recycled the threats he used to issue to his wife.

Hardship inspired Joyce. His first fiction publication, in 1904, was "The Sisters," a story about the death of a syphilitic priest as seen through the eyes of a boy. Father Flynn dies after erratic behavior and paralysis, though no one will name the cause, and the boy is left to guess at the truth beyond the halo of silence. Joyce thought of Dublin as a massive den of syphilis, metaphorically and literally. Europe as a whole was a "syphilisation," he would later joke, and the disease accounted for the continent's manias. He planned a collection of short stories capturing the syphilitic paralysis at the core of Dublin's moral life. He wrote about the city's petty thieves and political hacks, its laundresses, abusive fathers and boardinghouses. He called the collection *Dubliners,* and he would write it in fits and starts over the next decade.

One day he began composing elaborate sentences that barely settled into images and scenes. Rather than a story for *Dubliners,* he was writing an over-wrought announcement unmoored from his careful epiphanies. The speaker prophesies the overthrow of old orders and aristocracies and proclaims the rise of a new conscience. Joyce wanted to reveal multiple eternities to unborn generations. He wrote the eight-page piece in one day and called it "A Portrait of the Artist." When the editors of a Dublin magazine rejected it as incomprehensible, Joyce decided to turn his sketch into a novel—rejection inspired him even more than hardship. He wrote eleven chapters in two months.

Since Paris, Joyce had been searching for an epiphany in a person. He thought the world's radiance could emerge from an erotic connection with a woman who became in his mind an amalgam of women he had seen in Paris and in Nighttown, and the fact that she didn't exist made it easy to sentimentalize her. "Thy love," he wrote, "had made to arise in him the central torrents of life. Thou hadst put thine arms about him and, intimately prisoned as thou hadst been, in the soft stir of thy bosom, the raptures of silence, the murmured words, thy heart had spoken to his heart." Contempt for the trolls was no longer enough. Joyce believed he would achieve true artistry only if he could find a companion.

2.

NORA BARNACLE

———

Joyce moved out of the house in March 1904 and rented a room close to the Dublin docks. He declined the university's offer to teach French (he suspected it was the priests' way of controlling him) and cast about for other options. He wanted to start a newspaper called *The Goblin* with one of his friends—all they needed was £2,000. Joyce and Gogarty talked excitedly about compiling an anthology of poetry and witticisms gathered from public toilets. Joyce thought of turning himself into a joint-stock company and selling shares. He imagined that the prices would go up for his lucky investors as soon as his publications began to change Western civilization, and his lucky 1904 investors could get him at a bargain.

One Friday in June, Joyce was walking down Nassau Street, where carriages and bicycles made way for double-decker trams rounding the corner of Grafton Street—people rode up top in the pleasant weather, their heads swaying above the railing advertisements. The drivers wound brass handles to speed the trams forward beneath cables that were spread out over the streets like broken spider webs. Amid the urban tableau, Joyce saw a tall woman he had never seen before striding up the street with her long auburn hair pinned down over her ears. She had heavy-lidded eyes, a mischievous smile and she moved with confidence. Joyce approached her, and she glanced at his dirty canvas shoes. He had smooth, flushed skin, a bold chin and clear blue eyes with an earnest look about them. She thought he looked severe, yet like a little boy.

When he asked, she told him her name in her low, resonant voice. "Nora Barnacle," she said. It was beautiful and absurd. "Nora" was right out of Ibsen, and she pronounced her surname *"Bear*nacle," like someone from the west of Ireland. In fact, she was from Galway City, a town of less than fifteen thousand, and the Joyces originated in Galway, so he already had something to talk about. Nora mentioned that she was a chambermaid at Finn's Hotel just up the street. She cleaned rooms, waited tables and probably helped tend bar in the meager redbrick establishment.

Joyce asked her to meet him Tuesday evening in Merrion Square, just steps away from Finn's Hotel. He arrived on time, but she never came. The following night, he wrote Miss Barnacle a letter.

> *I may be blind. I looked for a long time at a head of reddish-brown hair and decided it was not yours. I went home quite dejected. I would like to make an appointment but it might not suit you. I hope you will be kind enough to make one with me—if you have not forgotten me!*
>
> *James A Joyce*

NORA BARNACLE CAME to Dublin to escape what little semblance of a family she had. When she was five years old, Nora's mother sent her to live with her grandmother. The Barnacles had been barely able to keep their house together, and they had to send Nora to her grandmother when twins arrived and Nora's father lost his bakery because of his drinking. Nora was thirteen when her grandmother died. After her grandmother, it was the convent, and after the convent, Uncle Tommy.

Nora's uncle was a disciplinarian who warned his niece to be home on time lest she get a beating. In the evenings, he went looking for her through the streets of Galway while swinging a blackthorn stick. Nora was usually with her friend Mary O'Holleran when Uncle Tommy couldn't find her, and the young women were more brazen together. They dared each other to use foul language, and Nora wasn't afraid to say "bloody" or "God" or "damn" the way men did. They sneaked into their neighbors' gardens and stole vegetables, because if they'd eat a head of cabbage while looking into the mirror they would see the face of their future husbands. They would stick nine pins into an apple, throw the tenth away, stuff the apple into their left stockings and tie it with their right garters—*not* the left. When they put the apple under their pillow, they would dream of the man they'd marry. But it only worked on Halloween.

Nora had gotten more than her share of attention from men. A young schoolteacher named Michael Feeney sang songs to her, but he succumbed to typhoid in the winter of 1897, the same winter her grandmother died. Sonny Bodkin gave Nora a bracelet when she was sixteen, but tuberculosis ended that courtship. At the convent, they called her the "man killer." A young priest once invited her to tea at the presbytery and then pulled her onto his lap. The priest's hand was already under her dress before she could push him away, and he told her that *she* was the one who sinned by tempting him.

Sometimes Nora and Mary would put on trousers, neckties and heavy boots. They would tuck their hair under their caps and roam around Galway's Eyre Square disguised as men. Mary remembered hearing Uncle Tommy whistling his favorite tune as he walked toward them one night. "My love, my pearl, my own dear girl." As they passed within the length of his blackthorn, Mary muttered in a husky voice, "Good night," as if the three of them had just finished a pint together. Uncle Tommy paused for a perplexed moment as the two figures walked quickly away, and when they turned the corner they broke into fits of laughter over their triumph.

NORA CHANGED her mind after receiving Joyce's letter. On June 16, 1904, she met him in Dublin's Merrion Square and walked with him to Ringsend, an empty field by the docks on the eastern edge of the city where the River Liffey opens into the bay. There were no streetlamps, and they were alone. As she drew closer he could smell the balsam and rose from the scented handkerchief she pinned into her clothes, and he blushed when he felt the gentle tugging at his buttons. She pulled his shirttails up, nimbly reached her fingers inside and began. When he moaned, she looked at Joyce and smirked, "What is it, dear?" It was an important moment in literary history.

Joyce, eager to remain aloof, kept up his carousing, but every now and then he strolled into Finn's to see Nora, and the sight of his clothes and shoes embarrassed her. Considering his appearance, his letters to her were oddly formal. He insisted on signing his name "James Joyce" or "J.A.J." or with joking pseudonyms—anything but "Jim." So she did the same. "N Barnacle," sometimes, or "Norah Barnacle" (Joyce found the *h* appalling). He insisted on calling her "Miss Barnacle" when they were together, and by August he was still unsure how to relinquish the formalities. "How am I to sign myself?" he once wrote before refusing to sign at all.

But he wrote to her about her deep voice, her brown shoes, and the kisses she placed upon his neck like small birds. And as the summer went on, the days without her became longer. By the end of July, Joyce was frustrated and suspicious when he couldn't see her for more than two consecutive evenings. He took one of her gloves to help him pass the time until their next meeting, and he slept with it unbuttoned beside him, where it was quite well behaved, he wrote, just like Nora herself.

Few people approved of what was happening between them. Miss Barnacle was, after all, just a chambermaid, and despite his family's travails, Dublin thought James Joyce could do better. His brother Stannie thought her face was rather "common." Joyce's father didn't take the match seriously, and he laughed when he heard her name. *Barn*acle? "Oh, she'll never leave him." Joyce's friends went so far as to insult her in front of him. They were surprised that Joyce could be interested in a woman so uneducated—the Galway girl never got past grammar school. Cosgrave insisted that it wouldn't last and called Miss Barnacle by her first name just to nettle Joyce, if not to remind him that he had met her first. Joyce pretended to have the same indifference for their opinions in this matter as he had in all other matters, but the act was more difficult. "Their least word," he confessed to her in a letter, "tumbles my heart about like a bird in a storm."

Joyce was unsure how a serious relationship would affect his life as a writer. Despite his affectations, being an artist was not a pose or a passing fancy. It was who he was. To declare yourself an artist in 1904 Dublin was not an embarrassment. An aspiring artist didn't fear accusations of pretentiousness or irrelevance. Even if, as Joyce insisted, Ireland had failed its writers, art mattered, and like all things that matter, it required sacrifice. The question nettling Joyce was whether Nora fit into his life as an artist. He was torn between the isolation he had cultivated since his banned essay and the companionship he had craved since writing "A Portrait."

He tried to explain this in a long, oblique letter to Nora. He had left the Catholic Church years ago, he wrote, and everything he did was a part of the battle he waged against it. But it was more than the Church. The whole order of life seemed flawed—so many nations like encampments containing families packed up like miserable parcels going nowhere. "How could I like the idea of home?" he asked her, after growing up with a dissolute father who slowly killed his wife and nearly ruined the children who managed to survive childhood. Joyce feared he was destined to relive his father's mistakes. She wanted stability, and he was a vagabond. Yet he insisted that he wanted more than her caresses. Joyce hinted that he was ready to give something up for Nora, though his letter offered little more than hints. He wanted her to search for him through his words and find him hiding there like a child.

Joyce demanded that Nora demonstrate her love in the most exacting terms possible. She would have to reject the conventions he resented—marriage, the Church and the home. He wanted her to spurn him or guide him through "the central torrents of life." Nora had to study his letter carefully because the pages read like a finished puzzle unsolving itself. Each revealing moment was followed by a turn that seemed deliberately vague. What, exactly, did he want beyond her caresses? When she didn't respond, he wrote another letter imploring her to write back quickly. He had *thirteen* letters from her.

JOYCE WAS EVICTED at the end of August, which forced him to venture out to Oliver Gogarty's watchtower by the sea. Gogarty was living in one of the many Martello towers that had been built along Ireland's eastern coastline to repel a Napoleonic invasion. In 1900, the British War Office had decommissioned the towers, removed the howitzers and swivel guns, emptied the gunpowder magazines and abandoned them. Gogarty rented the granite tower on Sandy-cove, nine miles south of Dublin, for eight pounds a year.

For Joyce, the shoreside tower was a last resort. For Gogarty, it was a boyhood bohemia by the sand grass. Their conversations swerved from steep philosophy to sacrilegious japes. Gogarty would close his eyes and summon all of his medico-spiritual powers to make sure he got all of Jesus' platelets and white corpuscles into the wine at consecration, and Joyce matched it with his venereal version of the prayer at the end of the Mass.

> Blessed Michael, the ass angel, propel us in the hour of contact; be our safeguard against the wickedness and snares of the Syph Fiend; May God rebuke him, we humbly pray, and do Thou, O Prince of the Heavenly Host, thrust Syphilis down to Hell and with him all the wicked spirits who wander through the world for the ruin of tools. Amen.

Joyce did not remain in the tower for long. A dispute, which Gogarty said involved his playfully firing a pistol above Joyce's head, gave Joyce the impetus to do what he had been planning for months: he walked the nine miles back to Dublin in the middle of the night to leave Ireland forever. Joyce waited for Nora in Merrion Square the following evening with the hope that she would give up everything to be with him. He didn't ask her directly if she would go. He asked, "Is there one who understands me?"

WHEN NORA BARNACLE LEFT GALWAY, she did it alone in the middle of the night. She didn't say good-bye to her mother or Mary O'Holleran. When she wanted only brief escapes from home, she would tell her mother and Uncle Tommy she was going to church in the evening with Mary. The two friends would walk to the Abbey Church near Eyre Square, and when Nora said enough prayers not to raise suspicions, she would slip away to meet Willy Mulvagh, the only Protestant on Mary Street, while her friend waited in the pew. Nora and Willy went places where Uncle Tommy wouldn't find them, and she would return to the church hours later with details and a box of cream sweets.

But Uncle Tommy couldn't be fooled forever. When he forbade her to see him, she saw him even more. She wasn't in love with Willy, but she enjoyed the freedom and thrill of their time alone, and she was happy. But one night as she walked home, Nora heard the tapping stick and "My love, my pearl, my own dear girl." She didn't even need to turn around. Uncle Tommy followed her home.

When he entered the house after her, Uncle Tommy ordered Nora's mother out of the room and began beating his insolent bitch of a niece with his blackthorn stick. Nora fell down screaming and clutched his knees while her mother listened through the door. The sharp blows fell on her back and ribs as she curled up on the floor and trembled like an angry fist.

The next day Nora began her secret plans—the inquiries about jobs, the furtive packing, the one-way ticket for Dublin—and by the end of the week she was gone. Nora Barnacle gave up everything she knew to go to a city she had never seen and start a new life where she knew no one. She was nineteen years old, and her life was finally her own.

So when Joyce asked Nora, "Is there one who understands me?" Nora said yes.

3

THE VORTEX

———

Ezra Pound pushed the furniture to the edges of the study in Sussex so that he would have enough room to teach William Butler Yeats how to fence. Pound would lunge and retreat across the room while Yeats, twenty years his senior, would slash the air with his foil. They met in London in 1909, shortly after Pound published his first collection of poetry. A glowing review appeared in London's *Evening Standard*: "Wild and haunting stuff, absolutely poetic, original imaginative, passionate, and spiritual. Those who do not consider it crazy may well consider it inspired . . . words are no good describing it." Pound had written the review himself.

Pound began attending Yeats's Monday dinner gatherings in London. He dashed about with his wild mane of hair, flung himself into fragile chairs, and leaned back in luxuriant repose. His black velvet jacket and facial hair—a long mustache and a tuft on his chin trimmed to a point—were part of his poetic regalia. His flowing capes, open-necked shirts and billiard-green felt trousers rankled London's staid sensibilities. At one of Yeats's gatherings, Pound began plucking the petals off the red tulips on the table and, one by one, he ate them. When the conversation paused, Pound asked, "Would anyone mind having the roof taken off the house?" At which point he stood up and began reading one of his poems in his unabashed American accent.

Yeats needed a secretary for the winter of 1913–14 so he could focus on his work. He wasn't sure Pound's nervous energy made him suitable for the job, but Pound admired Yeats, and Yeats, at the time, needed the admiration. He had written virtually no poetry in the seven years before he met Pound, and he was still fighting rumors that his career was waning. But the winter retreat deepened Yeats's concentration. After breakfast, Pound could hear him through the chimney humming and chanting his poetry. Yeats would write while Pound read Confucius and translated Japanese Noh plays. When the afternoon weather was good enough to put away the foils, they took long walks or drank cider at a nearby inn. In the evening, Pound would read to Yeats from Wordsworth, Rosicrucian philosophy and *The History of Magic* before talking late into the night.

Ezra Pound was a brilliant editor, a good essayist and a mediocre poet, which is to say he's famous for all the wrong reasons. He thought good poetry was economical. Adjectives, for example, often obscured the object they tried to describe. He once wrote to another poet in exasperation, "Have you ever let a noun out unchaperoned???" When Pound edited one of Yeats's poems, he cut the first seventeen lines down to seven and whittled the last fifteen to eight, slashing every unnecessary word he could find and getting rid of abstractions that he blamed on Yeats's admiration for Milton. Pound had no patience for grand gestures to emotion. He wanted poems to treat objects directly—poetic emotions emerged from things.

This hardnosed turn from the ornamental and symbolic toward direct-ness and geometric austerity—a precision suitable to the machine age—was happening in various artistic circles. Painters rediscovered hardness through cubism, and Pound drew inspiration from the stark lines of London artists like Wyndham Lewis, Jacob Epstein and Henri Gaudier-Brzeska. When Yeats met Pound, Yeats was already abandoning escapist lyrics for poetry with "more salt," as he put it. Mythical themes paled against dire news. "Romantic Ire-land's dead and gone," Yeats wrote in his poem "September 1913"—he was no longer, as Joyce had said, pandering to the Irish public.

For Pound, the hardness of art was something empirical. A good poem was not a matter of taste. It was either right or wrong, like mathematics or chemis-try. "Bad art is inaccurate art," he declared. To rail against adjectives was to defend the truth, though it was far easier for Pound to edit the truth than to render it. One day he stepped onto the platform of a Paris metro station, and in the bustle of people he caught a glimpse of a transcendent face. As he turned to follow it, he saw another, and then another. He labored over a thirty-line poem about it and reused repeatedly before tearing it up. He was still thinking about that moment six months later, but when he tried to write it again he failed. A year after that, Pound finally finished the poem, "In a Station of the Metro," that cost him so much effort.

The apparition of these faces in the crowd:
Petals on a wet, black bough.

Two juxtaposed images, sharp and direct. No long-winded elocution, no tricks or persuasion, no tinsel or frills—there was not even a *verb*. He peeled away layers of rhetoric until all that was left was the epiphany. He named his theory of poetry *Imagism,* and he promoted it vigorously. He gave prescriptions for would-be *Imagists.* "Use no superfluous word." "Go in fear of abstractions."

Pound was reacting to what he considered contemporary London's sloppy, ill-fitting verse—a hand-me-down romanticism—with a poetic style that was, above all, new. "The artist," Pound wrote in 1913, "is always beginning." Pound's polemicism was a way to summon kindred spirits—his enthusiasm and his love of novelty anchored itself in clannishness. England's literary world was a constellation of groups, and Pound wanted one of his own. By the end of 1913, he was compiling an anthology of *Imagist* poetry, and he asked Yeats if he knew anyone he should add to his collection. Yeats said that he did. There was a young Irishman, about Pound's age, named James Joyce, who was unknown outside of Dublin but who might suit Pound's tastes. Yeats talked about Joyce's style and, it seems, his defiance and his abrupt departure from Ireland with Nora Barnacle, which had been the talk of literary Dublin. Yeats recalled a particular poem Joyce had written in 1903, "I Hear an Army," and while he searched for it, Pound decided to type a letter to Mr. Joyce.

Dear Sir:

Mr Yeats has been speaking to me of your writing. I am informally
connected with a couple of new and impecunious papers . . . they are
about the only organs in England that stand and stand for free speech
and want—I don't say get—literature . . . we do it for larks and to have
a place for markedly modern stuff.

Pound's letter was an unlikely request for materials. He never wrote to people he didn't know, he informed Joyce, but he was willing to give him a try. Then he wrote out longhand, as an afterthought, "—don't in the least know that I can be of any use to you—or you to me. From what W.B.Y. says I imagine we have a hate or two in common—but that's a very problematical bond on introduction."

WHEN EZRA POUND was seven years old, his parents told him to rewrite his letter to Santa Claus more politely. "My Dear Mr Santa Claus," the revision began, "If it pleases you to send me the following list of articles I would be very much obliged if you would." He wanted a tool chest, a battle ax and "a toy World." He left the United States for London to plunge into the center of everything because provincialism was one of Pound's enduring hates.

London was the largest city in the history of the world. With over seven million people, it was more than twice as large as Paris (the second biggest city), and the population had grown by nearly a million every decade since 1880. London's spectacular productivity generated its growth. Forty percent of London workers manufactured goods (furniture, armaments, light bulbs) that were sold throughout the British Empire with the help of a merchant fleet that dominated the seas. Despite New York's growing prominence, London was the financial center of the world. The city's exchange markets set global commodities prices, and the world's governments came to London to finance their projects. London's unprecedented size made the British government a pioneer in law enforcement. The city established its first centralized police department in 1829, and Parliament empowered it with laws banning public prostitution, gambling and obscenity—all for the sake of controlling large populations.

Yet the years before World War I were among the most turbulent in the city's history. As other nations began to challenge Britain's economic dominance, real wages and employment rates began falling, which radicalized British trade unions. Coal miners, dockworkers and railroad employees struck simultaneously. Food lay rotting on the docks and London's coal supply (over three hundred thousand tons each week) ground to a halt. British industries lost thirty-eight million workdays in 1912 alone. The political climate was just as volatile. Liberal electoral landslides led Parliament to cripple the power of the unelected House of Lords in 1911. The British aristocracy suddenly found itself without its traditional power to veto tax and spending bills, and their Lordships' vetoes on all other measures became temporary. The fall of the House of Lords signaled the decline of the old social order. Ezra Pound came at just the right time.

The most disturbing change was a wave of radical attacks throughout England. Radicalism should not have been a surprise for a city that sheltered political refugees like Marx, Trotsky and Lenin, all of whom had lived among the socialists and anarchists in the East End. Bombs were planted to sabotage the water supply. Windows were smashed on Downing Street as well as in government buildings and shops across the country—they used bricks, stones and hammers. A steel spike was thrown through the window of Chancellor David Lloyd George's cab, striking him inches away from his eye and cutting his face. Winston Churchill was horsewhipped at a train station. Empty houses, garden pavilions and churches were burned. Bombs exploded in Westminster Abbey, in churches, trains, castles and houses. Scotland Yard purchased its first camera to take surveillance photos of the suspects. They were all women.

England's most determined radicals were suffragettes. Despite the decline of the House of Lords, Britain's politics lagged far behind its culture. Women were earning university degrees, refusing unwanted marriages and becoming financially independent. In 1911, more than a third of London's workforce was female—an increase of 22 percent over the past ten years. Women were more important to the empire than ever before only to find that they had no voice in national politics.

The suffragettes' campaign for voting rights gained momentum when they began disrupting Liberal Party meetings in 1905. Suffragettes had no choice but to force their way into the democratic process, going beyond parades and Votes for Women banners. In 1910 several hundred women trying to storm Parliament met violent resistance from the police and male bystanders. Several women were injured, and two died. When suffragettes began hunger strikes in prison, the guards put them in straitjackets and used funnels to force-feed them semolina through their noses. At least one woman's nasal membrane was torn away. The public outcry against force-feeding led Parliament to pass the Cat and Mouse Act, which allowed authorities to release a hunger-striking prisoner and rearrest her as soon as she was healthy again. Officials seized suffrage headquarters and intercepted their letters, but the hunger strikes continued, as did the arson campaign, the window smashing and the bombings. Several suffragettes plotted to assassinate the prime minister.

The revolutionary mood swept London culture as well. The first sign of change was the Grafton Gallery's 1910 exhibition, "Manet and the Post-Impressionists." Post-Impressionism was the catch-all term for a generation of artists experimenting in the wake of Impressionists like Monet and Renoir. Museumgoers muttered harsh judgments. "Admirably indecent" and "pure pornography." One wall displayed a portrait of Madame Cézanne with bluish tones shading her flattened face. Her hands and dress seemed to have been left unfinished, as if Cézanne did not love her. One man laughed so uncontrollably in front of the portrait that he had to be escorted out of the gallery.

The Post-Impressionist show was unsettling partly because Londoners hadn't absorbed Impressionism—England's art world was decades out of style. In fact, the Grafton Gallery show was rather tame. Many of the paintings on display were from the 1890s. Gauguin and Cézanne were dead, Van Gogh was two decades in the grave, and the two most radical Post-Impressionists, Picasso and Matisse, were barely represented. Nevertheless, Post-Impressionism seemed to be a harbinger of social turmoil, as if the sketched, indistinct hands of Cézanne's wife rejected centuries of Western civilization's accomplishments. "To revert in the name of 'novelty' to the aims of the savage and the child," one critic wrote, "is to act as the anarchist, who would destroy where he cannot change." Anarchists, suffragettes and Post-Impressionists were militating against civilization.

For people like Ezra Pound, however, the Post-Impressionist exhibit was just the retail version of an underground art scene developing in Soho nightclubs and cabarets. After midnight, as London's pubs issued their last calls, artists gathered in venues like the Cave of the Golden Calf at the end of a tiny lane off Regent Street, where a single electric light shone over the entrance of a cloth merchant's warehouse. After knocking on the door, members and their friends lowered themselves through an opening resembling a manhole and descended a flight of wooden stairs into a large cellar with exposed beams latticing the ceiling. The walls were covered with goblinesque figures in orange and purple performing grotesque gymnastic feats. Golden Calf patrons watched Spanish gypsy dances, shadow plays and poetry readings. Cabaret singers and ragtime bands took their turns on the small stage, and half-drunk couples danced the Turkey Trot and the Bunny Hug, their chests pressed together until dawn. Even the women smoked cigarettes, and their hemlines were well above the ankle.

One of the artists to appear at the Cave of the Golden Calf was Filippo Marinetti, the leader of the Italian Futurists, who celebrated violence and dynamism rendered through an aesthetic of noise and speed. The veins swelled in Marinetti's head when he imitated explosions and the ratatat of machine-gun fire. The Futurist manifesto advocated wholesale cultural destruction, as if the future would not arrive until the past was burned away: "Set fire to the shelves of the libraries!" the manifesto commanded. "Deviate the course of canals to flood the cellars of museums! Oh, may the glorious canvasses drift helplessly! Seize picks and hammers! Sap the foundations of venerable cities!"

That cultural destruction became literal when suffragettes began slashing paintings in museums across London. In 1914, a woman named Freda Graham walked into the Royal Academy, pulled out a hatchet concealed in her muff and sliced up a portrait of the Duke of Wellington. Another woman punched holes into Venetian paintings at the National Gallery with a loaded cane. Yet another slashed John Singer Sargent's portrait of Henry James with a butcher's cleaver. There would be no peace in England until women had the right to vote. It made sense, in the heady years before World War I, to wage war through art. To the radicals, high art was largely a political invention, a propaganda tool justifying empire, so to attack museum culture was to attack imperial power.

No one exemplified the interchange between radical politics and art more than Dora Marsden, a renegade suffragette who would radicalize Ezra Pound and publish James Joyce's first novel. In 1909, Marsden led a march of thirty women to Parliament and was charged with assaulting a police officer by hitting him with her banner (she claimed it was an accident). After spending a month in jail, Marsden broke up a Liberal Party meeting by throwing iron balls through a glass partition. That earned her two more months in prison, where she went on a hunger strike, smashed her cell windows and tore off her prison clothes to protest naked. When the guards forced her into a straitjacket, Dora Marsden, at four foot ten, squirmed her way out.

Liberal Party meetings routinely became suffragist protest sites. When a young Winston Churchill addressed an audience in Southport in 1909, police officers surrounded the hall so that Churchill could rally support for a budget bill that the House of Lords vetoed. When he argued that the Lords should acquiesce to the House of Commons because it represented the will of the electorate, a voice shouted out from a ceiling porthole, "But it does not represent the women, Mr. Churchill!" The audience flew in an uproar. Dora Marsden had eluded the tight security by hiding in the hall's attic space the previous day and waiting through a night of rain and freezing temperatures. After haranguing Churchill for several minutes, Marsden and two accomplices were dragged off the roof and arrested.

In 1911, Marsden resigned from England's radical suffrage organization, the Women's Social and Political Union, because it was trying to steer her toward nonjailable activities. Because her ambitions were far larger than organizing cake sales and plastering Votes for Women signs on boats, she decided to expand the feminist movement beyond politics altogether by starting a magazine called *The Freewoman*. A suitably radical magazine, she believed, would foment "a vast revolution in the entire field of human affairs, intellectual, sexual, domestic, economic, legal and political." In the pages of her magazine and in Freewoman Discussion Circles, suffragists encountered socialists and anarchists for debates about taboo subjects like divorce, venereal disease, same-sex relationships, birth control and free love.

Marsden opposed everything that threatened individual freedom, including governments, churches and collectivist concepts like class, gender and race. The "centre of the Universe," she declared, "lies in the desire of the individual." Marsden drifted from suffragism to individualist anarchism—expanding the vote merely expanded the government's myth of legitimacy. Before long, she rejected all movement politics (the goal was to "destroy Causes" rather than join them) as well as all abstractions, which meant fighting language itself. The word *woman* "should be banished from the language," she declared. "Our war is with words." Her search for precise language, for a way to change the world through writing, led Dora Marsden to Ezra Pound and James Joyce.

Marsden embraced literature as a weapon against abstraction. Only "poets and creative thinkers" reveal the individual's nature—poetry gives us access to the center of the universe. *The Freewoman* was not particularly literary until 1913, when Rebecca West, who helped edit the magazine, put Marsden in touch with Ezra Pound. Marsden pressed him on his philosophy before she would work with him, and Pound's response was uncharacteristically tentative. "I suppose I'm individualist," he wrote to Marsden. "I suppose I believe in the arts as the most effective propaganda for a sort of individual liberty." Marsden's sharp questions stayed with him, and a couple of months later he wrote a defense of poetry that followed Marsden's lead. In "The Serious Artist," Pound claimed that the artist "presents the image of his desire, of his hate, of his indifference as precisely that," and only a report on individual desires could illuminate human nature. Marsden published his essay in 1913, and a tense but fruitful partnership began. When Marsden changed the magazine's name to *The Egoist*, Ezra Pound approved.

MARSDEN'S ABILITY to connect clear poetry to radical politics helped instigate a new phase in Pound's career. His essay for Marsden marked the genesis of that phase, for it was here that Pound began to see that what mattered most about art was its peculiar energy. Images like "petals on a wet, black bough" were clear and immediate, but their stillness didn't capture the twentieth century's vitality. A couple of months later, he found a word for art's energy: "a VORTEX, from which, and through which, and into which, ideas are constantly rushing." Vorticism was Imagism with the verbs put back in.

The key to the Vortex was that its energy was collective. It drew its power not from individual genius but from a gathering swirl of talent, and a frenetic style would, ideally, begin to draw the movement together. In June 1914, Ezra Pound and Wyndham Lewis published an oversized, 160-page Vorticist magazine with the title thrown diagonally across the magenta cover in a screaming font: *BLAST*. "WE ONLY WANT THE WORLD TO LIVE," the Vorticists proclaimed, "and to feel its crude energy flowing through us." Vorticism combined Marinetti's belligerent triumphalism, suffragette radicalism and Dora Marsden's individualist anarchism. *Blast* was dedicated "TO THE INDIVIDUAL" and praised the suffragettes:

WE ADMIRE YOUR ENERGY. YOU AND ARTISTS

ARE THE ONLY THINGS (YOU DON'T MIND

BEING CALLED THINGS?) LEFT IN ENGLAND

WITH A LITTLE LIFE IN THEM.

Oversized type named everything the Vorticists would destroy. Blast the British Academy. Blast Henri Bergson, the Post Office and cod-liver oil. Blast every year between 1837 and 1900 (Queen Victoria's reign). After the blasted, the manifesto named the blessed. Bless England's great ports. Bless the hairdresser ("He attacks Mother Nature for a small fee"). Bless French pornography ("great enemy of progress"). Bless Oliver Cromwell and castor oil. Bless James Joyce.

Joyce had responded to Pound's letter in January 1914. He was in Trieste, the Austrian Empire's Mediterranean seaport, and he sent Pound a typescript of *Dubliners*, a detailed account of his publishing woes and the first chapter of his first novel, *A Portrait of the Artist as a Young Man*. He had spent the previous decade writing the thinly veiled autobiography, and the process was unforeseeably frustrating—at one point he threw his one-thousand-page manuscript into the fire (only half of the hastily rescued pages survive), and he wrote *Dubliners* partly as a diversion. But Joyce pared back the manuscript so that the artist's epiphanies studded Dublin's squalor, and when Pound read it he knew immediately that Joyce was among the blessed.

He sent chapters of *A Portrait* to *The Egoist* as soon as he received them, and he began thinking of ways to have Joyce paid for his work so that he wouldn't waste his time teaching English. He reached across Europe to pull Joyce into the Vortex. "I'm not supposed to know much about prose," Pound responded, "but I think your novel is damn fine stuff." And it would get better. The end of *A Portrait* is a series of diary entries from the artist, Stephen Dedalus, before he flees Dublin for Paris. The final pages were a stepping-stone toward the vast, unvarnished interior monologues that Joyce was just beginning to imagine. They were the first auspicious glimmers of a much larger novel gathering in the vortex of Joyce's mind.

4.

TRIESTE

———

James Joyce began writing *Ulysses* at the edge of a war that changed people's understanding of scale. In June 1914, a Serbian assassin walked up to Archduke Ferdinand's motorcade in Sarajevo with a semiautomatic pistol, and by the end of the summer bombs were rumbling across Europe. The benchmark for a destructive European conflict was the Franco-Prussian War in 1870. In the summer of 1914, that war's 250,000 dead soldiers seemed like victims of antiquated tactics. Modern weapons were so powerful that all anyone had to do was attack first to win—an invader would conquer in a matter of weeks. Everyone thought the same thing, and everyone was wrong by orders of magnitude. The Great War would last years. It would kill seven million civilians and ten million soldiers. And that was only part of it. The troop movements, the overflowing field hospitals and the miles of trenches laid the groundwork for the devastation of 1918, the Spanish flu. More than fifty million people were killed by particles too small for any existing microscope to see. The world was decimated by machine guns, fragmentation grenades and coiled packets of viral RNA.

Joyce never imagined the looming destruction when he left Ireland with Nora in 1904. They planned an unexceptional life in Paris's Left Bank, where he would write and teach English and she would become a laundress, perhaps, or a seamstress. Joyce contacted the Berlitz School for a job opening and spent weeks scraping together money from anyone who would help, but he never told his father he was leaving with Nora Barnacle. When they departed from Dublin, Nora watched Joyce take leave of his family from a distance before she went striding up the ferry's gangplank to start a life with a man she had known for less than four months. Joyce endured three years of silence before his father unburdened himself of his disappointment: "I saw a life of promise crossed and a future that might have been brilliant blasted in one breath." Nora had no one to be disappointed in her. Neither of them would ever live in Ireland again.

But they never made it to Paris. After taking a temporary job in Pula, a small outpost on the Istrian peninsula, Berlitz found Joyce a long-term position in Trieste, the Austrian Empire's only merchant seaport. Trieste was a gateway to Vienna, Ljubljana and Milan, and it was the second-largest port in the Mediterranean. Twelve thousand ships carrying 2.5 million tons of cargo passed through Trieste every year, and the city's population grew by over a third in the first decade of the twentieth century. By the time Joyce and Nora arrived in 1905, there was a large demand for foreign language instruction—one trip to the market indicated how polyglot the city was. Italian dialects clashed with German, Czech and Greek. Albanians and Serbs haggled over prices while Croatians and Slovenians half-guessed their way through conversations. If Joyce had wanted to escape Ireland's provinciality, he had found the perfect place.

Merchant ships from far-flung ports wedged themselves into the Grand Canal bringing fruits, spices, barrels of Arabian coffee and olive oil from around the Mediterranean. Steamships arrived with rubber and timber to build an empire, and Trieste's wealth accentuated the young Irish couple's poverty. They watched men in bowler hats tapping canes with handles made of ivory or gold rather than Joyce's humble ashplant. Women wore ample Viennese gowns with ostrich feathers soaring above their hats. They would nudge each other and laugh at Nora's cheap skirt, whispering words that, thankfully, she couldn't understand.

Nora was pregnant when they arrived in Trieste, and landladies balked when she began to show. There was no ring on her finger, and the backlash was nearly as bad in Trieste as it would have been in Dublin. Nevertheless,

Joyce remained adamant: asking a priest or a lawyer to ratify their relationship was out of the question. Joyce believed that marriage was the first step toward foisting upon their children the same nightmares of history and belief that they had traveled so far to escape. It was a coercive institution of property and power, and Nora's pregnancy made that coercion clear—the couple was forced to leave three different flats.

In late July 1905, Nora gave birth to a boy. The baby came a month earlier than expected (the new parents had miscalculated), and Joyce named his son Giorgio in honor of his deceased brother George. About a year later, Nora was pregnant again. When Lucia was born in the hospital's pauper's ward in June 1907, the nurses gave Nora twenty crowns. The Irish couple had officially become a charity case.

Fatherhood was a burden for Joyce. At twenty-three, he was unprepared for the responsibility, and the prospect of dragging children from one impoverished household to another, as his own father had done, haunted him. The passionate life with Nora was fading, and she was indifferent to his work, which was more vexing than if she had despised it. When she saw him copying small scenes into his manuscript from loose sheets, she asked, "Will all that paper be wasted?"

Joyce's brother Stannie joined them in Trieste a couple of months after Giorgio's birth. He took a job at Berlitz, and together they made eighty-five crowns a week. It was on the lower end of the average Triestine salary, but it would have been sufficient for a thrifty lifestyle. To save money, they shared a flat on the outskirts of town with the school's other English teacher, Alessandro Francini, and his wife. But Joyce was bad with money. Instead of saving the few spare crowns they had, he insisted that they dine out at restaurants, preferably the one with electric lighting. Later in the evenings, he would venture into the Cittavecchia, the old city, passing small wineshops and trundling oxcarts—some of the streets were too steep and narrow for carriages. He was drawn to working-class trattorias and grungy *osterie* where men shouted at one another in Czech or Hungarian. Joyce drank absinthe and sang songs with the wharf porters before making his way to the brothels.

When he didn't return home one night, Francini searched the Cittavecchia and found Joyce's limp body lying in the gutter. It was usually Stannie's job to find him. He would drag his older brother back home from a bar, and the Francinis would listen to the Irish brothers insulting each other in a lilting, Dante-esque Italian they had learned in school. Stannie once scolded him, "Do you want to go blind? Do you want to go about with a little dog?" Nora's barbs were sharper: "Faith I tell you I'll have the children baptized tomorrow." But no threat was effective. Joyce asked the Berlitz director for advances on his wages whenever the money ran out. He drank to evade the burden of father-hood, and the expenses of drinking increased his burden, which compelled him to drink more. One night, when Joyce came home insensibly drunk after squandering money they hadn't yet earned, Stannie began beating him. Francini could hear the awful sounds from his room. He got out of bed, despite his wife's objections, and told Stannie, "It's no use."

JOYCE TAUGHT ENGLISH by giving his students evocative, idiosyncratic passages to recite and copy down.

> Ireland is a great country. They call it the Emerald Isle. The Metropolitan Government, after so many centuries of having it by the throat, has reduced it to a specter. Now it is a briar patch. They sowed it with famine, syphilis, superstition, and alcoholism. Up sprouted Puritans, Jesuits, and bigots.

They were, at times, like epiphanies, commonplace observations leading to deep insight.

> The tax collector is an idiot who is always annoying me. He has filled my desk with little sheets marked "Warning," "Warning," "Warning." I told him that if he didn't stop it, I would send him to be f . . . ound out by that swindler, his master. Today, the swindler is the government of

Vienna. Tomorrow it could be the one in Rome. But whether in Vienna or Rome or London, to me governments are all the same, pirates.

His students, bewildered as they must have been, would not forget the word *swindler*.

Joyce thought governments were swindlers and pirates because their authority was nonnegotiable. To be a citizen of a state was to be its servant, which Joyce considered an affront to his individuality, the quality that made him an artist. *"Non serviam"* is the creed Stephen Dedalus, the budding artist of *A Portrait*, adopts, and it was simultaneously a political and artistic motto: "I will not serve that in which I no longer believe whether it call itself my home, my fatherland or my church."

Joyce's individualism derived partly from anarchism. He acquired books about anarchy in Trieste and began calling himself an anarchist as early as 1907, though he was a "philosophical" anarchist rather than a political one—and his stomach, he said, was an incorrigible capitalist. His interest in anarchism stemmed from the tenet that all authority—governmental or religious—boiled down to control without consent. To govern is to violate an individual's sovereignty.

We associate anarchists with chaos and bomb throwers, but their fervor derived from a rigid logic: if an agreement isn't voluntary, it's coercive. If you have not explicitly consented to an authority, then it is your master. Because all governments are compulsory, they are all oppressive. To overthrow a monarchy and create a democracy is merely to trade the tyranny of the king for the tyranny of the majority—if you happen to be in the minority, the distinction is irrelevant. Anarchists saw no real difference between limited and absolute authorities. Whether a law instituted traffic lights or a secret police, the violation of individuality was essentially the same.

For philosophical anarchists like Joyce, rejecting authority meant rejecting the entire conceptual category to which "authority" belonged: abstractions and foundational assumptions. Anarchists believed that states and churches rested upon phantom concepts (like legitimacy or moral obligation) masquerading as fundamental truths when they were really just inventions helping tyrants wield power. The philosophical core of anarchism was thus a skepticism of the ostensibly self-evident concepts that held sway over people. It was the conviction that big ideas could enslave, whether they be duty, rights or God; your home, your fatherland or your church.

Anarchism emerged as a response to the rapid growth of the modern state, and, more particularly, to the growth of one of the nineteenth century's biggest ideas: the police. When the British Parliament created the Metropolitan Police in 1829, it invented a form of state power that was diffused throughout the city. Ten years later, Parliament empowered the police to arrest loiterers, "riotous" drunkards and anyone committing a misdemeanor whose name and residence couldn't be verified. The act banned cockfighting and shooting firearms within three hundred yards of homes. It banned driving "furiously," wantonly ringing doorbells and flying annoying kites. It banned the sale and distribution of "profane, indecent, or obscene" books, and the laws would only get stronger over time. By 1878, the British government had passed more than one hundred laws expanding police powers, and Britain set the example for police expansion all around the world.

For people suspicious of authority, the multiplying laws were self-perpetuating: more ordinances created more criminals and, thus, the need for more police officers and an ever-exploding government. The professionalization of law enforcement made patrolmen seem like foot soldiers in an increasingly centralized apparatus staffed with detectives, jailers and bureaucrats who thought of state power as job security. To artists like Joyce, who considered free expression sacrosanct, censorship epitomized the tyranny of state power, for the state not only banned obscenity, it decided what obscenity was. Unlike firearms or kites, the violation was arbitrary—the law hemmed the government in with limits of the government's choosing—and the fact that censors acted as if indecency were self-evident only made the arbitrariness more blatant. To publish a gratuitously obscene text—to deny "obscenity" as a legitimate category altogether—was a way to expose and reject the arbitrary basis of all state power. It was a form of literary anarchy.

TRIESTE WAS FERTILE ground for anarchist ideas. The city's predominantly Italian population had been under Austrian rule for hundreds of years, but after the unification of Italy in 1861, Italian Triestines demanded inclusion in the new Italian state, and the divisions between Italians and Austrians became more palpable as the city became more prosperous. Italians resented the cultural infiltration of their city—a Germanic street name here, an Austrian monument there. Political plums and administrative favors all went to Austrians. When a fight broke out between German and Italian students at Trieste's law school in 1904, the 137 students arrested were all Italian. Whether the authorities were Italian or Austrian, some portion of the city would be governed against its wishes. To be an Irishman in Trieste was to see your own country's problems refracted through another empire. For Joyce, leaving home meant seeing global principles beneath local problems, seeing one collectivity pitted against another—Italianness and Austrianness, nationalism and empire. Individuals were crushed by big ideas.

Italy declared war on the Austrian Empire in May 1915. By June, the steamers and ships' masts in the Grand Canal dwindled. Wartime trade plummeted and mines were planted in the Adriatic to help starve Vienna into defeat, and Trieste was empty. The trams were gone—their cables commandeered by the military—the coaches and oxcarts were gone, and the multilingual shouts from the bars were replaced by the shouts of soldiers demanding documents. The last of those soldiers to be called up for duty patrolled the streets with rifles from the Franco-Prussian War dangling from their shoulders on knotted pieces of string. The sounds of their boots echoed off the shuttered shop fronts in the Cittavecchia. High up on a hill on the old city, the San Giusto Cathedral cast an afternoon shadow over the nearby streets, and in a small apartment on one of those streets, with books crammed into the bedroom and empty chairs in the drawing room where students used to sit, James Joyce was busy writing something new.

"Stately, plump Buck Mulligan came from the stairhead, bearing a bowl of lather on which a mirror and a razor lay crossed." In the opening chapter of

Ulysses, Joyce recalled his days with Oliver Gogarty (Buck Mulligan) at the Martello tower in Sandycove before leaving Ireland with Nora. Joyce finished the first chapter on June 16, 1915, and it could not have been easy. The Berlitz School where he was teaching closed indefinitely that same day. Most of the teachers were conscripted, and the students had either enlisted or fled. And yet as the cannonades and air raids came closer to his apartment in Trieste, Joyce tunneled deeper into his novel. He composed the young men's dialogue on the tower's parapet while small crowds gathered on Trieste's waterfront and listened to the gunfire coming from a town a few miles away. Austrian Triestines mocked the Italian battle cry by shouting, *"Avanti, Cagoia!"*— "Forward, snails!" The cheers grew louder with each explosion.

As an Austrian port with an Italian population and a mostly Slavic police force, the city began to tear itself apart. When news of Italy's declaration spread, Austrian mobs roamed through the streets attacking Italian nationalists and destroying Italian restaurants and cafés. Sailors vandalized the statue of Verdi in one of the piazzas, and when they burned the offices of pro-Italian newspapers, the police simply watched. The Joyce family was placed on a list of enemy aliens, and Stannie, who made his Italian sympathies clear, was arrested and placed in an internment camp. By the end of May, the Triestine authorities dissolved the municipal council, censored the press and the mails, deported Italians en masse and declared a state of siege. When the last train for Italy left, Trieste felt like an open-air prison. Shops were shuttered. Lines formed all night in front of the last open bakery, and food prices skyrocketed. "Whoever has the last sack of flour," Joyce said, "will win the war."

JOYCE WAS HARDLY in a position to embark upon a new novel, much less a novel as ambitious as *Ulysses*. In 1915, he was unemployed, perched on the edge of a battlefront with a wife and two children and as poor as he had ever been. *A Portrait* was unpublished, and *Dubliners* had appeared in bookstores two weeks before the archduke's assassination. At the end of 1914 only 499 copies had been sold (120 of which Joyce was required to purchase himself), and the sales were crawling to a standstill. In the first six months of 1915, twenty-six copies of *Dubliners* were sold. In the last six months, only seven.

Ulysses began as a whim. It was originally an idea for a short story to tag along in *Dubliners*. Alfred H. Hunter—the lonely, benevolent Jew in Dublin who had lifted Joyce from the dirt in St. Stephen's Green—was a hero of the Trojan War, the protagonist of Homer's greatest epic, the king of Ithaca, Ulysses. The Hunter-as-Ulysses equation was well suited for a short story, but the concept had undergone some unforeseeable growth in Joyce's mind. In 1914, he began gathering his ideas. Joyce mapped the events of the ancient tale of the *Odyssey* onto Dublin: a funeral in Glasnevin cemetery was a descent into Hades. His friend Byrne's little flat on Eccles Street was Ulysses' palace in Ithaca, and the barmaids at the Ormond Hotel were the Sirens. He had a name for his Ulysses: Leopold Bloom. Stephen Dedalus was Telemachus, Ulysses' son. Stephen was a son whose father was lost, and Bloom was a father finding his way back to his son. His wife, Molly, was Penelope patiently waiting for her husband's return from the Trojan War.

By the early twentieth century, the very idea of an epic seemed antiquated. The *Odyssey* represented the essence of a cohesive civilization, and if the war demonstrated anything, it was that Europe was fragmentary. An Irish *Odyssey* would be a mock epic, a tale that invoked classical comparisons to deride what civilization had become. For Joyce, there was a mischievous thrill in reimagining the epic stage as dowdy, dirty Dublin. Dublin's Ulysses is not a king but an ad canvasser for a newspaper, and he returns home not to a faithful queen but to a wife who cheated on him earlier that day. To see the life of Leopold Bloom through the adventures of Ulysses was to peer into the twentieth century through the cracked looking glass of antiquity.

But the other side of Joyce's thrill was transubstantiating the modern city's quotidian surroundings. Joyce slipped across centuries from the mundane to the mythical and back. For years, he thought of an epiphany's flash of insight as a moment revealing "the soul of the commonest object," as Stephen Dedalus puts it. But in *Ulysses*, Stephen tells us that the "intense instant of imagination" is an insight across and into time. "So in the future, the sister of the past,

I may see myself as I sit here now but by reflection from that which then I shall be." Everything we are, everything we do, acquires its more durable meaning in belated recognitions, which will themselves be fodder for more distant moments. The epiphany belongs to the future. Joyce could see himself as a young man in Dublin now that the bombs were falling around Trieste. And so it is with civilizations telling their stories. Dublin, crossing the threshold of the twentieth century, could gaze back to see itself on the Homeric stage at last.

And Joyce added yet another level of complexity—something that fused the modern world's disparate orders of magnitude. Instead of an epic unfolding over the course of years, *Ulysses* would take place on one day. In the twenty-first century, a circadian novel seems natural. We are accustomed to the tick-tock of live reports, RSS feeds, status updates, and twenty-four-hour news cycles feeding us the perception that global events turn on single days. Yet in 1915, the notion that a single day was an appropriate time frame for an extended novel, or that in the limits of smallness we could find a culture's grand pattern, was, to say the least, exotic. A few writers had written single-day novels before *Ulysses*, but none on the scale that Joyce imagined—no one thought of a day as an epic. Joyce was planning to turn a single day into a recursive unit of dazzling complexity in which the circadian part was simultaneously the epochal whole. A June day in Dublin would be a fractal of Western civilization.

Joyce continued the story of Stephen Dedalus in the opening chapters of *Ulysses*. Stephen is twenty-two years old and swimming in his ideas. He walks along the shore in Sandycove, and he thinks not so much about what he sees as the fact that he is seeing it.

> Ineluctable modality of the visible: at least that if no more, thought through my eyes. Signatures of all things I am here to read, seaspawn and seawrack, the nearing tide, that rusty boot. Snotgreen, bluesilver, rust: coloured signs. Limits of the diaphane.

It was not the type of prose that flew off the shelves. It was, however, a new rendering of the way people think. Thoughts don't flow like the luxuriant sentences of Henry James. Consciousness is not a stream. It is a brief assembly of fragments on the margins of the deep, a rusty boot briefly washed ashore before the tide reclaims it. Joyce wanted Stephen's thoughts to be clipped and prismatic. He wanted to strip thoughts and emotions down to their essentials. He wanted density, the bones of communication, the sharp utterance, the urgent telegram, the MOTHER DYING COME HOME FATHER.

5.

SMITHY OF SOULS

In 1913, Miss Harriet Weaver was just another *Freewoman* subscriber. Like Dora Marsden, she was a disaffected member of the Women's Social and Political Union, Britain's radical suffrage organization, and when she found Marsden's audacious magazine she knew she had discovered something vital. *The Freewoman* embraced unmentionable subjects, which, predictably, got the magazine in trouble. Newsstand sales plummeted in 1912 when the company that controlled train station bookstalls throughout England removed *The Freewoman* from its kiosks. Articles about divorce reform, contraception and free love were, according to the company, "unsuitable to be exposed on the bookstalls for general sale." Shortly thereafter, an anarchist publisher withdrew his offer to continue the magazine's publication because he feared being prosecuted for libel and sedition.

Miss Weaver was less daunted. When she read Marsden's appeal in *The Freewoman*'s final issue, she offered Marsden, whom she had never met, two hundred pounds to revive the magazine as *The New Freewoman*. The money was a pledge of support rather than a bid for control. *The Freewoman* already sounded to Miss Weaver as if it were "edited on a mountaintop." She merely wanted Marsden to continue her work. But Marsden began retreating into her own book, a sweeping philosophical treatise she hoped would synthesize philosophy, theology, mathematics and physics. To keep the magazine going,

Miss Weaver found herself donating more money, leasing a new office and hiring London printers to consolidate operations. In June 1914, after Ezra Pound allied with Marsden and *The New Freewoman* morphed into *The Egoist*, she reluctantly became the magazine's editor.

Miss Weaver was not one to quarrel. She preferred the harmonious order of her three-room flat in Marylebone, London, where she regularly arranged fresh flowers to balance the dark woods of her furniture. Miss Weaver was thirty-nine and an heir to her maternal grandfather's cotton fortune. She led a staid life. Miss Weaver waited until her mother died before she saw her first (and last) stage production. Her sitting room doubled as a dining room when she had company, and it became her study when she had extra work. At her Victorian desk, beside a wall of books, a Georgian dining table and chairs upholstered in blue and muted gold, Miss Weaver edited the most daring magazine in England. And if printers cut portions of the text she gave them, she fired them.

She took over *The Egoist* in trying circumstances. A reliable staff member resigned, as if jumping ship, as soon as Marsden stepped down, which left Weaver with a staff of one, Richard Aldington, to run a struggling magazine. The first *Egoist* print run in January 1914 was an optimistic two thousand copies. By September 1914, three months after Miss Weaver took over, they were printing half that number. She reduced issues from twenty pages to sixteen, and the biweekly became a monthly. The finances were abysmal. *The Egoist* earned £37 in revenue in the last six months of 1914, and the costs totaled £337. Miss Weaver paid the difference. Part of the problem was the war. Printers were difficult to obtain, contributors were enlisting in the military, wholesale prices more than doubled and no one wanted to advertise in an eccentric literary magazine in the middle of a national crisis.

In 1915, zeppelins began crossing the North Sea to drop bombs on houses, theaters and city buses. Thousands of Londoners rushed to catch a glimpse of the silver airships as they drifted eastward with the wind on moonless nights. London had not been attacked in centuries, and the city was not prepared. British pilots couldn't even see their targets, let alone fire at them. It took hours to prepare the antiaircraft batteries, and the falling artillery shrapnel caused more damage to the city than the zeppelins. The Great War was waged on armies and civilians alike, and the violence opened up like some monstrous epiphany in the European imagination. One of the zeppelin captains looked down at the explosions lighting up like a garland of flowers across the city. It was, he said, "indescribably beautiful."

After the fifth zeppelin raid, Dora Marsden wrote from England's northwest coast and begged Miss Weaver to flee London for the countryside—"Can't you? Won't you??" She would not. Even Ezra Pound suggested that she suspend *The Egoist* during the war. She did not. Miss Weaver would carry on with the magazine if for no other reason than to serialize James Joyce's *Portrait*. Her biggest threat was London's printers.

One of the paradoxes of the war was that while Londoners bravely faced the possibility of being burned alive by thermite every time they went to the pub, they were less willing than ever to risk moral offense. When *The Egoist*'s printer received chapter three of *A Portrait*, the manager refused to print an unseemly paragraph describing Stephen Dedalus's daydreams about Nighttown and soon began cutting small passages without so much as informing Miss Weaver. Her forbearance reached its limit when they cut two sentences from Joyce's fifth chapter, one of which described a girl standing in the middle of a rivulet near the ocean: "Her thighs, fuller and softhued as ivory, were bared almost to the hips where the white fringes of her drawers were like featherings of soft white down." Miss Weaver gave the printers a well-mannered dismissal: "we have decided to leave you," she wrote, "and are very sorry to have to leave."

A few months later, the replacement printers deleted two words (*fart* and *ballocks*) whose meanings Miss Weaver did not happen to know, which was, of course, beside the point. She fired them as well. Joyce's text forced *The Egoist* to go through four printers in Miss Weaver's first two years. She wrote to apologize to him for the "stupid censoring" of his novel, and she made it clear that, though there were only so many printers in London, she was determined to try them all.

Miss Weaver knew she was courting danger by publishing James Joyce's work. After all, the entire first printing of his debut book of fiction had been destroyed. In November 1905, when Joyce was twenty-three, he sent the manuscript of *Dubliners* to a London publisher named Grant Richards. Richards responded nearly three months later to say that *Dubliners* had many problems. It was about Ireland, and no one wanted to buy a book about Ireland. It was a collection of short stories, and no one wanted to buy a collection of short stories. But he admired it so much that he was willing to publish it under modest terms. Joyce would get no advance and no royalties from the first five hundred copies sold. He would receive 10 percent from the sales on the first one thousand copies after that, though he would omit every thirteenth copy from the total. Several weeks later, however, Richards returned his manuscript and demanded changes.

The printer cut several passages and refused to print the story "Two Gallants" altogether. Richards himself objected to the word *bloody* in one of the stories ("she did not wish to seem bloody-minded"), and the offensive word appeared several more times in *Dubliners*: "if any fellow tried that sort of game on with *his* sister he'd bloody well put his teeth down his throat, so he would." Joyce did his publisher the favor of listing every objectionable instance and, for good measure, pointing out the implicit danger of his story "An Encounter." The man by the docks with the gaps between his yellow teeth and the "bottle-green eyes" is entertaining immoral impulses as he talks to one of the two truants about whipping boys who misbehave. It was, a lawyer friend later told Joyce, "beyond anything in its outspokenness" he had ever read.

Joyce wrote to Richards that if they eliminated every offensive detail they'd be left with nothing but the title. He was writing hard truths about moral decay for the advancement of Irish civilization only to have his work weakened by a semiliterate London machinist armed with a blue pencil. "I cannot write without offending people," he concluded, and if he were forced to write his stories another way, he would not have written them at all.

Richards insisted that no legitimate publisher would touch Joyce's book without changes, and an illegitimate publisher would "do no good to your pocket." Joyce, impoverished as he was, fired back, "The appeal to my pocket has not much weight with me." He would be happy to make money from *Dubliners*, he wrote, but "I have very little intention of prostituting whatever talent I may have to the public." Richards presented himself as an editor challenging Joyce's versatility rather than an exploiter pimping his talent. "Remember," he wrote to Joyce, "it is only words and sentences that have to be altered; and it seems to me that the man who cannot convey his meaning by more than one set of words and sentences has not yet realized the possibilities of the English language." Joyce was unimpressed.

In September 1906, Richards informed Mr. Joyce that after "the very careful re-reading" of his manuscript, they could not publish *Dubliners*. The stories would not only damage the publisher's reputation, Richards wrote, they would impede Joyce's success for the rest of his career. Joyce, undeterred, sent *Dubliners* to several other publishers—John Long, Elkin Mathews, Alston Rivers, Edward Arnold, William Heinemann and Hutchinson & Company. They all rejected it.

Dubliners didn't find another publisher until 1909. George Roberts was a stocky Protestant from Belfast who set up a publishing house in Dublin called Maunsel & Company. Roberts favored younger Irish writers, so Joyce's story collection was a natural fit, but the same objections about *Dubliners* soon resurfaced. In "Ivy Day in the Committee Room," an Irish nationalist mentions Prince Edward's late ascension to the throne after the death of his long-lived mother, Queen Victoria: "Here's this fellow come to the throne after his bloody owl' mother keeping him out of it till the man was grey." After Richards had withdrawn his offer, Joyce embellished the Queen Victoria reference from "bloody owl' mother" to (and why not?) "bloody old bitch of a mother."

When Roberts demanded changes, Joyce became defiant. He sent a public letter to Irish newspapers airing his grievances. He threatened to sue Maunsel & Company for breach of contract. He wrote to King George V asking for His Majesty's official permission to print the stories (the king's secretary declined to comment). He returned to Ireland from Trieste (a five-day journey) to settle the dispute in person. When Roberts worried about libel suits from people and establishments mentioned in *Dubliners* by their real names, Joyce offered to secure written authorization from every individual, publican and restaurateur himself. Dublin booksellers, unfortunately, hesitated when Joyce asked if they would sell his book. One manager said that a couple of young men had recently told him to remove a risqué French novel from his window display and that if he didn't, he'd find his windows smashed.

In August 1912, after three years of haggling, Roberts wrote the most forceful rejection letter of his career: "the publication of the book by Maunsel & Co. is out of the question . . . even if the objectionable parts were struck out, there would still remain the risk of some of them having been overlooked." And even if they were to consider publishing his stories, which they would not, Joyce would have to deposit one thousand pounds (an exorbitant amount) as insurance against lawsuits. But that wasn't all. Roberts claimed Joyce had breached their contract by submitting a "clearly libelous" manuscript and threatened to sue *him* for the printing costs of a book he refused to publish. So Joyce, hoping to have the pages bound and published in London, went to the printer's shop on O'Connell Street, where an elderly, ruddy-faced man named Falconer gave Joyce a sample copy of his book but refused to hand over the printed sheets for any price. After Joyce left, Falconer and his Scottish foreman destroyed every page of *Dubliners* they had printed. They weren't burned. They were "guillotined."

Joyce's nine-year struggle to publish *Dubliners* was his first lesson in the way governments controlled words. Sometimes it was about policemen barging through doors and burning books, but more often it was about coercion and intimidation. The mere threat of lawsuits and criminal charges against publishers, printers or booksellers—they were all liable—was enough to halt the sale of a book. Even if there were no criminal charges, small publishers like Richards and Roberts had to worry that critics, reporters and clergymen scouring their books for obscenity would sound a moral alarm and provoke protests and boycotts that would bankrupt them.

THE BRITISH CENSORSHIP REGIME had grown more powerful during the war years. In 1915, the London police seized a thousand copies of D. H. Lawrence's *The Rainbow* ("a monotonous wilderness of phallicism," as the *London Daily News* put it) from the warehouse of a reputable publisher, Methuen, and burned them. And yet seizures and burnings were not the gravest threat: British authorities demonstrated that they were willing put people in prison for distributing immoral material, and they would not be deterred by publishers or printers who insisted that their obscenity was "art."

Obscenity had long been a common law offense, but explicit statutes banning immoral books didn't appear in the United States and the United Kingdom until the nineteenth century, when rising literacy rates met with urbanization and a burgeoning market of publications that were affordable to the youth and the urban poor. Salacious literature was widespread enough in the mid-nineteenth century to start a moral panic that culminated in the Obscene Publications Act of 1857. Lord Campbell, the chief justice of the Queen's Bench, drafted a bill that empowered the police, with proper warrants, to enter private homes and businesses (by force, if necessary), search for and seize immoral literature. If the seized material was intended for sale or distribution, magistrates could imprison the owner and burn the obscenity. The law expanded police powers in a way that few English people could have imagined twenty years earlier. Search and seizure authority was generally reserved for customs officials and the military, but London's growing police force—which didn't even exist before 1829—suddenly found itself vested with the same powers.

Before 1857, police search and seizure authority was limited to illegal gambling dens and ships carrying arms down the Thames. The Obscene Publications Act, however, allowed the police to rifle through books and papers in any home, shop or private office based on little more than a citizen's complaint. The government had shifted its focus from criminals to words themselves. It was not enough to put offenders behind bars. The books had to be tracked down and burned, and the law made no distinctions among printers, publishers and booksellers—that's why Miss Weaver's printers cut every off-color word they found.

And yet the Obscene Publications Act didn't give magistrates and policemen any guidelines regarding what to search for, seize and destroy, which meant that obscenity was whatever the most motivated enforcers thought it was. This did not seem problematic in mid-Victorian England. During the parliamentary debate over the Obscene Publications Act, Lord Campbell waved a copy of Alexandre Dumas's *Lady of the Camellias* as an example of a dirty book that nevertheless would not be banned. The law, he said, would target books with "no artistic merit or aspiration at all," and the public had good reasons to think it would remain that way. Literary London didn't object to the anti-obscenity law because no one could think of an English novel that would unjustly fall under the ban. At midcentury, English writing was so circumspect that mentioning sex seemed contrary to artistic intentions almost by definition—it just wasn't something a legitimate novelist portrayed. There were respectable English novels from the likes of Dickens, Trollope and Thackeray and then there was pornography.

And the qualms about the Obscene Publications Act were misdirected, for the real power behind Britain's censorship regime was not the police. It was the London Society for the Suppression of Vice, which began fighting obscene and blasphemous texts in 1802. Two years later, the Society had nearly nine hundred members, and by midcentury they more or less controlled the enforcement of obscenity laws. The SSV shaped public opinion and cowed publishers through shame and potential boycotts. Salaried agents performed undercover investigations, and when they discovered particularly offensive books (the works of Thomas Paine, for example), they pressed charges and put offenders behind bars. The Society helped Lord Campbell draft the Obscene Publications Act and wasted no time implementing it. In 1817 the Society had brought a few dozen pornographers to trial. The year the law passed, they prosecuted 159, and in nearly every case they won convictions resulting in fines, seizures, prison sentences and hard labor.

By the late nineteenth century, Britain's growing literary life found itself tethered to standards carved out by the SSV in the 1850s. When a widening spectrum of books began to address sexuality as a subject of art, science, psychology and public health, the law began to reach beyond the underground pornography market. In the 1880s, a vogue for French realist novelists like

Flaubert, Maupassant, and Zola swept Britain, and their candid depictions of everyday working-class life went well beyond Britain's decorous fiction. One infamous passage from Émile Zola's *La Terre* describes a girl bringing her cow to mate with a bull on a neighboring farm: "She had to reach right across with her arm as she grasped the bull's penis firmly in her hand and lifted it up. And when the bull felt that he was near the edge, he gathered his strength and, with one simple thrust of his loins, pushed his penis right in."

An English publisher named Henry Vizetelly specialized in producing U.K. editions of realist fiction. Vizetelly & Company published translations of Dostoevsky, Tolstoy, Gogol and several of Zola's novels, including *La Terre*. In 1884, the Irish novelist George Moore, who was having trouble getting his first novel circulated, turned to Vizetelly & Company to publish his next novel in a two-shilling edition, less than one-tenth of the inflated industry-standard price. Vizetelly boasted in the press that he had sold more than a million copies of French novels, including a thousand copies of Zola's books every week. When Lord Tennyson, England's poet laureate, condemned "the troughs of Zolaism" in verse, the outlines of a cultural divide were clear: Vizetelly's cheap foreign books were arrayed against standardized three-volume novels, whose high prices bought cultural legitimacy.

The Vigilance Association, the successor to the SSV, organized a boycott against Vizetelly, mounted a publicity campaign that reached the floor of Parliament, and, in 1888, it pressed obscenity charges against him repeatedly for publishing Zola. Vizetelly pleaded guilty and was sentenced to three months in prison. His stock of Zola novels was destroyed, and his publishing house— thriving only a year before—went bankrupt.

When Zola died in 1902, London's literary journals remembered the novelist as a towering figure of nineteenth-century literature, but what printers and publishers remembered was the power of the vice societies and their willingness to crack down on risqué material even if it called itself art. It was Vizetelly's prison sentence that was in the back of the publishers' and printers' minds when they began poring over everything Joyce wrote, from *Dubliners* to *Portrait* to *Ulysses*. Joyce could only have made things worse when he told

George Roberts that the worst outcome of publishing *Dubliners* was that "some critic will allude to me as the 'Irish Zola'!" No one wanted to be another Vizetelly.

MISS WEAVER, prim, fastidious, repeatedly mistaken for a Quaker, was willing to risk jail time. She was one of eight children in a devout Church of England family, and when she was not quietly listening to her father's twice-daily prayers, she drove him frantic by climbing the trees, walls and cliffs around their Cheshire estate. The Weavers forbade dancing, shunned unnecessary luxuries, banished exotic vegetables like asparagus from their table and considered novels an idle pleasure to be avoided as much as possible. Miss Weaver openly devoured books from the likes of Ralph Waldo Emerson, Oliver Wendell Holmes and John Stuart Mill while concealing the novels from her parents and the servants. When she was nineteen, her mother caught her reading George Eliot's *Adam Bede*. Jane Austen and the Brontës were irksome enough, so far as her mother was concerned, but Eliot was worse. George Eliot was, in fact, a woman who had been living openly with a married man, and *Adam Bede* is about a young woman who gives birth to an illegitimate child and leaves it in a field to die.

Mrs. Weaver told her daughter to go to her room and remain there until she was summoned. She must have anticipated a stern talk from her father, but when they finally called her downstairs, the man waiting to speak to her was the vicar of Hampstead. The reprimand from the Church of England was supposed to drive home a lesson about the hazards of novels, but instead it made reading a rebellion. And some writers were worth fighting for.

The first thing Miss Weaver heard about Mr. James Joyce was that the entire first printing of *Dubliners* had been destroyed for being unprintably obscene. He had exiled himself from Ireland for over a decade and had, as Dora Marsden later wrote to Miss Weaver, a "reputation for quarrelling with all the world." That was part of the allure. By the time Miss Weaver began reading *A Portrait* in *The Egoist*, he was a man with an aura gathering around him, and the idea of the artist as an individual defying empires, churches and conventions developed in the monthly installments.

The opening scenes depicted a sensitive boy with feeble eyes hiding under a table and pasting inside his boarding school desk the number of days left until Christmas vacation. Dora Marsden's writing was idealistic and yet prone to the abstractions it railed against. Joyce's writing, on the other hand, had a quality Miss Weaver could not fully articulate, something she described vaguely as "a searching, piercing spirit," a capacity for "scorching truth" and "startling penetration." By the time she read about Stephen Dedalus's struggle with his faith, his excursions into Nighttown and his flight from Ireland "to forge in the smithy of my soul the uncreated conscience of my race," as Stephen puts it, she was captivated. Despite his vulnerabilities, he would never ensconce himself in the upholstery. To read Joyce was to escape from family prayers, to climb the highest tree and to behold the disquieting panorama across the bluff and the river Weaver coursing below it.

Joyce's publishing woes only enhanced his appeal, for one of the only emotions more powerful to Miss Weaver than her awe of artistic talent was her unbounded empathy for hardship. When Miss Weaver and Ezra Pound began searching for a publisher for Joyce's *Portrait*, they got a stream of rejections—from Secker, from Jenkins, from Duckworth. Herbert Cape said he hoped Joyce would abandon the novel and start something new. Grant Richards sent the manuscript back to Miss Weaver without so much as commenting (privately, he called the manuscript "hopeless"). Pound sent it to Werner Laurie, Ltd., who he thought could tolerate frankness, but Laurie wrote back that publishing Joyce's book in wartime London was "quite impossible"—he was so sure it would be banned that he wouldn't even recommend other publishers. In January 1916, Pound prevailed upon Duckworth to reconsider, and the publisher sent back a withering evaluation of James Joyce's first novel:

> *It is too discursive, formless, unrestrained, and ugly things, ugly words, are too prominent; indeed at times they seem to be shoved in one's face, on purpose, unnecessarily. The point of view will be voted "a little*

sordid." The picture of life is good; the period well brought to the reader's eye, and the types and characters well drawn, but it is too "unconventional." . . . At the end of the book there is a complete falling to bits; the pieces of writing and the thoughts are all in pieces and they fall like damp, ineffective rockets.

Pound was disgusted. "These vermin crawl over and be-slime our literature with their pulings," he told Joyce's agent. For Pound, the rejection of a writer like Joyce was the latest evidence that the Allies were fighting the wrong enemies. "You English will get no prose till you exterminate this breed . . . Why can't you send the publishers' readers to the Serbian front and get some good out of the war."

Pound advocated for Joyce as if he were protecting someone who belonged to him. Joyce was a long-lost Imagist, a blessed Vorticist, a kindred spirit writing fiction just as Pound himself would have written it. His keen eye penetrated the people and objects around him and extracted, as Pound put it, "the universal element" inside them all. *A Portrait* gave him the feeling that he was reading something "absolutely permanent," something that would never die, and finding that immortality in a manuscript before it was published—before anyone even *wanted* to publish it—summoned Pound's thrill of discovery and his missionary zeal. For what Joyce really gave Pound was a galvanized sense of confidence, a reassurance strong enough to overcome any nagging doubts about his highest literary ambitions: if an artist could write such prose in the middle of a brutal war, then Pound's plans for a twentieth-century renaissance were not as fanciful as they seemed. And if *A Portrait* couldn't find a publisher, then it was clear beyond all doubt that his primary obstacle was not talent or vision or even money but the rank stupidity of the vermin infesting the publishing industry.

Miss Weaver's reaction was more temperate. When she exhausted publishing options in England, she raised one last possibility with Joyce: "I have been wondering whether *The Egoist* could do it." The Egoist Press had published only the magazine and a pamphlet of poems, and Miss Weaver emphasized that their edition could not approach anything produced by an actual book publisher. Since that possibility seemed closed, she ventured that the Egoist Press might risk publishing Joyce's book, assuming she was granted the authority from "the other members of our staff and the directors of our small publishing company"—namely, Dora Marsden.

It was a bold plan. But even Miss Weaver's fortitude could only go so far, for while *The Egoist* could take care of financing, advertising and distribution, someone needed to print it. Weaver approached printer after printer only to have each one refuse, sometimes brusquely. "We could not for one moment entertain any idea of printing such a production," Billing & Sons wrote to her. "We are convinced that you would run very great risk in putting such a book on the market," and they advised her to scour the text and cut any objectionable passages. Over the next few months, thirteen printers refused to print *A Portrait* in its entirety. Every time a printer suggested an expurgated version, Miss Weaver declined.

Pound, who was nothing if not resourceful, came up with an idea: they could leave large blank spaces in the text wherever a printer wished to cut words or passages. Then they could type out all of the deleted portions on quality paper and paste the omitted words into every single copy—"And damn the censors." Joyce thought it was ingenious. The printers, unfortunately, thought it was madcap.

England's rejection of *A Portrait* made Pound feel that, after years of relentless socializing, he was still an outsider. He had insinuated himself, to one degree or another, into an array of modernist magazines—*The Egoist, The New Age, Poetry, Poetry and Drama, North American Review* and others—only to find that he was still at the mercy of "Victorian-minded" editors, printers and publishers. When Joyce implored Pound in 1916 to get a handful of his poems published in any magazine that could pay, Pound responded that he had run out of connections in England. "There is no editor whom I wouldn't cheerfully fry in oil and none who wouldn't as cheerfully do the same by me." What Ezra Pound wanted was his own magazine, a magazine that would bring the Vortex together and publish their material without fear of censorship.

It was difficult to see, but prospects were beginning to turn for Pound and his young cohort, and no one's prospects had shifted more dramatically than Joyce's. In just two years, he had gone from being an unpublished novelist teaching Berlitz classes to being a writer with zealous allies, a small but avid magazine audience and—rarest of all assets—a fearless, accommodating publisher. After so many years toiling in exile, a viable future as a writer was starting to seem real. It may not have been much—Pound, Weaver and Dora Marsden were only marginal figures in a world preoccupied by war—but a supportive coterie was enough to encourage Joyce to venture much further out into his writing than he ever had before.

6.

LITTLE MODERNISMS

———

What we now call modernism was a loose collection of small cultural insurgencies driven by a broad, sometimes inchoate discontent with Western civilization—from the way poems were written to the way governments functioned and capital flowed. Suffragettes, anarchists, Imagists and socialists rarely formed tight bonds, but they were a part of the same guerrilla band. The outposts of modernism were small, do-it-yourself magazines. The serial format encouraged shifting allegiances and sudden rifts like Pound's leap from Imagism to Vorticism. Writers could argue, experiment and change their minds from one month to the next. Timeless names shared pages with amateurs and eccentrics long since forgotten. Writers were rarely paid, and their contributions were uneven, but they were plentiful. Pound submitted 117 magazine contributions in 1918 alone. Portions of virtually everything Joyce wrote—including *Dubliners*, *A Portrait*, *Ulysses* and *Finnegans Wake*—appeared as experiments in magazines before they were finalized in books. The "little magazines," as they were called, were a misnomer—their biggest asset was space. They published hasty drafts, unfinished work and immoderate opinions. They traded free ads with other magazines to create a network of experimental outlets with overlapping readerships. Magazines were modernism's blogosphere.

The Egoist took material that other London magazines like *The English Review* and *The New Age* wouldn't publish. In Chicago, Harriet Monroe's

Poetry shared readers with *The Dial*. A Dublin little magazine called *Dana* published three of Joyce's poems—all inspired by Nora—shortly after they rejected his first prose piece, "A Portrait of the Artist," in 1904. But the most important magazine for Joyce, for *Ulysses* and possibly for modernism, was a homespun Chicago monthly called *The Little Review*, which drew small circles of devoted readers who sustained themselves on discussions of Nietzsche, Bergson and H. G. Wells. Headlines like "Feminism and New Music" appeared alongside coverage of Chicago's first citywide election in which women had the right to vote (male turnout soared). *The Little Review* published an astounding field of contributors over the years: Hemingway, Yeats, T. S. Eliot, Djuna Barnes, Sherwood Anderson, Marianne Moore, William Carlos Williams and Wallace Stevens, to name just a few. It reproduced artwork from Brancusi, Cocteau and Picabia.

One of the magazine's biggest draws was the bold enthusiasm of its founding editor, Margaret Anderson, the woman destined to bring *Ulysses* to the public, no matter how controversial it was. In the March 1915 issue, Anderson became possibly the first woman to advocate gay rights in print when she protested the fact that people were "tortured and crucified every day *for their love*—because it is not expressed according to conventional morality." "With us," she wrote, "love is just as punishable as murder or robbery." People walked up to the magazine's graceful editor on the street and said, "Aren't you Margaret Anderson? Congratulations!" Letters to *The Little Review* trickled in from kindred spirits in Wyoming, Kansas and Ontario. "I feel as if I had found my companions . . . I believe that you can become the heart of our new age of letters—if you are true."

Margaret Anderson recalled her decision to start her own magazine as a flash of inspiration in the middle of the night: "I demand that life be inspired every moment." The problem was that no one had the time or stamina for the work that inspiration requires. *"If I had a magazine,"* she thought, *"I could spend my time filling it up with the best conversation the world has to offer."* Anderson cut her teeth in the magazine business in 1910 as a staff assistant for *The Dial*, where she learned her way around the printing room before the editor's unwanted advances compelled her to quit. She was there just long enough to know how heedless it was to start her own magazine. She was horrible with finances and deadlines. She knew little about layouts, marketing and publicity, and she had no money.

What she had was conviction. She traveled to Boston and New York and extracted $450 in revenue from skeptical advertising managers at places like Houghton Mifflin, Scribner's and Goodyear ("A New Day Dawns in Tires"). She arranged a fundraising dinner at Chicago's preeminent literary salon, the Little Room. A writer named Eunice Tietjens remembered how Anderson "stood pouring out such a flood of high-hearted enthusiasm that we were all swept after her into some dream of a magazine where Art with a capital A and Beauty with a still bigger B were to reign supreme." Anderson secured several financial backers, including DeWitt Wing, an enthusiast of Nietzsche and bird watching, who promised to pay the magazine's office rent and printing costs.

In March 1914, Margaret C. Anderson's name appeared on the cover of the first issue of *The Little Review.* "*Little*" wasn't diminutive. It was intimate. The title was printed on a vellum label hand-pasted onto a plain, tan cover, and the issue's first pages carried the editor's stirring announcement:

> If you've ever read poetry with a feeling that it was your religion, if you've ever come suddenly upon the whiteness of a Venus in a dim, deep room, if, in the early morning, you've watched a bird with great white wings fly straight up into the rose-colored sun . . . If these things have happened to you and continue to happen until you're left quite speechless with the wonder of it all, then you will understand our hope to bring them nearer to the common experience of the people who read us.

Anderson grew up in Indiana and attended Ohio's Western College for Women, an offshoot of Mount Holyoke. A university education was rare for a woman at the turn of the century, and her degree was supposed to be a social token for an affluent family or, at most, a palliative for a bright young woman when she would not tolerate attending a finishing school. As soon as she graduated, Anderson's parents brought her back home to Indiana, where, from an upstairs room overlooking lilac bushes, she plotted her next escape. She would type out twenty-page letters detailing the household's routine injustices and place them on her father's desk in the early morning so that he could read them at his earliest convenience. Carbon copies appeared on her sisters' beds.

When Anderson came across the opportunity to write book reviews for a small Christian weekly in Chicago, she assembled the family on the couch and delivered a rousing argument for her departure as if performing before a rapt crowd. A few weeks later, when Anderson's father heard that she was smoking cigarettes and racking up debts at a candy store, he rushed to the Chicago YWCA and packed her bags. Anderson vowed to escape Indiana again and, as she put it, "conquer the world."

CIGARETTES AND CANDY STORE debts were quaint compared to Anderson's association with Emma Goldman, the most notorious anarchist in the United States. At the time, Americans considered anarchism a more dangerous threat to democracy than socialism. And for good reason. In 1901, a young man claiming to be inspired by Goldman wrapped a revolver in a handkerchief, walked up to President McKinley at an exposition in Buffalo and shot him twice in the stomach. Two years after the assassination, Teddy Roosevelt signed a law authorizing the government to bar or deport noncitizen anarchists, and Goldman, who was born in Russia, went into hiding.

Being persecuted only spurred Emma Goldman's defiance. When she re-emerged from hiding in 1906, her lectures drew thousands of people across the country, and by 1914, as the world was about to wage war for reasons that were murky, if not opaque, Goldman's clarity was appealing. She spoke in stirring absolutes: The individual was spontaneous and free. Governments were coercive and violent. "The State," she declared, "is organized exploitation, organized force, and crime." Governments were not even a necessary evil. The crime and poverty they claimed to control were in fact created by governments themselves when they corrupted the individual's natural goodness with artificial laws. Insofar as we believe that the State maintains the order that makes individual freedom possible, the State has us hoodwinked.

Structures of oppression were embedded in corporations, churches and an entire array of institutions, from marriage to the media, and what was remarkable about Goldman was that her sweeping critiques gave way to a relentless optimism about anarchy. Emma Goldman gave anarchism its charisma. Rather than politicizing a rigid logic, she was a defender of dreams. She transformed skepticism into a fighting faith, a philosophy of the self into something larger than the self. She thought of the individual as an embodiment of natural law, a "living force" and, invoking Walt Whitman, "a cosmos." Anarchism was about more than the defiance of all laws. It was about "the salvation of man."

Margaret Anderson attended two Goldman lectures when she toured Chicago in 1914, and like so many others, she was captivated by her brio and idealism. More important, she showed Anderson how to bridge radical politics and radical art: one lecture railed against Christianity while the other examined modern drama. Art, for Goldman, was an individualist deed as integral to anarchism as a bomb or a labor strike. She gave speeches about Chekhov and Ibsen as well as Yeats, Lady Gregory and George Bernard Shaw.

In other words, Emma Goldman was doing what Marsden and Pound were trying to do in *The Egoist*, and it was suddenly what Margaret Anderson wanted to do in *The Little Review*. After hearing Goldman speak, Anderson had just enough time to commit to anarchism before the May 1914 issue went to press. She had known nothing about Goldman when she started *The Little Review*. Six months later, she was hosting the Queen of the Anarchists and her radical associates in her apartment.

Anderson declared *The Little Review*'s credo to be "Applied Anarchism," and she called Goldman's philosophy the highest human ideal. High as it was, Anderson applied the ideal rather lightly. On Christmas Day 1914, she and a friend freed themselves from property rights by cutting down a Christmas tree from a publisher's carefully landscaped estate. A few days later, a constable served Anderson with a warrant at a train station, and the judge fined her ten dollars despite her rousing defense ("We thought we were in the primeval forest"). Anderson resumed cigarette smoking and began wearing trousers, which, as the editor of a quasi-anarchist magazine, earned her national attention. *The Washington Post* quoted her protest: "Why shouldn't women do anything they want to do? . . . We are all in bondage to social convention, and only by rebellion may we break those bonds. I have been in revolt since I was eight." A Mississippi paper called Miss Anderson the "missing link of humanity." The paper didn't object to rebellion; it insisted, "but we draw the line at cigarette smoking and long pants for the women folks."

Sometimes the rebellions were less innocent. In 1915, *The Little Review* printed one of Goldman's speeches urging people to prepare for the "overthrow of both capitalism and the state." That same year, the state of Utah executed a labor activist for murder despite scant evidence, and Anderson protested, "why didn't someone shoot the governor of Utah before he could shoot Joe Hill?" She ended the article in exasperation: "For God's sake, why doesn't someone start the Revolution?" Statements like this were provocative even in tranquil times. To publish them while the skittish country was edging toward war was reckless. Detectives showed up at the *Little Review* office to investigate.

Patrons and advertisers withdrew their support as soon as the magazine became anarchistic. Anderson was kicked out of her apartment before the end of 1914, so she moved to a community north of Chicago nicknamed "Editors' Row," where she joined people associated with various Chicago magazines, including *The Dial* and *Poetry*. When the Christmas Tree Heist deprived her of that home, too (the tree belonged to her landlord), Anderson set up camp with her two sisters on the Lake Michigan shore. Their tents had wooden floors and oriental rugs. They roasted corn by the fire, baked potatoes in the ashes and washed their dishes and clothes with sand ("the original cleansing powder," Anderson called it). Friends visited over the next six months. The writer Sherwood Anderson told stories by the campfire, and other writers pinned poems to the tents like valentines.

IN 1916, Anderson met Jane Heap. She seemed intimidating at first, and she was husky, owned a revolver, looked squarely at everyone she spoke to, had short hair she swept across her broad forehead and full lips that reminded Anderson of Oscar Wilde. Jane Heap was from Topeka, Kansas. She grew up next door to a mental institution, which, to Jane, was Topeka's only point of interest. She responded to the isolation of Kansas by being more exotic. She imagined her ancestral home as the Arctic Circle, where her mother's Norwegian family once lived. She and her friends wore trousers and neckties and called one another by masculine names such as "Richard" and "James." After high school, she left Kansas, studied painting at the Art Institute of Chicago, affiliated herself with Chicago's Little Theatre and devoted her life to the beautiful. "I know that if everyone felt Beauty strongly," she wrote to a woman she met in Chicago, "felt that everything beautiful was god and all things not beautiful not God, that woman was the nearest Symbol for Beauty, if one could see this—there would be no sin, or squalor, or unhappiness in the whole world."

Margaret Anderson recognized herself in Jane's lonely idealism, and she had never heard anyone talk the way she did. Emma Goldman delivered spine-tingling speeches, but Jane had a knack for conversation. Anderson used to think of speaking as a stage performance—as a lecture to her family assembled on the couch—so she went browsing for wisdom. She recited poetry and quoted philosophers, but Jane never quoted anyone. Everything she said seemed like a revelation in progress. Martie, as Jane called her, jotted down their conversations and begged her to write for *The Little Review*. Jane resisted at first, but before long she became the de facto art editor. She transformed the magazine's design, altered the page headers and discarded the bland tan covers for striking colors and better layouts. *The Little Review* was no longer just Margaret Anderson's.

Jane reminded Anderson that revolution was subservient to art, not the other way around, and when Anderson saw Goldman in July, it became clear that Anderson had been pulled into a different orbit. Jane thought Goldman's ideas were vague and illogical, and the Queen of the Anarchists thought Jane was too aggressive. "I felt as if she were pushing me against a wall," Goldman said later. When Goldman's friends began praising "The Ballad of Reading Gaol," Oscar Wilde's sentimental lament drawing from his imprisonment, Anderson scoffed at their ideologically driven appraisal of a bad poem. The anarchists thought Anderson was corrupted by bourgeois aestheticism, and

Anderson thought they were trapped by radical kitsch. Each thought the other insulted individualism.

Anderson's initial enthusiasm for Goldman had masked the differences between them. She didn't share Goldman's unshakable faith in the individual. Goldman thought the public's resistance to individualism was a by-product of a conformist power structure, but Anderson thought it was endemic. "Our culture—or what little we have of such a thing—is clogged by masses of dead people who have no conscious inner life," she wrote in 1914, and her contempt deepened into disgust. "'People' has become to me a word that—crawls," she wrote in 1915. "*Peo-pul.*" She saw the public as "a cosmic squirming mass of black caterpillars" writhing in protest against the rare butterfly. Whenever Goldman praised the individual, Anderson imagined the artist, a person not just incidentally exceptional—not someone who summoned the virtues everyone possesses—but fundamentally, almost biologically exceptional.

Anderson folded Goldman's defiant politics into an expansive conception of artistic genius, the purest form of individualism. "The ultimate reason for life is Art," Anderson declared in the August 1916 issue. "And revolution? Revolution is Art." By then, *The Little Review* seemed feeble, so feeble, in fact, that Anderson threatened to leave the pages blank—an empty magazine was better than a bad magazine. She threw down the gauntlet before the public: "Now we shall have Art in this magazine or we shall stop publishing it. I don't care where it comes from—America or the South Sea Islands. I don't care whether it is brought by youth or age. I only want the miracle!

"Where are the artists?"

THE DISPUTE BETWEEN Emma Goldman and Margaret Anderson dramatized tensions that rippled through the various modernist insurgencies and began to influence Joyce's new book. It was not clear how the exceptional and the mundane—the artist and the ad man—could interact, or how individuals could be revolutionary when revolutions were almost by definition the work of collectives. One solution was to change the understanding of revolution altogether. For modernists like Anderson and Joyce, the greatest individualist triumph was to bypass the political struggles Goldman ceaselessly fought, to sweep away conformity and subservience with mighty works of art. The dispute about individualism arose from precisely the thing that made individualism captivating: an overweening faith in the individual's power.

Part of what made the tension so fraught was that both political and artistic individualists drew much of their faith from the same source, an 1844 treatise by Max Stirner called *The Ego and His Own*. Stirner maintained that the individual was the only source of virtue and the only reality—everything else was an abstraction, and all abstractions were "spooks," ghosts vexing the ego. Anti-individual forces—corporations, bureaucracies, churches, states—were not merely unjust. They were *unreal*. Such sweeping skepticism generated sweeping dismissals of higher causes and concepts like God, truth and freedom. Stirner concluded his book with the declaration, "All things are nothing to me."

The Ego and His Own went through forty-nine printings from 1900 to 1929, and its ideas united an array of modernists. Joyce read Stirner. So did Emma Goldman. So did Nietzsche. So did Miss Weaver. Ezra Pound and Margaret Anderson encountered his ideas through other writers, and Dora Marsden called *The Ego and His Own* the "most powerful work that has ever emerged from a single human mind." It inspired her choice to rechristen *The New Freewoman* as *The Egoist*. Shrinking the world down to the ego made the twentieth century manageable. It fueled Goldman's optimism and Joyce's dogged determination.

Egoism appealed to modernists who found politics hopeless. In what seemed to be a permanent era of corporations and jostling empires, egoism provided anarchism with a way to retreat into culture while making that retreat seem like a more principled defiance. The individual would defeat collectivism not through protests and dynamite but through philosophy, art and literature. Turn-of-the-century individualist anarchists rejected political violence, deemphasized communal associations and celebrated a tradition of anarchist ideas already in circulation, from Wordsworth, Whitman and Zola to Thomas Paine, Rousseau, Nietzsche and Ibsen. It suited Joyce perfectly.

Joyce was steeped in individualist modernism in his formative years—

A Portrait depicts the development of his egoism in Stephen's defiance of home, fatherland and Church—and yet in 1914 he began to alter the entire tradition. *Ulysses* swerves from Stephen's heady defiance toward Leopold Bloom's humbler individualism. The novel opens with Stephen back in Dublin where he started, but Bloom never tries to leave. His individuality resides resolutely within a mental and municipal matrix. Bloom's qualms and jokes, his fears and memories, his errors, insights and half-pursued speculations help him navigate the delicate spaces that separate him from the Dubliners around him and, crucially, from himself.

When Bloom gazes out of a carriage window on his way to a funeral and sees Stephen, skinny and alone and in the garb of someone in mourning, it is Joyce looking at himself. Stephen and Bloom, the young Joyce and the older Joyce, wander through Dublin, obliquely aware of each other, and cross paths briefly before moving onward. *Ulysses* split the ego that *A Portrait* built, and that split is the fission through which the world bursts forth. Joyce began to write *Ulysses* thinking that a person is more than a singularity sweeping away a world of abstractions. The individual is something fraught, multiple, contradictory, something deceptively small, something already marbled with abstractions. In *Ulysses*, Joyce was exploring what egoism always was: a way to find God in atoms. It was one of modernism's greatest insurgencies.

7.

THE MEDICI OF
MODERNISM

The modernist milieu was small enough to be shaped by the haphazard connections that place an old book in a new reader's hands or bring a bright-eyed editor to an unforgettable lecture. One of the small connections that brought cultural and political individualists together—and put the first pages of *Ulysses* in to print—came in the form of a personal response to an offensive magazine article. In 1915, Ezra Pound received a letter from a piqued subscriber to *The New Age* who happened to be a prominent New York art collector. John Quinn was a finance lawyer with connections to Wall Street, Tammany Hall and Washington, D.C. He started his own law firm when he was thirty-six, and he worked tirelessly. He dictated letters and memoranda to stenographers arranged around his desk in his Nassau Street office, and at the end of the day an assistant would lug a leather briefcase filled with unfinished business to Quinn's apartment overlooking Central Park so he could work through the evening. In the morning, another stenographer would arrive and take dictation while Quinn dressed and shaved.

John Quinn used his clout for modernism. He spent his precious spare time collecting art and manuscripts, sometimes at above-market prices. In 1912, Quinn legally incorporated a group of dissident New York artists who split from the fusty National Academy of Design and helped them secure a space for the most ambitious art show anyone had seen in decades. The exhibition was housed in the new armory of the New York National Guard's 69th Regiment (Quinn liked the fact that the regiment was known as "The Fighting Irish"). They divided up the cavernous space into eighteen rooms, covered the partitions in burlap and squeezed in as many artworks as they could. Next to established masters like Monet and Renoir they hung the work of radical artists like Kandinsky, Matisse, Munch, Duchamp and two young artists who called themselves Cubists, Braque and Picasso.

It became known as the Armory Show, and John Quinn was its biggest single contributor. He loaned seventy-seven artworks from his collection, including a Gauguin, a Van Gogh self-portrait, and one of Cézanne's portraits of his wife. At the unveiling, Quinn declared the show "epoch making in the history of American art . . . the most complete art exhibition that has been held in the world during the last quarter century." It was probably an understatement. The Post-Impressionist show that rocked London in 1910 included fewer than 250 artworks from twenty-five artists. The Armory Show displayed about 1,300 artworks from more than three hundred artists, and its sheer size was enough to grab headlines. Four thousand people saw the show on opening night, and by the time it finished touring Boston and Chicago (where Matisse and Brancusi were burned in effigy), three hundred thousand people beheld the monumental survey of established and experimental art.

Teddy Roosevelt, John Quinn's friend, said he detected "a lunatic fringe" in the exhibition and worried that the country was being infiltrated by "European extremists." Nevertheless, the Armory Show marked the New York art world's coming of age, and it changed the American art market forever. Before 1913, Quinn had had somewhat conservative tastes, but the show fired his enthusiasm for more audacious artwork, and his purchases were substantial enough to create a ripple effect in the market. When one Chicago collector heard about Quinn's early buying spree, he rushed to New York and nearly matched his expenditures. In 1914, Quinn bought more art than anyone else in the United States, and he moved to a larger apartment on Central Park West just to store it all (displaying it all was impossible).

So when Quinn read an article by Ezra Pound in 1915 that mocked American art collectors who were buying outdated artworks and manuscripts, Quinn suspected Pound was referring to him, and he defended himself in a letter to Pound as a patron of "live" artists. "If there is a 'liver' collector of vital contemporary art in this country, for a man of moderate means," he wrote, "I should like to meet him." No one helped artists more than he did, he said. He testified before Congress, called in favors with politicians, and mounted a press campaign to change the prohibitive tariff law on art imports—in fact, he *wrote* the new tariff law. Instead of paying a 15 percent duty, collectors in United States who bought work directly from artists could now import it without charge.

Ezra Pound quickly understood the type of man he was dealing with. Quinn not only cared about art, he had the means and connections to make art happen. Pound wrote back to offer his apologies. "If there were more like you we should get on with our renaissance," he said, roping him in with *our*. After a couple of letters, Pound was more direct. If he were an editor of a literary magazine that published writers no one would print, what kind of support would he have from New York? "Are there any damd female tea parties who will committeeize themselves and try to sell the paper?" Wartime London was muzzling him, and the only solution was complete financial and editorial control of his own magazine. Of course, Pound wasn't interested in the help of tea party committees. He was asking for a patron, and he approached John Quinn with measured compliments and competitive swagger: "I don't want or need a popular success, I need say a thousand or two new subscribers. Who is there in New York (with the sole exception of a certain J.Q.) who has any gutttts?"

London was not enough. Without an "official organ" in New York, Pound's renaissance would be just another parochial experiment, a lively footnote in the history of Western culture, and he intended to make a permanent mark on global centers of power. Pound imagined a magazine that would gather far-flung writers in a single location and deliver them regularly to an elite audience—"The rest are sheep," Pound insisted. The magazine wouldn't help the Vortex. It would *be* the Vortex. He told Quinn that they would have all of James Joyce's work, D. H. Lawrence's novels, Wyndham Lewis's stories and the poetry of "a young chap named Eliot . . . I have more or less discovered him." And "Joyce," Pound assured him, "is probably the most significant prose writer of my generation." Quinn probably hadn't read anything by Joyce, and the name itself would have meant little to anyone beyond the small *Egoist* readership—he was the most significant prose writer no one had ever heard of—but Quinn remembered hearing Yeats and George Russell talking about a young man named Joyce back when he visited Dublin in 1904, and whatever they said had left an impression on the wealthy American.

Pound bandied about ideas for a title. *The Alliance. The Vortex. The Hammer.* He sent a magazine prospectus for Quinn to show potential donors, and it included a decidedly masculine list of potential contributors. "I think active America is getting fed up on gynocracy and that it's time for a male review," he informed Quinn. Magazines had long been seen as feminized objects with content and advertising targeting women, and Pound imagined himself invading that gendered domain.

Pound told Quinn they should make an official announcement: "No woman shall be allowed to write for this magazine." They would, of course, have sworn enemies from the outset. "BUT," Pound banged on his typewriter, "most of the ills of american magazines (the rot of mediaeval literature before them, for that matter) are (or were) due to women"—women of both genders, he emphasized. *The Hammer, The Vortex*—whatever they called it—would be a force against the feminization of culture. When he finished the letter he realized that even sending it was dangerous, and he wrote out in large letters at the bottom of the page:

> IF THIS DOCUMENT
> GETS OUT OF
> your HANDS INTO
> THOSE OF MINE
> ENEMIES I SHALL
> STARVE OR BE HUNG
> AT ONCE.

Quinn must have realized what was happening. This was the sort of screed that strained Ezra Pound's ties in London, yet beneath his bluster was an offer of friendship. The young firebrand was making himself vulnerable to Quinn.

SEXISM WAS A FACET of Pound's elitism, and while elitism made Pound abrasive, it also made him relentlessly productive. In a world overrun by mediocrity, individuals with extraordinary talent had extraordinary responsibility. Pound thought civilization depended upon a cultural vanguard leading the sheep onward. Good art was not a luxury or a recreation cordoned off from the business of life. It *was* the business of life. Even the Great War stemmed from bad literature. Pound argued in *The Egoist* that Germany's belligerence was the result of "the non-existence of decent prose in the German language." "Clear thought and sanity depend on clear prose . . . A nation that cannot write clearly cannot be trusted to govern nor yet to think." The bombs and bullets rattling Europe were the consequences of bad poems and novels.

The trouble with Pound's elitism was money. No one could make a living on a subscription list as meager as Pound was imagining, so his solution was to bypass mass-market publishing and rely upon the patronage model of the Italian Renaissance: artists would make a living not by pandering to the sheep but by creating an aristocracy of taste. What the aristocracy needed, he insisted, was an unscrupulous magazine backed by patrons who didn't care about sales or popularity or politesse. Pound was transforming Quinn's concept of patronage. Instead of buying the paintings and manuscripts of established or dead artists, Pound wanted him to support younger artists. This way, Quinn could be more than a cultural bystander, a mere collector of property like Isabella Stewart Gardner. When a patron's money buys time and food, Pound argued, "the patron then makes himself equal to the artist, he is building art into the world. He creates." Pound was inviting Quinn into the Vortex.

In 1916, Quinn began to gather contributions for Pound's magazine with instructions that the editors were to remain *"absolutely free."* Quinn himself gave Pound one hundred pounds per year for his work with *The Egoist*, and if he needed more, he need only say the word. This was a good start. In April 1916, Pound, unbeknownst to Joyce, implored Quinn to send Joyce some money. Joyce and his family income had fled to Zurich, where he had no students and no income, and he was desperate. "Ten years teaching in Trieste," Pound told Quinn, "so as to be able to write as he liked without listening to editors so as to be independent. Ousted by war, sick, subject to eye-rheumatism or something or other that makes him temporarily blind or at least too blind to keep most jobs." For years, artists pestered Quinn for favors, and here was Ezra Pound writing frantic letters to help his friends.

Quinn began to live through Pound's ambitions. By the summer of 1916, he planned magazine offices in London and New York. He wanted each issue to have 96 to 128 pages, far more than the 30 to 40 pages Pound was imagining. Quinn thought each issue should cost fifty cents instead of thirty-five. He calculated costs (about $6,880 per year), rattled off his shortlist of potential donors and searched for like-minded staff members. "We want a little savagery and some fierceness," he told a friend.

But the plans never materialized. Pound didn't have the patience, the salesmanship or the business sense to run a magazine—conquering the world required more than a battle ax and a globe. It was easier, of course, to take over an existing magazine than begin one from scratch. In November 1916, Pound went through some back issues of *The Little Review* since Miss Margaret Anderson had taken it upon herself to send him the copies. Pound wrote to say that her magazine "seems to be looking up," but it was still "rather scrappy and unselective." She printed his letter. The magazine continued to improve. There were bombastic contributions about anarchism and prison letters from Emma Goldman, but the June-July issue devoted sixteen pages to Imagism that rounded out forty-five pages of respectable work. Yet the August 1916 issue was only twenty-five pages, and Anderson's lead article, "A Real Magazine," caught his attention.

I loathe compromise, and yet I have been compromising in every issue by putting in things that were "almost good" or "interesting enough" or "important." There will be no more of it. If there is only one really beautiful thing for the September number it shall go in and the other pages will be left blank.

Come on, all of you!

Pound dredged up the September issue and discovered that she actually did it. The first half of the magazine was blank. And that's when it occurred to him that the only person who had any guts was a woman.

EZRA POUND HAD A VEHICLE to bring Joyce's work to America, but he had to improve it first. As soon as Pound saw the blank pages of *The Little Review*, he wrote to Margaret Anderson and asked if there was any way he could help. They wanted the same things: experimentation, unfettered thought and individualism. The editor of *The Little Review* was outspoken, uncompromising and willing to curry Pound's favor. She had two thousand subscribers, which was exactly what he wanted. *The Little Review* was desperate for money and new material, and Pound had John Quinn and a stable of young talent. Anderson seemed amenable to his suggestions, and Pound had plenty to give. In other words, they were a perfect match.

In Pound's second letter to Anderson, he told her he wanted *The Little Review* to be his "official organ" in the United States. He peppered her with questions. How many words per issue could he have? How often would the review appear? How much capital did they need? His unnamed guarantor would offer £150 per year to pay contributors, expenses and Anderson's and Heap's salaries (ten dollars a week), and he wanted all of his contributors to appear at once. "BOMM! Simultaneous arrival of new force in pages of *Little Review*." Pound wrote to Quinn that same day. And the next day. And then three days after that. *The Little Review* published only glimmers of talent, he admitted to Quinn, but it had enthusiasm, and enthusiasm was enough. Quinn had misgivings. He suspected that Miss Anderson was a nauseating "Washington Squareite," and their Fourteenth Street basement office (with no telephone) deepened his suspicions. "The thing I really want to find out," he wrote to Pound, "is whether the woman has not merely discrimination but whether it is possible to work with her; whether she is neurotic or not; whether she is decent and bathes."

Margaret Anderson and Jane Heap had moved to New York in 1917. They lived in a four-room apartment above an undertaker and a pest control company on Sixteenth Street. One of the rooms was *The Little Review*'s literary salon, where poets, painters and anarchists could gather for inspiration and ideas. They papered the walls with long sheets of gold Chinese paper. Old mahogany furniture and a dark plum floor absorbed the light reflecting off the shimmering walls, and a large blue divan hung from the ceiling by chains. The poet William Carlos Williams found it intimidating.

Anderson and Heap believed the people who possessed *The Little Review*'s élan would come to them, and they did. An eighteen-year-old Hart Crane arrived at their apartment with some of his early poems. Crane became the magazine's advertising manager, sold one ad in two months and quit. After that, he rented two rooms above the *Little Review* office to remain in its orbit. Young writers were especially drawn to the magazine. Once, a young woman knocked on their door to beg them for advice.

"What shall I do to become a good writer?" she asked Anderson. She wrote heartbreaking short stories about mining tragedies and other proletarian disasters.

"First," the editor counseled, "disabuse yourself of the national idea that genius is a capacity for hard work. The meaning of genius is that it doesn't have to work to attain what people without it must labor for—and not attain."

Bemused but undeterred, the young woman repeated, "Yes, but what shall I do?"

Miss Anderson looked down at the girl, "Use a little lip rouge, to begin with. Beauty may bring you experiences to write about."

EZRA POUND BECAME *The Little Review*'s foreign editor in May 1917, and he wasted no time. That summer, the magazine published fourteen poems by W. B. Yeats, including "The Wild Swans at Coole." They published work from T. S. Eliot and Wyndham Lewis. James Joyce wrote to *The Little Review* from Zurich and promised to send new fiction as soon as he recovered from an undisclosed illness. Anderson and Heap increased the magazine's size and tightened the layout, and even then some issues topped sixty pages. They tracked down the cheapest printer in New York, a Serbian immigrant named Popovitch, and on the Sundays before an issue was scheduled to go out they rushed to his shop on Twenty-third Street to help set the type, correct the proofs and prepare pages for the binder.

The editors were optimistic. At the end of 1917, they announced wartime price increases and planned to double their subscription list while shedding political affiliations. In the August 1917 issue, Anderson casually referred to "the simple and beautiful but quite uninteresting tenets of anarchism. I have long given them up." That was news to her subscribers, but *The Little Review* was willing to alienate readers. The magazine had a new motto emblazoned across its title page: "Making No Compromise with the Public Taste."

For the first time, Margaret Anderson felt as she had when she was making speeches in front of her family in the hopes of conquering the world. "I want to absorb everything," she wrote to Pound. He wrote back, "I don't want to sleep until we can steam-roller over the *Century* in a magazine using just as much paper."

The tension within modernist magazines was that while they coveted the freedom that smallness gave them—independence from both conflict-averse advertisers and the moderating influence of large readerships—they really wanted to be big magazines, and the industry seemed to offer ample opportunities for aggressive visionaries. In the late nineteenth century, magazines began slashing their prices to increase their circulation. Monthlies that cost twenty-five to thirty-five cents in the United States began selling for less than half that price. Higher advertising revenues outweighed the money they lost on sales because businesses paid more to reach readerships that grew to the hundreds of thousands.

Press advertising, virtually nonexistent before the Civil War, became a billion-dollar industry by World War I. Magazine circulation tripled in the

United States between 1890 and 1905. At the beginning of the twentieth century, there were thirty-five hundred different magazines with an aggregate circulation of sixty-five million—about one for every American who could read. As the magazines grew, so did the businesses that advertised in them. Lower prices, expanding ad revenues and wider audiences became a feedback loop. The print industry invented mass culture.

The modernist magazines tried to imitate the mass-market model of heavy advertising, posters, circulars, branding slogans and publicity stunts—Anderson's encampment on Lake Michigan was, to some degree, a media event. To publicize *The Egoist*, Harriet Weaver hired two "sandwichmen," men with billboards strapped to their shoulders, to sell the magazine on the streets. But experimental magazines would never get the readership of *Cosmopolitan* or *McClure's* (both in the hundreds of thousands). From 1916 until the magazine's demise, *The Egoist* averaged sales of two hundred copies per issue, and advertisers fled *The Egoist* and *The Little Review* in a matter of months. Modernist magazines were the misfit pieces of mass culture's engine. Patronage was their only option.

In MAY 1917, John Quinn invited Anderson and Heap to dine at his penthouse apartment on Central Park West. A French manservant led them down a long, high corridor squeezed tight with six or seven thousand books, and in the drawing rooms overlooking the park there were paintings covering every inch of space. Manet's *L'Amazone*, which Quinn had just purchased for four thousand dollars, enjoyed prominent real estate, but probably not for long. The apartment was an overgrown museum. Paintings were standing in disorderly ranks in corners and alcoves. They were piled up in the bedrooms, in closets and under beds. Anderson recognized the Van Gogh self-portrait and Cézanne's portrait of his wife from the Armory Show. In fact, the excitement surrounding the Amory Show—the sense that something special was happening in the American art world—was partly why she began *The Little Review* in the first place. Four years later, she was dining with the three men who had orchestrated the show, for John Quinn's other guests that evening were Walt Kuhn and Arthur Davies, the show's organizers.

Anderson and Heap enjoyed Quinn's irascibility, but he was more prone to diatribe than dialogue, and he had a crude art vocabulary. The "pictures" he admired the most were "kicking" and "full of radium." He was the type of man who kept his art stacked like piles of money. Quinn, for his part, thought Miss Anderson was beautiful. Her buoyant hair and lustrous blue eyes were allur-ing. She was buxom and refined—"a damned attractive young woman," he wrote to Pound, "one of the handsomest I have ever seen." Miss Heap, on the other hand, had a broad body and a mannish haircut—"a typical Washington Squareite." Quinn examined back issues of *The Little Review* and found swarming misprints, ecstatic articles about mediocre artists and tasteless an-nouncements about financial problems. To save money, one of the issues was printed on butcher's paper, and they turned their office into a small bookshop where, he informed Pound, people "could come in and *have tea*."

Quinn wanted Kuhn and Davies to take over a portion of the magazine for art criticism and reproductions—but art editing was Jane's territory, and the editors had no intention of relinquishing it. When Quinn told Anderson to "go ahead" with the magazine anyway, he received not a word of gratitude. He warned Pound about Miss Anderson: "a firm hand with a willful lady is, it seems to me, what she requires."

Pound tried to stage-manage the partnership from across the Atlantic. Quinn might not have the ability to talk fluently about art, he told Anderson, but he had instinctive taste. Besides, "he expresses approval and says you are intelligent." He encouraged her to visit him every once in a while and to "be a comfort to Quinn. He is about the best thing in America," and he wrote the same conciliatory letters to Quinn. She has an "amiable spirit," he wrote, and she wasn't deferential because "she hadn't any real idea who you are when she met you." That was a lie, but it was necessary. For the first time in his literary career, Ezra Pound was a peacemaker.

Despite Quinn's misgivings, he helped secure advertisements from his publishing friends. He offered to pay their rent if they were in trouble, and, he wrote to Anderson, "I shall, of course, be glad to give you the benefit of my expert advice re any question of censorship." Word of Quinn's association with *The Little Review* eventually got around to Mitchell Kennerley, a publisher Quinn had defended against obscenity charges. Kennerley asked him, "Will you defend *The Little Review* if it is attacked?"

Quinn didn't hesitate. "I certainly will."

8.

ZURICH

————

In June 1915, Joyce was unemployed, two months' salary in debt and a British citizen residing in enemy territory. He put up his furniture as collateral to purchase train fare from Trieste to neutral Switzerland for himself, his wife and his two children, ten-year-old Giorgio and eight-year-old Lucia. The circuitous route through the Austrian war zone took three nerve-racking days before they arrived in Zurich, which had become a haven for smugglers and spies, forgers and deserters, propagandists and black market tycoons. Food was scarce, especially in winter, when the corn and potatoes planted along the lake were dormant. When meat wasn't available, people ate boiled chestnuts and frog legs. Instead of sugar cubes, cafés served coffee with saccharine pills.

The war gave Zurich a surreal atmosphere. In July 1916, Hugo Ball read out the Dada Manifesto in a Zurich guild house: "How does one achieve eternal bliss? By saying dada. How does one become famous? By saying dada. With a noble gesture and delicate propriety. Till one goes crazy. Till one loses consciousness." Dadaists wearing masks and outlandish costumes performed dances bordering on madness in the Cabaret Voltaire. They recited poems of nonsense words, hiccups, whistles, moos and meows. Dadaism was Futurism with buffoonery instead of violence. What the two movements shared was a desire to start from scratch. In the midst of a war of unprecedented scale, they wanted to begin civilization anew.

The Swiss did not approve. Cavalrymen with swords and plumed hats rode through the streets to maintain order, and the police eyed the hordes of refugees (nearly half of the city's population) for signs of suspicious activity. Saboteurs traded troop movements, discreet gentlemen bartered forged documents for milk and butter, and Lenin played chess at the Café Odéon before boarding a sealed train back to Moscow to start a revolution. Everyone was potentially a spy, and James Joyce, a skinny Irishman from Trieste, was no different.

The Austrian government suspected that Joyce was relaying letters from Austria to Italy for a man named Adolf Mordo, and they believed Mordo, who fled Trieste, was aiding an underground Italian resistance. Joyce was indeed relaying correspondence between enemy countries, but the letters were not coded communications to Mordo. They were love letters written to Mordo's daughter from one of Joyce's former students. Nevertheless, when the police in Graz discovered the communications, they wanted information about Joyce, and the subsequent government report from Trieste stated, "As a foreigner and as far as his political opinions were concerned, he had a doubtful reputation. While he was a resident in Trieste, however, he never gave cause for any suspicions." But after the official thought about it, he crossed out the second sentence. A later report indicated that Joyce and his creative associates in Zurich were "most undesirable people."

In 1916, the Austrian government sent an undercover agent to pose as a student wishing to take English lessons from Joyce in order to ascertain his allegiances and activities. Was he plotting against the Central Powers? Joyce apparently knew what was happening because he told the spy what he wanted to hear: he was an ardent Irish nationalist—a member of Sinn Fein—bent on the destruction of Britain. He wrote anti-British articles in a London magazine called *The Egoist* and was under British surveillance. It wasn't true, but it was convincing. The spy reported to his superiors at the Royal Defense Headquarters that "Professor Joice" could be quite helpful to the Austrian war effort: "the pen of this man could be used by us."

But Joyce wanted nothing to do with the war. For years, he avoided the pestering British Consulate's requests to return to the United Kingdom, to enlist or to report to their doctor to verify his medical exemptions. "As an artist I am against every state," he told a friend. "The state is concentric, man is eccentric. Thence arises an eternal struggle. The monk, the bachelor, and the anarchist are in the same category." He didn't approve of revolutionaries throwing bombs in theaters, and yet, he said, "have those states behaved any better which drowned the world in a bloodbath?"

In Zurich, Joyce was in exile from his exile. He walked through the streets with an ill-fitting brown overcoat and a scraggly beard cut to a point. A friend's Bavarian landlady was afraid of him, and the Stadttheater's chorus girls called him "Herr Satan." Joyce lived in Zurich without much of the ballast of his life: his books, his manuscripts, and the cherished family portraits all stayed in Trieste (no one imagined the war would last very long). Per usual, the Joyces inhabited a series of apartments, the most comfortable and expensive of which was a two-room segment of a five-room flat they shared with strangers. Lucia slept in a bedroom with her parents while Giorgio had a cot in the living room. The Joyces, according to the Austrian spy, appeared to be surviving on the breadline.

And yet Joyce was beginning to make a name for himself in the literary world. *The Egoist* completed serialization of *A Portrait* in 1915, and he found avid supporters among influential writers like H. G. Wells and H. L. Mencken. Ezra Pound and W. B. Yeats helped secure him small institutional grants—seventy-five pounds from the Royal Literary Fund, fifty-two pounds from the Society of Authors and one hundred pounds from the Civil List, a gift endorsed by Prime Minister H. H. Asquith, though he had his reservations. The grants gave Joyce time to write *Ulysses* and to frequent Zurich's cafés and restaurants, where he drank regularly with a small group of international refugees who called themselves the "Club des Étrangers."

Nora frequented the cafés as well, even if leaving the children home alone disturbed middle-class Zurich sensibilities, but Joyce's revels were difficult to match. During late-night festivities he would break into his signature dance, an inspired approximation of a jig that he honed, it seems, over the course of the next decade (every art form requires patience). Joyce's jumps, whirling arms and rubber-legged kicks somehow managed to appear both clownish and graceful to delighted onlookers. Sooner or later, Nora would coax him homeward, though he displayed the same tireless enthusiasm at the parties they hosted over the years. Joyce would sing Irish ballads and accompany himself on the piano in impromptu recitals that went far too late into the evening. One guest remembered the rich brogue in Nora's exasperation as Joyce began another song. "Ther-r-r-re he goes again!" she exclaimed, plugging her ears with her fingers, "and will the man never learn?"

Whatever else happened, the Joyces always ate dinner as a family. Mother and father spoke Triestino with Giorgio and Lucia at various restaurants as if sharing a secret argot, a verbal performance of a shared life far from Zurich. And yet Joyce was able to offer his family little more than this tendril of intimacy during the war. Among Lucia's few enduring memories of her father in Zurich was the sight of him writing on the floor of their flat—notebooks, pens, crayons and papers arranged out around him like obstacles, and the words on all the pages slashed through in red.

Joyce was working with a scaffold, a schematic understanding of his novel's events loosely tied to episodes from Homer's *Odyssey*, so that his writing had become a painstaking process of fitting details into a broad schema. "I write and think and write and think all day and part of the night," Joyce wrote to Pound. "But the ingredients will not fuse until they have reached a certain temperature." By 1917, nearly three years after beginning *Ulysses*, Joyce was still not quite finished with a single episode, but when plans to serialize *Ulysses* in *The Little Review* solidified in 1917, he focused on finishing publishable drafts chronologically. Publication, after all, would break the cycle of writing and thinking, and an audience might help fuse the melding ingredients.

THE WRITING WAS GOING reasonably well until Joyce collapsed on the sidewalk in February 1917. A spasm of pain shot through his right eye—it felt like it was going to burst open—and a wave of agony left him unable to move for twenty minutes. Joyce's iris, the blue part of his eye, was swollen from iritis, and the swelling pushed his iris forward, perhaps less than a millimeter, which blocked the drainage of ocular fluid. When the pressure spiked inside his eye,

Joyce found himself in the throes of his first attack of glaucoma. The episode was, more than financial troubles and world war, the gravest threat to the book Joyce had barely begun to write. If untreated, glaucomatic pressure would slowly kill his optic nerve cells until the eye went blind, and Joyce had every reason to think that both eyes would suffer before long. After giving up a settled life to be a writer, glaucoma threatened to take away something he had not anticipated losing. Joyce had guarded himself carefully against the national, imperial and religious enemies of his artistic independence only to discover that his iconoclastic masterpiece might be at the mercy of periodic inflammations within his own eyes.

Joyce had suffered from iritis several times before. In 1907, his eyes became so inflamed that he couldn't read, write or teach. A doctor repeatedly disinfected them with silver nitrate, but even if the treatment had helped (it didn't), Joyce had other symptoms to contend with. He had inexplicable pains in his back and stomach. He was bedridden by the end of the first week, and when he walked he shuffled around like an old man. He suffered from mild panics and had difficulty breathing. Something was wrong with his skin—Stannie rubbed his brother's body down with a noxious lotion mixed with salt. His right arm had become, as Stannie put it in his diary, "disabled" for weeks. The illness dragged on for over two months. While Nora was giving birth to Lucia in the pauper's ward of the Triestine hospital, Joyce was undergoing electrotherapy treatment, which, like everything else, didn't help. Stannie thought it was a particularly nasty case of rheumatic fever. Joyce suffered twelve more acute bouts of iritis over the next fifteen years, and the development of each "eye attack," as he called them, was maddeningly unpredictable. Sometimes the pressure built slowly, beginning with a nagging discomfort creeping into either or both of his eyes in the middle of the night. The pain could subside spontaneously or intensify in a matter of days, hours or minutes.

Once his iritis became glaucomatic, the only effective treatment was an iridectomy: a surgeon cuts away a small piece of the iris to help drain the eye and reduce its pressure. Needless to say, Joyce resisted surgery and convinced himself that the best cure was a warmer climate. He wore black glasses whenever he went outside to make the sunlight bearable and begged Dr. Sidler, the director of the Augenklinik at the University of Zurich, not to operate. The doctor consented, but Joyce's condition was deteriorating.

A sticky fluid of fibrin and pus was accumulating inside his eye, and it glued a portion of his iris down to the lens capsule behind it, forming a synechia. The adhesion was a serious problem. It warped the pupil's contractions and dilations and further impeded the drainage of intraocular fluid, which increased the chances of another attack of glaucoma.

Cases like Joyce's presented doctors with two bad options. Surgically separating the synechia could tear away pieces of Joyce's iris and damage his vision permanently, but if the synechia wasn't removed, the entire margin of the iris might stick to the lens, making Joyce's pupil immovable and his right eye blind. The most appealing treatment for synechia at the time was a drug called atropine. With luck, atropine would separate the synechia, paralyze Joyce's strained ciliary muscles, sedate his irritated nerve endings and relieve his dilated blood vessels—all without surgery. The problem with atropine, however, was that it increased intraocular pressure, risking an "eye attack" yet again. Joyce could take the risk of surgically damaged vision or medically induced glaucoma.

Dr. Sidler decided to give Joyce atropine, though two months later, in April, Joyce developed glaucoma again, and as his illness continued through the summer and fall, he discovered another problem with atropine: it was poisonous. Atropine is derived from a plant called belladonna, or deadly nightshade, and its roots, berries and leaves contain a chemical that disrupts the parasympathetic nervous system. Eating a single leaf could be fatal, and an excessive amount of atropine—one or two too many eyedrops per day or a slightly stronger solution—could cause fainting, headaches, throat irritation, delirium and hallucinations. During the months Joyce spent avoiding surgery, the amount of atropine he took became toxic. He complained of fevers and an irritated throat. He began hallucinating.

Word of Joyce's condition spread. John Quinn purchased some of Joyce's manuscripts to help him financially, and knowing Joyce was unable to read, he wrote to Nora to explain the seriousness of glaucoma and the importance of obtaining Switzerland's best doctors—advice from friends or a priest or the British consul, he said, would do no good. Quinn cabled ten pounds to help pay for the medical fee, and he consulted America's "best eye expert" about Joyce's case. "Poor fellow," he wrote to Pound, "one can tell from his letters that he is a sick man and worried and harassed and depressed."

Pound had worried about Joyce's eyes ever since Joyce sent a picture of himself in 1916. "Thanks for the photograph," Pound responded. "It is a bit terrifying." He was alarmed that Joyce's eyes were so distorted, and he offered his own alternatives to surgery. He suggested squinting through cylindrical lenses used to correct astigmatism and twisting them around to see if they helped. He should also track down an osteopath in Zurich instead of a typical M.D. He might be cured, he wrote, "by having a vertebra set right side up and thus relieving blood or nerve pressures." Like Quinn, Pound consulted his own medical expert for advice. Quinn's expert didn't like Pound's expert.

SOMEHOW—DESPITE WAR, pain, atropine hallucinations and his inability to earn an income—Joyce found ways to write *Ulysses*. There were small moments of health stolen in early afternoons, days of reduced pain and functioning pupils, a week or two of optimism inspired by Dr. Sidler's confidence. Joyce scrawled phrases on slips of paper that he left like Easter eggs in unlikely spots around the apartment. He would try to find them when he was better and piece together the lives of Stephen Dedalus and Leopold Bloom from scraps. It continued like this for years. There were few, if any, bursts of inspiration that set him composing paragraphs at a time. *Ulysses* was a procession of drafts, a sedimentary novel that gained its mass one grain at a time.

Joyce kept notebooks and large sheets of paper crammed with character descriptions, lists of rhetorical devices, notes on mathematics, facts about ancient Greece and Homer's *Odyssey*. Sometimes the notes were arranged by chapter or subject: "Names and Places," "Gulls," "Theosophy," "Blind" and "Recipes." He wrote down phrases and single words, seemingly at random—"tainted curds," "heaventree," "knight of the razor," "boiled shirt," "toro"—and collected them in notebooks, where they waited to be inserted into his manuscript like pieces in a jigsaw puzzle. Big or small (one of his entries was simply "We"), Joyce seems to have known exactly where the fragments would go (Bloom must use the royal We, the embodied collective, at a certain moment in the "Circe" episode). Each time he inserted a detail into a draft, he crossed it out with a crayon until he had notebooks filled with large Xs and lists of insertions struck through with red, blue and green slashes.

As time went on, Joyce's note taking increased. There was a torrent of notes—he made notes from his notes—all of them together, he said, would fill a small suitcase. He stopped drafting on both sides of his notebook pages so that he could use the left pages (the versos) entirely for additions. Joyce built *Ulysses* phrase by phrase.

Though he was far from Dublin, Joyce found his material everywhere. He mined the Club des Étrangers for information and manipulated conversations so that they would bear upon the subjects discussed in his novel. Everything around him, anything people talked about, had a potential place in his scheme—a Swiss pun, an idle gesture, the name of a poison, an item of physiology or folklore. Joyce was voracious. In the middle of a conversation, or at dinner, or while walking down the street, he would stop and produce a small notebook from his vest pocket and bend forward until his face approached the end of his twitching pencil while he jotted down a fortuitous word or phrase. In August, after Nora took the children to Locarno to give Joyce the space he seemed to need, he wrote alone and talked to the cat. "Mrkgnao!" said the cat. He wrote it down.

Nora wrote from Locarno about how much the marketplace reminded her of Trieste, and she told him about the thunderstorms, which would have terrified him. "I shall wait at the telephone at Eleven if you telephone well and good if not dosent matter." Nora's letters, though short and infrequent, were like Joyce's. The tenderness was half concealed. "I hope you are writing Ulisses dont stay up too late at night I suppose you havent bought any close for yourself be sure and do so[.]" If it was strange to be in Zurich without his family, it became easier as he ambled through the city, swinging his ashplant cane just as he did in Dublin. Joyce walked down Bahnhofstrasse in the late summer afternoon and listened to the languages populating the sidewalks. He could smell the linden trees along the street, and behind their slender trunks were Zurich's blue and white trams, the same colors as the trams on Nassau Street.

Pain—without warning—struck Joyce's head like lightning. The face of the stranger who carried him to a nearby bench was blurry, and Joyce saw halos around the streetlamps radiating outward from red to yellow to green. When he gathered his senses, the dread of knowing what the doctor would say when he returned to the Augenklinik must have washed over him. Dr. Sidler would have tapped on his eyelids and felt the retinal arteries throbbing against the wall of Joyce's eye. He decided that an operation was unavoidable.

Joyce was conscious during his surgery. The nurse medicated him with atropine and cocaine before the blepharostats pried his eyelids open. The surgeon held Joyce's eyeball with fixation forceps so that his eye, riveted in the surgical light, watched the blade advancing like a bayonet. The cornea resisted for a moment before the blade pierced the surface and slid into the eye's anterior chamber. Exudate flowed over into the incision. The nurse took the fixation forceps, turned Joyce's eye downward and handed Dr. Sidler the iris forceps. The prongs entered the chamber and pulled the top edge of Joyce's iris out through the incision like a tissue from a box. The nurse handed the doctor the iris scissors, and after warning Joyce to hold still, he cut away a triangular piece of his iris and pushed the severed edge back inside with a spatula.

When it was over, Joyce had a nervous breakdown. Perhaps it was the trauma of the procedure—the sound of the instruments clinking in the tray, taking their turns at him. Perhaps as he lay in bed, the cocaine fading and his single eye darting around the room to follow atropine hallucinations flitting into corners like ghosts, he had too many hours to imagine the prospect of a life spent groping for scraps of paper like an old man. Perhaps it was the burden of writing an exhaustive story of a single day in Dublin, a day that he insisted on narrating minute by minute and wouldn't end until well past midnight. After three years of work, it was still only eight in the morning—and he did not have a single completed episode. Perhaps it was the strain of warfare, of never having money, of children to feed and the mounting quotidian problems he could barely manage when he was healthy. Perhaps it was guilt. Nora rushed back from Locarno to be with him in the recovery room, but the doctors refused all visitors until his emotional collapse subsided. It took three days. She wrote letters on his behalf and nursed him while his eye bled for two weeks.

THE SURGERY MIGHT have provided Nora with some small measure of hope, for Joyce had been ensconcing himself in a private world with little room for her or the children. Perhaps his pain would bring him back to her and to the world outside of *Ulysses*. Since fleeing to Switzerland, Joyce had begun to treat his life as a feeding ground for his book. At one point, he asked Nora to cheat on him so that he might understand more completely Leopold Bloom's life as a cuckold. Nora's trip to Locarno with the children was a tactical retreat to coax out a man steadily withdrawing into his work, but neither the retreat nor his illness brought him back.

The family's more practical problem was that Joyce fervently pursued his writing despite the fact that his career, well over ten years in the making, provided so little. Though Joyce was gaining recognition, the possibility of making a living as a writer seemed as distant now as it had ever been. By mid-1917, Joyce had earned exactly two and a half shillings in royalties on *Dubliners*—a fraction of one pound. *A Portrait* was published in the United States at the end of 1916, and Miss Weaver published a British edition by persuading the U.S. publisher, Ben Huebsch, to ship extra copies to England. Though Joyce's first novel was buoyed by a raft of good reviews, it took several months for the British edition to sell only 750 copies. Joyce was mystified, but Pound reminded him just what sort of writers they were. "How many intelligent people do you think there are in England and America? If *you will* write for the intelligent, how THE HELL do you expect your books to sell by the 100,000???????"

Joyce expected little more than enough income to make wartime inflation manageable, and yet even elemental concerns (paying the rent, keeping his family warm, his eyes) were lost in his pressing desire to create one permanent work of art. While writing *Dubliners* and the first draft of *A Portrait*, he told Stannie that he wanted to transubstantiate "the bread of everyday life" into something immortal. As time went on, the quest for artistic permanence grew into the desire to write a novel in a language "above all languages," to speak beyond the vocabulary that tradition handed to him. The war had given Joyce what it gave the Dadaists and the anarchists, what it gave Lenin and Freud: the sense that everything was about to change, that the crackup of Europe and the fall of empires portended something truly revolutionary, and if a novel were skillful enough, it could advance all of civilization. For what mattered about being an egoist and an artist was that the pure, self-directed individual would abandon the self, would delve back into the far reaches of culture, the broad collectives and abstractions, the imperial traditions, the conscience of a race, and transform it all.

Luckily, money arrived from various sources. Supporters in New York (including Scofield Thayer, the editor of *The Dial*) donated a thousand dollars to help. One of John D. Rockefeller's daughters, Edith McCormick, gave Joyce a thousand Swiss francs a month for over a year. A few days after the publication of *A Portrait*, Joyce received a letter from a London law firm while he was convalescing in a darkened room—someone else had to read it to him. The letter informed him that an anonymous "admirer" was giving him two hundred pounds, equivalent to his annual salary before the war. Neither Joyce nor Pound could guess who the donor was.

Wartime patronage made it easier for Joyce to indulge his artistic ambitions, but the grandeur of his ambition meant that there was little room in his life for anything other than *Ulysses*. He read portions of his manuscript to Nora, who remained indifferent, and when he couldn't talk to her about *Ulysses*, he found little to say to her at all. It was no coincidence that one of Joyce's closest friends in Zurich, an English painter named Frank Budgen, wanted to hear all about his book. Budgen remembered how he first saw Joyce in the summer of 1918. Joyce was a slender man with pants cut narrow at the legs "wading like a heron," navigating around chairs and tables in a darkened garden with his head tilted upward and his irregular eyes peering out from behind thick lenses. Joyce and Budgen drank carafes of white wine (always white wine, which tasted, Joyce said, like electricity) at their regular table at the Pfauen. Joyce would throw his head back, and the café would echo with his outburst of a laugh.

They had conversations with sculptors and poets, intellectuals, expats, communists and Freudians. "Why all this fuss and bother about the mystery of the unconscious?" Joyce asked Budgen. "What about the mystery of the conscious?" Once, to liven up the mood, Joyce took from his pocket a tiny pair of a doll's underwear, put the frilly garment on his fingers and walked them seductively across the table toward a poet, who became red with embarrassment.

Budgen was eager to hear about *Ulysses*. "Among other things," Joyce told him, "my book is the epic of the human body." Budgen looked on skeptically as Joyce continued. "In my book the body lives in and moves through space and is the home of a full human personality."

"But the minds, the thoughts of the characters—"

"If they had no body they would have no mind," Joyce said. "It's all one."

What Budgen admired most about Joyce was his zeal, his boyish excitement about small things—he could work all day on two sentences. He read portions of his manuscript to Budgen in a muted, far-off voice, as if he were reading only to himself. He seemed to be discovering something no one had ever found, like a new continent or a cure to a dreadful disease.

Once, Joyce handed Budgen a piece of graph paper torn from his notebook. "Can you read it?" Joyce asked. He couldn't. "There are about a dozen words written in all directions, up, down and across." Joyce pulled out his magnifying glass and asked him to try with that—even a few letters would help. The glass enlarged a thicket of writing. Was there an "e"? Or a "c"? A "c-l"? Budgen discerned a few letters appearing like deer in the woods, and that was good enough. Joyce took back his paper and magnifying glass and waded on. He was one word further into the day.

PART II

It was like a burning at the stake as far as I was concerned. The care we had taken to preserve Joyce's text intact; the worry over the ills that accumulated when we had no advance funds; the technique I used on the printer, bookbinders, paper houses—tears, prayers, hysterics or rages—to make them push ahead without a guarantee of money; the addressing, wrapping, stamping, mailing; the excitement of anticipating the world's response to the literary masterpiece of our generation . . . and then a notice from the Post Office: BURNED.

—MARGARET ANDERSON

9.

POWER AND POSTAGE

———

The United States declared war on the German Empire on April 6, 1917. One week later, a bomb exploded in a munitions plant in Philadelphia, killing 130 people, the result of a German plot. After nearly three years of isolation, the war had come home. "German agents are everywhere," ads warned in newspapers and magazines. Government notices encouraged citizens to send names of potential enemies and, in some cases, to take suspicious individuals by the collar and turn them over to the police: "The only badge needed is your patriotic fervor."

Vigilance organizations—the Minute Women, the Sedition Slammers, the Boy Spies of America—sprouted up around the country looking for German spies, enemy sympathizers and draft dodgers. The most extensive organization was the American Protective League, a quasi-official auxiliary to the Justice Department. For a seventy-five-cent fee, many members received "U.S. Secret Service" badges, despite protests from the actual Secret Service. The APL made arrests, patrolled with sidearms and coordinated with local, state and federal officials. Members had no training and little oversight, and the loose organizational structure allowed them to engage in blackmail, wiretapping, burglaries, kidnappings and lynchings. By the end of the war, the APL had investigated roughly three million "character and loyalty" cases. They found zero German spies.

Some of the German spies were Irish. The most ardent Irish nationalists hoped a British defeat would give Ireland its independence, and a few plotted to use Ireland as a staging ground for German attacks on Britain—one of the conspirators was New York Supreme Court Justice Daniel Cohalan. In 1916, three months after the plot was uncovered, a cargo ship carrying two million pounds of munitions headed for Britain exploded in New York Harbor, and the resulting blast measured 5.0 on the Richter scale. Irish dockworkers had planted the firebombs. Like Justice Cohalan, the dockworkers were probably members of the Clan-na-Gael, a militant Irish nationalist group operating in semisecrecy in several U.S. cities.

In June 1917, Congress passed the Espionage Act, which banned any activity hindering the U.S. armed forces or helping its enemies during the war. Citizens could be imprisoned for up to twenty years for using language that might provoke draft dodging or military insubordination. Congress amended the law to criminalize "any disloyal, profane, scurrilous, or abusive language about the form of government of the United States," and over the next three years the government waged the largest crackdown on political dissent in U.S. history. The highest government official enforcing the Espionage Act was the postmaster general, and he directed local postmasters around the country to inspect all newspapers and magazines—anything unsealed—for material that would "embarrass or hamper" the war effort. The prime enforcer of political control was neither a federal intelligence agency nor a league of citizen spies. It was an army of three hundred thousand civil servants.

It's strange to think of it now, but the Post Office Department was a major federal law enforcement agency. On the eve of World War I, the FBI (then called the Bureau of Investigation) was a fledgling subsidiary of the Justice Department. When the Espionage Act was signed in 1917, there were only three hundred Bureau of Investigation agents, and the Secret Service had only eleven counterespionage agents in New York. But the Post Office (an executive branch department in those days) was well established. It had 300,000 employees, including 422 inspectors and 56,000 postmasters overseeing the circulation of fourteen billion pieces of mail every year. The Post Office reached the far corners of the country, and it had been that way for decades.

Long before there were highways and telephones there were postal roads and mail couriers. Small towns had post offices before they had cemeteries.

So when the United States entered World War I and the government wanted to censor dangerous words with a nationwide mechanism that had a long history of constitutional authority, it turned to the Post Office. The government gained the power to censor words by mastering the ability to circulate them, and warfare—the other foundation of big government—justified more censorship. This was how the government found James Joyce. The censorship troubles of *Ulysses* began not because vigilantes were searching for pornography but because government censors in the Post Office were searching for foreign spies, radicals and anarchists, and it made no difference if they were political or philosophical or if they considered themselves artists.

THE GROWTH of the federal government is largely a story of the growth of the Post Office, and a powerful Post Office was the cornerstone of the U.S. censorship regime. Since its establishment in 1782, the Post Office had a legal monopoly over mail circulation, but the government didn't exercise that power until 1844, when Congress declared that the system's purpose was "elevating our people in the scale of civilization and bringing them together in patriotic affection." Out of a diverse population sprawling across the continent, the mail would make Americans. This policy began a half-century expansion during which the Post Office built roads, slashed postage rates and stiffened penalties for private carriers violating the government's monopoly. From 1845 to 1890, mail volume increased one hundred times over.

The Post Office garnered most of its strength by slashing postage rates. In 1844, it charged twenty-five cents to carry a letter four hundred miles, and if the letter had two sheets, the postage doubled (envelopes counted as another sheet). Seven years later, that same letter could be delivered nearly across the continent for only three cents. Newspapers and magazines enjoyed reduced rates since before the days of Ben Franklin, and yet periodical postage also plummeted. By 1879, newspapers and magazines were grouped as "second-class mail" and delivered anywhere for two cents per pound. If the recipient lived in the same county as the sender, delivery was free. Rates didn't hit rock bottom until 1885, when periodicals were delivered anywhere in the country for one cent per pound, and it remained that way until 1918.

The infrastructure that made Americans also made modernists. The Post Office enabled little magazines on shoestring budgets to reach nationwide audiences. If half of *The Little Review*'s subscribers were in Manhattan and the other half scattered around the country, Anderson and Heap could distribute two thousand copies of an issue for $3.33. Their postage bill for the October 1917 issue was $2.50—the price of just one Joyce fan's subscription. And yet all the Post Office needed to do to control a magazine like *The Little Review* was revoke its second-class status. First-class postage was eight to fifteen times higher—an unsustainable cost for a little magazine—and the Supreme Court ruled that postal bans and rate increases didn't infringe on free speech because publishers had other distribution options, even if denying a magazine's second-class rates would bankrupt it.

World War I dramatically expanded postal censorship. Postmaster General Albert Burleson claimed the Espionage Act gave him the authority to judge mailed material without court approval or congressional oversight. When Congress asked Burleson to disclose his surveillance instructions to the nation's postmasters, he simply refused. The Post Office decided who broke the law, who deserved rate increases or outright bans and who deserved criminal prosecution. Burleson was a man to be reckoned with. He wore a black coat to match the black umbrella he carried at all times, and one of the president's advisers called him "the most belligerent member of the cabinet," which was saying a lot in 1918. He once complained about a socialist newspaper's "insidious attempt to keep within the letter of the law."

Under Burleson's direction, Post Office inspectors began leafing through newspapers and magazines for unpatriotic material. Within a year, the government suppressed more than four hundred different issues from scores of publications for a range of political statements, ranging from a poem praising Emma Goldman to a reprint of Thomas Jefferson's opinion that Ireland should be a republic. By the end of the war, more than a thousand people were convicted of violating the Espionage Act, and hundreds received prison sentences.

The foundation of this systematic suppression of political speech was a particular reading strategy that government officials used when considering allegedly treasonous texts: intentions and effects were secondary to an inherently dangerous nature. It didn't matter if a magazine or pamphlet *actually* led people to avoid the draft or aid the nation's enemies. It was enough if the Post Office decided that the words could potentially cause trouble. The basis of political censorship was the self-evident danger of words, their ability to provoke illicit actions in anyone who might read them. In other words, the government read a treasonous text the same way it read pornography. You knew it when you saw it.

But it wasn't supposed to be this way. The government applied the Espionage Act well beyond the authority of the statute itself. Judges granted the Post Office broad power to crack down on the corrupting tendency of radical speech partly because they had been so accustomed to granting that same power over obscenity. By the time James Joyce's *Ulysses* began to appear in *The Little Review* in 1918, the Post Office was in a position to ban the circulation of several of the novel's chapters for being both obscene *and* anarchistic. In fact, the government's reaction to *Ulysses* reveals how much nineteenth-century ideas about obscenity shaped twentieth-century ideas about radicalism. The threat of political words corrupting a vulnerable nation of immigrants might have seemed critical after President Wilson's declaration of war in 1917, but the threat of sexual words—and the fight against them—had been established for decades.

THE HISTORY of the U.S. censorship regime began in earnest in 1873, when Anthony Comstock boarded a train to Washington, D.C., with a draft of a new federal law in his pocket and a satchel filled with his dirtiest pornography. Comstock was the head of the New York Society for the Suppression of Vice, and because he understood the power of words, he understood the power of the Post Office. The government's postal expansion began the year Comstock was born, and his lifetime corresponded with the emergence of mass print markets. Cheap reading material was flooding the country because distribution costs were plummeting as quickly as production costs. "The daily papers are turned out by hundreds of thousands each day," he wrote,

> and while the ink is not yet dry the United States mails, the express and railroad companies, catch them up and with almost lightning rapidity scatter them from Maine to California. Into every city, and from every city, this daily stream of printed matter pours, reaching every village, town, hamlet, and almost every home in the land.

Circulation was insidious. Comstock wanted the government to ban not just immoral books and pictures but also circulars and advertisements—everything that kept pornographers in business. A book like *Lord K's Rapes and Seductions* wasn't the only problem. They had to outlaw the catalog listing the book for sale and the newspapers printing the ads that told people where to find it. The law also had to ban contraception and abortion-related articles—birth control, after all, was part of the same avaricious business of lust. Pharmacists and smut peddlers profited from the same fantasy of sin without consequences.

On March 3, 1873, after nearly a month of lobbying, Ulysses S. Grant signed Comstock's bill banning any "obscene, lewd, or lascivious book, pamphlet, picture, paper, print or other publication of an indecent character" as well as anything intended to prevent conception or induce abortion. And it wasn't just illegal to mail indecent things. It was illegal for anyone—even a doctor—to mail information *about* indecent things. Advertisements for condoms, for example, or instructional manuals explaining how to use a condom (or what a condom *is*) were now criminal if sent through the mail, whether in a magazine or a private letter. The Comstock Act, as it was called, granted search and seizure powers with warrants based on nothing more than the sworn complaint of one individual (Comstock, for example), and the penalties for mailing obscene material were much harsher: the maximum fine was now five thousand dollars instead of five hundred, and the maximum prison sentence increased from one year to ten.

States across the country exercised even more power. New York's anti-obscenity statute criminalized the sale, production, advertisement and possession of immoral material with intent to distribute. It gave the police search and seizure powers and allowed courts to order the destruction of books and property. This federal patchwork of obscenity laws had perverse effects. A man was free to visit a brothel, but if he wrote a *story* about visiting a brothel he could go to prison—immoral words became more punishable than immoral acts. An office clerk who mailed an obscene book faced a heavier sentence than the book's author, publisher and seller because the Comstock Act wasn't about raiding bookshops. It was about raiding the nation's most powerful distribution network.

When President Grant signed the bill, Comstock was sworn in as a special agent of the Post Office Department. He carried a gun and a badge, and he was one of only a handful of special agents empowered to make arrests across the United States. In retrospect, Comstock's special agent appointment was as important as the law that bears his name, for he single-handedly transformed postal law enforcement. Previously, the Post Office's special agents collected debts, supervised delivery service and arrested mail thieves. Post–Civil War obscenity regulations required the government to supervise far more than the distribution of the mail. It supervised the *content* of the mail. And yet no one exercised that power until Comstock was sworn in. Since Abraham Lincoln signed the first postal obscenity law in 1865, officials prosecuted about one person per year. In Comstock's first nine months as a special agent, he prosecuted fifty-five. The country's largest bureaucracy suddenly had an attack dog, and the circulation of words was never the same again.

WORLD WAR I exacerbated the resentment of the government's growing authority, for nothing represents authority quite like military conscription. On draft registration day in 1917, Emma Goldman held protest rallies in New York. A few days later, eight policemen raided the office of her magazine, *Mother Earth*, on 125th Street. They searched for the names and addresses of anti-conscription supporters, radicals and anarchists. Goldman and her partner, Alexander Berkman, were arrested for conspiring to prevent registration and for advocating violent resistance to the U.S. government.

The Little Review was one of their most vocal defenders. Margaret Anderson and Jane Heap circulated an open protest letter claiming that the anarchists faced imprisonment and deportation "for the hideous crime of free speech," and they listed the addresses of the judge and the U.S. district attorney so that sympathizers could demand a fair trial. The judge and prosecutor received scores of letters and telegrams. Some of them, apparently, were threatening, and six officers were detailed to protect the judge's life. The press reprinted the protest letter and quoted old issues of *The Little Review* featuring Anderson's praise of Goldman, and federal authorities took note.

The trial of Goldman and Berkman was the first high-profile prosecution of anarchists in decades. By the end, Anderson and Heap were among Goldman's only friends who weren't thrown out of the courtroom (standing for "The Star-Spangled Banner" was mandatory), and they were sitting at the defendants' table when the jury found them guilty. Goldman and Berkman received ten-thousand-dollar fines and two years in prison.

THE CLIMATE OF SUPPRESSION had a chilling effect throughout the publishing industry. To avoid an Espionage Act prosecution, Ezra Pound made sure *The Little Review* didn't talk about the war, but the editors felt a wartime backlash anyway. In September 1917, a longtime reader protested the "Ezraized *Little Review*," and a reader from Chicago was blunt: "I wish you didn't have such a craze for foreigners and self-exiled Americans. I think you have missed your chance right here in your own country . . . I am tired of these floods of Russian, French, Scandanavian [sic], Irish and Hindoo stuff that have swept the country." Subscriptions dwindled, and *The Little Review*'s support of Emma Goldman got the editors evicted from their Fourteenth Street office. They scrounged for money and subsisted on potatoes for days. Nevertheless, Margaret Anderson, determined to live beautifully, dressed for their potato and biscuit dinners in a crepe de chine chemise and a fur scarf.

Then the legal problems started. The October 1917 issue of *The Little Review* included a short story by Wyndham Lewis about a British soldier who impregnates a woman and ignores her letters while he's off fighting in the trenches. "And when he beat a German's brains out, it was with the same impartial malignity that he had displayed in the English night with his Springmate." Comstock Act or Espionage Act—you could take your pick. Three thousand copies of the October 1917 *Little Review* were halted in the weighing room of the Post Office while the New York postmaster sent a copy to Washington for inspection. The issue circulated to Postmaster General Burleson, the attorney general's office and, finally, to the solicitor general of the Post Office, William H. Lamar.

In 1918, the law codified what had already been standard procedure: the solicitor general held the final authority to judge dangerous words, ban publications and begin criminal prosecutions over anything obscene or treasonous sent through the mail. The solicitor's purview was massive and uncontested. When William Lamar took the job, the volume of publications circulating through the mail was increasing at a rate of thirty-five million pounds per year, and even liberal courts considered his censorship decisions "conclusive" unless they were "clearly wrong."

Lamar did not take his responsibilities lightly. He had been a preacher from Alabama before he turned to the law in the 1880s, and he believed in the power of words. "Words are the first and last weapon of all fakers," he told *The Boston Globe*, "big words, extravagant words, mysterious words." Dealing with mysterious words was simply a matter of "reading between the lines," he said, and he knew what radicalism looked like. "You know I am not working in the dark on this censorship thing," he wrote to a journalist. "I am after three things and only three things—pro germanism, pacifism, and high browism."

John Quinn wrote a legal brief defending *The Little Review*, and he appended a letter to William Lamar. "The foreign editor is Ezra Pound, Esq.,

who is a very distinguished writer and poet and is a personal friend of mine."
He informed Lamar that he was quite familiar with obscenity law and had a
proven track record: when Anthony Comstock brought charges against another friend of his, Mitchell Kennerley, he won the case easily, and in his professional opinion the short story in question "does not come within gunshot of
violating the statute or any Federal statute. I know the writer, Wyndham
Lewis, personally." Quinn kindly asked Lamar to cable his authorization for
the magazine's circulation to the New York postmaster and to do so quickly.
Quinn was going to Washington to meet with the attorney general and the
chairman of the Foreign Affairs Committee, and after that he planned to speak
with Lamar in person.

Quinn's influence didn't work. Lamar declared the October issue of *The
Little Review* obscene under Section 211 of the U.S. Criminal Code, an updated version of the Comstock Act. Quinn filed a motion to restrain the Post
Office, but Judge Augustus Hand ruled against it. There was more detail than
necessary in Lewis's story, and while there were legal books more salacious
than this magazine, Judge Hand argued, they escaped government bans "because they come within the term 'classics,'" which were justifiable exceptions
"because they have the sanction of age and fame and usually appeal to a com-
paratively limited number of readers." In other words, salacious classics were
legal because they were old and most people didn't read them.

The defeat was an embarrassment to Quinn. The postal ban associated
him and *The Little Review* with radical magazines like *Mother Earth* and *The
Masses*, and he kept news of the decision out of the papers. When the embarrassment subsided, he suspected something was amiss. Lewis's story wasn't
particularly obscene, his direct appeals to Lamar hadn't worked and his brief's
argument about the story's moral lesson for unwed women had fallen on deaf
ears. Quinn concluded that someone must have put pressure on the postmaster general. Then it suddenly made sense.

"Alas!" he wrote to Pound. "Here's the fact, as I believe it: Miss Anderson
broke into the papers last spring over that lousy old anarchist Berkman and
that old slut Emma Goldman; in court every day; greatly excited and all 'hot
up'; thought Goldman a 'great woman'—ad nauseam." *The Little Review*'s an-

tics attracted the attention of federal officials, Quinn wrote to Pound, and Anderson was now known as a pacifist, which was barely distinguishable from a
traitor. "So there you are!! Attention centered on her! The country going
through a spasm of spy-hunting and a greater spasm of 'virtue.'" That's why
the magazine was confiscated. And he was right. The Bureau of Investigation
opened a file on Margaret Anderson, and Lewis's short story was just an
excuse to harass a radical magazine. Lamar declared the October 1917 issue
unmailable not for being obscene but for being a "Publication of Anarchistic
tendency." The Post Office banned its circulation under the auspices of the
Espionage Act.

POUND WAS ALARMED. His literary renaissance, only months old, was already in jeopardy. He was worried not just because Quinn's displeasure
threatened the magazine's finances, but also because he had recently received
the first chapters of James Joyce's *Ulysses*. And they were magnificent. Given
the news from New York, however, he wasn't sure it would survive the spasms
of spy-hunting and virtue. He wrote to Joyce in mid-December 1917:

> *I suppose we'll damn well be suppressed if we print the text as it
> stands. BUT it is damn wellworth it. I see no reason why the nations
> should sit in darkness merely because Anthony Comstock was horrified
> at the sight of his grandparents in copulation, and thereafter ran
> wode in a loin cloth . . . Wall, Mr. Joice, I recon you're a damn fine
> writer, that's what I recon'. An' I recon' this here work o' yourn is some
> concarn'd litterchure. You can take it from me, an I'm a jedge.*

Pound sent the typescripts to Margaret Anderson in February 1918,
though he warned Anderson, in Chaucerian English, that "Joyce has run
wode" in the third chapter—it was madness, even if different from the Com-
stock-in-loincloth variety. The chapter was, he said, "magnificent in spots,
and mostly incomprehensible" (he later changed his mind). Stephen's thoughts
morph and proliferate without any gloss or mediation—Joyce did not adjust

his content or style to assuage the inherent difficulty of overhearing someone's mind. In the "Proteus" episode, Stephen walks alone on the beach, and as the exterior action falls away, his thoughts touch upon his family's dissolution, the conversations he had earlier in the day, his silly childhood prayers, *Hamlet* and Shelley and Aristotle, his own pretentiousness, arias and nursery rhymes, last night's dream about Baghdad, a newspaper report of a murder, the murderer's imagined thoughts and the possibility of walking out into eternity from the shore.

As conceptual as the episode is, Stephen's thoughts begin with (and return to) the visible world: "Ineluctable modality of the visible: at least that if no more, thought through my eyes. Signatures of all things I am here to read, seaspawn and seawrack, the nearing tide, that rusty boot." The reader doesn't know it yet, but Stephen broke his glasses the day before—he can barely *see* the rusty boot. He thinks about seeing because it helps him cope with blindness. For Joyce, writing Stephen's stream of consciousness was partly a way to go beyond the visible world by thinking about it.

Margaret Anderson had always wanted to peer into the mind of the artist. She and Jane Heap spent hours exploring relevant questions. *"By what touch does one immortalize objects? By what power does one create in one's own image?"* Anderson wanted to weigh the content of a person's mind, to examine "the poignant human being" and distill the secrets of creativity. Here at last she had a key to the artist's laboratory. Anderson read the manuscript straight through to the opening of "Proteus," and when she came to the rusty boot, she stopped reading, looked up at Jane and said, "This is the most beautiful thing we'll ever have. We'll print it if it's the last effort of our lives."

Pound had no idea how the law would apply to *Ulysses*. He suggested they mail only three hundred copies of each Joyce issue. If the Post Office didn't confiscate them, they could send out the rest. He asked Quinn if mentioning urination was illegal. What about mocking transubstantiation? Were there any statutes prohibiting blasphemy? He wanted to know where the line was so they wouldn't cross it again. "When dealing with religious maniacs, one NEVER can tell." Pound refused to let *The Little Review* fall apart before *Ulysses* was in print. "For God's sake," he wrote to Anderson, "do something to cheer Quinn. He is the best and most effective friend I have in America." Since Quinn's faith in the magazine was shattered, he tried to salvage his faith in *Ulysses*. All their troubles, he wrote to Quinn, would be worthwhile "even if we go bust and die in a blaze of suppression over Joyce's new novel."

For Pound, the fight for *Ulysses* was fueled by his outrage that a government capable of banning a writer like James Joyce even existed. When he saw the text of the Comstock Act, he wanted to reprint the statute in every issue as an example of the institutional mediocrity that their renaissance should vanquish. Pound tried to convince Quinn that their aristocracy of taste required a new law: "I think the statute which lumps literature and instruments for abortion into one clause is so fine a piece of propaganda for the Germans that it would be disloyal to publish it here till after the war." The law encapsulated the country's ignorance. It was "grotesque, barbarous, ridiculous, risible, Gargantuan, idiotic, wilsonian, american, Concordia Emersonian, VanDykian, Hamilton-Mabiean, pissian, pharrrtian, monstrous, aborted, contorted, distorted, merdicious, stinkiferous, pestilent and marasmic." Never had adjectives seemed so weak.

Pound wrote a letter to William Lamar "man to man" ("I trust you are proud of your handiwork," he wrote) and asked Quinn to forward it (he didn't). He wrote a *Little Review* article denouncing the legal system that could treat art like "the inventions of the late Dr. Condom," and he skewered the judge's argument that the "classics" escaped censorship because so few people read them. Pound thought that the reasoning thwarted literature's development. Any contemporary writer who wanted to write a classic that violated social conventions would have to endure being outlawed—and therefore impoverished—until official approval arrived decades or centuries later. Until then, writers were at the mercy of an unaccountable authority like Lamar with no literary training.

Quinn wanted to drop the matter entirely. What seemed charmingly cavalier about Pound's rants when his subject was art or poetry became petulant when he talked about the law, and *The Little Review* had enough problems without encouraging more scrutiny from federal officials. Quinn informed Pound that his intemperate article against the Comstock Law "might be the last straw"—his quip about "the inventions of the late Dr. Condom" was itself potentially illegal. Pound didn't seem to grasp how quixotic his protest was in the middle of a war. The only way the government would change the law, he told Pound, would be to make it stronger.

"There is nothing in the anti-Comstock business. People are sick and tired of it," and he warned Pound not to ruin his own reputation just as he was making a name for himself in the United States. "In the minds of nine hundred and ninety-nine people out of a thousand your campaign for free literature would be lumped in at once with pro-Sanger, pro-Washington Square, pro-free love, pro-anti-Comstock propaganda, pro-birth control propaganda, pro-socialist propaganda." Once you were assigned to a group like that, it was impossible to get out.

THE GROWING SCHISM between the two men was fundamental: Quinn was practical, and Pound was an ideologue trying to turn art into power. Imagism and Vorticism were his attempts to remove the barriers between the word and the world. Pound's renaissance in art was trying to colonize the world of politics, and yet his reaction to the Comstock Act proved he was trapped inside the art world no matter what—he was reading the statute as if it were a *poem*. Pound was horrified not so much by the fact that immoral books and condoms were outlawed as that they were "lumped" into the same clause, as if the meanings of the listed items shaped one another like couplets in a stanza. Quinn didn't want to change society or international relations through his patronage. He just wanted to change art. And it unnerved him to think that Pound's creative spirit, his pugnacious honesty and his freedom to flee to China or Alaska were inseparable from his incompetence.

But he still had faith in Pound's opinions about art, and Joyce's work confirmed it. Quinn declared *Dubliners* "one of the most sincere and realistic books ever written." When *A Portrait* was published in 1917, the U.S. publisher, Ben Huebsch, sent Quinn a copy and referred to it as a novel that "very nearly approaches genius." Quinn no longer needed convincing. He bought about thirty copies of *A Portrait* for his friends and wrote an article praising James Joyce in *Vanity Fair*: "A new star has appeared in the firmament of Irish letters, a star of the first magnitude." Quinn's Joyce was Pound's Joyce. His article praised the Irish writer's newness and honesty, his rejection of ornament, rhetoric and compromise—he went so far as to copy portions of Pound's letters verbatim.

National ties turned his appreciation for Joyce into devotion. Quinn was the son of Irish immigrants. His mother, whom he adored, was an orphan from Cork who had arrived on U.S. shores when she was fourteen, and Quinn visited Ireland for the first time only weeks after she died in 1902. The Irish became an extended family for a man who had lost his parents and whose closest ties were to a couple of siblings and a bevy of mistresses. With no children of his own, John Quinn began to think of his patronage of great Irish writers as a part of both his heritage and his legacy.

Quinn, in fact, suspected he was dying. He discovered that he had a malignant tumor in his large intestine and needed surgery to remove a section of his colon. For months, Quinn's assistant was the only one who knew, but the reality was setting in. He was only forty-eight years old. "I am still interested in life," he wrote to Pound, "still feel its sap, the world seems good to me, and I don't want to go for a long, long time yet." He prepared his will and squared away unfinished business before checking into the hospital. In March 1918, he sent Pound the remaining $750 he promised for his work for *The Little Review*, and he gathered an additional subsidy of $1,600 from himself and three of his friends. He did not intend to help the magazine any further.

So when Quinn's assistant delivered his mail to his hospital room and Quinn, recovering from surgery, flipped through the March 1918 issue of *The Little Review* containing the debut installment of James Joyce's new novel, *Ulysses*—the long-awaited masterpiece guaranteed to make all their troubles worthwhile—the references to "snotgreen" noserags and "the scrotumtightening sea" disgusted him. There was a joking ballad that included a line about Jesus urinating. The burden of Quinn's sickness likely made every unpleasant detail unbearable, and he dictated an angry letter from his hospital bed. "That is what I call toilet-room literature, pissoir art. It doesn't even rise to the dignity of boudoir art or whorehouse art or cabaret art." He could have *The Little Review* convicted in thirty seconds before any judge or jury in the country.

THE FIRST PERSON to censor *Ulysses* was Ezra Pound. Joyce sent the fourth chapter while Quinn was in the hospital, and the text was substantially worse than "snotgreen" and "scrotumtightening." Leopold Bloom takes his morning trip to the outhouse in the small back garden of his Eccles Street flat. "He felt heavy, full: then a gentle loosening of his bowels. He stood up, undoing the waistband of his trousers. The cat mewed to him." Ezra Pound took out his blue pencil and struck a line through the phrase "of his bowels" and another through "undoing the waistband of his trousers." He cut about thirty lines before sending it to Anderson and Heap.

Pound told Joyce they could print the unexpurgated text in a Greek or Bulgarian translation someday, but Joyce was not amused. "I shall see that the few passages excised are restored if it costs me another ten years," he vowed. Pound justified his deletions on artistic grounds. It was bad writing, he told Joyce in a letter. "Bad because you waste the violence. You use a stronger word than you need, and this is bad art, just as any needless superlative is bad art." Pound didn't want Quinn agitated any more than was absolutely necessary, and if *The Little Review* were suppressed too often it would be suppressed permanently. "I can't have our august editress jailed, NOT at any rate for a passage which I do not think written with utter maestria."

Pound sensed that *The Little Review* was falling apart just as *Ulysses* was starting to see the light of day. He went months without hearing from Anderson and Heap, and the situation in New York was worse than he knew. They were behind on rent, malnourished and sick. Jane wrote to a friend back in Kansas about their squalid apartment. "It is so dirty—and everything is broken or scuffed or bent and useless—and a perfect pest of mice—hordes of them. I can't bear to look at my room, or put it in order." Jane lost fifteen pounds from dysentery and had fever blisters on her face. Anderson caught the Spanish flu and began seeing someone else. She would lock herself in a room to proofread upcoming issues while Jane ensconced herself in some far corner of the apartment to avoid catching a glimpse of the other woman, half-naked, darting to and from the bathroom. Jane alternately entertained and avoided the advances of her own love interest, Djuna Barnes, but she was heartbroken and, eventually, suicidal. And *The Little Review*'s troubles were just beginning.

THE U.S. GOVERNMENT'S censorship of *Ulysses* began with an offhand note about the novel's unusual style. In March 1919, a copy of *The Little Review* landed in the Translation Bureau of the Post Office Department because the magazine contained pages of French prose. The Translation Bureau was tasked with sifting through foreign-language texts for wartime crimes, and it was still operating in 1919. The official inspecting *The Little Review* read the five-page installment of *Ulysses*, in which Leopold Bloom helps a blind man cross the street and wonders what it would be like not to see. The Translation Bureau official wrote to his supervisor, "The Creature who writes this *Ulysses* stuff should be put under a glass jar for examination. He'd make a lovely exhibit!"

The issue was perfectly legal, but the supervisor decided to examine the Creature more closely, and he discovered that the January issue of *The Little Review* was more offensive than peculiar. Leopold Bloom orders a gorgonzola sandwich for lunch at Davy Byrne's pub and sips a glass of burgundy. The taste makes him think of the grapes in the Burgundy sun, which reminds him of a bright day on a hillside outside of Dublin. Molly kissed him with seedcake in her mouth, and he began to chew it.

High on Ben Howth rhododendrons a nannygoat walking surefooted, dropping currants. Screened under ferns she laughed warm folded. Wildly I lay on her, kissed her: eyes, her lips, her stretched neck beating, woman's breasts full in her blouse of nun's veiling, fat nipples upright. Hot I tongued her. She kissed me. I was kissed. All yielding she tossed my hair. Kissed, she kissed me.

The Post Office notified *The Little Review* that the January 1919 issue was henceforth forbidden from the U.S. mail—the censorship of *Ulysses* began with the novel's central scene of affection.

Since the issues had already been sent to subscribers, the ban was effectively a warning. The second ban was more punctual. The Post Office notified Anderson that the May 1919 issue was being inspected in Washington, D.C., to determine whether Episode IX of *Ulysses* was obscene, lewd, lascivious and filthy, and therefore in violation of the Comstock Act. John Quinn was the only person who could help, and his appreciation for Joyce—despite some of his nauseating details—made him feel as if he had no other option. Quinn spent nearly an hour and a half dictating a legal brief defending *Ulysses*, and Lamar gave him the courtesy of making his decision over the weekend. By Tuesday morning, Quinn heard that the issue was banned.

Quinn prepared to catalog the offenses to Ezra Pound, but he couldn't bear to dictate the magazine's illegal passages to his young female stenographer, so he dismissed her and composed the letter himself. There was an assortment of small objections. Stephen Dedalus mentions the "incests and bestialities" that stain "the criminal annals of the world[.]" He declares, "It is an age of exhausted whoredom groping for its god." Buck Mulligan jokes about visiting Stephen "at his summer residence" in Nighttown, where he was "deep in the study of the *Summa contra Gentiles* in the company of two gonorrheal ladies, Fresh Nelly and Rosalie, the coalquay whore." Buck shares a title for a masturbatory play: "*Everyman His own Wife (a national immorality in three orgasms) by Ballocky Mulligan.*" All of this, mind you, was happening in the course of a discussion of Shakespeare—at one point, Buck cheerfully brings up "the charge of pederasty brought against the bard." Quinn wondered if Pound had even read the banned issue.

As with previous episodes, Pound had not only read it, he had censored it—he simply hadn't gone far enough. Anderson informed her readers that the magazine "ruined" Joyce's writing by "omitting certain passages in which he mentions natural facts known to everyone." Whether pederasty, masturbation and incest were known to everyone was beside the point, Quinn wrote to Pound. "The fact of s—t—g being a common practice every day and hence must be 'a natural fact known to everyone' is no reason why it should be put upon a printed page of a magazine." Perhaps Joyce's conversations had been acceptable among students and librarians in the National Library of Ireland in 1904. They were not acceptable for a magazine sent through the U.S. mail system in 1919.

Pound resorted to flattery. He told Quinn that his legal brief was one of the most brilliant defenses of realist literature he had ever read, and he was sending it to T. S. Eliot (*The Egoist*'s current literary editor) for publication. Eliot wrote to Quinn from London a few days later to say that the suppression of *Ulysses* was "a national scandal . . . The part of *Ulysses* in question struck me as almost the finest I have read: I have lived on it ever since I read it." Eliot pledged to do everything he could for Joyce in England, but he felt like a lone evangelist in a particularly hostile country. In London, he wrote to Quinn, "the forces of conservatism and obstruction are more intelligent, better educated, and more formidable."

10

THE WOOLFS

In the spring of 1918, before *Ulysses* caught the eye of the U.S. Post Office Department, Miss Weaver was trying to serialize Joyce's novel in *The Egoist*. She sat at Virginia Woolf's tea table and placed her gray woolen gloves neatly beside her plate. She wore a buttoned mauve suit and habitually tugged her collar more closely around her neck. The sun arrived briefly that day, streaming through the windows of Hogarth House, in southwest London, but it was still unseasonably cold for April. Miss Weaver looked directly at her hostess's large eyes and answered questions scrupulously, "Yes, Mrs. Woolf."

Virginia Woolf was born into the world of arts and letters. She was the daughter of Sir Leslie Stephen, a well-known writer and editor, and Julia Prinsep Stephen, who had served as a model for Pre-Raphaelite painters. Her half brother was Gerald Duckworth, one of the many publishers who rejected Joyce's *Portrait*. Woolf was a core member of the Bloomsbury Group, a collection of London artists and intellectuals that included E. M. Forster, the economist John Maynard Keynes, and the painter and art critic Roger Fry, whose infamous 1910 Post-Impressionist exhibition gave the group sudden prominence. Woolf's Bloomsbury affiliation was, at the time, more influential than her fiction, which was just beginning to appear, but she had been writing reviews for the *Times Literary Supplement* for over a decade, and by 1918 her bold pronouncements on novelists old and new were appearing nearly every week. She declared H. G. Wells (immensely popular at the time) "curiously disappointing" while the Victorian Charlotte Brontë was a renegade: "Every one of her books seems to be a superb gesture of defiance." When Woolf declared that "on or about December 1910, human character changed" her long-time readers may have found it arch, but they could not dismiss it.

Virginia Woolf had only heard of Harriet Weaver, and though she ventured helpful questions at tea, her guest seemed incapable of maintaining a conversation. Miss Weaver was an enigma. The daring editor of *The Egoist*—the eccentric successor to *The Freewoman*, an organ of social rebellion—was rather like a "well-bred hen," as she described her in her diary, a woman who comes to tea wearing woolen gloves.

On the other side of Miss Weaver's plate sat the parcel Virginia Woolf was expecting. The neat brown paper wrapping contained the first portion of Mr. Joyce's *Ulysses*. Miss Weaver explained that she was having difficulty finding someone in London willing to print it. A few weeks earlier, the printer for *The Egoist* set up the type for the first episode, but as they reconsidered a few of the more colorful words ("snotgreen" and "scrotumtightening") and remembered what type of material they could expect from Joyce, they refused to print it even with deletions. By 1918, Miss Weaver was acquainted with nearly every printer in the London area, and she wasn't willing to go through the frustrating round of acceptances and retractions again. But T. S. Eliot told Miss Weaver that the Woolfs had started their own press. On a whim, they had purchased a small handpress along with letters and chases and a sixteen-page pamphlet explaining the basics of printing. They operated it out of their home and called it Hogarth Press.

Miss Weaver wanted Hogarth Press to print *Ulysses*, chapter by chapter, in a series of booklets. It would be, she said, a "supplement" to *The Egoist*, for the magazine had become too small for *Ulysses*, the format having dwindled from sixteen pages down to twelve or fourteen. Joyce was not yet finished with his novel, she told the Woolfs, but she estimated the full text would be around three hundred pages. They could examine the first four episodes she brought with her, and she would forward the following episodes as soon as Joyce produced them.

It occurred to Woolf that Miss Weaver was an incompetent businesswoman—her supplement plan was bizarre and the arrangements hazy or non-existent. She puzzled over the woman before her, with her hair pulled back in a bun and her spine keeping its distance from the back of the chair. "How did she ever come in contact with Joyce & the rest?" she wrote in her diary. "Why does their filth seek exit from her mouth?" Virginia and Leonard Woolf agreed, skeptical as they were, to consider Mr. Joyce's manuscript.

A few days later, Desmond MacCarthy, another Bloomsbury member—a literary critic serving in the navy during the war—visited Hogarth House after dinner. As they grew listless, MacCarthy happened to pick up Joyce's manuscript lying about, and he read the beginning of the fourth episode.

> Mr Leopold Bloom ate with relish the inner organs of beasts and fowls. He liked thick giblet soup, nutty gizzards, a stuffed roast heart, liver-slices fried with crustcrumbs, fried hencods' roes. Most of all he liked grilled mutton kidneys which gave to his palate a fine tang of faintly scented urine.

It was *highly* amusing. MacCarthy began reading aloud with dramatic flourishes.

> Kidneys were in his mind as he moved about the kitchen softly, righting her breakfast things on the humpy tray. Gelid light and air were in the kitchen but out of doors gentle summer morning everywhere.

MacCarthy took particular delight in imitating Mr. Leopold Bloom's cat as she circled the legs of the breakfast table. "Mkgnao!" He gave it his best effort, and there were subtle changes, a veritable feline vocabulary. "Mrkgnao!" said MacCarthy. Virginia Woolf found the performance quite satisfying.

MacCarthy wasn't the only guest to ridicule. The Woolfs had recently befriended Katherine Mansfield, a twenty-nine-year-old writer from New Zealand, and when she noticed that they had a portion of Joyce's forthcoming book, she couldn't help but begin reading. It didn't take her long to decide that *Ulysses* was disgusting, unhealthy and too repellent to read. "I can't get over the feeling of wet linoleum and unemptied pails and far worse horrors in the house of his mind," she later wrote to a friend. Yet she turned to Virginia Woolf and said, "But there's something in this: a scene that should figure I suppose in the history of literature." It was difficult to name that something.

For several reasons, Hogarth Press, like so many other London printers, refused to print *Ulysses*. There were obvious practical problems. The Woolfs' longest publication at the time was a pair of short stories (one by Virginia, the other by Leonard) that amounted to thirty-one pages. Leonard's hands trembled so much that Woolf had to set every page herself, letter by letter. A few days before Miss Weaver's visit, she set a personal record when she completed a single page in an hour and fifteen minutes. They started their press in 1917 to give themselves freedom from editorial constraints, and when their work began, Virginia Woolf was, as she wrote in her diary, "the only woman in England free to write what I like." They published authors that trade publishers didn't find remunerative (like Joyce, perhaps), but Hogarth Press was not meant to be a printer for someone else's imprint.

The Woolfs were also afraid to print *Ulysses*. Leonard Woolf showed the episodes to a couple of printers he knew, and both insisted that no reputable printer would touch it. The publisher and the printer, he was told, would face certain prosecution. To be free, apparently, one needed more than a press of one's own.

Virginia Woolf cited only the practical reasons when she typed her cordial letter to Miss Weaver: "We have read the chapters of Mr Joyce's novel with great interest, and we wish that we could offer to print it. But the length is an insuperable difficulty to us at present." A novel of three hundred pages would take them at least two years to produce, she said, because they had a small handpress and no help. They regretted the decision very much, and she instructed her servants to return the manuscript quickly.

And there was yet another reason for the rejection, something more elemental: Virginia Woolf did not like *Ulysses*. A year later, she wrote a review in *The Times Literary Supplement* that initially praised Joyce as a writer who wished "to reveal the flickerings of that inmost flame which flashes its myriad messages through the brain." He was, she wrote, admirably willing to disregard "coherence or any other of the handrails" that readers crave, and her backhanded praise led to a direct strike: *Ulysses* "fails, one might say simply, because of the comparative poverty of the writer's mind." She didn't mean to disparage Joyce's intellect. Rather, she meant that his imagination had gotten away from him—the magnitude of *Ulysses* outstripped the capacity of his mind to harness it.

Virginia Woolf didn't know it yet, but her own mind was just beginning to work through Joyce's project. Over a year later, after she had stopped paying attention to the installments in *The Little Review*, T. S. Eliot dined with the Woolfs and couldn't stop raving about *Ulysses*. It was after that meeting that she confessed in her diary, "what I'm doing is probably being better done by Mr Joyce." She then began to wonder exactly what it was she was trying to do.

READERS FAR LESS DISCERNING than Virginia Woolf have a right to feel alienated. At times, *Ulysses* reads like a book that wants *not* to communicate. A government official told Ezra Pound that British war censors were convinced the *Ulysses* installments were an elaborate spy code, and a reporter in Chicago said some of the episodes were so outlandish that, as Pound put it, they "had bitched the American market" for Joyce's work.

The whole project of Homeric correspondences—embedding references to the *Odyssey* in modern Dublin—seems indulgent, and Joyce executes it so subtly that the novel can become a scavenger hunt for pedants. Leopold Bloom does not sail an Irish Aegean or vanquish cycloptic tyrants in Sandycove. Rather, glimmers of the *Odyssey* shine through in everyday gestures—a secondhand reference to Bloom's "knockmedown cigar" is the burning pike that blinds the Cyclops, who is now the unnamed "Citizen" ("broadshouldered deepchested stronglimbed frankeyed"). A newspaper editor who speeds Bloom on his way to pick up an order for an ad is Aeolus, the god of the winds. The deafening sound of the presses churning out copy for the *Evening Telegraph* and the *Freeman's Journal*, the endless rhetorical devices and the bloviating newspaper headlines throughout the chapter allude to Aeolus's windbag foolishly opened by Ulysses' men. But even astute readers wouldn't necessarily know to look for windiness (metaphorical or literal) in the "Aeolus" episode because Joyce refused to have the Homeric chapter titles printed. As an added challenge, Joyce's chapters aren't even in the epic's original order. The only Homeric handrail is the title of the book itself.

Some allusions are so obscure that their pleasure seems to reside in their remaining hidden. How were readers supposed to know that the directions Bloom and Stephen travel across Dublin to the *Evening Telegraph* offices correspond to the directions Ulysses and the Phoenician sailors travel as they approach the Aeolian Islands? Even beyond the Homeric parallels, *Ulysses* was bewildering. Each chapter was different. Month after month, another experiment appeared like a bizarre new creature from an unknown country. In 1919, Miss Weaver read the manuscript of the eleventh episode, "Sirens," which begins:

> Bronze by gold heard the hoofirons, steelyringing.
> Imperthnthn thnthnthn.
> Chips, picking chips off rocky thumbnail, chips.
> Horrid! And gold flushed more.
> A husky fifenote blew.
> Blew. Blue bloom is on the
> Goldpinnacled hair.
> A jumping rose on satiny breast of satin, rose of Castile.
> Trilling, trilling: Idolores.
> Peep! Who's in the. . . . peepofgold?
> Tink cried to bronze in pity.
> And a call, pure, long and throbbing. Longindying call.
> Decoy. Soft word. But look: the bright stars fade. Notes
>   chirruping answer.
> O rose! Castile. The morn is breaking.
> Jingle jingle jaunted jingling.
> Coin rang. Clock clacked.

It continues like that for two vertiginous pages. Miss Weaver began to worry about Joyce, and her response was delicate. "I think I can see that your writing has been affected to some extent by your worries," and she repeated her hope that his health would improve as soon as he was able to leave Zurich's poor climate. Pound was less delicate. He wrote to ask if he had "got knocked on the head or bit by a wild dog and gone dotty"—as soon as Joyce sent him something brilliant, he got rabid prose like this. Then it occurred to him. "*Caro mio*," Pound wrote, "are you sending this chapter because you feel bound to send in copy on time?" He urged Joyce to take as much time as he needed.

But Joyce wasn't rushing. In fact, he had begun working on the "Sirens" episode as early as 1915. Lydia Douce (with her bronze hair) and Mina Kennedy (with her golden hair) are barmaids at the Ormond Hotel, and Joyce imagined them as Sirens singing out to Ulysses as his ship passes their island. The chapter itself was a song: it was modeled after the eight-part structure of a fugue, and in those first pages Joyce adds an overture, an introduction to the musical sounds and phrases that would be repeated, contextualized and vested with meaning over the course of the chapter. In the opening of "Sirens," the pure sound of the words is what matters. As the episode unfolds, those sounds find their locations in a narrative: the ringing steel of the horse's hoofs carrying the viceroy past the hotel, the "long in dying" resonance of the blind man's tuning fork, the jingle of coins in Blazes Boylan's pocket as he leaves to see Molly Bloom in her bedroom at four o'clock—a meeting Bloom knows about. The overture requires readers to read in bewilderment as the meanings of words dissolve into their sounds. It requires readers to abandon, for a moment, their expectations of what words are supposed to do. They would have meaning in retrospect.

Ulysses was changing radically in 1919. In the second half of the novel, Joyce began to move beyond Leopold Bloom and Stephen Dedalus. In "Wandering Rocks," the tenth episode, an all-seeing eye follows twenty-seven characters over an hour and five minutes (Joyce calculated the actions precisely) in nineteen imbricated sections. Each moment includes a flashing glance at another event happening simultaneously somewhere else in Dublin. A one-legged sailor looking for alms passes two of the Dedalus sisters on their way home. Five sandwichmen plod down the street advertising a stationery store called Hely's (each man bears a scarlet letter) while Blazes Boylan's secretary wonders if a character in the novel she reads is in love with a woman named Marion.

The undertaker closes his daybook while an arm on Eccles Street (Molly's) tosses a coin to the one-legged sailor. Young Patrick Dignam, with his collar sticking up, carries pork steaks home for a wake and remembers the last time he saw his father, heading back to the pub. He hopes he's now in purgatory.

"Wandering Rocks" is a montage of the city, and Bloom and Stephen become background figures caught in the frame as the camera pans across Dublin. Bloom is a "darkbacked figure" looking for a book for Molly in a hawker's cart as Boylan buys a basket of fruit for her, coins already jingling in his pocket. At home, eleven minutes later, the Dedalus sisters eat yellow pea soup donated by a nun while a crumpled YMCA pamphlet declaring "Elijah is coming" floats down the Liffey, where Bloom threw it two chapters earlier. Joyce's tendency to shift seamlessly from one perspective to another began with his long-standing objection to quotation marks. He thought they were unnatural—"perverted commas"—because they barricaded voices from narrative text, and he wanted words to flow through and around characters like water. *Ulysses* was becoming a river of voices.

ONE OF THE NEW VOICES was Gerty MacDowell's. In the late fall and winter of 1919, Joyce was writing the "Nausicaa" episode in small purple notebooks bound with string while harvesting inserts from various note sheets. In "Nausicaa," Gerty MacDowell, perhaps seventeen years old, sits on a beachside rock near a church. It is eight in the evening, and Gerty is aware that a man (Leopold Bloom) is watching her from a distance. She fantasizes that he is a gentleman in one of the sentimental novels or magazine romances she reads. Joyce wrote Gerty's thoughts:

> Dearer than the whole world would she be to him and gild his days with happiness. Nothing else mattered. Come what might she would be wild, untrammelled, free.

But Gerty's happiness would have to be a hard-won thing. As Joyce thought more about that moment, he began to imagine the arduous paths her thoughts would take, the difficulties she and the mysterious gentleman must surmount before their gilded days of freedom together. Gerty's thoughts gathered like clouds. Joyce marked a letter *M* after the word *happiness,* wrote another *M* on the blank left page, and began writing. "There was the allimportant question was he a married man. But even if—what then? Perhaps it was an old flame he was in mourning for from the days beyond recall." "Allimportant" was not enough for Gerty. Joyce drew an arrow up and inserted "and she was dying to know."

Her curiosity leads her beyond the question of whether the man looking at her is married, for there are more poignant obstacles than matrimony. Joyce drew another arrow farther up: "or a widower who had lost his wife or some tragedy." What kind of tragedy? Joyce drew yet another arrow up. A tragedy "like the nobleman in that novel that had to have her put into a madhouse, cruel only to be kind." As the nobleman on the beach came into focus, Joyce added one last flourish at the top left corner of the page. The man looking at her was like the nobleman "with the foreign name from the land of song."

With that small phrase—an insert to an insert to an insert—Gerty's imagination captures something of who Leopold Bloom actually is. "Leopold" is foreign to Ireland, of course, and yet his family name is still more foreign, though dressed in native garb. When Leopold's father immigrated to Ireland, he anglicized his surname to "Bloom" from "Virag," the Hungarian word for flower. Bloom's Jewishness is well known in Dublin, but his foreign name is half obscured. Gerty, in her fantasy, stumbles upon his secret. There are several other moments of insight lurking in their thoughts. Bloom guesses that she's about to have her period, and she is. Gerty guesses that he is a cuckold, and he is. They are blind epiphanies.

Joyce returned to the beginning of Gerty's new excursion where it began lower down on the left page. "But even if—what then?" Gerty would push on. What *if* he were married? He marked the letter *W* and began another insertion at the left edge of the page. "Would it make a very great difference?" He wrote another sentence he discarded, but the misstep took him in a new direction. He began a larger answer to the question in another insert at the bottom of the page.

From everything in the least indelicate her finebred nature instinctively recoiled. She loathed that sort of person, the fallen women off the accommodation walk beside the Dodder that went with the soldiers and coarse men, degrading the sex and being taken up to the police station. No, no: not that. They would be just good friends in spite of the conventions of Society with a big ess.

Like the "Sirens" overture, Gerty's mind becomes clearer in retrospect. Now when Joyce imagines her fantasizing about the man watching her on the beach, she conjures possible worlds (a marriage, an affair, the awful consequences) and pulls back toward virtue. Friendship is, nevertheless, a dead end for Gerty. The promise that "she would be wild, untrammelled, free" is still on the horizon of her thoughts, and Joyce would take her there.

She finds another way to get close to the man on the beach while avoiding the shame of the fallen women in the Ringsend tenements. Joyce went all the way back to the "allimportant question" and her first thought: "Perhaps it was an old flame. . . ." Gerty would understand his loss. She imagines the ghost of the woman who stands between them. "The old love was waiting, waiting with little white hands stretched out, with blue appealing eyes. Heart of mine! She would follow, her dream of love, the dictates of her heart that told her he was her all in all, the only man in all the world for her for love was the master guide." She enjoys the way a small word like *all* can do so much.

"Nothing else mattered." Gerty finally arrives at her destination, only now she would be "wild, untrammelled, free" whether she is with him or not. Her fantasy about the nobleman has freed her from him. Joyce opened up an excursion to a madhouse, a foreign nobleman, fallen tenement women, a police station and a dead lover's ghost all in the period between "gild his days with happiness" and "Nothing else mattered." To build this passage, he incorporated fifteen insertions from his "Nausicaa" note sheets. He had 879 more. Joyce didn't revise *Ulysses*. It was revisionary through and through.

11

BRUTAL MADNESS

For all of its obscurities, Joyce's book is more sentimental than erudite, more elemental than cerebral. The origin of his interest in the *Odyssey* wasn't lofty. It was a children's book. Joyce was eleven years old when an English teacher at his Jesuit school asked his class to write an essay about their favorite hero. Joyce thought of Charles Lamb's *The Adventures of Ulysses*. It was about the wily Greek warrior traveling home from the Trojan War, a king who was, according to Lamb's version, "inflamed with a desire of seeing again, after a ten years' absence, his wife and native country, Ithaca." It was a tale of superhuman feats, magical spells, banquets and treasures, terrifying monsters, fair princesses and thwarted villains.

Ulysses heard the song of the Sirens (a song so beautiful that men abandoned their families forever) by plugging his crew's ears with wax and having them tie him to the ship's mast. He survived the storm that killed his crew by clinging to that same mast for nine days. When Ulysses returned to Ithaca, he disguised himself as a beggar and slaughtered his wife's suitors to be reunited with his wife and only son at last. The teacher, after reading Joyce's essay, frowned at the young man and said, "Ulysses is not a hero."

But to Joyce, he was. Ulysses was the "world-troubling seaman" and the most complete human being in all of literature. He was a father to Telemachus and a son to Laertes. He was a friend, a soldier, a lover and a husband. Joyce thought of him as Europe's first gentleman, but he was also a rebel. Ulysses was the only man in Hellas who opposed the Trojan War. He knew the official reasons were "only a pretext for Greek merchants, who were seeking new markets," Joyce said, but when he fought, Ulysses was an ingenious warrior. He invented the first tank, he reasoned, the Trojan horse. Yet beyond all of the adventures—beyond the hard work, the detours, the challenges, the schemes and disguises, the spells and the riches given and lost—the story of Ulysses is a story about going home.

IN 1909, years before the First World War, Joyce returned home to Dublin with his son Giorgio. After five years abroad, *Dubliners* was unpublished, *A Portrait* was a mess, and *Ulysses* was merely an idea. Joyce could not properly call himself a writer, though he could call himself a father, and he made the rounds in Dublin displaying his four-year-old boy. One afternoon he met Vincent Cosgrave and boasted of his life in Trieste sipping coffee on the Adriatic and coming home to Nora. Cosgrave agreed that Joyce was lucky to be with Nora—he himself, he told Joyce, was fortunate enough to have met Nora in front of the National Museum steps several nights a week back in 1904. And they, too, had walked out to Ringsend.

Joyce's mind tumbled through the implications. There *were* many nights when she couldn't meet him, and Finn's Hotel couldn't have been that busy. She might have walked with Cosgrave down the same streets even as Joyce was in his room writing her letters. He wondered if she whispered the same things in Cosgrave's ear that she whispered to him and if, perhaps, she had taken things further.

Joyce did the math before he wrote to her. They had first slept together three nights after leaving Dublin—October 11, 1904. Giorgio was born on July 27. That was nine months and sixteen days (and what's two weeks to a jealous mind?). He remembered how small the bloodstain was on their hotel sheets, and the baby came much earlier than expected. In the upstairs room of his father's house in Dublin, Joyce got a pen and paper. "Is Georgie my son?" he wrote to Nora. "Were you fucked by anyone before you came to me?" Joyce, who despised violence, wanted to stop a man's beating heart with a bullet.

After nearly two weeks of silence from Trieste, Joyce visited his friend John Byrne in his row house on Eccles Street and broke down in a fit of sobbing. Byrne later wrote that he had never seen anyone so thoroughly shattered. He listened to Joyce's story before concluding that it was all a "blasted lie." Cosgrave and Gogarty, his ne'er-do-well Nighttown companions, were conspiring against him to destroy his happiness. They were simply jealous. Whether or not Byrne was right, he was telling Joyce what he wanted to hear. Byrne's assurances sank into Joyce's beaten frame over the course of the evening. He slept at Eccles Street and woke up the next morning in a new mood.

Joyce begged Nora for her forgiveness, and for perhaps the first time in his life, his tenacious superiority dissolved. The defiant individualist so eager to cast off home, fatherland and church found relief in helplessness. He thought of Nora holding him "in her hand like a pebble." To feel belittled by her was to sense something larger than himself, something approaching awe—this is what happened when the ego splits. Like the imaginary woman in his first prose sketch who "made to arise in him the central torrents of life," Joyce believed Nora was making him a writer, and he idolized her for it. "Guide me, my saint, my angel," he wrote to her. "*Everything* that is noble and exalted and deep and true and moving in what I write comes, I believe, from you." He imagined curling up in her womb like her unborn child, as if she were bringing him into the world at last.

It was Joyce's first time away from Nora, and he wrote to her constantly. He sent her gloves and Donegal tweed for a new dress. He bought her an ivory necklace with an inscription etched into one of the pieces. "Love Is Unhappy," it said on one side, "When Love Is Away" on the other. He sent her money to buy lingerie. He wanted to see her in a woman's ample undergarments—nothing skimpy and tight like a schoolgirl's things, nothing with silly lace trim or fabric thin enough to see through. He wanted her in full, roomy lingerie bedecked with "great crimson bows" and three or four layers of frills at the knees and thighs. He sent her packages of cocoa and told Stannie to make sure she drank it twice a day and ate plentifully so that when he returned to Trieste her body would be as ample and as womanly as her underclothes. Joyce enjoyed the complex secrecy of lingerie. He enjoyed the public glimpse of a private article. He imagined smelling her perfume on the cloth blended with her heavier smells beneath it. He imagined pristine white fabric bearing stains.

At first, he didn't dare mention the mad images welling up in his mind, but when he wrote to Nora near the end of November he alluded to a certain kind of letter that he wished she would write. He wanted her to lead the way. So she did. She began by giving him instructions and telling him what she would do to him if he disobeyed her. The letter was so dirty that we will never know what her instructions were. Nora destroyed her letters years later. Only one item survives—Joyce cherished it in a white leather pouch lined with satin. It was a one-word telegram from Nora: "*Sì*."

Most of Joyce's letters remain, and in December 1909 they began to evolve. One of the effects of his declarations of devotion is that they allowed him to give himself over to a fierce abandon. "Inside this spiritual love I have for you," he wrote, "there is also a wild beast-like craving for every inch of your body, for every secret and shameful part of it, for every odour and act of it." He had previously alluded to the various acts and positions that flashed across his mind, and now he went so far as to describe them. He imagined, he wrote, "your hot lips sucking off my cock while my head is wedged in between your fat thighs, my hands clutching the round cushions of your bum and my tongue licking ravenously up your rank red cunt."

Joyce was trying to take language as far as it could go, and in doing so he was crossing a threshold he had wanted to cross for years. When he was struggling in Paris in 1902, Yeats wrote to tell him that a poem he sent was amateurish. It was the poetry "of a young man who is practicing his instrument, taking pleasure in the mere handling of the stops." Now Joyce was sounding the deepest notes. He was beginning to say everything, to write the unwritten thoughts that go on in the mind.

He wanted, he wrote to Nora, "to fuck between your two rosy-tipped bubbies, to come on your face and squirt it over your hot cheeks and eyes." Each articulated desire compelled him to write more, as if his letters could give Nora a complete inventory of his thoughts. He listed all the places she should fuck him. He wanted her to ride him in a chair, on the floor, over the back of the sofa. He wanted her to pull him on top of her on the kitchen table. "Fuck me into you arseways," he wrote. He wanted her to ride him with a red rose sticking out behind her. He wanted her to hike up her clothes and squat over him, "grunting like a young sow doing her dung, and a big fat dirty snaking thing coming slowly out of your backside." He wanted her to take him on a darkened staircase while she whispered into his ear all the filthy words and stories she and other girls told each other.

The things he wrote would mortify him the next day, and brief silences from Trieste sparked fears that he had gravely offended her. Joyce was, for the first time in his life, afraid of the power of his words. When he was not worried that his letters would estrange Nora, he was terrified that their intensity would provoke her to throw herself at someone out of sheer lust. While Nora telegrammed Joyce, "*Sì*," he telegrammed, "*Be careful*." And yet the thrill of their erotic letters depended upon dismissing caution. His extravagant words deliberately risked his own rejection so that the arrival of her next letter in the mail could usher him all the more dramatically to the safe intimacy of acceptance. Nora Barnacle guided Joyce to his most noble and exalted writing by letting him be obscene.

Nora's acceptance and encouragement were exactly what he needed after those first few years of lonely struggle with his writing, and to magnify her encouragement Joyce made her the face of all women. She was a schoolgirl, a mother, a queen, a mistress and a muse. When Joyce first imagined a woman's love releasing "the central torrents of life" within him, he had it backwards. The torrents within him were compressed into Nora. She was the sublime and the obscene, an angel and a whore. She was, in fact, the first one to say dirty things. In the middle of the night, not long after they left Ireland, she "tore off" her chemise, as he reminded her, climbed on top of him, slid him inside of her, and when the thrust of her hips down onto him was not enough, she bent closer and pleaded, "Fuck up, love! Fuck up, love!"

Nora's letters were similarly unabashed. One was written with such abandon that Joyce called it "disjointed." Another letter described something she would do with her tongue, something she had never done before. Joyce wrote carefully in his tiny script—very few words are changed or crossed out—with her letter open in front of him. He fixated on one particular word she wrote. He contemplated the curves of the letters, the shapes they must have compelled her mouth to make, the ink sinking into the paper as she wrote them, the sound of the letters as brutal as the act they named. The word was bigger than the others, and she underlined it. The thin arcs of the cursive *f* soared above her writing's gentler slopes and plunged down below them. It had the symmetry of a bow on her blue chemise with one of the ribbon ends pulled toward the upturned vowel. Joyce lifted her letter to his lips, and he kissed the word. He wanted pages more.

For someone who fussed and toiled over the smallest lines and passages of his poetry and fiction, the unbridled excesses of their letters felt triumphant. The achievement lay not just in their letters' seamy details but also in their torrential violence, in the waves of "wild brutal madness" Joyce felt sweeping over him when he sat down to write, a madness forceful enough to wrench language out of its self-enclosed world. Obscene words became indistinguishable from obscene acts in his mind. The paradigmatic scene of Joyce's sexual imagination (and a point of origin for the literary imagination of his greatest years) was the thought of hearing Nora uttering dirty things, watching her mouth forming the words, while, he wrote, he could simultaneously "hear and smell the dirty fat girlish farts going pop pop out of your pretty bare girlish bum and *fuck fuck fuck fuck* my naughty little hot fuckbird's cunt for ever."

JOYCE'S RECORD of foul language began when he was seven years old. His parents sent him to a boarding school twenty miles from Dublin, and the Jesuit institution's punishment book notes that one of the priests paddled him four times on the hands for "vulgar language." Joyce was the youngest boy in the school. He proudly announced his age as "half past six," and the other boys turned it into his first nickname, another kind of punishment. Words were integral to the architecture of power before Joyce could understand it. They had erotic strength not because they were filthy, but because filthy words weren't very different from moral words. The alphabet that described his depravity also spelled out laws and commandments—the same fabric had innocent frills and shameful stains. What made their letters so thrilling for Joyce was the way they careened between innocence and guilt, the sublime and the obscene.

Passion, shame, love and jealousy roiled painfully in him throughout his most reckless letters to Nora. When he wasn't declaring his love, he demanded to know her every transgression. When Cosgrave had his hand under her dress did his fingers go inside of her? If so, how far? And for how long? Did he make her come? And what did she do? What did he ask her to do? Joyce was trying to master the past by possessing all of its details. "When you were with him in the dark at night did your fingers *never, never* unbutton his trousers and slip inside like mice?" The undertow of guilt was never far behind. "I love you, Nora, and it seems that this too is part of my love. Forgive me! forgive me!"

Joyce was turning his moral outrage against himself. Letters to Nora functioned as confessions of his depravity and pleas for the punishment he deserved: he wanted her to whip him with a cane. He imagined what it would be like to have done something bad, to see her summoning him with a flushed angry face, an ample bosom, her massive thighs spread open, and, he wrote, "to feel you bending down (like an angry nurse whipping a child's bottom) until your big full bubbies almost touched me and to feel you flog, flog, flog me viciously on my naked quivering flesh!!" To detail his punishment was to degrade himself further and thus to require yet more ruthless punishment— Joyce enjoyed breaking the rules because he honored them. And yet the brutal repetition of his words, which conjured the most depraved masochism, all resolved, in the end, into his letters' more comforting and sonorous refrains: "Nora, Nora mia, Norina, Noretta, Norella, Noruccia . . ." Any words—all words—seemed more powerful and real because of her. What he wanted, he wrote to her, beyond the fucking and flogging, was to go back to her in Trieste and to sit for hours, "*talking, talking, talking, talking* to you." If only such fleeting moments could go on endlessly.

Ulysses was for Nora. The book he was writing—the novel that tried to say everything—was a monument to their first evening together. The day Joyce was immortalizing in *Ulysses* was the day he walked with Nora beyond the docks, where they were alone for the first time. June 16, 1904. The ink of each word in his manuscript made those fugitive moments incrementally more indelible. *Ulysses* was his final love letter.

The erotic letters between James Joyce and Nora Barnacle are one of the secret headwaters of modern literature. For it was here that Joyce had an epiphany about language itself: the souls of the commonest words illuminated the fact that the ultimate power of writing is its ability, like love, to render the writer helpless. His most intrepid letters dissolved into abject pleas ("Forgive me!") and feeble iterations of Nora's name. Joyce was discovering the paradox of words when he was most apt to benefit from it—he had left Dublin to become a writer only to return five years later as an agent for a short-lived cinema. He had spent those years belaboring a novel that no one had read—that perhaps no one would ever read. But with Nora, Joyce had an audience. She was not a scholar or an aesthete, not a patron or a literary critic, but she was devoted, and she read his letters carefully. It was in their secret exchanges in 1909 that Joyce, who spent so much time gaining mastery over words, abruptly found himself mastered by them. That helplessness gave his diligent craftsmanship a dimension of awe, a fear and a thrilling freedom, a recklessness and an openness that must have felt like endless talking.

An intellectual gulf separated the Galway girl from the artist, and yet in some ways she became a model for every reader he ever wanted. The "ideal reader," Joyce would write years later, suffers from "an ideal insomnia." He wanted people to read novels as carefully, as ardently and as sleeplessly as they would read dirty letters sent from abroad. It was one of modernism's great insights. James Joyce treated readers as if they were lovers.

12

SHAKESPEARE AND COMPANY

T he candle flame burned closer to Sylvia Beach's hand as she searched for hours through the piles of books. By the mid-1920s, Sylvia Beach was, as one writer called her, "probably the best known woman in Paris," and her career had begun in the unlit cellar beneath the Boiveau and Chevillet bookshop. She had filled two trunks with poetry in London and scoured the bookstalls along the Seine for any English or American book she could find, but her biggest discoveries were in the shadows of M. Chevillet's cluttered cellar, where she salvaged a Twain, an Austen, a Whitman and a family of Henry Jameses with sturdy bindings. Abandoned Kiplings and Dickinsons peeked out like survivors in the paper rubble.

The idea of her own bookstore had taken shape in Belgrade. In the winter of 1919, Sylvia Beach was trudging through Belgrade's snowy streets in the aftermath of World War I. Serbia's capital was a linchpin of the Balkans, Europe's most vexing tangle of ethnicities. The war that began when a Serbian nationalist walked up to the archduke's motorcade in Sarajevo ended five years later with more than seven hundred thousand Serbs dead, most of them civilians. Nearly a fifth of the Serbian population was gone (the war's highest casualty rate), and Belgrade was still in ruins. Victorious survivors wandered along the trenches collecting shrapnel and battlefield souvenirs. Independence still felt new. Serbia had endured centuries of alternating control by the Ottomans and Austrians, and each conquest had destroyed Belgrade all over again. Buildings over two stories high were rare.

When Sylvia Beach arrived with the American Red Cross, she saw the skeletons of horses strewn along the roadside—she couldn't tell if they had been killed or euthanized or if they had starved to death. Serbia was stagnant. There was no electricity or running water. There were no schools, factories, airports or bridges, and she navigated around mortar shell craters on her way to the market. She struggled with the language, but she learned three important phrases: "Please," "How many" and "Cream puffs."

The market vendors hailed from all around the Balkans. Serbs, Albanians, Macedonians and Bosnians came to town in their national clothing, and so to walk through the Belgrade marketplace was to wade through turbans, head-dresses, fezzes and Astrakhan hats. Gypsy women in colorful layers smoked pipes as they traveled through town. Women carried egg-filled baskets dangling from both ends of a pole resting on a shoulder. People kept warm with a drink called *salep* that was made from the dried tubers of orchids and boiled in tin cans over bits of charcoal. There was little else to buy.

Beach's sister Holly was a Red Cross translator, and she got Sylvia a job as an administrator. She handed out pajamas, blankets and condensed milk to underweight Serbs standing barefoot in the snow—she didn't know why they didn't bring shoes. The Red Cross funneled columns of German and Austrian prisoners into Belgrade's delousing plant, where their tattered uniforms were baked and their bodies scrubbed clean. The Red Cross opened hospitals and orphanages, and the nurses went from house to house documenting inhabitants, medical conditions and primary needs. Beach produced the survey forms on a groaning mimeograph machine and filed them when the nurses returned each day.

Despite all the work they did, the women controlled nothing in postwar Belgrade. Beach found it nettlesome at first, but it soon became infuriating. "The Red Cross has made a regular feminist of me," she wrote to her mother in New Jersey. "It's seeing men doing all the managing and helping themselves to all the pleasant things that come along." The women, she said, "rank as buck privates—are ordered hither & thither, forced to obey unquestioningly." Their treatment was especially galling for a woman who had grown up in Princeton and Paris. Beach's father was a Presbyterian pastor (President Woodrow Wilson's pastor, actually), and the last of nine generations of clergymen. Sylvester Beach was a community leader, a women's suffrage advocate and a firm believer in the independence of his wife and three daughters. His second daughter changed her name from Nancy to Sylvia in his honor.

Sylvia Beach settled in Europe permanently in 1914, and in 1917 she volunteered to work twelve hours a day on a farm in Touraine while the men fought in the trenches. She was proud of her khaki uniform, though the women picking grapes and bundling wheat alongside her disapproved of her bobbed hair and trousers. It could have been worse. When she was in Spain in 1915, villagers threw rocks at her and her sister Cyprian because they were wearing riding pants. But the desolation of postwar Belgrade deepened her perspective as nothing else had. The low mountains surrounding Belgrade trapped the cold Black Sea wind as it carried storms into the city. Snow collected in the crevices between the low-roofed houses and melted down the sloping streets to the muddy Sava River, which curved below the city to meet the brown Danube.

Postwar Belgrade's dreadful beauty gave Sylvia Beach a new resolve. For years, she imagined running a bookshop that would be more than a business or a showroom for books. She imagined an alcove for a literary community, a place where readers and books could find one another, where writers lifted off the page and became real people walking through the door to greet their readers. The money she had been saving wasn't sufficient, but she was willing to write to her mother for help. "I'm sure you would approve of my wanting to make a supreme effort to take something interesting and worthwhile for a life work instead of working under someone at an uninspiring task—with ideas and art taboo and you might as well be a squirrel in a wheel." Her mother was skeptical. It "would be such hard indoor work," she reminded her daughter. Sylvia was small, and her parents always thought of her as delicate.

Nevertheless, she telegrammed her mother when she returned to France: "Opening bookshop in Paris. Please send money." Until then, her prospective bookstore was to be in London, but a trip to England convinced her that the rents were too high and the market already saturated. More important, Sylvia had fallen in love. In March 1917, before leaving Paris for volunteer work, she visited La Maison des Amis des Livres. It was, strangely, both a bookshop and a lending library. She walked in to find the friendly round face of Adrienne Monnier. Her eyes, she remembered, were alive like William Blake's.

After the war, Monnier suggested that Beach open an English bookshop in Paris so they could have sister shops on the Left Bank. Adrienne would lend and sell French books, and Sylvia would lend and sell English books. Monnier could teach her about the book trade in Paris, and without good advice a bookshop in any city would be daunting. By the time Monnier found a vacant storefront in a former laundry around the corner from her shop, Beach was convinced. A few days after her pleading telegram, her mother sent three thousand dollars over the Reverend Beach's objections.

Beach went to the flea market for a table and comfortable antique armchairs that would invite people to stay and read. She purchased drawings by William Blake and portraits of Oscar Wilde and Walt Whitman. Beige sackcloth covered the walls, and Serbian rugs blanketed the hardwood floor. The lion's share of the money went to books. She purchased essential modernist titles in London, and her sister Cyprian sent books from New York. By the time she searched the cellar of Boiveau and Chevillet, she was piecing together the backbone of her shop—the secondhand books that comprised her lending library.

Adrienne Monnier's shop was the first lending library in France, and her success convinced Beach that there was room in Paris for her. The plunging value of the franc made foreign books too expensive to buy—this was, after all, before the paperback revolution—yet there was a growing demand for English-language books in Paris, and she could meet it by lending instead of selling. Members could take out as many books as they wanted, one at a time, for seven francs per month (about fifty cents). To save money, the shop doubled as Beach's apartment. She put a cot in a small back room with an adjoining kitchenette and slept against a barred window that looked out to the courtyard's water closet. At night she watched the rats "running up and down the bars like fingers on a harp," but she didn't care. She had a bookshop of her own.

On a Monday morning in November 1919, Sylvia Beach hung a small wooden sign above her door and opened the shutters to Shakespeare and Company. The signboard was a painting of the bard. Monnier helped spread the word, and members of the French literati came immediately, including André Gide, Georges Duhamel, Jules Romains and Valery Larbaud, all prominent French writers. English and American writers weren't far behind. Shortly after Ezra Pound moved to Paris in 1920 (England had become too docile, he complained), he sauntered into Shakespeare and Company, surveyed the premises and asked Miss Beach if there was anything he could fix for her. He applied his expertise to a cigarette box from Sarajevo and a wobbly chair.

Sylvia Beach had impeccable timing. The First World War had created a generation of transnationalists. Young men and women who never thought of leaving their hometowns found themselves serving in allied or enemy countries and imagining cosmopolitan lives. The booming American and British economies and the plummeting franc made Paris the perfect cosmopolis. Between 1915 and 1920, the franc lost nearly two-thirds of its value against the dollar, and Paris's affordability made its charms irresistible. Only fifteen thousand Americans had visited France annually before the war. In 1925, American tourists numbered four hundred thousand, and many of them stayed. There were eight thousand American permanent residents in Paris in 1920. Three years later, there were thirty-two thousand. The influx made Paris's changes seem like Americanizations. One-way streets and electric signs appeared along with English-language newspapers. There were American churches and grocery stores, Masonic lodges and basketball leagues. Cabarets and café concerts were supplanted by large music halls where expatriates listened to jazz while sipping bright jumbles of alcohol they called "cocktails" without having to worry about federal raids.

Shakespeare and Company transformed an Anglophone convergence into a community. It was, in fact, a thinly monetized social center. Library membership fees barely covered expenses, and the shop made only one hundred dollars in profit in 1921. The importance of Shakespeare and Company had nothing to do with money. By the end of the year, it was a place where readers and writers could talk to one another, where older and younger people exchanged ideas and where Sylvia Beach introduced writers to editors and publishers. If you wrote or read literature and found yourself in Paris—for a week, a month or a decade—you knew where to go. Shakespeare and Company became a literary node in a cultural metropolis.

Culture needs locations. It is not a seamless backdrop so much as a patchwork of local phenomena. Cultures have centers, specific arenas where artists join institutions, where people influence and repel one another, where activities change because of planned and unplanned events and where one can be exposed to people and ideas from Japan, Moscow, West Africa and Dublin all in the same day—cultural centers exist because they are hubs for the peripheries. If modernism had a preeminent location, it was Paris: atop Montmartre before the war and then, when prices became too high, the Left Bank, less than two square miles of narrow streets and wide boulevards south of the arcing River Seine.

Left Bank neighborhoods were diverse, inexpensive and saturated with cafés. This was especially true of Montparnasse, a Left Bank neighborhood where working-class people, immigrants and political refugees mixed with artists and the bourgeoisie as well as students from the adjacent Latin Quarter. Artists like Chagall and Brancusi drank with butchers at the Café Dantzig because Montparnasse's major artist colony was next to a slaughterhouse.

Cafés were more than just the accoutrements of Paris's cultural life. In the nineteenth and early twentieth centuries, there were more drinking establishments in Paris than in any other city in the world—one for about every three hundred people. That was three times as many per capita as in New York and more than ten times as many as in London. The sheer number of Parisian cafés facilitated the formation of small groups in uncrowded spaces, which allowed people to talk, plan and argue freely. If the arguments became fierce, the café culture helped with that, too—there was always another one down the street, and their sidewalk access facilitated the chance encounters that allow groups to form, dissolve and reconfigure. Though fluid, café interactions were far from frivolous. They thrived in France partly because they were havens from stringent nineteenth-century assembly laws. Uprisings from 1848 to the Paris Commune to 1919 arose seemingly spontaneously because workers organized in cafés rather than through unions. Left Bank cafés were at once intimate and ephemeral, playful and consequential, semipublic proving grounds for ideas and semiprivate sanctuaries from the state. They were the perfect spaces for modernism and for a book as urban as *Ulysses*.

Shakespeare and Company was a hybrid space, something between an open café and an ensconced literary salon, which suited Anglophone patrons for whom café culture was always adoptive. Sylvia Beach's bookshop gave British and American travelers a dose of the stability that cafés didn't provide. Several members had their mail sent to Shakespeare and Company (for some writers it was their only reliable address), and Beach used a pigeonhole box to sort their mail alphabetically. The Lost Generation had a home.

On a hot Sunday afternoon in July 1920, Adrienne invited Sylvia Beach to an early dinner party at the home of a French poet named André Spire. Beach didn't want to go. She admired Spire's poetry, but she didn't know him personally, and he hadn't invited her. Adrienne nevertheless insisted and, as usual, she had her way. Spire's warm welcome put his American guest at ease, but as they entered, he pulled her aside and whispered something that terrified her. "The Irish writer James Joyce is here."

The dinner was a welcoming party for Joyce, who had just arrived in the city he would call home for the next twenty years. The move had been unplanned. Ezra Pound had convinced Joyce to relocate to Paris when the two men met for the first time in Italy the previous month. Pound detected the sensitive man beneath the "cantankerous" Irish shell and urged him to move closer to the center of modernism. It was a good time to relocate. Joyce had just finished the fourteenth episode of *Ulysses*, "Oxen of the Sun," which takes place in a maternity hospital, and its nine-part structure links the development of the English language to the gestation of a fetus. Joyce mimicked dozens of styles, from Anglo-Saxon to Middle English to Elizabethan prose to Milton,

Swift, Dickens and others before unraveling into Irish, Cockney and Bowery slang. The episode cost him a thousand hours of work, and he expected the next one, "Circe," to be even more challenging.

Pound prepared the city for Joyce. He sent copies of his work and favorable news clippings to important individuals. He found a French translator for *A Portrait* and a furnished three-bedroom apartment free of charge (for a few months, at least). The final touch was a sumptuous literary dinner to introduce Joyce to Paris's literati. Beach saw Pound slung across an armchair in a velvet jacket and a blue shirt with the collar open wide, and Dorothy Pound, Ezra's wife, was speaking to a statuesque woman with full auburn hair. Dorothy introduced Miss Beach to Nora, and Beach perceived a certain dignity to Joyce's wife. Nora was happy to find someone with whom she could speak English, and Beach was happy to approach Joyce indirectly, as if by his reflected light.

Spire announced the meal and began loading plates with cold cuts, fish and meat pies. Salads and baguettes circulated around the long table, and the host filled glasses with red and white wine. Only one guest was not drinking. As the man in the ill-fitting suit kept declining Spire's repeated offers, the other guests began to watch. James Joyce turned his glass upside down to prove that he meant it. He never drank before eight in the evening. As a jest, Ezra Pound lined up all the bottles in front of Joyce's plate in case he should change his mind. Everyone laughed, but Joyce was red with embarrassment.

After dinner, he slipped away as the conversation turned to literature, and Beach wandered into Spire's small library after him. When she saw Joyce hunched in the corner between two bookcases, with his hair swept back from his forehead, she began trembling.

"Is this the great James Joyce?"

He peered up from the book at the petite American woman with the resolute chin. He extended his limp hand and said simply, "James Joyce."

He expressed himself with careful precision, as if speaking to an audience still learning English. She admired his gentle voice and Irish accent. He pronounced "book" to rhyme with "fluke." "Thick" was sharpened to "tick," and his r's trilled upward. The novel he was writing was "*Oolissays.*" Joyce's skin was fair and flushed. He had a small goatee, and there were lines etched into his forehead. She thought about how handsome he must have been as a young man. But there was something abnormal about his right eye, something magnified or distorted by his thick glasses. It was nearly grotesque.

The name Shakespeare and Company made him smile, almost as much, perhaps, as "Sylvia Beach." He was looking for signs of luck in Paris, and these were auspicious names. As she told him about her bookstore, he pulled a small notebook out of his pocket and held it close to his eyes so he could write down the address. It was heartbreaking. Just then, Joyce jumped at the sound of barking from across the road. She went to the window and saw Spire's tiny dog bounding after a ball.

"Is it coming in? Is it *feerrce?*"

She assured Mr. Joyce that the dog did not look at all fierce, and he was certainly not charging toward the library. He had been bitten by a dog on the chin when he was a boy, he explained, and they had terrified him ever since. The great James Joyce was a blushing, trembling man with weak eyes and a fear of dogs. He was adorable.

The next day, Joyce walked into Shakespeare and Company wearing a dark blue serge suit and a black felt hat. He had a slender cane and a regal bearing undercut by dirty canvas shoes. He ambled over to the photographs of Oscar Wilde and Walt Whitman, and if she wondered in those brief moments what he thought about her small bookshop, her anxiety was relieved as he sat down in an armchair and asked to join Miss Beach's lending library. He could afford a subscription for one month.

Sylvia Beach saw Joyce as sensitive and vulnerable. His list of fears included the ocean, heights, horses, machinery and, above all, thunderstorms. As a child, he hid in the cupboard at the sound of thunder, and the tempests seemed to pursue him all his life. Beach remembered him cowering in his hallway during thunderstorms, which he blamed on the preponderance of Parisian radio broadcasts. Beach encouraged Joyce to talk about his troubles, and he had a few to discuss. The apartment that Pound got for Joyce and his family was a small, fifth-floor servants' flat in Passy. It had one double bed, no bathtub and no electricity. Joyce was in the midst of borrowing a desk, linens, blankets and money. He was also, of course, writing *Ulysses*, and he believed the strain of writing at night exacerbated his eye troubles.

Joyce sketched a picture of an iridectomy on the back of one of the bookshop's circulars. He drew two amoeboid circles, one inside the other, and a few erratic scribbles for iris tissue. Sylvia stared at what appeared to be a drawing by an eight-year-old (this was not, after all, Joyce's medium). He scored five quick lines radiating out from the eye (to signify pain? eyelashes?) and dug the lead of the pencil into the paper as he described the Swiss surgeon's incisions from the edge of the iris to the margin of the pupil. To clarify, it seems, he drew the eye again—circles, scribbles, slashes and all—though the second time he added a heavy dot on the iris. She kept both drawings.

He claimed his eye surgery in Zurich was poorly timed. They should have waited until the iritis subsided, and the doctor's haste impaired his vision. Wasn't it difficult to write? Couldn't he dictate? That was out of the question, he said. He wanted to be in contact with the words, to shape each letter with his hand. Nora groused about how single-minded he had become with his writing. In the morning, barely awake, his first impulse was to reach for his pencil and paper on the floor, and his novel would distract him for the rest of the day. He'd stroll out of the house just as Nora was about to serve lunch because he was oblivious to the time. "Look at him now!" she complained to Beach. "Leeching on the bed and scribbling away!" She wished he could have been something other than a writer. Sylvia Beach could not agree.

13.

HELL IN NEW YORK

———

The end of World War I did not bring peace. The cost of living doubled in five years, which led to thirty-six hundred strikes in the United States in 1919 alone. On May Day of that year, anarchists sent more than thirty green boxes disguised as department store toys to prominent men around the country, including Attorney General Mitchell Palmer, Postmaster General Burleson and Solicitor General William Lamar. Most of them were lucky. When the first few packages detonated in the hands of their recipients, sixteen bombs were still sitting in the General Post Office because they had insufficient postage.

The following month, ten bombs went off simultaneously in several cities, including San Francisco, Milwaukee, Cleveland and New York, and this time they weren't mailed. In Washington, D.C., a man carrying a large suitcase apparently tripped on one of the steps leading to the attorney general's front door, and the bomb exploded in his yard. A neighbor across the street, an ambitious assistant secretary of the Navy named Franklin D. Roosevelt, strode through shards of glass in his living room, stepped over a body part thrown against his doorstep and ran to the attorney general's house. Dozens of pink leaflets were fluttering down the street. "We have been dreaming of freedom, we have talked of liberty, we have aspired to a better world, and you jailed us, you clubbed us, you deported us, you murdered us whenever you could." The bombers promised to destroy all tyrannical institutions. "Never hope that your cops and your hounds will ever succeed in ridding the country of the anarchistic germ that pulses in our veins."

The next day, the police found what was left of the bomber's head on the roof of a three-story mansion a block away. They linked the bomber to an Italian anarchist named Luigi Galleani, who was tracked down and deported days after the June bombings. But that was just the beginning. Attorney General Palmer, who survived his second assassination attempt unscathed, amassed a federal crime-fighting force four times larger than that during the war. Officials estimated that New York City housed "more than twenty thousand persons of extreme radical views." They were mostly foreigners, and the distinctions between anarchists and communists, Galleanists and Bolsheviks became meaningless. "On a certain day in the future, which we have been advised of," Palmer warned Congress, "there will be another serious, and probably much larger, effort of the same character which the wild fellows of this movement describe as revolution, a proposition to rise up and destroy the government at one fell swoop."

The government responded to the bombings with "Red Raids" throughout the country. In the fall of 1919 and early 1920, authorities ransacked offices, confiscated files, destroyed property, roughed up presumed radicals, arrested more than ten thousand suspects and deported hundreds of foreigners in massive roundups. Emma Goldman and three hundred other radicals were deported on a ship under security so tight that no one, not even the U.S. Marines guarding the prisoners, knew the ship's destination. The captain was instructed not to open his sailing orders until he was twenty-four hours at sea.

The biggest Red Raid started at exactly nine p.m. Eastern Time on January 2, 1920. Agents arrested more than three thousand people in thirty-five cities around the country—not just in likely enclaves along the eastern seaboard, but in places like Toledo, Des Moines, Louisville and Kansas City. In New York, more than one hundred Justice Department agents paired up with plainclothes policemen and fanned out across the city in army trucks and hired cars. When harsh interrogations didn't yield the right answers, investigators manufactured confessions of violent antigovernment conspiracies and forged suspects' signatures. Attorney General Palmer claimed to be acting under the authority of the Espionage Act—the U.S. Senate never ratified the Treaty of Versailles, which meant that the country was still technically at war.

The Red Raids fed information to an obscure new wing of the Bureau of Investigation (the precursor to the FBI) called the General Intelligence Division. Wherever its agents went, they confiscated files, books, newspapers and magazines connecting radicals across the country in a community of words (the Communist Party alone had twenty-five newspapers). Bookshops were hubs of subversive activity. It was a sign of the times that a former YWCA on Fifteenth Street in New York was now a shop selling radical literature. The government located underground print shops and leafed through publications sent through the mail to piece together the network of publishers, writers, bookstores, comrades and sympathizers.

The Little Review was one of the magazines caught up in the dragnet, which jeopardized the only platform for James Joyce's growing opus. The Post Office banned the January 1920 issue because barroom Dubliners in the *Ulysses* installment refer to Queen Victoria as "the flatulent old bitch that's dead" and a "sausageeating" German on top of it. They joke about the potential medical consequences of her son King Edward VII riding more women than horses: "There's a bloody sight more pox than pax about that boyo." The references were disparaging enough to be illegal if a federal official wanted them to be. Years after its support for Emma Goldman and anarchism, *The Little Review* was still under scrutiny.

By 1921, the General Intelligence Division had files on nearly half a million subversives, and that was just a start. Ezra Pound would have a file. So would Ernest Hemingway, Theodore Dreiser, Langston Hughes and John Steinbeck. So would James Joyce. The files were methodically cataloged and cross-referenced by the division's ambitious young director, J. Edgar Hoover. He had received his appointment on the eve of the Red Raids, when he was twenty-four years old, and he got his start as a government librarian.

But radicalism was not rooted out easily. On September 16, 1920, a skinny, unshaven man in workman's clothes drove an open wagon through downtown Manhattan. He stopped across the street from the J.P. Morgan building on Wall Street, close to the New York Stock Exchange, set a time bomb wired to a hundred pounds of dynamite and disappeared back into the city. The blast shook Wall Street's financial buildings to their foundations and threw people to the ground before they even heard the explosion. Glass from buildings as far as Broadway fell down on the heads of bankers and clerks like jagged snow. The bomb was packed with five hundred pounds of iron slugs the size of walnuts. Whoever made the bomb broke apart cast-iron window weights with a sledgehammer so that the pieces would gouge into granite buildings and skulls. Hundreds of wounded survivors staggered for safety amid flames, overturned cars and mutilated bodies. Thirty-eight people died, and pieces of a horse lay all along Wall Street.

John Quinn was in his Nassau Street office when the bomb shook the building. He saw a cloud of greenish yellow smoke rising above the roof of the Assay building a couple of blocks away as well as the shattered glass dome on top of the Morgan building. Seconds later, crowds surged up the street, and Quinn watched the people down below pushing one another forward and toppling like tall grass in the wind.

The financial center attack was payback for the government raids. The devastation, Quinn wrote to the artist Jacob Epstein, was "a horrible price to pay on account of anarchists, mostly Russian anarchists, and nearly all Russian Jews, I am sorry to say." Quinn felt trapped on an island teeming with the world's unwanted biology, and he ranted to Ezra Pound about what New York had become in the last decade. The city was bursting with "seven or eight hundred thousand dagos, a couple of hundred thousand Slovaks, fifty or sixty thousand Croats and seven or eight hundred thousand sweating, pissing Germans." It was a city of infernal noise and voracious, mongrel crowds. The Jews swarming into New York from all over Eastern Europe, he wrote to Pound, are "nothing but walking appetites."

THE RADICALS THREATENING New York were also, more often than not, the city's sexual iconoclasts. They attacked marriage, fought for birth control, examined, explored and celebrated sexualities. Anarchists, communists and sexual liberators shared neighborhoods, ideas, readers and publishers. Ben

Huebsch published D. H. Lawrence and James Joyce alongside unabashedly communist books like *The Truth About Socialism*. *Mother Earth* and *The Masses* advocated tirelessly for greater sexual freedom. In March 1916, the month before the United States entered the war, *The Masses* published an editorial defending Germany. "Militarism is not a trait of any race or nation," it said. "Do not let them make you hate Germany. Hate militarism."

Next to the editorial was an attack on John Sumner, Anthony Comstock's newly appointed successor at the NYSSV, protesting the fact that Sumner could censor whatever he wanted, including any issue of *The Masses* he didn't like. The magazine declared him "the supreme power in American publishing life." Five months later, Sumner arrested the magazine's circulation manager. He confiscated all copies of the September issue of *The Masses* as well as copies of Dr. Auguste Forel's five-hundred-page medical treatise, *The Sexual Question: A Scientific, Psychological, Hygienic and Sociological Study for the Cultured Classes*. The Swiss doctor's prose was not exactly racy ("Copulation, or coitus, takes place as follows . . . "), but Sumner was settling scores.

Sumner was an unassuming man in spectacles, a thirty-nine-year-old lawyer who was married and the president of the men's club of his Long Island Episcopal church three years running. His demeanor was not calm, exactly, so much as relentlessly procedural. Sumner had the look of a bureaucrat who arrived early for work and ate his lunch at his desk.

He took over Comstock's work at the beginning of literary obscenity's golden age. Novelists, activists, doctors and scholars were beginning to address sexual matters more frankly, and the U.S. censorship regime was tested as never before. At the end of the nineteenth century, burning books had hardly been necessary. Comstock's power drew from a combination of legal threats and moral suasion to cow publishers who were already more or less compliant. Even if blueblood publishers like Putnam and Houghton were willing to risk their sterling reputations to publish provocative novels, fighting the Society's standards meant risking an expensive legal battle to sell a book whose profit margins were likely to be razor thin no matter what. The economics left morally questionable books to fly-by-night operations with underground handpresses that would pirate books published in Paris. While they would remain a problem, they would be marginal.

All of that was changing. Cheaper books and higher literacy rates meant that the nation's readers were younger, poorer, more urban and more diverse, and they demanded stories that resembled the world around them. It was only a matter of time before books began to change. In the 1910s and 1920s, a spate of new novels appeared that would have been unthinkable a decade before. *Hagar Revelly, The "Genius," Jurgen, The Story of a Lover, The Well of Loneliness, Lady Chatterley's Lover.*

Ulysses was the most spectacular example of a scandalous book gaining praise in respectable circles, and though some of those books were illegal, daring authors could rely upon a new generation of publishers who were willing to risk prosecution and fight charges in court in order to serve the country's urban readers. Ben Huebsch, Horace Liveright, Alfred Knopf, Max Schuster and Bennett Cerf. The list itself was a sign of the changing industry. One of the old book dealers privately complained, "They're all goddamn Jews!"

Sumner knew the ground was shifting beneath the NYSSV, and he exploited the Red Scare to regain control. He began talking about obscenity not as the work of the devil but as the work of anarchists, Bolsheviks, radical feminists and family planners clustering in urban immigrant enclaves. "Just as we have the parlor Anarchist and the parlor Bolshevist in political life," Sumner declared during the Red Raids, "so we have the parlor Bolshevist in literary and art circles, and they are just as great a menace."

There was little difference between the dangerous words that the government found treasonable and the salacious words that the NYSSV found morally corrupt. The vice society, in other words, was strengthening national security, and as the Bureau of Investigation's work mounted, so did the Society's. In the thick of the Red Raids, Sumner and his men raided radical bookshops for sexual material—according to the society, the Yiddish translation of Forel's *The Sexual Question* was now an anarchist book. In 1912 the NYSSV arrested seventy-six people across the country. In 1920 it arrested 184, more than any in the vice society's history. Sumner noted that less than a third of the criminals were of "real American stock." As the Society's records made clear, most were German and Irish.

Sumner worried that foreign ideas about sex were infiltrating the legal system. When the Nineteenth Amendment to the U.S. Constitution seemed poised to become law in 1920, guaranteeing women the right to vote, Sumner warned that "radical feminists" wanted to establish separate, antagonistic powers. They wanted the government to legitimize children born out of wedlock, which would encourage pregnant women to remain unmarried and give birth to "promiscuous children"—the nation's home life would crumble. At the moment, such women were marginal, he said, "but they are shrewd, and one finds them writing insidious and widely read books on the freedom of the modern woman, and advocating still greater sex freedom." As if they didn't already have enough.

JOHN SUMNER SEARCHED for opportunities to combine the fight against radicals and sex liberators, and he soon had his chance. One day in the summer of 1920, the New York district attorney telephoned Sumner to discuss a disturbing issue of *The Little Review*. In the latest installment of *Ulysses*, Gerty MacDowell is sitting on a rock on the beach while a choir sings in a nearby church. Her friends Edy and Cissy are watching Cissy's twin brothers, Tommy and Jacky, play along the shore in their sailor suits, and Gerty watches herself being watched by a man farther up the beach, Leopold Bloom. As fireworks go off in the distance, Gerty leans back and Bloom catches a glimpse of her blue garters.

> And she saw a long Roman candle going up over the trees up, up, and they were all breathless with excitement as it went higher and higher and she had to lean back more and more to look up after it, high, high, almost out of sight, and her face was suffused with a divine, an entrancing blush from straining back and he could see her other things too, nainsook knickers, four and eleven, on account of being white and she let him and she saw that he saw.

The way the girl encourages the man, leaning back to reveal her undergarments, was appalling—and that was only part of it. The scene was blasphemous. To imagine such things happening within earshot of a church service, to say nothing of the children playing in the distance, made the story gratuitously offensive. It simultaneously desecrated the young woman, the Catholic mass and childhood itself. Sumner read the rest of the episode carefully.

And then a rocket sprang and bang shot blind blank and O! then the Roman candle burst and it was like a sigh of O! and everyone cried O! O! and it gushed out of it a stream of rain gold hair threads and they shed and ah! they were all greeny dewy stars falling with golden, O so lovely! O so soft, sweet, soft!

It was, it seemed, an entirely new species of smut. What completed Joyce's disturbing tableau on the beach was the unsettling way that the girl's "innocent" thoughts ("a man of honour to his fingertips") coincided with the man's lascivious thoughts ("Swell of her calf. Transparent stockings, stretched to breaking point"). If Sumner wanted a rendering of how easy moral corruption was—a portrait of lust's slippery slope from mawkish romance to pornography and promiscuity—this was it. Young ladies didn't just need to be protected from Bloom. They needed to be protected from *Gerty*.

Sumner must have pieced it all together when he began his investigation. *The Little Review* was a Washington Square magazine repeatedly banned from the mails for sedition and obscenity. As he pored over previous issues, he would have noticed ads for the Washington Square Book Shop, which had been so closely aligned to the radical Liberal Club next door that the two establishments had cut through their shared wall to create a doorway. A little bit of digging revealed that Josephine Bell was the bookshop's proprietor, the same woman indicted for wartime conspiracy in *The Masses* case for writing a poem honoring Emma Goldman.

And that's when it dawned on him, how he'd heard of *The Little Review*. The editors had been among Emma Goldman's supporters during her 1917 espionage trial. A glance at their magazine was enough to indicate that Margaret Anderson and Jane Heap were feminists of the most radical kind. Far beyond legitimizing the children of unwed mothers, they openly supported anarchism and homosexual rights. They eschewed marriage. And they lived together. The magazine was loaded with foreign contributors. The July–August issue that the DA gave him featured several un-American names: Ben Hecht, Djuna Barnes, Elsa von Freytag-Loringhoven. And there, just inside the cover, adoringly pasted in, was a picture of the writer James Joyce—the glasses, the slicked-back hair, the mustache and pointed beard. His heavy coat was pulled up at the neck as he gazed off, unsmiling, into the distance, like some sort of Irish Trotsky. You could tell a radical just by looking at him.

A criminal conviction against *The Little Review*, the Washington Square Book Shop and James Joyce would be a moral trifecta: a single conviction could be a victory against the immorality, radicalism and foreign ideas beleaguering the country in 1920. Hours after the Wall Street bombing in September, hundreds of men worked through the night to clear away the wreckage and replace shattered windowpanes twenty stories high so the financial district could open for business the next day. When morning came, a crowd of more than one hundred thousand people flocked downtown to sing "The Star-Spangled Banner" near the Wall Street statue of George Washington, and John Sumner walked into the Washington Square Book Shop to purchase incriminating copies of *The Little Review*.

TWO WEEKS LATER, John Quinn received a telegram from Margaret Anderson informing him that a warrant had been issued for the arrest of Josephine Bell of the Washington Square Book Shop for selling *The Little Review* to an undercover agent of the New York Society for the Suppression of Vice. The sale, according to the warrant, violated New York State law, and the offensive material was the latest installment of James Joyce's *Ulysses*. Quinn heard the news while working on a case challenging the constitutionality of the government's wartime seizure powers. His fee was $174,000, and the case was headed to the U.S. Supreme Court.

So one can imagine how much patience Quinn had when the *Little Review* "editrix" and her assistant showed up at his austere office with Josephine Bell and her lawyer. Something about Washington Square bohemianism triggered Quinn's disgust of bodies, the smell of immigrants, sexualities and death. *The Little Review* suited the square perfectly, he told Pound. It was devoted "to urine and feces and sweat and armpits and piss and orgasms and masturbations and buggeries and Lesbianisms and God knows what." Anderson and Heap, he thought, would use the trial to promote themselves while he took on all the work pro bono.

"What did I tell you?" Quinn told them. "You're damned fools trying to get away with such a thing as *Ulysses* in this puritan-ridden country." Knowing that Quinn's allegiances were with Pound and Joyce, they tried to pacify him by reminding him of their larger goals—publishing *Ulysses* was part of the reason why he financed *The Little Review* in the first place, and Pound and Joyce had insisted on printing the installment. Quinn responded that their job was to exercise editorial judgment, not to follow directions from Pound and Joyce. "An artist might paint a picture of two women doing the Lesbian business," Quinn said, "but the owner of a gallery would be an idiot if he hung it." Anderson and Heap thought publishing *Ulysses* was worth any trouble they might encounter, and they insisted on the importance of broadening the public mind. Quinn fired back, "You'll be broadening the matron at Blackwell's Island one of these days, and serve you damn well right."

Quinn got the judge to transfer the charges from the bookstore to Anderson and Heap. The case was adjourned for two weeks, and as they left the Jefferson Market Courthouse, Anderson and Heap began arguing with Sumner. They were not ashamed of publishing *Ulysses*. "We glory in it," Anderson said. "This trial will be the making of *The Little Review*." To their surprise, Sumner was happy to carry the argument down Eighth Street, and when they entered the Washington Square Book Shop, the scene of the crime, Sumner followed them inside.

As eager as he was to debate the vice society's principles, Anderson thought he was amenable to her vision, that he would be converted to the cause of

Beauty if only she could sit down to tea with him every day for a month. She could not have been more mistaken. Quinn, like Anderson, did everything he could to persuade Sumner over a lunch meeting; he gave Sumner a sense of who he was (in case he didn't know) and furnished him with a glowing review of Joyce's work in *The Dial*. "I don't give a damn for these women," he told Sumner, "but I do want to save James Joyce from the stigma of indecent writings if I can." He asked the NYSSV to drop the charges, and in exchange Quinn would halt the publication of *Ulysses* in *The Little Review*.

Sumner listened patiently before informing Quinn that the case hadn't originated with the vice society. It originated with the New York district attorney's office. That summer, a businessman named Ogden Brower had flipped through one of his teenage daughter's magazines and found the passage where Gerty MacDowell reveals her nainsook knickers,

> and she was trembling in every limb from being bent so far back that he could see high up above her knee where no-one ever and she wasn't ashamed and he wasn't either to look in that immodest way like that because he couldn't resist the sight like those skirtdancers behaving so immodest before gentlemen looking and he kept on looking, looking.

When Brower asked his daughter how she had heard about *The Little Review*, she said that she hadn't heard about it, and she certainly hadn't ordered the magazine—it was an unsolicited package sent like an explosive through the mail. Her father was outraged. He marked four of the dirty pages and wrote a letter to the district attorney.

> *If such indecencies don't come within the provisions of the Postal Laws then isn't there some way in which the circulation of such things can be confined among the people who buy or subscribe to a publication of this kind? Surely there must be some way of keeping such "literature" out of the homes of people who don't want it even if, in the interests of morality, there is no means of suppressing it.*

A complaint like this from a prominent businessman was an embarrassment, for surely there *were* means of suppressing the magazine, and the DA's office asked the secretary of the NYSSV for his opinion.

Sumner wasn't going to drop the charges. He doubted that Quinn could end the serialization of *Ulysses* altogether, and Anderson's "defiant" attitude suggested that Quinn's clients were more unruly than he realized. But Quinn insisted that Joyce was nothing like the editors. He was an artist, whereas Anderson and Heap were "sheer self-exploiters. Too damn fresh." And he would see to it that Joyce himself canceled further publication.

When the meeting was over, Quinn dictated a letter to Pound in a flourishing attempt to unburden himself from years of aggravation.

> *If Joyce wants to help them who haven't helped him; if he wants to do something for those who have been living upon his work for months without paying for it; if he wants to have that number condemned, and hence the book as a book automatically condemned; if he wants to prevent its being published as a book here; if he wants to deprive himself of royalties anywhere from $1500 to $2000 or $2500, for the benefit of these two rabbits; if he wants to set himself up as an expert on American law against my opinion as an expert of experience; if he wants to go off half cocked and construe this as persecution of him, when Sumner didn't know of his existence, and hardly knows how to spell his name; if you should get the idea into your head that there is any principle involved in this thing or that the freedom of literature is at stake; if you still are under the impression that "The Little Review" ought to be encouraged, and not shut up like any other female urinal that is unwashed and rancid, then I have nothing more to say.*

He went on for sixteen more pages.

Quinn knew the magazine would be convicted if the DA didn't drop the charges himself, and a conviction against a portion of *Ulysses* would criminalize the entire book. As soon as the press caught wind of the charges, Sumner's attack upon *The Little Review* would link James Joyce to Bolsheviks and bomb throwers and birth controllers. Joyce would lose everything for a Washington Square rag. It infuriated Quinn that the editrixes' ineptitude could topple Joyce's genius, that a snippet—a mere sixteen pages—might end the publication of a book that Joyce had been working on for six years.

Ezra Pound was taken aback by the news. As willing as he was to turn aesthetic disagreements into angry screeds against the Post Office and the Comstock Act, he wasn't prepared for arrests, indictments and potential prison sentences. "'Nausikaa' has been pinched by the PO-lice," he wrote to Joyce. "Only way to get *Ulysses* printed in book form will be to agree not to print any more of it in *The Little Review* . . . the only thing to be done now is to give Quinn an absolutely free hand."

When Pound first told Quinn about "Nausicaa," he had been enthusiastic: "Perhaps everything ought to be said ONCE in the English language." After the arrest, however, even he began to distance himself from its excesses. He told Quinn he deleted a few risqué passages, and he suspected Anderson and Heap ignored his deletions (they hadn't). Pound insisted that the two women were, as Quinn knew, willful, if not reckless. And so was Joyce. When Pound suggested changes to the manuscript, Joyce sent him an intemperate letter that Pound attributed to Joyce's persistent illness and "overwrought nerves," but Pound offered Quinn, in strict confidence, his general estimation of Joyce: "He is not a particularly reasonable person."

ON OCTOBER 21, 1920, the front two rows of the Jefferson Market Courthouse were filled with fashionable women who came to protest the obscenity charges against *The Little Review*. John Quinn walked in wearing a three-piece suit with a gold watch chain dangling from his vest. He looked around at the burglars and vagrants corralled by police officers with glinting buttons and stars. Two days before, he had been in Washington, D.C., preparing his Supreme Court case, and now he was beset by immigrants, Negroes and Italians in a judicial factory.

Quinn never intended to be there. It was just a preliminary hearing, but the young lawyer handling it had telephoned Quinn's office when he gathered that the judge, Joseph Corrigan, had a personal animus against Sumner. Judge Corrigan already had several exasperating exchanges with vice societies, and he was unwilling to uphold charges based on nothing more than Sumner's word, which was exactly what Sumner was asking him to do. His deposition claimed that *Ulysses* was "so obscene, lewd, lascivious, filthy, indecent and disgusting, that a minute description of the same would be offensive to the Court and improper to be placed upon the record thereof."

In other words, Sumner refused to list any of the offensive passages. The New York Comstock Act criminalized anyone "who writes, prints, publishes, or utters, or causes to be written . . . any obscene, lewd, lascivious, filthy disgusting or indecent book, picture, writing, paper." This meant that if passages in *Ulysses* were obscene, it would be illegal to utter those obscenities in court or cause a stenographer to record them. The vice society thought that upholding the law meant not examining any of the material the law condemned—the accusation was the evidence. Sumner's argument was not eccentric. In 1895 the Supreme Court ruled, "It is unnecessary to spread the obscene matter in all its filthiness upon the record." It was enough to describe the matter's "obnoxious character" in order to ascertain "the gist of the offense."

Judge Corrigan had heard it before (it was the Society's habitual gambit), but he insisted on examining the magazine himself. Quinn rushed to the courthouse while the judge read *The Little Review* in his chambers, and when Corrigan emerged, he greeted the lawyer with a smile—they happened to be old friends.

Hearings like this were usually formalities, but Joyce's legal problems might all end here if Judge Corrigan would simply dismiss the charges—though he could do that only if he deemed *Ulysses* patently innocent, and only a personal favor could inspire such an unlikely judgment. If Quinn were more pessimistic, he might have concluded that his loyalty to Joyce had shackled him to a sinking ship. Ezra Pound had resigned from *The Little Review* in frustration the previous year (the resignation didn't last long), but the serialization of *Ulysses* continued. Quinn might have thought it fitting that Joyce and *The Little Review* could go down together because *Ulysses* and Margaret Anderson filled him with the same volatile mixture of disgust and attraction.

They forced him to think of the human body as something simultaneously teeming and thwarted. The image of Gerty MacDowell straining against the fabric of her clothing resembled what Quinn imagined was Anderson's frustrated fertility. He wrote to Pound that her virginity, if she were a virgin, was "over-ripe, the thing that burst itself." The "Lesbianisms" of Greenwich Village, the scrotumtightening sea of Manhattan's immigrants and James Joyce's epic of the human body all reminded Quinn of his own failing body and the lethal rupture to come. Joyce seemed to be making an art form out of the many ways death and decay could bloom within the living. Quinn's mortality pursued him no matter how many artworks he purchased or how many cases he won.

A stirring courtroom argument did nevertheless stave off the feeling of death, and a defense of Joyce against obscenity charges required the sophisticated legal creativity he found envigorating. Quinn had to base his courtroom argument on mid-nineteenth-century British law, for the definition of obscenity that guided Anglo-American jurisprudence in 1920 was articulated by a British judge in 1868: "I think the test of obscenity is this, whether the tendency of the matter charged as obscenity is to deprave and corrupt those whose minds are open to such immoral influences and into whose hands a publication of this sort may fall." This definition of obscenity became known as the Hicklin Rule, and it transformed obscenity law. Instead of targeting pornographers profiting from books that were offensive to "any well-regulated mind," as the author of the Obscene Publications Act put it, the Hicklin Rule defined obscenity by a book's effects on society's most susceptible readers— anyone with a mind "open" to "immoral influences." The purview of the law shifted from protecting well-regulated minds to sheltering ill-regulated minds. Lecherous readers and excitable teenage daughters could deprave and corrupt the most sophisticated literary intent.

The Hicklin Rule inspired Quinn to argue that a book couldn't be filthy if it was unintelligible or disgusting or private. "You could not take a piece of literature up in an aeroplane fifteen thousand feet into the blue sky, where there would be no spectator, and let the pilot of the machine read it out and have it denounced as 'filthy,' within the meaning of the law." It had to "corrupt" or "deprave" a mind, and judges generally read "corruption" as a synonym for "arousal." What this implied was that if Gerty were ugly—if she were entirely unarousing—she would be legal. Quinn continued: "If a young man is in love with a woman and his mother should write to him saying: 'My boy, the woman you are infatuated with is not a beautiful woman . . . She sweats, she stinks, she is flatulent. Her flesh is discolored, her breath is bad. She makes ugly noises when she eats and discharges other natural functions'"—the mother would be writing ugly truths for her son's moral benefit. Gerty MacDowell, Quinn argued, similarly sends men running toward virtue. He insisted that Joyce was like Swift or Rabelais: he was not an artist of corrupting beauty. He was an artist of ugly truths.

It was not clear what, precisely, Quinn found so disgusting about Gerty MacDowell.

She leaned back far to look up where the fireworks were and she caught her knee in her hands so as not to fall back looking up and there was no one to see only him and her when she revealed all her graceful beautifully shaped legs like that, supply soft and delicately rounded, and she seemed to hear the panting of his heart his hoarse breathing.

Were readers supposed to be disgusted by Gerty because she is mawkish or because, as we discover later in the chapter, she is lame? One of the Joycean touches is that reality topples Bloom's fantasy when Gerty limps away pages after her beautifully shaped legs appear. If that's what makes her unappealing, surely Joyce's story was at least plausibly filthy under the law.

A single word in the Hicklin Rule—a word that Quinn studiously ignored—dramatically expanded judges' authority by making censorship a preemptive activity. Publishers, booksellers, printers and writers were liable not just for corrupted readers but for a publication's "*tendency*" to corrupt. By focusing on a book's hypothetical effects on hypothetical readers, the Hicklin Rule made an obscenity judgment a feat of the imagination—for certainly the judge himself was above such "immoral influences." Rather, it was his task to determine whether the book would deprave someone entirely unlike him. Judge Corrigan would have to peer into the mind of Ogden Brower's young daughter (herself peering into the mind of Gerty MacDowell) and imagine her potential reactions. The law required the judge to be a bit like Joyce.

Quinn could be right about Joyce's moral lessons and ugly truths, and it still wouldn't matter. So long as there was some measure—any measure—of potentially corrupting beauty, Joyce's episode was illegal. Gerty's charms got *Ulysses* indicted for obscenity as Judge Corrigan decided to hold the editors of *The Little Review* for trial. Quinn retorted that his decision proved he had a dirty mind. It was a sly comment—almost a jab. Was Corrigan *aroused* when he read the magazine in his chambers? Corrigan merely smiled as he made out the warrant for the imprisonment of Anderson and Heap and set their bail at twenty-five dollars each, which Quinn reluctantly paid.

Quinn didn't even entertain the possibility of an acquittal. He had warned Joyce about the cultural climate: "There have been a good many arrests and prosecutions of publishers of books in New York recently. There was a perfect orgy of sex stuff published," and if Joyce tried publishing *Ulysses* without deletions, the copies and plates would be seized and destroyed, the book would be banned from both the mail system and the private express companies, and the publisher would face a heavy fine and jail sentence. No American publisher would touch Joyce's book once the "Nausicaa" episode was convicted. And Sumner was determined to convict it.

14.

THE GHOST OF
COMSTOCK

John Sumner patrolled the streets of New York City, and if he found indecent artworks or window displays, he ordered proprietors to remove them. He wasn't a special agent of the Post Office like Comstock, but he assumed quasi-official powers anyway. He unlocked and searched mailboxes for felonious packages. He accompanied officers on raids and stakeouts. He gathered evidence, obtained warrants, seized materials, arrested suspects and served as the complaining witness in court when the DA prosecuted. And when books were deemed obscene, he supervised the burnings himself. Sumner cast a wide net. He would threaten fourteen-year-olds with jail time in order to find out exactly where they got the dirty books and pictures hidden in their desks. In 1919, one of his men teamed up with an officer to eject six male cross-dressers and several scantily clad women from an indecent party. It was Tammany Hall's Halloween Ball.

Sumner operated like a single-minded intelligence officer piecing together a network of urban vice, and the biggest trove of information came from letters, phone calls and anonymous tips about nuisances ranging from immoral neighbors and exhibitionists to obscene bathroom drawings and garden statuary. People asked the New York Society for the Suppression of Vice to track down unfaithful spouses, eloping teenagers and perverts harassing innocent sailors on shore leave. Sumner watched countless plays, musicals, movies and burlesque performances. He bought every questionable book and magazine issue he could find. He served as a conduit of information for smaller vice societies and law enforcement officials around the country, and he lobbied senators, governors and mayors for stronger laws.

John Sumner's great virtue was that he professionalized Anthony Comstock's belligerence. "Years ago fighting methods had to be used," Sumner said when he assumed his office. "Now it is brains." The NYSSV hired Sumner as an assistant secretary in 1913 because they thought his mild demeanor would moderate Comstock's excesses. Soon after Sumner joined the Society, he found himself breaking up fights between Comstock and his own men— their accountant used to peek through his keyhole to avoid his boss lumbering down the hallway. When Sumner took charge of the Society in 1915, he was still contending with the forty-year legacy of a single man—with the specter of Comstock himself.

In 1872, Anthony Comstock was a barrel-chested, small-town upstart with extravagant muttonchops and a tense upper lip. He was twenty-eight years old, going bald before his time, and he brought down New York's pornography industry single-handedly. He waded through basement shops in the Lower East Side, asked for items behind counters and in back rooms, feigned interest with every peddler and crony who approached him and rummaged through desultory stacks of magazines and novels in newsstands. Comstock declared 165 different books indisputably obscene and began escorting police officers to pornographers to ensure their arrest. He interrogated suspects and traced the supply chain back to middlemen, publishers, printers and bookbinders in order to find the criminals and destroy the inventory. He once hijacked a wagon filled with steel and copper printing plates and took them to the Polytechnic Institute of Brooklyn, where a professor destroyed them with acid. In eight months, Comstock had forty-five people arrested. Two months after the Comstock Act was signed in 1873, the YMCA's financial backers founded the New York Society for the Suppression of Vice, and Anthony Comstock became the head of what would soon be the most powerful vice society in the United States. He was, as he put it, "a weeder in the garden of the Lord."

Moral reformers like Comstock took matters into their own hands because the New York City police were corrupt, ineffective and barely professionalized. New York didn't even have a police department until 1845, partly because New Yorkers were afraid of what a mayoral despot could do with a club-wielding army. The qualms subsided by the 1870s. Before long, Comstock could arrest pornographers as either a special agent of the Post Office or as a deputy sheriff, and by the end of his career he claimed more than three thousand convictions totaling 565 years, eleven months and twenty days of prison time. Comstock enjoyed measuring the dimensions of his righteousness. He counted 2,948,168 obscene pictures burned. 28,428 pounds of stereotype printing plates destroyed. 318,336 "obscene rubber articles" confiscated. Sixteen dead bodies. He measured the books he destroyed by the ton: fifty.

But stamping out obscenity was surprisingly dangerous. NYSSV agents received death threats. Packages addressed to Comstock contained poisons, infected bandages and collections of smallpox scabs. One day, while opening a heavy box, he heard an ominous click. The box contained shards of glass packed tightly between canisters of rifle powder and sulfuric acid. A piece of emery swung across match ends by a rubber band was supposed to ignite a fuse when the box was opened. The explosion would launch the shards of glass into his chest and face. Then the sulfuric acid would eat away at the wounds.

In 1874, Comstock apprehended a one-handed man named Charles Conroy for the third time, and when the carriage halted at the jailhouse gates, Conroy pulled a three-inch blade from his coat pocket and swung for Comstock's head, cutting through his hat and grazing his scalp. Comstock had a badge, but he didn't know how to search a prisoner properly. As he fumbled for the door latch, Conroy plunged the knife into his face, severing an artery and opening the flesh to the bone. Comstock threw open the carriage door, and as the prisoner emerged behind him, he drew his revolver and placed it against Conroy's head. Blood was still spurting from the gash in Comstock's face when the jailer ran out to assist him.

To VICE HUNTERS like Comstock and Sumner, violence was a manifestation of the chaos that obscenity created. Censorship was preemptive—judges and juries banned books based on their tendencies rather than their consequences—because governments saw pornography as a threat to civil society. The basis of the Hicklin Rule was an eighteenth-century legal treatise declaring that banning words with "a pernicious tendency is necessary for the preservation of peace and good order, of government and religion—the only solid foundation of civil liberty." Censorship wasn't just about sex. It was about preserving a tenuous public order.

The absence of strong law enforcement made obscenity seem more alarming because officials relied on moral rectitude to help regulate the excesses of urban life. Explicitly sexual material—whether it was written by James Joyce or a knife-wielding smut peddler—threatened that moral order. A character like Gerty MacDowell, it seemed, would lure young women to unwed motherhood, where they would raise morally stunted children. To broadcast Gerty's behavior in a magazine would create more young women just like her, and a generation of Gerty MacDowells was enough to honeycomb the foundations of society. Moral reformers like Comstock had always seen the fight against obscene literature as more than a moral crusade. They saw it as an essential civic duty.

In fact, the Anglo-American definition of obscenity was so strict because it was written not to contain an outbreak of lustful readers but to quell widespread civil disorder in Victorian England. After British Parliament passed the Obscene Publications Act in 1857, British courts still had to decide what obscenity was, and the opportunity came in an 1868 case against an anti-Catholic pamphlet entitled *The Confessional Unmasked*. The pamphlet was a series of excerpts from theological tracts designed to prepare Catholic priests for questions they might receive from parishioners confessing their sins. Are looks or filthy words between married couples sinful? (Sometimes.) Does a husband sin mortally if he does not spend his seed after commencing copulation? (Not if both parties consent.) Was it a sin to think about your deceased wife while having intercourse with your second wife? (Yes.) Does a widow sin by deriving pleasure from memories of intercourse? (Yes, grievously.) Is it *always* a mortal sin if a husband "introduces his ——— into the mouth of the wife?" (Opinions vary.)

It's doubtful anyone would have bothered to read the legalistic prose had *The Confessional Unmasked* been about anything other than illicit sex: "It is asked, 2ndly, whether, and in what manner, married parties sin by copulating in an unnatural posture?" The answer was that "an unnatural position is, if coition takes place in a different manner, viz., by sitting, standing, lying on the side, or from behind, after the manner of cattle; or if the man lies under the woman." All of these positions were sinful.

The Confessional Unmasked was an exposé of Catholicism's lecherous sacraments, and it was incontestably obscene. To Victorians, any discussion of unnatural sexual practices (even in the most unarousing terms) was more than depraved. For some of the pamphlet's readers, it was a revelation of depravity—it would conjure thoughts that people would not have otherwise imagined.

When the case came before the Queen's Bench, the justices of the high court summarily outlawed the pamphlet. And while they were at it, the Lord Chief Justice of England, Alexander Cockburn, crafted the stringent Hicklin Rule, though he was by no means a prude. In fact, Cockburn earned a reputation as a mediocre judge, a social gadabout and a philanderer (he once climbed through the window of Rougemont Castle's robing room to escape being caught in a tryst). Though he never married, he fathered two illegitimate children, and when the prime minister offered him a peerage in 1864, Queen Victoria refused him the honor, citing his "notoriously bad moral character." Yet the disquieting circumstances surrounding *The Confessional Unmasked* turned even Lord Cockburn into a moralist. During the trial, the defense attorney avoided discussing the pamphlet's consequences as much as possible, but it didn't matter because everyone in the courtroom already knew: the consequence of *The Confessional Unmasked* was widespread rioting.

The case began when a police officer in the midland city of Wolverhampton seized 252 copies of the pamphlet from a metal broker who was selling them for a shilling. The seller was a member of the Protestant Electoral Union, whose goal was to elect members of Parliament who would "maintain the Protestantism of the Bible and the LIBERTY OF BRITAIN." The Union specialized in incendiary propaganda, and its most notorious speaker was an Irishman named William Murphy, who railed against Catholic depredations and incited angry Irish mobs wherever he went. It wasn't until his visit to Wolverhampton in 1867 that the authorities and the British press began paying closer attention. During Murphy's first lecture, Irishmen hurled stones through the lecture hall's windows, injuring several people, and Murphy was able to lecture on *The Confessional Unmasked* only by turning the lecture hall into a citadel surrounded by hundreds of police officers, military cavalrymen and recently sworn-in constables. The sectarian tension was intolerable, so when local authorities discovered who was selling *The Confessional Unmasked*, they searched his house and seized his copies.

While the Union appealed the obscenity charges, Catholic-Protestant tensions worsened. Murphy promised to prove to the people of Birmingham that "every Popish priest is a murderer, a cannibal, a liar and a pickpocket." When his lecture was over, Catholics invaded Protestant houses and broke apart the furniture. Protestants retaliated by vandalizing a Catholic church, marching to Birmingham's Irish district with staves, breaking into houses and carrying off furniture while singing "Glory, Glory Hallelujah." During the week of rioting, the Union sold roughly thirty thousand copies of *The Confessional Unmasked*. Purchasing the pamphlet became an act of solidarity.

By the time the case came before the Queen's Bench, *The Confessional Unmasked* was indeed a threat to peace and good order throughout the midlands. Murphy's lectures in Ashton-under-Lyne spurred Protestant uprisings that left twenty Irish houses ransacked and one Irishman dead, and the sectarian anger became fodder for a group of Irish nationalists called the Fenians, who, in 1867, attacked Chester Castle, shot a police sergeant dead and bombed Clerkenwell Prison, killing twelve and wounding fifty. The riots and bombs made the pamphlet's political intentions irrelevant. What mattered were its consequences.

The fact that a sexually explicit pamphlet could cause such mayhem drove

Cockburn to a conclusion about all texts in a literate society: words were dangerous, and the law had to guard against their damaging effects before the public suffered from them. But what would happen when the effects of a book weren't so clear—when there weren't riots in the streets? Everything that made the Hicklin case compelling also made it difficult for Lord Cockburn to craft a broad legal principle. It was easy, in the wake of the Murphy Riots, to forget that a "pernicious tendency" was difficult to spot. It was easy to insist that a book should be burned before it had a chance to be read.

JUDGE COCKBURN'S rule of preemptive censorship dovetailed perfectly with a religious zealot's anxieties about purity in a world of sin. Anthony Comstock and John Sumner fought so ardently to eliminate immoral books and images because they believed the most effective way to serve God was to attack the seeds of sin before they could be sown—to quash a book's pernicious tendencies before they could destroy families and communities. Lust was the most pernicious of sins. It was the first stumble that could drag a sinner into a life of evil. Lust led to the brothel, and the brothel led to disease. Lust weakened both the body and the mind. It ruined marriages. It compelled deceit. It promoted indolence and reckless behavior. It blinded its victims to consequences and sapped the sense of responsibility that kept society from anarchy.

Comstock's understanding of lust's destructiveness was a more colorful version of the beliefs written into the British and American legal traditions: "There is," Comstock wrote, "no other force at work in the community more insidious, more constant in its demands, or more powerful and far-reaching than lust." It was, he wrote, "*the boon companion of all other crimes.*" Lust's influence was strongest on the young. Comstock imagined it as a vulture plunging into children's entrails, or a terrifying monster standing over the beds of sleeping children and waiting to slip into their minds as soon as they awoke. It was advertised everywhere, and society's most precious citizens were the most vulnerable to the lures of the imagination.

The fear of pornography was neither ignorant nor blindly dogmatic. In fact, Comstock was applying the wisdom of the past two centuries. Since the Enlightenment, philosophers emphasized the importance of education and exterior influences on who we are. Our minds and moral habits arose from our responses to the outside world. Consciousness was like a blanket of snow waiting to receive the slightest impressions. We weren't born as the people we are today. We were, for the most part, made. Comstock quoted the philosopher John Locke to underscore the consequences of the smallest impressions on "our tender infancies." Locke thought people resembled rivers in the way that slight adjustments at their origins could lead them to vastly different destinations. "I imagine the minds of children as easily turned this way or that, as water itself," Locke wrote. His insight wasn't liberating. It was terrifying. When virtue and vice do not arise exclusively from within—when the influences of an entire community play a role in each individual's struggle of conscience—then one was not merely responsible for oneself. One was responsible for everyone. This was Anthony Comstock's moral burden, and the load would never lighten.

The most diabolical aspect of pornography was that it exploited the mind's gifts. Memory and imagination tormented the lust-ridden individual. Years after a sinner embarked upon a virtuous life, the smallest cue—a gesture, a name, a song—could unleash words and images planted in the mind like time bombs. A drunk could sober up. A glutton could fast. An infidel could find God. But one could never be free from the impression that an obscene image or story made—a book read once will stay with you forever.

In 1915, Comstock was dying of pneumonia. His hacking cough brought up blood, and though he found it difficult to breathe, let alone speak, he requested a stenographer to come to his bedside so he could dictate his last instructions to his successor. John Sumner was appointed to lead the NYSSV the following morning, September 22 (his birthday), and regardless of the instructions he was given, he abandoned Comstock's policy of prosecuting contraceptive manufacturers and returned the NYSSV to its original mission: the pursuit of dirty books, magazines and pictures. Any vice society leader had to be as dogged as the pornographers he pursued, but Sumner would do it with more finesse than brutality. He emphasized public outreach by writing open letters to newspapers and engaging in high-profile debates with people like Clarence Darrow in the hopes of winning approval through the force of reason. And yet Sumner's sensible veneer covered an intensity that made him more akin to Comstock than he would ever admit. As John Sumner patrolled New York, threatening high school students, raiding parties and burning books, Anthony Comstock loomed over his shoulder like a ghost.

15.

ELIJAH IS COMING

———

I am working like a galley-slave, an ass, a brute," James Joyce wrote in a letter. "I cannot even sleep. The episode of *Circe* has changed me too into an animal." By December 1920, he was suffering from another episode of iritis in a dark apartment on rue Raspail. His eyes had gotten worse since his surgery, and the heat from the gas stove, he thought, was the only thing warding off a full-blown attack of glaucoma. Joyce was so cold in their last residential hotel that he wrote with blankets over his shoulders and a shawl wrapped around his head. He wrote whenever he wasn't bedridden with fits of pain, and he thought about writing whenever he was. He started "Circe" in April 1920 and estimated it would take three months to complete. By December, he was on his ninth draft, and "Circe" was still expanding, insert by insert, as he drove his pen late into the night, his pupils gaping in the room's meager light.

Joyce finally reached the midnight of his book. In the "Circe" episode, Leopold Bloom follows Stephen Dedalus into Nighttown, where an elaborate fantasy unfolds in Bella Cohen's brothel on Tyrone Street before Bloom rescues Stephen from a fight with British soldiers, brushes the dirt off his shoulders and walks him home. Nothing was interior now—there were no thoughts, no fears, no memories or nightmares that were not acted out for the people in the brothel to see, and the brothel contained everyone.

The presiding spirit was the enchantress in Homer's epic who turns Ulysses' men into swine. Before wily Ulysses approaches Circe's hall to rescue his men, the god Hermes gives him an herb that will protect him from her spell. The herb that saves Ulysses is called Moly (things like this were no coincidence). Joyce wondered if the word *syphilis* had its origins in Circe—perhaps it was Greek: συφιλια. *Su* + *philis*. "Swine love," the spell that drove men to brute madness. After Ulysses compels Circe to transform his men back into humans, she regales them with a celebration that lasts a full year. Joyce toiled on "Circe" months longer than he planned. The episode became at turns a carnival, a nightmare, a phantasmagoria and a hallucination. Miracles are performed and humiliations enacted. Genders change. Hours dance. Moths speak.

Nearly everything and everyone the reader has seen through the day returns as a nightmare. Gerty MacDowell reproaches Bloom ("Dirty married man! I love you for doing that to me."). Blazes Boylan tosses him a coin and hangs his hat on Bloom's antlered head ("I have a little private business with your wife, you understand?"). Bloom shakes hands with the blind stripling ("My more than brother!"). "Bronze by gold," the prostitutes whisper. The nanny goat, dropping currants, ambles by. Father Dolan emerges to upbraid Stephen for the glasses he broke in *A Portrait* when he was six years old ("lazy idle little schemer"). The ghost of Stephen's mother, like Joyce's mother, appears with green bile trickling from her mouth (he asks her to tell him that she loves him). Bloom's father, who committed suicide years ago, touches Bloom's face with "vulture talons." The long-awaited Elijah finally arrives and begins to dispense judgment ("No yapping, if you please . . . "). Rudy, Bloom's son, appears as he would have if he had survived infancy.

JOYCE TOOK NEARLY A MONTH to respond to Quinn's urgent letter about the charges against the "Nausicaa" episode, and when he did, he sent a coded telegram.

SCOTTS TETTOJA MOIEDURA GEIZLSUND. JOYCE

Quinn's office clerk, Mr. Watson, obtained a copy of the Scott's code manual and translated Joyce's message. "I have not received the telegram you mention. You will be receiving a letter upon this subject in a few days giving information and my views pretty fully. I think a little delay will not be disadvantageous."

Quinn cabled back and insisted that Joyce cease serial publication immediately. If they were lucky, the DA might drop the charges. If they were unlucky, he would add more counts to the indictment. But Joyce wanted to keep his *Little Review* audience, and if he was unwilling to compromise for editors and printers, he was even more unwilling to compromise for law enforcement officials, no matter what his lawyer's advice. Quinn received another telegram from Paris.

MACILENZA PAVENTAVA MEHLSUPPE MOGOSTOKOS.

Watson decoded it: "Private and reliable information received. Number in dispute has been issued. Pending receipt of your letter matter will remain over."

But the matter was far from over, and Quinn had to come up with a plan. The case was scheduled to go before a panel of three judges in December, and he decided he would file a motion for a jury trial instead, which would slow the process down. The transfer motion would have to be filed and scheduled for a hearing before an overworked grand jury could get around to issuing an indictment. By the time a jury of twelve was selected and the magazine convicted after a full trial, it would be the autumn of 1921, and as long as the legal proceedings were grinding forward, they could publish a private edition of *Ulysses*. That is, instead of selling the novel in bookstores, a publisher would print around one thousand high-quality copies and mail them directly to readers placing orders in advance.

Technically, the book would be legal before the ruling against *The Little Review* was handed down, and Quinn figured Sumner and the DA were less likely to prosecute a book circulating privately than a magazine available to unsuspecting young women. A deluxe private publication could sell for as much as eight to ten dollars per copy, about four times more than the average book. At 15 to 20 percent royalties, Joyce could earn as much as two thousand dollars. All he would have to do is finish his novel before the legal clock ran out.

Quinn was trying to convince Ben Huebsch to publish a private edition of *Ulysses*, but the impending trial was making him leery. Huebsch was the obvious option for Joyce. He had published *Dubliners* and *A Portrait*, and he admired Joyce's new book. Quinn urged him to sign a contract even before *The Little Review* landed in court, and by December 1920 he decided that he and Huebsch needed to have "a showdown." He wanted Huebsch to make an offer for *Ulysses* while the risks appeared as minimal as possible—the last thing Huebsch needed was to see the details of the trial in the newspapers.

The showdown was at Quinn's apartment, and Quinn drew first: Joyce would never agree to any cuts or alterations, he told Huebsch, and it was a "practical certainty that if *Ulysses* were published here without any alteration of the text, it would be suppressed, involving your arrest and trial." Quinn was starting, apparently, with the bad news. Huebsch already knew the good news. Boni & Liveright sold private editions of several daring books, and they escaped prosecution every time. While none of their books had indicted excerpts, Quinn assured Huebsch that magazines and books were judged by different legal standards: the more discreetly something circulated, the more likely it would escape prosecution. And a conviction against *The Little Review* could be a *good* thing. It would end the serialization of *Ulysses*, and the demand would be higher if a few chapters hadn't seen the light of day.

Quinn wanted fifteen hundred copies printed on high-quality paper and priced somewhere around ten dollars so that Joyce could get a royalty of two dollars per copy. That would give him three thousand dollars for *Ulysses*, more than Quinn mentioned to Joyce. But Huebsch was nervous, and when Quinn sensed that he wanted to see how the trial played out, he planned to approach Boni & Liveright for a quick contract. But without Joyce's approval, he had to keep stalling.

QUINN FILED THE MOTION for a jury trial in January 1921, and in a concluding flourish he argued that the charges caused *The Little Review* "serious financial loss." The longer the ban continued, he claimed, the more it would damage their finances. *The Little Review* struggled through 1920, and it went into a tailspin after Sumner walked into the Washington Square Book Shop. Quinn and his friends had withdrawn their financial support, leaving Anderson and Heap desperate for subscribers and benefactors. Over dinner with Anderson one night, a patron demanded sexual favors for his continued support. She was furious. *The Little Review* also needed content. *Ulysses* was, more or less, keeping the magazine afloat.

Jane Heap wrote to Joyce for the first time: "We cannot apologize for the recent deletions," she wrote in green ink. "We can only suffer with you. Our entire May issue *was* burned by the Postal department and we were told brutally that we would be put out of business altogether if we didn't stop 'pulling that stuff.'" Then she turned to the pressing issue: the *Ulysses* installments were coming too slowly. They were parceling out the text in smaller chunks, but it wasn't enough. Could he send short stories or poems? "We cannot pay well at present," she confided. "We live only because we are able to fight like devils."

Following the obscenity charges, Anderson and Heap halted publication for three months. In December 1920, they interrupted a performance of Eugene O'Neill's *The Emperor Jones* at Washington Square's Provincetown Playhouse and asked the audience for contributions to defend *Ulysses* and save the magazine from bankruptcy. Whatever they gathered at the theater, it was just enough to publish a December issue. The editors announced that the charges forced them to raise subscription prices from $2.50 to $4.00.

Meanwhile, Quinn pressed Joyce to finish *Ulysses* quickly. Sumner and the DA were increasingly impatient with procedural delays, and Huebsch, still inching toward an agreement, needed to publish it by the fall to avoid censorship. Joyce answered with another coded telegram saying that the finished manuscript was only a few months off, but he wanted more than two dollars per copy. "Make following counter proposal: $3 $3.50. Withdraw offer unless accepted immediately."

Joyce reasoned that a limited edition of *Ulysses*—already longer than most private editions—could retail for more than ten dollars. But nobody made agreements like this "immediately"—even when the book *didn't* have legal problems. Whether Joyce was too far removed from the situation in New York or too absorbed in his own writing, he simply wasn't worried. He cabled again five days later in code: "In financial difficulties. Remit by telegraph as soon as possible two hundred dollars pending completion of contract."

Quinn was astonished. Here was an impoverished author—barely able to afford a telegram—with criminal charges against a portion of what was already a long and difficult manuscript. The editors publishing his fiction were facing jail time for it, and instead of seizing any publication offer he could get— instead of thanking Quinn for trying to strong-arm a publisher into offering a contract for what would probably be a financial loss even if it *wasn't* a legal mess—Joyce demanded nearly double the royalties and a two-hundred-dollar advance on a contract that didn't even exist. Pound was right. James Joyce was completely unreasonable.

CABLING MONEY REQUESTED WILL ENDEAVOR WRITE NEXT
THREE OR FOUR WEEKS DO NOT CABLE ME AGAIN ANY
SUBJECT HAVE ENDEAVORED MAKE YOU AND POUND UNDER-
STAND AM WORKING LIMIT MY ENDURANCE   QUINN

THE *LITTLE REVIEW* TRIAL could not have happened at a worse time. Not only was Quinn shuttling back and forth to Washington, D.C., to prepare for the most important case of his life, but the country had fallen into an economic depression. Throughout 1920, wholesale prices were plunging due to a sudden drop in demand for U.S. products after the war. European agriculture recovered faster than anyone expected, and American farmers were left with large surpluses and crushing debt that ravaged both the farmers and the banks that financed them. Commodity prices dropped 46 percent in less than a year, and by 1921 Quinn found himself in the middle of a disaster. One of his biggest clients, the National Bank of Commerce, had holdings in hundreds of agriculture companies, all on the brink of collapse. Quinn himself lost thirty thousand dollars in securities that year, and there was no end in sight. "Clients, banks, corporations have lost money right and left. Soft spots developed where the surface seemed to be clean and hard. Failures, failures, failures!" Bankruptcies multiplied till corporate officers became hysterical. It was the third financial panic he had been through, and it was by far the worst—"a financial reign of terror."

Quinn's employees were at their wits' end. One of his junior partners quit, and the other couldn't handle his work because he was having domestic problems, spending late nights in Washington Square and, like Joyce, suffering acute attacks of iritis. Quinn worked on Sundays, Christmas and New Year's Eve. He worked nights, canceled all private engagements and gave up daytime smoking breaks. The time he took to defend *The Little Review* was costing him his sanity, not to mention thousands of dollars in lost fees from other cases, but he was unable to say no to an artist like Joyce. "The trouble with me," he wrote to J. B. Yeats, the poet's father, "is that I am too damned good-natured."

But it was Miss Weaver's good nature, above all, that allowed Joyce to write *Ulysses* amid war and recession, and she tried desperately to insulate him from the financial difficulties he created for himself. Miss Weaver had begun her patronage modestly. In 1916 she sent Joyce fifty pounds, ostensibly for serializing *A Portrait* in *The Egoist*, though it was nearly as much money as the magazine grossed in a year. In February 1917, the Egoist Press published *A Portrait* with Huebsch's sheets, but circumstances dulled the occasion's triumph. Joyce's letters over the previous three months detailed his ongoing affliction, including several collapses he said were due to a nervous breakdown, and she got her first glimpse of Joyce's likeness when he sent her the photograph that Pound had called "terrifying," though the sight of Joyce's eyes moved her to compassion rather than terror.

By 1919, Miss Weaver was collecting every press clipping about Joyce she could find and losing sleep over the draft episodes of *Ulysses*, but Joyce was still struggling. The Egoist Press's second edition of *A Portrait* sold only 314 copies in over a year, and Joyce suffered multiple eye attacks in 1918 followed by yet another in February 1919. So at the end of that month, Miss Weaver became Joyce's anonymous donor by giving him a £5,000 war bond yielding

£250 in income annually. When Nora received the letter from Miss Weaver's law firm, she rushed to meet Joyce in Zurich and danced a jig on the steps of the tram. Two months later, Miss Weaver revealed herself as the donor and begged him to forgive her lack of "delicacy and self-effacement."

From that point forward, Miss Weaver's patronage was candid. In August 1920 she bestowed another capital gift of £2,000. During the late stages of drafts and revisions on *Ulysses*, Joyce was earning £350 per year (equivalent to more than £11,000 today) from Miss Weaver's two capital donations, and she padded this with several small gifts over the years. She wanted to repay Joyce for the freedom she felt when she read *A Portrait* by giving him the freedom to write a book unfettered by marketplace constraints. And she was not disappointed, for the new novel he was writing appeared to be constrained by nothing, to be the most ambitious novel anyone had ever written. Her investment also would have granted Joyce peace of mind if he were capable of living within his means, but the apartment he rented in Paris in December 1920 cost £300 per year, nearly everything she gave him, and a high rent was not the only indulgence. Nora dressed the family in fashionable clothes. Joyce was fond of fine restaurants, taxicabs and, of course, considerable drinking. He tipped everyone extravagantly—five-franc tips for one-franc drinks, as if he distrusted the money. Add Joyce's medical bills and it's easy to see how he was desperate for an advance on *Ulysses* by the beginning of 1921.

Years of patronage attenuated Joyce's already weak sense of practicality, which is part of the reason he thought *The Little Review* should continue serializing *Ulysses* while John Quinn fought criminal charges. Ezra Pound was less concerned about *The Little Review* charges now that Joyce had a patron—that, in Pound's opinion, only made severing his connection with the magazine easier. Quinn, in fact, was the only person who understood the gravity of Joyce's immediate legal problems, and the situation in New York became worse when Quinn's motion for a jury trial was denied in February 1921. The judge sympathized with Quinn's claims about the magazine's finances, but the argument was a bit too clever. The judge sympathized so much that he decided to do the editors a favor: by denying a jury trial and holding the trial before the three judges of Special Sessions, the editors would get an earlier judgment and be back in business much sooner. Quinn received two days' notice: *The Little Review* was scheduled for trial on Friday, February 4.

Quinn rushed to the DA's office, found the prosecutor in charge of the case, Assistant DA Joseph Forrester, and introduced himself in a half whisper. For the past week, Quinn had been suffering from laryngitis, and his doctor forbade him to speak. He asked for another adjournment, and Forrester actually told John Quinn that there would be no more delays unless Sumner agreed to it. Quinn had the ear of U.S. Attorney General Palmer, testified regularly before congressional committees, changed the nation's copyright and tariff laws, was almost single-handedly defending the federal government in the U.S. Supreme Court, and now an assistant New York DA was telling him that he couldn't get an adjournment in the Jefferson Market Courthouse unless some functionary from the vice society would allow it.

And Sumner refused. There had been at least six adjournments already, and he appeared in court for each one of them. The case should have been heard back in October, and now that it was February, he had run out of patience. Besides, Sumner told him, it was an open-and-shut case—it would be over as soon as the judges read the magazine. So Quinn was, more or less, forced to get a note from his doctor. He drew up an affidavit certifying his laryngitis in order to request an adjournment directly from the judge, and the court granted him ten more days.

Quinn told Anderson and Heap to start thinking about character witnesses, people who could vouch for their motives in order to limit the penalty. They were definitely going to be found guilty—"There isn't the slightest shade of a doubt of that," he told Anderson—and because they had a history of violations, they would be treated like "old and callous offenders." They were lucky to be prosecuted under the state law, where the maximum penalty at the time was only a thousand-dollar fine and a year in prison. If they were luckier, their punishment might be a permanent postal ban. But if they were defiant in court, he said, they might go to prison.

Sumner's prosecutions routinely put people behind bars, even when the offenders were more important than the *Little Review* editors. When he prosecuted the president of Harper & Brothers for publishing an obscene book earlier that year, the company's president was ordered to pay a thousand dollars or spend three months in prison. Quinn might post fifty dollars in bail for Anderson and Heap, but he was not about to give them two thousand dollars for their freedom.

THE LITTLE REVIEW was inundated with angry letters about *Ulysses*. The editors generally ignored them, but one envelope featured such beautiful handwriting that Margaret Anderson opened it. A woman in Chicago wished to share her thoughts about Mr. Bloom's encounter with Gerty on the beach:

> *Damnable, hellish filth from the gutter of a human mind born and bred in contamination. There are no words I know to describe, even vaguely, how disgusted I am; not with the mire of his effusion but with all those whose minds are so putrid that they dare allow such muck and sewage of the human mind to besmirch the world by repeating it—and in print, through which medium it may reach young minds. Oh my God, the horror of it . . . It has done something tragic to my illusions about America. How could you?*

Anderson stayed awake all night trying to write an answer large enough to encompass her indignation over the writer's "profound ignorance of all branches of art, science, life," though in the end she could only be dismissive: "It is not important that you dislike James Joyce," she wrote back. "He is not writing for you. He is writing for himself."

Anderson courted hardship and ostracism partly, as Quinn suspected, for self-advertisement, but mostly because she saw it as the key to independence. Anderson broke away from her family only to find that she had shifted her dependence to contributors, advertisers, patrons and foreign editors. She envied the fact that people like James Joyce and Emma Goldman were in exile or in prison for something bigger than themselves. The image of Joyce toiling through war, illness and penury to follow his own vision—publishers, readers and puritanical policemen be damned—was, for Anderson, the essence of art.

Now that she had criminal charges against her, she shared Joyce's defiance and with it, she hoped, his independence. In the belated *The Little Review* issue following the charges, Anderson insisted that genuine art rested upon two principles: *"First, the artist has no responsibility to the public whatever."* The public, in fact, was responsible to the artist. *"Second,"* she emphasized, *"the position of the great artist is impregnable* . . . You can no more limit his expression, patronizingly suggest that his genius present itself in channels personally pleasing to you, than you can eat the stars."

The Little Review existed for genius—that was why Anderson and Heap "fought like devils" for every issue. Anderson wanted, as she later wrote to a friend, to be "the arranger of life, the killer of the philistine, *the favorite enemy of the bourgeoisie."* Whereas Ezra Pound wanted an aristocracy of taste, Margaret Anderson wanted an autocracy, a society in which the exceptional would rule over the unexceptional. "Anything else," she wrote, "means that the exceptional people must suffer with the average people—from the average people." For Anderson, the obscenity trial against *Ulysses* and *The Little Review* was not a fight for the freedom of speech. It was a fight for the freedom of genius.

16.

THE PEOPLE OF THE STATE OF NEW YORK V. MARGARET ANDERSON AND JANE HEAP

———

The courtroom was packed with spectators drawn by Margaret Anderson's refined looks and reporters eager to get the scoop on the "Greenwich Girl Editors." The previous week, a judge threatened another Village editor with psychiatric observation at Bellevue, and this week's show was even more promising. Anderson and Heap were defending a book rumored to be radical Freudianism, impenetrable madness and what one reporter called "ultra-violet sex fiction." But Quinn was determined that there wouldn't be a scene. He told Anderson and Heap that they had two responsibilities: to shut their mouths and to surround themselves with "window trimmings." Any Washington Squareites they brought to court were to dress like demure, tasteful ladies rather than the women who showed up at the preliminary hearing looking, he said, like they were rustled into court after a whorehouse raid. Anderson was determined to follow his advice, but it only made her more contemptuous of the proceedings.

"Everyone stands up as the three judges enter," she recounted in *The Little Review*. "Why must I stand up as a tribute to three men who wouldn't understand my simplest remark?" When she wasn't outraged by the proceedings, she tried not to be bored by them. "Perhaps one can be enlivened by speculating as to whether they will swerve the fraction of an inch from their predestined stupidity."

The men overseeing the stupidity were Special Sessions Chief Justice Frederic Kernochan and two white-haired judges, John J. McInerney and Joseph Moss. Assistant DA Forrester called only one witness, John Sumner. All Sumner had to do was explain the circumstances of the suppression—the troubled daughter, the outraged father and the undercover purchase in the bookstore on Eighth Street, where any young woman might find it—and James Joyce's obscenity would speak for itself.

It occurred to Quinn that the trial was a demoralizing squabble among Irishmen. Two of the three judges were Irish. The indictment was handed down by Corrigan, an Irishman, against James Joyce, another Irishman, and in the middle of it all was John Quinn squaring off against an assistant DA who presented himself, Quinn thought, as "a one hundred and thirty percent Irish Republican" defending Ireland's dignity against betrayers like Quinn and Joyce.

Quinn argued that Joyce was an artist matching the caliber of Shakespeare, Dante, Fielding and Blake. He was a satirist like Swift and Oscar Wilde, and there was less "filth" in *Ulysses* than there was in Broadway performances and Fifth Avenue window displays. Quinn initially thought the case was so hopeless that he wouldn't even bother calling witnesses to defend *Ulysses'* literary merits, but as the trial approached, the desire to win (or to mitigate sentencing) got the better of him, and he convinced the judges to hear expert testimony. One witness, a British lecturer named John Cowper Powys, testified that Joyce's fusion of dialogue and narrative, thought and action, made his style too obscure to deprave and corrupt the public—the average reader would find it repellent. *Ulysses,* Powys testified, was "in no way capable of corrupting the minds of young girls." He used to teach at a girls' school, so he knew.

When Quinn's second witness took the stand, the judges grew impatient with so-called experts. Philip Moeller was one of the founders of New York's Theatre Guild, and he asked the judges if he might use technical terminology to explain how Joyce applied Freudian psychology. The scene between Gerty and Bloom on the beach was really "an unveiling of the subconscious mind." Joyce's chapter, he testified, "most emphatically is not aphrodisiac."

"What's this!" Judge Kernochan interrupted. "What's that?"

Quinn tried to help, "Well, if I may explain your honor, an aphrodisiac is an adjective derived from the noun Aphrodite, supposed to be the goddess of beauty or love—"

"I understand that," said Kernochan, "but I don't understand what this man is talking about. He might as well be talking in Russian."

When the judges proceeded without hearing from the rest of Quinn's experts, it occurred to Anderson and Heap that *Ulysses* was trapped in a foreign country where beauty and craftsmanship were meaningless. One of the judges declared (without shame, apparently), "We don't care who James Joyce is or whether he has written the finest books in the world."

And yet the trial was going better than it seemed. The fact that there were witnesses at all was a victory. Courts typically ignored literary merit in obscenity cases, but Quinn cited an obscure 1913 ruling by Judge Learned Hand to secure an exception. Hand was a cousin of the judge who had ruled against *The Little Review* in 1917, but he was no friend of Anthony Comstock ("When I wish to hear from you," he once told the bullying crusader in his courtroom, "I will let you know!"), nor did he approve of the Hicklin Rule. Hand was suspicious of judicial hunts for hidden tendencies in books, especially when they focused on anyone "into whose hands" a book "may fall." The Hicklin Rule requires us, the judge wrote in 1913, "to reduce our treatment of sex to the standard of a child's library." The government had an interest in protecting valuable literature, he argued, and artists needed freedom to portray the full scope of human nature because "truth and beauty are too precious to society at large to be mutilated." The Hicklin Rule's tendency to tether modern society to Victorian values made it an instrument of immorality.

Learned Hand proposed his own definition of obscenity—it was the first time in over forty years that a federal judge questioned the reigning standards: "Should not the word 'obscene' be allowed to indicate the present critical point in the compromise between candor and shame at which the community may have arrived here and now?" The meanings of *obscene* and *lewd* and *lascivious* weren't set in stone. They were fluid and local, hashed out by communities from year to year.

Though this seems like a small point to make, it was radical. To suggest that what corrupts a reader's mind changes over time is to imply that what is natural about a mind—its uncorrupted state—also changes. If you read it carefully, Learned Hand's ruling didn't just make obscenity malleable. It made human nature malleable. But no one read it carefully, and Hand's decision fell into obscurity. It was, after all, only a preliminary ruling on a savvy defense attorney's motion to bypass a jury trial. John Quinn was the only person who paid attention to Hand's argument—he quoted it at length in his memorandum—because Quinn himself was the savvy defense attorney.

THE COURT ADJOURNED for a week so that the judges could read *The Little Review* themselves. When the proceedings resumed, the Assistant DA Forrester prepared to read some of the offensive passages out loud, but one of the white-haired judges stopped him. There were ladies in the courtroom. Everyone turned to the statuesque woman in the high-collared coat, her clear eyes gazing steadily from behind heavy lids. Margaret Anderson's virtuously dressed supporters were clustered behind her. Quinn turned back to the judge and smiled. The attentive women in the front rows didn't need to be protected from the filth of *The Little Review*, he explained, and the woman who had caught his eye was the magazine's *editor*.

The judge couldn't believe it. "I am sure she didn't know the significance of what she was publishing," he said. "I myself do not understand *Ulysses*—I think Joyce has carried his method too far in this experiment."

"Yes," Judge McInerney said, "it sounds to me like the ravings of a disordered mind—I can't see why anyone would want to publish it."

The courtroom exercise infuriated Anderson. Even if the judges *could* understand Joyce, they would insist on applying incommensurable standards. It was like having your outfit for the day judged by a trio of weathermen. Anderson was on the verge of shouting out to the judges. "Let me tell you *why* I regard it as the prose masterpiece of my generation," she wanted to say, "and why you have no right to pit the dullness of your brains against the fineness of mine." Jane, eager to avoid prison, was poking Anderson in the ribs, whispering, "Don't try to talk. Don't put yourself into their hands."

Quinn was pleased with the judges' bewilderment—it was the cornerstone of his argument. So long as Joyce's writing was unintelligible it couldn't be obscene. *Ulysses* was "cubism in literature," he said, trying to balance its seriousness with its obscurity, and he read a passage of Bloom's thoughts to illustrate his point:

A monkey puzzle rocket burst, spluttering in darting crackles. Zrads and zrads, zrads, zrads. And Cissy and Tommy ran out to see and Edy after with the pushcar and then Gerty beyond the curve of the rocks. Will she? Watch! Watch! See! Looked round. She smelt an onion. Darling, I saw your. I saw all.

Joyce baffled. The text didn't even have proper punctuation, which, Quinn suggested, was the unfortunate result of Joyce's poor eyesight. The DA became so outraged at this insult to the court's intelligence that he launched into a red-faced invective, at which point Quinn broke in and pointed to the prosecutor, "This is my best exhibit! There is proof *Ulysses* does not corrupt or fill people full of lascivious thoughts. Look at him!" Almost involuntarily, they looked. "Does a reading of that chapter want to send him to the arms of a whore? Is he filled with sexual desire? Not at all. He wants to murder somebody! He wants to send Joyce to jail. He wants to send those two women to prison. He would like to disbar me. He is full of hatred, venom, anger and uncharitableness. But lust? There is not a drop of lust or an ounce of sex passion in his whole body. . . . . *He* is my chief exhibit as to the effect of *Ulysses*."

In his concluding statements, Quinn tried to put the prosecution in a logical bind. Readers would either understand the episode from *Ulysses* or they wouldn't. The readers who couldn't understand *Ulysses* would, by definition, not be corrupted by it. And the few readers who could understand it would either be captivated by its "experimental, tentative, revolutionary" style or else they would be repulsed or bored. Either way, the vulnerable young women of

New York were protected from corruption by their own naïveté. Joyce's chapter was inscrutable to all but the most sophisticated readers, readers that the state of New York did not need to worry about.

"It's just the story of a lady's lingerie," Quinn said.

"The lady is *in* the lingerie," a judge responded.

Quinn had the two older judges exactly where he wanted them—befuddled and amenable to his authority, but Judge Kernochan was different. "He is an ass without the slightest glimmer of culture, but he knows the meaning of words," Quinn later wrote to Joyce.

After the judges conferred, Kernochan pronounced Margaret Anderson and Jane Heap guilty of violating the New York state law against obscenity. To keep the editors out of prison, Quinn certified that "Nausicaa" was the most offensive chapter in the book, but the judges still weren't sure how seriously the women should be punished. One of them asked Sumner if there were any prior complaints regarding the magazine. Sumner glanced at Margaret Anderson, her full lips heavily rouged. Sensing the stakes of the question, he gallantly pushed the other suppressed issues under the pile of papers in front of him. "Not at all," he said.

Whether it was because it was their first time in court or because the judges pitied their ignorance, Judge McInerney announced a penalty he considered "very lenient." The judges ordered Anderson and Heap to serve ten days in prison or pay a fine of one hundred dollars, an amount they almost certainly didn't have. Luckily, one of the ladies gathered in the courtroom, a wealthy Chicagoan named Joanna Fortune, kept Anderson and Heap out of jail by paying the fine herself.

Newspaper reporters and Greenwich Villagers crowded around as the Girl Editors were hauled off to be fingerprinted. Somewhere in the bustle of the crowd a young man called out, "That chapter was a bit disgusting."

Jane Heap shouted back, "Is it a crime to be disgusting?"

Now that the proceedings were over, they were eager to break their silence. The question of obscenity "should be left to us experts," Anderson told the newsmen, rather than to smut hounds like Sumner. "Give an artist a moral and he will lose his art." And then she gave a plug: "*The Little Review* is the only medium through which the artist may enjoy his place in the sun."

Anderson decided that if the law insisted on treating her like a delicate creature, then the men would have to take a delicate creature's fingerprints. She examined the inkpad. She wanted more towels, she said, and one of the men hastened to retrieve them. She wanted better soap, she said, and they managed to find something more suitable. She wanted a nail brush, she said, and by some feat of resourcefulness they supplied even that. Miss Margaret C. Anderson reluctantly submitted her hands to the pad while the men assured her that the ink wouldn't stain.

The prospects for the publication of *Ulysses* in the United States were bleak, and Quinn felt genuine remorse. He wrote to Anderson, "I thought of Joyce and of his need for the money and that he was abroad and out of touch with things here, and perhaps not in the best of health. And I remembered how hard it was for serious writers to live in these years and months and days . . . I have done the best I could, and I failed." Word spread that the Post Office had sent the seized copies of *The Little Review* to the Salvation Army, where fallen women in reform programs were instructed to tear them apart.

ANDERSON AND HEAP were lucky. No one at the *Little Review* trial noticed the most scandalous aspect of "Nausicaa," the obscurity at the heart of the episode: while Gerty MacDowell is leaning back on the rocks, Leopold Bloom is masturbating. The judges, the reporters, the innocent girl's father and John Sumner himself missed it, which is understandable. Even if one were looking for something so improbably, outlandishly offensive, it wasn't easy to find. When Gerty limps away, Bloom "recomposed his wet shirt," but Pound had cut the word *wet*. A few pages later, the manuscript read, "O sweety. All your little white up I saw. Dirty girl. Made me do love sticky." Pound crossed out "up I saw. Dirty girl" and, prudently, "love sticky" so that *The Little Review*'s version was more discreet though less coherent: "O sweety all your little white I made me do we too naughty darling." An especially astute reader might connect Bloom's "hoarse breathing" and his face's "whitehot passion" several pages earlier, but the blue garters and nainsook knickers tend to steal the show.

If Anderson and Heap knew, they pretended not to, and Quinn himself may not have noticed if Pound hadn't clued him in. Joyce, he told Quinn, was bent on mentioning "every possible physical secretion." One of the only people who detected it was Judge Corrigan at the preliminary hearing. He held the editors for trial, despite knowing Quinn, because, he said, of "the episode where the man went off in his pants," which was illegal beyond all doubt. When Quinn mocked Corrigan for having a dirty mind, what he meant was that an innocent judge wouldn't have seen it—after all, it took a lascivious mind to find an orgasm in those bursting Roman candles.

So in the wake of the "Nausicaa" conviction, Joyce decided to make the tableau a bit more explicit. He restored "love sticky" and the wetness to Bloom's shirt, of course, and he added a new insert as Gerty leans back: "His hands and face were working and a tremour went over her." As with all of his revisions, Joyce was recalibrating: he wanted the details of his story to be just obscure enough to be found. He had a childlike desire to be searched for and discovered behind the couch or in a cupboard. When people couldn't see the Homeric correspondences in *Ulysses*, Joyce tabulated them in a handy chart. And when the key he provided threatened to become too public, he forbade publishers from printing it.

The question Joyce had asked Nora before they left Ireland remained with him his entire life: "Is there one who understands me?" The coins jingling in Boylan's pocket, Gerty's fantasy about Bloom's foreign name, the knock-me-down cigar hinting at the blinded Cyclops and Bloom's hoarse breathing are secrets waiting to be understood. Meanings in *Ulysses* are coy thrills. They are only partially revealed so as to draw people closer. *Ulysses* is difficult because Joyce was lonely. He was sentimental, prone to fantasy as well as rumination, and he beckoned readers onward through teases written into his book inch by inch. If Joyce resembles someone on that beach, it is not Leopold Bloom. Joyce is Gerty.

James Joyce in Dublin, 1904.

Nora Barnacle in 1904, the year she left Ireland with Joyce despite his refusal to marry her. *Ulysses* takes place on June 16, 1904, the day they had their first date.

James Joyce in 1919. Some of the women in Zürich called him "Herr Satan."

Ezra Pound pulled Joyce from obscurity and arranged for *The Little Review* to serialize *Ulysses*. When legal troubles loomed for the magazine, he insisted on printing Joyce's novel "even if we go bust and die in a blaze of suppression."

Margaret Anderson, the founder and editor of *The Little Review*, which serialized much of *Ulysses* from 1918 to 1921.

Dora Marsden, founder and editor of *The Egoist,* arrested for suffrage activism in London, 1909.

T. S. Eliot and Virginia Woolf in 1924. Woolf declined to print the first chapters of *Ulysses* in 1918, though she changed her mind about Joyce's novel after Eliot insisted that she read it in its entirety. "It is," Eliot claimed, "a book to which we are all indebted and from which none of us can escape."

John Sumner (wearing hat and glasses) burning obscene books in New York, 1935. Sumner and the New York Society for the Suppression of Vice instigated obscenity proceedings against *The Little Review* in 1921.

Anthony Comstock, founder of the New York Society of the Suppression of Vice. The scar on his left cheek was from a pornographer's knife.

The seal of the New York Society for the Suppression of Vice.

John Quinn, a wealthy New York lawyer and art collector,
defended *Ulysses* against obscenity charges in 1921.

James Joyce, Ezra Pound, Ford Madox Ford and John Quinn
in 1923. Pound brought writers and patrons together.

Sylvia Beach, founder of Shakespeare and Company and the first publisher of *Ulysses*.

When Sylvia Beach opened her Paris bookshop in 1919, she slept on a cot in the back room.

James Joyce and Sylvia Beach at Shakespeare and Company.

Ernest Hemingway was twenty-two years old when he walked into Shakespeare and Company in 1921. The following year, he helped smuggle copies of *Ulysses* across the Canadian border.

Harriet Shaw Weaver, Joyce's patron and the publisher of the first UK edition of *Ulysses*, which was partially burned, and the second UK edition, which was entirely burned. Weaver's association with Joyce scandalized her devout family.

Sylvia Beach and James Joyce (with mounting eye problems)
at Shakespeare and Company in 1922.

Sir Archibald Bodkin, director of public prosecutions and British censor of *Ulysses*.

Morris Ernst, ACLU co-founder and Random House's legal counsel. Ernst defended *Ulysses* as a "modern classic."

Random House co-founder Bennett Cerf and Ernst orchestrated the 1933 federal court case by importing one copy of *Ulysses* from Paris. *Ulysses*, Cerf said, was Random House's "first really important trade publication." © Bettman/CORBIS

Judge John Woolsey in New York, circa 1931. Woolsey's famous 1933 decision effectively legalized Joyce's novel in the United States.

Nora Barnacle with Joyce after eye surgery in 1930. Joyce endured at least eleven surgeries to save his eyesight.

The legalization of *Ulysses* gave Joyce widespread attention.

James Joyce circa 1922.

17.

CIRCE BURNING

————

One night in April 1921, Joyce heard a frantic knocking at his door. The unexpected guest was Mrs. Harrison, the "Circe" episode's ninth typist. The last time a typist rang his doorbell, she had thrown the manuscript at his feet and fled before he could say a word. Typists expected to work from a fair copy, a neatly rewritten draft, but Joyce sent the "Circe" fair copy to John Quinn as soon as it was finished. Quinn was purchasing the manuscript bit by bit, and Joyce needed the money, so the remaining manuscript was nearly one hundred pages of sclerotic handwriting with arrows and inserts loaded onto the pages. Four typists flatly refused the job when they saw it. Joyce told Sylvia Beach that another typist "threatened in despair to throw herself out of the window."

Beach took this as Joyce's way of asking for help, so she gave the manuscript to her sister Cyprian, a silent-film actress. Cyprian would wake up before dawn and decipher Joyce's writing line by line before going to the movie studio. When her film took her to other locations, she gave the manuscript to Raymonde Linossier, one of the only female barristers in Paris. Linossier's father, a famous physician, forbade her from consorting with Left Bank artists, and to evade her father's control she became secretive with her talents. She enrolled in law school partly to use studying as an alibi for literary trysts at La Maison des Amis des Livres and Shakespeare and Company. When *The Little Review* published Linossier's five-page "novel" under a pseudonym, she kept her copies hidden and never wrote again. Nevertheless, when Cyprian Beach gave her the "Circe" manuscript she typed out the eccentric brothel scenes while her suddenly ill father convalesced in the next room. She admired *Ulysses*, but after forty-five pages, even she had to quit.

The wandering manuscript then fell into the hands of Mrs. Harrison, Linossier's friend and the wife of a gentleman employed at the British embassy. When Mr. Harrison found portions of Joyce's manuscript on his wife's desk he began reading what appeared to be a delusional play in Dublin's red-light district. The characters included "A Whore," "Biddy the Clap" and "Cunty Kate." Lord Tennyson appears out of nowhere wearing a Union Jack blazer and cricket flannels. King Edward VII shows up sucking on a red date and officiates a fight. Moments later, he's levitating. A soldier tugs at his belt and threatens, "I'll wring the neck of any fucking bastard says a word against my bleeding fucking king."

A few pages later, Dublin is on fire. Amid the pandemonium (warfare, mortal shrieks, brimstone fires), Father Malachi O'Flynn celebrates a black mass.

FATHER O'FLYNN
Introibo ad altare diaboli.

THE REVEREND MR LOVE
To the devil which hath made glad my youth.

FATHER O'FLYNN
(takes from the chalice and elevates a blooddripping host)
Corpus meum.

THE REVEREND MR LOVE
*(raises high behind the celebrant's petticoats revealing his grey
bare hairy buttocks between which a carrot is stuck)*
My body.

The soldier shouts out again, "I'll do him in, so help me fucking Christ! I'll wring the bastard fucker's bleeding blasted fucking windpipe!"

Harrison flew into a rage. He began tearing up the manuscript, throwing pages into the fire. His wife heard the commotion, rushed into the room to stop him and hid what was left of "Circe" before he could burn any more of it. "Hysterical scenes followed," Joyce explained to Quinn, "in the house and in the street." Joyce begged Mrs. Harrison to retrieve the rest of the manuscript as quickly as possible. When she returned the next morning with the remnants, Joyce discovered that the husband had burned several pages of material from both his wife's typescript *and* the original manuscript. The only complete copy of "Circe" was on a steamship bound for New York.

John Quinn was in the midst of his last-ditch efforts to get a contract for *Ulysses* with Ben Huebsch, who, despite the *Little Review* conviction, did not want to relinquish his rights. When Quinn forced a decision, Huebsch finally refused to publish *Ulysses* in any edition, public or private, unless Joyce agreed to deletions. Quinn thought it was a wise decision. As remarkable as Joyce's book was, Quinn wrote to Huebsch, "it is better to lose twenty *Ulysses* than spend thirty days in Blackwell's Island for one." Joyce was not the only one who took pleasure in searing honesty.

Quinn called up Horace Liveright to secure an immediate deal for a private edition of *Ulysses*, and he was not disappointed. On April 21, Boni & Liveright made the offer that Quinn had been trying to pull off for the better part of a year. But the deal fell apart in a few hours. That same day, a package from Paris arrived at Quinn's office containing the long-awaited manuscript of "Circe," and Quinn was aghast. One scene details Bloom's masochistic punishment, in which the prostitutes in Bella Cohen's brothel hold him down (the cook comes out to help) while Bella, who transformed into a man a few pages earlier, squats over Bloom, smothers him with her/his buttocks and farts in his face. Bloom is then commanded to empty the brothel's piss pots or else "lap it up like champagne" shortly before he turns into a woman and is auctioned off as a sex slave. Anyone who published it—publicly, privately, in an aeroplane at fifteen thousand feet—would be convicted. He called Liveright back and told him to forget about *Ulysses*. The book was a legal nightmare. Liveright was disappointed, "but I guess you're right," he wrote to Quinn. "We'd all go to jail in a hurry if we published it except in a horribly castrated edition."

Days later, when Quinn read Joyce's distressed letter informing him that the original "Circe" manuscript had been burned, he was pleased. He hoped the hysteria in the Harrison household would bring Joyce to his senses. "I rather admire that husband," he wrote to Joyce. "He was playing the game right, shielding her, protecting her, guarding her, and learning what she was doing, and disapproving where disapproval was due." If an obscenity conviction in a New York court didn't halt *Ulysses'* prospects, the spell of Circe did. With Huebsch and Liveright out of the picture, and London printers unwilling to set even the "decorous" episodes, the novel had no viable publishing options in the United States or Britain. And the worst of *Ulysses* was yet to come.

SYLVIA BEACH'S OFFER happened casually, as if she and Joyce had been preparing themselves since they shook hands in André Spire's library and now all they needed to do to launch the ship was break the bottle. Joyce, disconsolate, went to Shakespeare and Company and told Miss Beach about the "Nausicaa" conviction in New York. "My book will never come out now," he said. Her question, when she asked it, was an answer to Joyce's unspoken proposal. "Would you like me to publish *Ulysses*?"

"I would."

Sylvia Beach had never published so much as a pamphlet. She had no experience marketing or publicizing a new book, no background with distributors or printers, no familiarity with plates or proofs or galleys. She had no capital, and she could only guess about costs and financing. Advertising would have to be based on circulars, charitable press and word of mouth. She knew almost nothing about the legal complications of the publishing industry, in France or anywhere else, to say nothing of the complications facing a book convicted of obscenity before it was even a book. She knew the "Circe" episode was more offensive than anything in *The Little Review*, and she knew it would get worse.

Despite all of this, she decided that Shakespeare and Company—a company of one, after all, of a thirty-four-year-old American expatriate who was, until recently, sleeping on a cot in the back room of a diminutive bookshop on a street nobody could find—would issue the single most difficult book anyone had published in decades. It would be monstrously large, prohibitively expensive and impossible to proofread. It was a book without a home, an Irish novel written in Trieste, Zurich and Paris to be published in France in riddling English by a bookseller from New Jersey. Joyce's readership was scattered. The book was at turns obscure and outrageous, its beauty and pleasures were so coy, its tenderness so hidden by erudition, that when it did not estrange its readers it provoked them. *Ulysses* was not even finished, and already it had been declared obscene in New York and burned in anger in Paris.

None of this mattered. Sylvia Beach wanted to be closer to Joyce and to the center of contemporary literature. She wanted to be successful and to repay the money her mother had given her. She wanted to give the world something more than pajamas and condensed milk. Beach and Joyce worked through the details themselves. Shakespeare and Company would publish a high-quality private edition of one thousand copies. She would send out announcements and gather orders by mail before publication and pay the printer in installments as the money came in. When the book was ready, she would mail copies by registered post to readers around the world.

She borrowed Quinn's idea of a private publication, but her prices were more ambitious. Instead of a ten-dollar edition, Shakespeare and Company would offer three versions of varying quality. The cheapest would be 150 francs, or $12. Another set of 150 copies printed on higher-quality paper would sell for 250 francs each—$20. The premium copies would be a set of one hundred books printed on Dutch handmade paper and signed by Joyce for 350 francs—$28. Even for an oversized, deluxe, private first edition, it was an extraordinary amount, the equivalent of about $400 today. The entire edition would earn $14,800, and Joyce would receive 66 percent of the profits. Neither of them thought about signing a contract.

Sylvia Beach was facing extraordinary problems. Six months before the announced publication date, the manuscript was far from complete, portions had been burned and she was having difficulty retrieving the only surviving copy. She wrote letters and sent cables to John Quinn in New York. Would he send the missing pages to Joyce? No. Would he let someone come to his office to copy the pages by hand? No. Sylvia's mother called him from Princeton. She was sailing for Paris in May and asked Mr. Quinn if she might please take the missing pages with her—her daughter would send them back as quickly as possible. Mr. Quinn refused. On the day her ship set off, she called him several times, nearly in tears, and the answer was still no. "He will get the missing pages," Quinn wrote to a friend, "but at my convenience." That was the gist of his message, anyway. Beach recalled that he "used language unfit for a lady like my mother."

As frustrating as it was (it took Quinn six weeks to send copies of the pages), Sylvia Beach was almost too busy advertising *Ulysses* to be preoccupied with the text itself. She drew up a circular announcing the plans.

ULYSSES suppressed four times during serial publication in 'The Little Review' will be published by 'SHAKESPEARE AND COMPANY' complete as written.

The circular said Joyce's book would be six hundred pages long and appear in the autumn of 1921. Beach's sisters and friends drummed up buyers in the States. The regular patrons of Shakespeare and Company subscribed immediately and submitted the names and addresses of other likely buyers. Robert McAlmon, an American writer newly arrived in Paris, gathered orders from patrons in Paris nightclubs and dropped the order forms off on his way home in the early morning. Beach could barely make out the handwriting on some of them. Joyce showed up at Shakespeare and Company to wait for orders to arrive, and Beach recorded the names in a green notebook. Hart Crane. W. B. Yeats. Ivor Winters. William Carlos Williams. Wallace Stevens. Winston Churchill. John Quinn ordered fourteen copies. And despite Josephine Bell's arrest, the Washington Square Book Shop ordered twenty-five—the largest single order.

The news spread quickly. Shakespeare and Company was mobbed with people, and the shop more than doubled its normal revenues. Sylvia boasted to her mother that less than two years after opening her shop, she was publishing "the most important book of the age . . . it's going to make us famous rah rah!" Articles about Beach and Shakespeare and Company began to appear in the press. "American Girl Conducts Novel Bookstore Here," *The Paris Tribune* announced. The article included a picture of the American Girl and reported rumors that the publication of *Ulysses* "may mean that Miss Beach will not be allowed to return to America."

Some people were not pleased to hear the news. George Bernard Shaw responded to the announcement by saying that he had already read portions of *Ulysses*. "It is a revolting record of a disgusting phase of civilization," he wrote, "but it is a truthful one." Shaw was one of Anthony Comstock's old victims—when his play *Mrs. Warren's Profession* was produced in New York in 1905, the cast and crew were arrested (Mrs. Warren is a brothel madam)—so one would think that a truthful record, disgusting or otherwise, had a lot to recommend it. Not enough, apparently. Shaw speculated that Sylvia Beach was "a young barbarian beglamoured by the excitements and enthusiasms that art stirs up in passionate material, but to me," Shaw wrote, "it is all hideously real." He had, thankfully, escaped that hideous island for the sweetness and light of England, where his play had also been banned. Shaw wanted to force young Dublin men to read *Ulysses* as a sort of immersive punishment, though this did not mean that he was going to purchase a copy. "I am an elderly Irish gentleman," he reminded Beach, and "if you imagine that any Irishman, much less an elderly one, would pay 150 francs for a book, you little know my countrymen." When Ezra Pound read the letter, he called Shaw "a ninth rate coward" in *The Dial*—he was too afraid to look the truth in the face.

JOYCE'S FEVERISH WRITING PACE increased in 1921, but the end of *Ulysses* kept receding like a horizon. In 1917 he had planned to finish in 1918. In 1918 he had planned to finish in the summer of 1919. By the time he was writing "Circe," with a shawl wrapped around his head, he planned to finish in early 1921. In January 1921 he planned to finish in April or May. In October he needed only three more weeks. By the end of November, just fifty or sixty more hours. Despite the circulars and newspaper reports, *Ulysses* would not appear in the autumn. Joyce was, nevertheless, rushing to have it published on his fortieth birthday, February 2, 1922.

Joyce was writing the final two episodes, "Ithaca" and "Penelope," simultaneously in the spring and summer of 1921. By then, the novel's perspectives and voices had multiplied, the Homeric correspondences were more elaborate, Dublin's June day was becoming a map of civilization and his characters' flesh and blood were being subsumed into a mythology. By the time Leopold Bloom wends his way home at two in the morning, events unfold as a series of questions and answers, cold and distant, as if spoken by gods looking down upon Dublin from Olympus. In "Ithaca," Bloom brings a weary Stephen Dedalus to his Eccles Street home after their adventure in Nighttown.

What act did Bloom make on their arrival at their destination?

At the housesteps of the 4th of the equidifferent uneven numbers, number 7 Eccles street, he inserted his hand mechanically into the back pocket of his trousers to obtain his latchkey.

Was it there?

It was in the corresponding pocket of the trousers which he had worn on the day but one preceding.

Why was he doubly irritated?

Because he had forgotten and because he remembered that he had reminded himself twice not to forget.

What were then the alternatives before the, premeditatedly (respectively) and inadvertently, keyless couple?

To enter or not to enter. To knock or not to knock.

The secrets were no longer in the inches. The chapter's impersonal style hides its sentimental content. A fatherless son and a sonless father, crossing paths throughout the day, arrive together at the father's home and finagle their way inside without the key. They discuss Paris, friendship and Stephen's prospective careers. Bloom makes Stephen cocoa and encourages him to sing quietly, which he does. Bloom recalls that once, when Stephen was ten, he invited Mr. Bloom to his house for dinner, which he politely declined. Now, after their long day, Bloom invites Stephen to spend the night at his house, which Stephen politely declines. And as the young man departs, the touch of Stephen's hand and the diminishing sound of his footsteps makes Bloom, for a brief moment, feel terribly alone. Yet all of this is told as if echoing off the walls of a white empty room.

The final chapter was the opposite. "Penelope" was lyrical and fluid. Joyce planned to end *Ulysses* with a series of letters from Molly, and he asked a friend in Trieste to deliver a briefcase he needed in order to write it. The briefcase, held closed by a rubber band, arrived in March 1921, and it contained the letters he and Nora had written to each other in 1909 (she had not yet burned hers). The sight of them—a large, red express stamp affixed sideways on an envelope, the thick, twice-folded pages filled on both sides, her neat handwriting without punctuation—would have been enough to remind him of the nights they spent apart.

She told him how much she liked being "fucked arseways." She described one particular night they shared, and she told him to pull himself off as he thought about it. "Yes," Joyce wrote back, "now I can remember that night when I fucked you for so long backwards. It was the dirtiest fucking I ever gave you, darling. My prick was stuck up in you for hours, fucking in and out under your upturned rump. I felt your fat sweaty buttocks under my belly and saw your flushed face and mad eyes." He detailed the variety of Nora's farts that night and declared how thrilling it was "to fuck a farting woman when every fuck drives one out of her."

To read their letters twelve years later was to encounter more than an archive of their abandonment. It was to return to a moment when he had risked far more than government censorship. Joyce had risked Nora's rejection by writing letters that were at once more visceral and more permanent than they had any right to be. It occurred to Joyce, in one of his letters, that their bodies would be gone someday and that perhaps the only thing left of them would be their words. As a 1909 Christmas gift, he sent Nora a bound manuscript of his poems and imagined their grandchildren turning the pages. Perhaps their words were more durable than anything else about them.

Whatever else dirty words may do, they turn words into bodies. The word *fuck* offends for what it denotes, but it also offends as an assembly of four particular letters on a page. This is why *f**k* is more printable than the unobscured expletive. We insist that the sight of the word's letters is more transgressive than a coy gesture to them because the word is important purely as a word. *Fuck* does more than transmit an idea. It is a sign whose very shape becomes a spectacle, a nude figure to be clothed in asterisks. Nora's words were sacred because they were so shamelessly physical. "Write the dirty words big," he instructed her "and underline them and kiss them and hold them for a moment to your sweet hot cunt, darling, and also pull up your dress a moment and hold them in under your dear little farting bum."

The final words of *Ulysses* would be Molly Bloom's unbroken stream of thoughts. At three in the morning, as Bloom falls asleep next to her, his head at her feet, Molly lies awake. Unlike the clipped interior monologues elsewhere in the novel, Molly's consciousness unspools without punctuation in eight grand movements. Joyce thought of her voice as full, relentless and indifferent, more geological than human—not only physical but an icon of physicality. Her body was spread out over the cardinal directions like some Vitruvian Woman looming in his mind, and her thoughts and memories swelled like tides. Since the bombs began falling around Trieste in 1915, the perspectives of his story had multiplied and expanded until now, nearing the end in Paris, "Penelope" completed what Joyce imagined to be his novel's cosmic dyad. After "Ithaca" tells the story from the edge of the galaxy, "Penelope" turns back to Molly as if to the warm earth revolving in the interstellar freeze.

Molly's thoughts about Stephen Dedalus entering her house after midnight merge with memories of years-old conversations with her husband.

Id confuse him a little alone with him if we were Id let him see my garters the new ones and make him turn red looking at him seduce him I know what boys feel with that down on their cheek doing that frigging drawing out the thing by the hour question and answer would you do this that and the other with the coalman yes with a bishop yes I would because I told him about some dean or bishop was sitting beside me in the jews temples gardens when I was knitting that woollen thing a stranger to Dublin what place was it and so on about the monuments and he tired me out with statues encouraging him making him worse than he is who is in your mind now tell me who are you thinking of who is it tell me his name who tell me who the german Emperor is it yes imagine Im him think of him can you feel him trying to make a whore of me what he never will he ought to give it up now at this age of his life simply ruination for any woman and no satisfaction in it pretending to like it till he comes and then finish it off myself anyway

If words can be bodies, Molly Bloom's soliloquy enters Joyce's novel like a gathering crowd.

THE PRESSURE OF WRITING enhanced Joyce's superstitions. Opening an umbrella inside, placing a man's hat on a bed and two nuns walking down the street were all bad luck. Black cats and Greeks were good luck. He wore certain colors to ward off blindness. A whole minefield of numbers and dates were good or bad. Once, while the Joyces were hosting dinner, two people unexpectedly called to say that they were on their way, bringing the dinner party to thirteen, so Joyce frantically tried to find another last-minute guest while imploring someone to leave. "Nausicaa," unsurprisingly, was the thirteenth episode, and Joyce took note of the ill-omened sum of the year's digits: $1+9+2+1$.

Superstitions gave Joyce the feeling of control, the illusion that he could place a finger on the tiller of fortune to help steer a life that seemed blown by chance—money arriving just when the cupboards were bare, an apartment found days before homelessness, fortuitous details gathered on scraps of paper despite eye attacks that came and went without warning. It was comforting to think that all the world's details were like the details of a novel, that they had meaning and that they could be altered by marginal revisions like replacing a hat or adding a fourteenth dinner guest.

Valery Larbaud was one of the lucky turns. Larbaud was a prominent French novelist and a friend of Shakespeare and Company. In February 1921, Sylvia Beach sent him the *Little Review* issues containing *Ulysses*. He stayed up entire nights reading it. "I am raving mad over *Ulysses*," he told her. "I cannot read anything else, cannot even think of anything else." When Larbaud left Paris for the summer, he offered Joyce his Left Bank apartment, rent free, so that he could have a more comfortable place to write. Joyce, Nora and the children moved into Larbaud's luxurious apartment complete with a leafy courtyard, a servant and polished floors. It was the twenty-second address to host Joyce's growing manuscript, and the nicest port on the voyage. Among Larbaud's rare objects and leather-bound books, there were thousands of soldiers—troops, divisions, battalions of hand-painted toy soldiers from all over the world.

Robert McAlmon was another lucky turn. He was a regular at Shakespeare and Company, and he did more than gather orders for *Ulysses* at nightclubs. He started giving Joyce money (about $150 a month) to carry him through the last stages of his manuscript. Joyce drank much of it, often with McAlmon himself at bars haunted by prostitutes and mediocre jazz until they were thrown out in the morning. McAlmon recalled Nora's disapproval. "Jim, what is it all ye find to jabber about the nights you're brought home drunk for me to look after? You're dumb as an oyster now, so God help me."

One night at a brasserie, Joyce was particularly nervous, and he saw omens in everything—the way his knife and fork were arranged on the table, the way McAlmon poured wine into his glass. A rat scampered down the stairs, which was extraordinarily bad luck. McAlmon shrugged it off as a Joycean quirk until Joyce's body went limp at the table—he had fainted. Joyce had an eye attack the following day. The pressure inside his eye mounted in a matter of hours, and he was rolling on the floor in pain. A week later, McAlmon went to his bedside, and as he looked down at Joyce's face, a mask of skin stretched over a skull, the sight of his suffering terrified him. He vowed never to drink with Joyce again.

Joyce's 1921 bout of iritis lasted more than a month. His eyes were bandaged (light itself was painful) and writing was out of the question. As he lay in bed, Larbaud's maid whispered to Joyce's daughter in the next room. "How is he now?" "What is he doing?" "What does he say?" "Is he going to get up?" "Is he ever hungry?" "Does he suffer?" Joyce could hear it all.

Blindness may also have been good luck. It forced Joyce away from the minutiae of his manuscript and into his imagination, where he could survey his novel from a distance. The larger structure became more apparent in his blindness. He discerned faint motifs and larger themes as he lay in a darkened room among Larbaud's tiny soldiers charging toward cabinet edges, bayonets like toothpicks fixed in the air. In August, when the pain was bearable, Joyce began revising ten different episodes simultaneously. He expanded "Hades." He seeded the book with Stephen's phrase "Agenbite of inwit" (Middle English for "Remorse of conscience") so that it became one of the book's refrains. He suspected his twelve-hour days were making his eyes worse, but he couldn't help himself.

Joyce wrote an elaborate new scene in "Circe." Bloom transforms into a king wearing a crimson mantle trimmed with ermine and becomes the object of anger and admiration for all—even Margaret Anderson appears. Joyce had noticed her defiant boast in John Sumner's deposition against *The Little Review* and decided to adapt it: "I'm a Bloomite and I glory in it," a Veiled Sibyl declares as she stabs herself and dies. Her death prompts a wave of devotional suicides by drowning, arsenic and starvation. Beautiful women throw themselves under steamrollers and hang themselves with "stylish garters." When someone suggests that Bloom is the messiah, he performs miracles for the crowd's delight. He "passes through several walls, climbs Nelson's Pillar, hangs from the top ledge by his eyelids, eats twelve dozen oysters (shells included)[.]" He contorts his face to resemble Moses, Lord Byron, Rip van Winkle and Sherlock Holmes. A few lines later, Leopold Bloom is defiled by dogs and set on fire.

PART III

"May I kiss the hand that wrote *Ulysses*?"
"No, it did other things too."

18.

THE BIBLE OF
THE OUTCASTS

Maurice Darantière, master printer of Dijon, was a relic of the past. His old machinery sat in a small vine-covered printing house that had changed little, if at all, since his father's days as a master printer. On Sunday afternoons, Darantière darned socks in an antique chair while his printing companion and housemate prepared afternoon meals that stretched into the evening with pastries, coffee and liqueurs. In the fall of 1921, Darantière worked through many of those meals. Sylvia Beach warned him about the unique challenges of printing *Ulysses*, but he could not have been prepared. For decades, printers had been using linotype machines to cast entire lines of text at once, but the typesetters at Imprimerie Darantière spent hours plucking tiny metal blocks out of large pigeonhole cases. They were assembling *Ulysses* by hand, one letter at a time.

The typescripts they received from Paris appeared rushed. Some of the lines were repeated, others ran off the pages, and still others were illegible because the typists had doubled over the words. The typesetters were forced to leave blank spaces wherever the text was inscrutable, and that was just the beginning. In June 1921, Darantière began sending Joyce the galleys of the first episodes. The galleys were large sheets of what would eventually be eight pages of text with wide margins for corrections. They were unpaged and easier to alter than page proofs, which would come later. Printers expected a few changes in the galleys, but Joyce filled them with arrows and inserts, new clauses and sentences. Joyce wasn't proofreading. He was still writing. Darantière repeatedly warned Sylvia Beach that Joyce's additions would be expensive because they were so time consuming. If a writer wished to insert a sentence, several lines or pages beneath it might have to move. One addition could cause an avalanche of changes.

Darantière began sending back more galleys instead of committing to page proofs, which meant that one galley revision turned into a rondo of three or four iterations—Beach told Darantière to give Joyce all the galleys he wanted. Joyce complicated matters by asking for multiple copies simultaneously and marking different additions to each one. To stay one step ahead, the typesetters began inserting blank pieces of type between lines or at the bottoms of paragraphs so that Joyce's additions would fill the space built into a galley instead of spilling over to another page, which would compound the work.

Then Darantière began sending page proofs, where an author corrects small errors like a missing comma or transposed letters. When Joyce returned them, Darantière was flabbergasted by *"le* très grand nombre *de corrections"* scrawled all over the pages. Joyce, even then, was still writing. Galley revisions in one episode inspired proof revisions in earlier episodes—printing *Ulysses* was like trying to cast a moving object. And yet Darantière's small printing house was beleaguered by more than onerous revisions to the most experimental prose in literary history. The typesetters piecing together *Ulysses* could not even speak English.

The mounting costs made Darantière anxious. He initially agreed to wait for payment until the book's subscriptions came in. The generous terms were based partly on his friendship with Adrienne Monnier and partly on the book's unusual back story—the years of work, the trial in New York, the protests of printers and angry husbands. Darantière was intrigued almost as much by the book's troubled circumstances as by the American woman's devotion to it. He was not, however, prepared to be a part of the creative process.

Darantière demanded five thousand francs in December, which was more than Shakespeare and Company's typical monthly revenue, but with the help of Miss Weaver, Beach paid it. Joyce went through as many as four galleys and five page proofs for every page of *Ulysses*. He wrote almost a third of his novel, including nearly half of "Penelope," on the galleys and proofs, and by the end of the year the alterations alone cost about four thousand francs. *Ulysses* exists as it does today partly because of Sylvia Beach's willingness to grant Joyce's wishes. She didn't just publish his book. She gave it room to grow.

Nora complained to friends about the revisions. "It's the great fanaticism is on him, and it is coming to no end." Joyce's demands were increasingly unreasonable. He requested a solid blue cover with white letters, but he wanted the blue to match the Greek flag. Darantière had to go to Germany to find the precise shade. Joyce didn't send the book's final page proofs until January 31, 1922. To keep his promise to Sylvia Beach, Darantière had to reset and print portions of the last two episodes in less than two days. And as the most laborious job that Imprimerie Darantière ever attempted was coming to a close, Darantière received a telegram from Paris. Monsieur Joyce wished to add just one more word.

ON THE MORNING of February 2, 1922, Sylvia Beach went to Gare de Lyons and waited for the Dijon-Paris express train to pull into the station. After the doors opened, she saw the conductor making his way through the harried morning travelers with a bulky parcel. Later that morning, when Joyce opened the door to his flat, Sylvia Beach stood proudly in front of him with his birthday present, the first two copies of *Ulysses*.

Beach placed one of the copies in the window of Shakespeare and Company. Primed by newspaper reports about the impending publication, the news spread overnight that James Joyce's *Ulysses* had arrived at last. The following morning, a crowd formed to gaze at the mighty tome in the front window. It was an imposing book: a bold blue cover, 732 pages, three inches thick and nearly three and a half pounds. People could only speculate about the rumored scenes in the final chapters. When Beach opened the shop for business, the crowd rushed in to receive its long-awaited copies. But *Ulysses*, she tried to explain, was not yet published—only two copies had been printed, but that only led everyone to claim the display copy. As they became more insistent, Beach grew afraid they were going to tear the book from its binding and divide the sections amongst themselves, so she grabbed Joyce's novel and hid it in the back room.

As copies trickled in from Dijon in February and March, Joyce signed the one hundred deluxe copies and helped Beach and others address and wrap the packages. He wanted copies mailed to his Irish readers as quickly as possible—before authorities realized they were circulating—because, he wrote to Beach, with the moralistic Vigilance Committee in Dublin and a new postmaster general "you never know from one day to the next what may occur." In the rush, he managed to slather glue on the labels, the table, the floor and in his hair.

On Sunday, March 5, 1922, the first review of *Ulysses* appeared in the London *Observer*. "Mr. James Joyce is a man of genius," Sisley Huddleston declared. The book was "the vilest, according to ordinary standards, in all literature. And yet its very obscenity is somehow beautiful and wrings the soul to pity." Six weeks of silence followed (Joyce thought there was a boycott against him) before a review appeared in *The Nation and Athenaeum* that called Joyce's quest for freedom herculean, though the reviewer had misgivings. *Ulysses* is "a prodigious self-laceration, the tearing-away from himself, by a half-demented man of genius," J. Middleton Murry wrote. Joyce was sensitive to earthly and spiritual beauty, but the book contained *too much*. "Mr. Joyce has made the superhuman effort to empty the whole of his consciousness into it." *Ulysses* had every thought a human being could have. It was bursting at the seams. Its content ravaged its form. After the tight prose of *Dubliners* and *A Portrait*, Joyce had become "the victim of his own anarchy."

Arnold Bennett's review the following week declared Joyce "dazzlingly original. If he does not see life whole he sees it piercingly." The final chapter was unmatched by anything else he had ever read. *Ulysses* is not pornographic, Bennett emphasized, and yet "it is more indecent, obscene, scatological, and licentious than the majority of professedly pornographical books." A consensus began to form as Bennett agreed that *Ulysses* was a work of genius written by an artist whose talents had gotten beyond his control. If only Joyce had harnessed his powers, Bennett lamented, "he would have stood a chance of being one of the greatest novelists that ever lived."

The reviews could not have been better. The week after the first critic weighed in, Beach received nearly three hundred new orders, including 136 orders in one day. By the end of March, the twelve-dollar version of *Ulysses* was sold out, and the rest were purchased in the next two months. Paris bookshops, all of which balked at Sylvia Beach's prices, were desperate to get copies, but they were too late, and the scarcity of Joyce's novel solidified its legendary status. Perhaps you didn't own *Ulysses*, but you knew someone who did, and maybe you read portions of it, or maybe you only saw it high atop someone's bookcase like some cerulean bird alighting from a canopy—and even that, over drinks with a friend, would be something to talk about. James Joyce had become Paris's newest literary celebrity. He avoided dining at his regular restaurants because people would gawk.

The backlash wasn't far behind. A headline splashed across the entire front page of London's *Sporting Times*: "THE SCANDAL OF ULYSSES." Even D. H. Lawrence, who would later write his own unprintably obscene novel, *Lady Chatterley's Lover*, said that the final chapter was "the dirtiest, most indecent, obscene thing ever written." Reporters wanted to know just what Miss Beach's father thought about it (she never asked). One paper labeled *Ulysses* "a freak production." Another called Joyce's rendition of Molly Bloom's consciousness a feat of "diabolic clairvoyance, black magic." Yet another declared *Ulysses* "the maddest, muddiest, most loathsome book issued in our own or any other time—inartistic, incoherent, unquotably nasty—a book that one would have thought could only emanate from a criminal lunatic asylum." The asylum image became a staple of Joyce reviews.

For the people most disturbed by *Ulysses*, the scandal had nothing to do with an isolated madman. In May, James Douglas, the well-known editor of *The Sunday Express* in London, wrote as scathing a diatribe as he could muster.

I say deliberately that it is the most infamously obscene book in ancient or modern literature . . . All the secret sewers of vice are canalized in its flood of unimaginable thoughts, images and pornographic words. And its unclean lunacies are larded with appalling and revolting blasphemies directed against the Christian religion and against the name of Christ—blasphemies hitherto associated with the most degraded orgies of Satanism and the Black Mass.

Douglas claimed to have evidence that *Ulysses* "is already the Bible of beings who are exiles and outcasts in this and every other civilized country," and it was galvanizing them all.

What made Joyce so appalling was that so-called men of letters in respectable journals were praising him as a genius. "Our critics are apologising for his anarchy," Douglas said. They were shirking their social responsibilities by flinging readers "to the hyenas and werewolves of literature." For people like Douglas, the arrival of *Ulysses* crystallized an elemental struggle in Western civilization, a struggle in which satanic anarchy was arrayed against God's civilizing influence.

> We must make our choice between the devil's disciples and the disciples of God, between Satanism and Christianity, between the sanctions of morality and the anarchy of art. The artist must be treated like any lesser criminal who tries to break the Christian code. For this is a battle that must be fought out to a clean finish: we cannot trust the soul of Europe to the guardianship of the police and the Post Office.

The sum of *Ulysses'* objectionable parts amounted to a transgression that the word *obscene* did not nearly cover, and it was difficult to find a word that did. Two critics resorted to calling Joyce's novel "literary Bolshevism," but several readers, perhaps intuitively, thought of it as anarchism. The editor of London's *Daily Express* referred to Joyce as "the man with the bomb who would blow what remains of Europe into the sky . . . His intention, so far as he has any social intention, is completely anarchic." Edmund Gosse, who had helped Joyce financially through the war, considered the Irish writer an extremist after *Ulysses*. It was, he said, "an anarchical production, infamous in taste, in style, in everything."

The reaction in Ireland was no better. *The Dublin Review* lambasted the novel's "devilish drench" and urged the government to destroy the book and asked the Vatican to place it on the Index Expurgatorius—merely reading *Ulysses* amounted to sinning against the Holy Ghost, the only sin beyond the reach of God's mercy. A former Irish diplomat claimed in *The Quarterly Review* that *Ulysses* would compel Irish writers to resent the English language. Some of those writers, he predicted, would plot the literary equivalent of the Clerkenwell prison bombing (the Victorian era's iconic Fenian assault) and blow a hole through "the well-guarded, well-built, classical prison of English literature." But those literary terrorists could consider themselves too late, for with the publication of *Ulysses*, he announced, "the bomb has exploded."

Even Joyce's family was unsupportive. His aunt Josephine hid her copy when she received it and told her daughters it wasn't fit to read. She eventually gave it away so that it wouldn't pollute her house. Stannie, who hadn't seen his older brother in years, predicted that "Circe" would be remembered as the most horrible moment in literary history (it seems he had not yet read "Penelope"), and he advised his brother to return to writing poetry. "I should think you would need something to restore your self respect after this last inspection of the stinkpots."

The most painful reaction was Nora's indifference. As a tribute to her importance, Joyce inscribed copy number 1,000 and presented it to her at a dinner party. She immediately offered to sell it. In November, Joyce lamented that she had still read only twenty-seven pages "counting the cover." When a revised edition appeared, he cut the pages for her, hoping that the added convenience would encourage her to open the book. At some point, she read the final chapter, which elicited her signature contribution to Joyce literary criticism: "I guess the man's a genius, but what a dirty mind he has, hasn't he?"

THE MOST IMPORTANT RESPONSES to *Ulysses* came from other writers. William Faulkner, whose novel *The Sound and the Fury* was, to some degree, an American rendition of Joyce's techniques, advised, "You should approach Joyce's *Ulysses* as the illiterate Baptist preacher approaches the Old Testament:

with faith." F. Scott Fitzgerald agreed. He gave Sylvia Beach a copy of *The Great Gatsby* when he met her, and inside the front cover he drew a picture of himself kneeling beside Joyce, who was rendered as a pair of oversized spectacles beneath a halo. Fitzgerald got his copy of *Ulysses* signed when he finally met Joyce in 1928, and to prove his devotion he offered to jump out of a window if Joyce would only ask. "That young man must be mad," Joyce said. "I'm afraid he'll do himself some injury."

Djuna Barnes was overwhelmed by *Ulysses*. "I shall never write another line," she declared. "Who has the nerve to after that?" It was as if the era of the novel were over. Ezra Pound thought an era of civilization was over. Pound declared in *The Little Review* that "the Christian era came definitely to an END" when Joyce finished the drafts of the last two chapters around midnight at the end of October 1921. He celebrated the epochal change by rewriting the Julian calendar. Year One P.S.U. (*Post Scriptum Ulysses*) began on November first, which was now Hephaistos. December was now Zeus, January was Hermes, and so on—the index of time shifted from the Roman politicians to the Roman gods. He told Margaret Anderson to reprint the calendar in every autumn issue from 1922 onward.

The magnitude of *Ulysses* was enough to force Pound to take stock of his life. Since the winter of 1914, when Yeats first mentioned the name of James Joyce as a kindred Imagist, Joyce had written an epoch-changing novel—a novel, Pound said, that lanced "the whole boil of the European mind"—and Pound had barely started his long series of poems, *The Cantos*. As selfless as he may have been, helping other writers was also a way to avoid his own writing. So Pound decided to fake his own death. Anderson and Heap received a letter ostensibly written by Pound's wife informing *The Little Review* that he was no longer among the living. The letter included a picture of his death mask and a request that they print it in the magazine. Pound sent the letter on Good Friday as a gesture to his second coming. He wanted the era *Post Scriptum Ulysses* to be the Pound Era.

T. S. Eliot also spoke of a new era. He wrote in *The Dial* that *Ulysses* was "a step toward making the modern world possible for art" (not, importantly, the other way around) because it gave an order, "a shape and a significance to the immense panorama of futility and anarchy which is contemporary history." Where others found *Ulysses* incomprehensible, Eliot saw a new mode of comprehension. The narrative method was obsolete, and Joyce replaced it with "the mythical method."

Virginia Woolf marveled at T. S. Eliot's rapturous praise on his visits to her house—she had never seen him that way before. "How could anyone write again after achieving the immense prodigy of the last chapter?" he said. Eliot had been trying to convince her about the importance of *Ulysses* for years. "It destroyed the whole of the 19th Century," he told her. "It left Joyce himself with nothing to write another book on. It showed up the futility of all the English styles." Though *Ulysses* made modernity coherent, Eliot considered its influence as daunting as it was liberating. It is, he wrote, "a book to which we are all indebted and from which none of us can escape."

Virginia Woolf was not as impressed. It had been four years since she refused to print the first few chapters of *Ulysses* for Harriet Weaver, and she remained skeptical. Nevertheless, near the end of the summer of 1922, she decided to find out for herself. Woolf put aside the second volume of Proust and began reading the copy of *Ulysses* she had purchased for the remarkable sum of four pounds. In August, after reading two hundred pages, she wrote in her diary that she was "amused, stimulated, charmed" at first "& then puzzled, bored, irritated, & disillusioned as by a queasy undergraduate scratching his pimples." Her repulsion went beyond aesthetic distaste or visceral shock. It was personal. "An illiterate, underbred book it seems to me: the book of a self taught working man, & we all know how distressing they are, how egotistic, insistent, raw, striking, & ultimately nauseating." As if he were unaware of the etiquette between readers and writers, Mr. Joyce came to the table and ate with his fingers. She felt sorry for him.

Joyce's experiment had gone wrong. "I feel that myriads of tiny bullets pepper one & spatter one," Woolf wrote privately, "but one does not get one deadly wound straight in the face." Yet something about *Ulysses* worked upon the mind slowly, as if the thousands of stalwart particles began to organize themselves in her sleep. Woolf found herself thinking about *Ulysses* long after she thought she was through with it. It was, as Katherine Mansfield said, "as though one's mind goes on quivering afterwards." W. B. Yeats had been reading *Ulysses* in *The Little Review* in 1918, and his first thought was "A mad book!" Later he confessed to a friend, "I have made a terrible mistake. It is a work perhaps of genius." Carl Jung, the eminent Swiss psychologist, experienced the same reversal. When he first read portions of *Ulysses*, he thought Joyce was schizophrenic, but after rereading it years later he exclaimed that it was an alchemical laboratory in which "a new, universal consciousness is distilled!"

Virginia Woolf's opinions also changed. The day after she finished *Ulysses*, Leonard showed her a review describing the book as a burlesque of the *Odyssey* woven out of the consciousnesses of three radically different characters. "I must read some of the chapters again," she wrote in her diary. Perhaps modern literature was not a fatal wound to the face. Perhaps those tiny bullets were the point. She had, in fact, said so herself after reading Joyce a few years earlier: the mind, she wrote, receives impressions like "an incessant shower of innumerable atoms" that fall upon us with "the sharpness of steel." But by 1922, after reading all of *Ulysses*, those steely atoms felt too innumerable to amount to anything cohesive. To stand at last in the mind's shower of atoms was to lose sight of any principle that could encompass either the mind or modern fiction.

Like Eliot and Pound, Woolf was working through the ramifications of *Ulysses*. Months later, she returned to a short story she had been writing when she read Joyce, and she began turning it into a novel. She realized that she could be more ambitious, that she could approach the "cheapness" of reality and the "central things" in life even if those things could not be made beautiful. Two years later, in 1924, she finished a novel that delves into the consciousnesses of three characters during a single day in London. She thought of calling it *The Hours*. Eventually, she named it *Mrs. Dalloway*. Joyce's tiny bullets had entered Virginia Woolf's bloodstream and felled her from the inside out.

NEARLY A CENTURY LATER, the reactions to *Ulysses* can feel overblown—like hype from like-minded friends and bombast from journalists trying to sell papers. These days, *Ulysses* may seem more eccentric than epoch changing, and it can be difficult to see how Joyce's novel (how any novel, perhaps) could have been revolutionary. This is because all revolutions look tame from the other side. They change our perspectives so thoroughly that their innovations become platitudes. We forget what the old world was like, forget even that things could have been another way. And yet they were. To understand how thoroughly Joyce broke conventions, it helps to remember how stringent they were. Molly Bloom lies awake at night and thinks about getting "fucked yes and well fucked too up to my neck nearly" by Blazes Boylan. Ten years earlier, Joyce couldn't publish *Dubliners* in part because he used the word *bloody*.

The world *Pre Scriptum Ulysses* was beset by restrictions on the printed word that seem quaint only because we no longer live with them. Print was the way an idea entered the culture's bloodstream, and literary bans ensured that the culture would never absorb dangerous subjects and concepts. Because bans were nebulous (censorship was never as simple as a list of unmentionable words), the influence they had over the culture became chillingly wide. The memory of publishers like Henry Vizetelly sitting in prison for publishing Émile Zola and the prospect of the censor bearing down on authors as they write can stifle books before they become books.

What made *Ulysses* revolutionary was that it was more than a bid for marginally wider freedom. It demanded complete freedom. It swept away all silences. An angry soldier's threats in Nighttown ("I'll wring the bastard fucker's bleeding blasted fucking windpipe"), Molly's imaginary demands ("lick my shit") and Bloom's appalling image of the Dead Sea ("the grey sunken cunt of the world") are declarations that henceforth there would be no more unspeakable thoughts, no restrictions on the expression of ideas. This is why printing the word *fuck* was more than schoolboy mischief. "He says everything— everything," Arnold Bennett marveled. "The code is smashed to bits." *Ulysses* made everything possible.

Dirty words were only part of the code-smashing liberation (*Mrs. Dalloway*, after all, didn't need to be dirty to need *Ulysses*). The code that *Ulysses* smashed was conceptual. For beyond liberation from silence, *Ulysses* offered liberation from what we might call the tyranny of style: from the manners, conventions and forms that govern texts almost without our realizing it. The novel as an art form had long been about breaking the tyranny of style, but

Ulysses removed narrative elements no one had considered removable. A single narrator guiding the reader through the story was gone. The contextual armature that helps a reader make sense of events was gone. Clear distinctions between thoughts and the exterior world were gone. Quotation marks were gone. Sentences were gone. In the place of style we are left with borrowed voices and provisional modes, all of which are fleeting, all of which, as Eliot told Woolf, reduce style to "futility."

But why should it matter? The end of style seems a long way from Fenian bombs and the collapse of civilization, yet the critics' comparisons were trying to capture the novel's apparent recklessness. To turn style into futility, it seemed, was to lay waste to all foundations. When a well-known poet named Alfred Noyes delivered a lecture in front of the Royal Society of Literature in October 1922, he launched into a familiar diatribe about the unprecedented obscenity of *Ulysses*. But what infuriated Noyes most was that Joyce's emergence signaled the degradation of the United Kingdom's foundational values. Literary critics were casting aside the best of English literary tradition for madmen calling themselves modernists. It was as if an entire civilization were in the process of forgetting itself.

To be oblivious of English values did not strike Noyes as a matter of losing the past. It struck him as a matter of losing grasp of reality. "The lack of any conviction that there are realities, standards, and enduring foundations in literature has had a deadly effect," he told the Royal Society. Groundless literary criticism was introducing "elements of chaos" into the minds of the younger generation.

He had a point. Narratives are the way we make sense of the world. We parcel existence into events and string them into cause-and-effect sequences. The chemist comparing controls and variables and the child scalded by a hot stove are both understanding the world through narrative. Novels are important because they turn that basic conceptual framework into an art form. A beautiful narrative arc reassures us that the baffling events around us are meaningful—and this is why *Ulysses* appeared to be an instrument of chaos, an anarchist bomb. To disrupt the narrative method was to disrupt the order of things. Joyce, it seemed, wasn't devoted to reality. He appeared to be sweeping it away.

If you were a modernist—if you believed the order of things was already gone—you thought differently. T. S. Eliot defended *Ulysses* by objecting to its critics' premise. Life in the age of world war was no longer amenable to the narrative method, and yet *Ulysses* showed us that narratives weren't the only way to create order. Existence could be layered. Instead of a sequence, the world was an epiphany. Instead of a tradition, civilization was a day. The chaos of modernity demanded a new conceptual method to make sense of the contemporary world, to make life possible for art. And that is what *Ulysses* gave us.

19.

THE BOOKLEGGER

A fter nearly eight years of writing, *Ulysses* was finally navigating the world, and no one knew what would happen next. It had been convicted of obscenity in New York the previous year, and its publication in Paris led to cries of scandal on the front pages of British newspapers. While it was possible that U.S. authorities would turn a blind eye to Gerty MacDowell once she was bound in an expensive book rather than a cheap magazine, Molly Bloom and the outrageous spectacles of the "Circe" episode pushed Joyce's novel beyond the pale. Obscenity laws were enforced so inconsistently that it was impossible to tell if the safe delivery of the first copies meant that *Ulysses* was tacitly sanctioned or if authorities simply didn't notice it. And if authorities *were* inclined to sanction Joyce's book, it was anyone's guess when, where or how they would respond. Officials could notify readers of a book's seizure and, in the absence of a legal challenge, its destruction, or they could press criminal charges against an unlucky bookseller. Copies could sell freely in the spring only to be seized in the fall. British authorities could object even if U.S. authorities did not, and an enforcement action anywhere—by a customs agent in Ireland, a police officer in Ohio or a postal inspector in London—could trigger bans in countries around the globe. Neither Sylvia Beach nor Joyce had the resources to fight for *Ulysses* in court, and Miss Weaver did not have the will.

Nevertheless, in the spring of 1922 copies of James Joyce's big blue book made their way into the United States as parcels from Paris marked *UN LIVRE*.

John Quinn saw his first copy of *Ulysses* in March at Drake's Book Shop on Fortieth Street. Quinn, who had been receiving the manuscript in batches for months, felt the gentle striations of the handmade pages and admitted, begrudgingly, that Sylvia Beach had managed to publish a beautiful book. The demand for *Ulysses* was unprecedented. Drake sold Shakespeare and Company's twelve-dollar copies for twenty dollars, and that was nothing. Brentano's, one of New York's major bookstores, was selling them for thirty-five dollars. Near the end of March, Quinn heard that a copy sold for fifty, and by October the rumored prices for the more expensive versions were as high as one hundred dollars in New York and an astonishing forty pounds in London. Everyone was talking about *Ulysses*.

And that was the problem. John Sumner and the NYSSV would soon discover that copies of *Ulysses* were landing on American shores. Anderson and Heap printed a full-page advertisement for *Ulysses* in *The Little Review*, and since Sumner and the Post Office Department were almost certainly keeping their eye on the magazine, the announcement must have sounded like a taunt. The NYSSV was extending its aggressive campaign against the wave of obscenity sweeping the nation—especially the "high filth" imported from overseas—and Sumner would be on the phone with postal inspectors and customs officials in every major port in the United States, urging them to seize any copies they could find. Quinn admired the fact that someone like Sylvia Beach could publish *Ulysses*. "She has tackled, with the audacity, if not the ignorance of amateurs, a really tough job," he wrote to Joyce. "That is the job of beating the United States Federal and State laws." But publishing Joyce's novel was only the first obstacle. The fight to get *Ulysses* into the hands of readers had just begun.

John Quinn contacted Mitchell Kennerley, the publisher he had defended against obscenity charges in 1913, because Kennerley knew the captain of an Atlantic transport liner who would smuggle books into the country. But if his smuggler were going to take on a job like *Ulysses*, they would have to send the books slowly—twenty or thirty a month—to avoid detection. The idea was that Shakespeare and Company would ship the books in bulk from Paris to London while Kennerley would collect money from buyers, ship the copies to readers by private carrier (never touching a postman's hands) and send the proceeds to Beach. Remaining inconspicuous was challenging, considering the book's size. The key to the plan was importing the books by freight, where it was easier for customs agents to overlook them. If they were found, Kennerley said, they would probably be returned to London instead of being burned. He would do the job for only 10 percent of the retail value—as a favor to Quinn.

Under normal circumstances, Quinn wouldn't consider such a scheme, but the *Little Review* trial and the book's publication had received so much press that there was little choice. Quinn wrote to persuade Sylvia Beach by emphasizing the plan's irresistible benefit: Kennerley was willing to break federal and state laws and risk arrest so that she wouldn't have to, and if he were arrested, "there wouldn't be a ghost of a shade of a shadow of a chance of acquitting Kennerley." In fact, Quinn told her not to send his fourteen copies of *Ulysses* until he could devise his own smuggling plan.

Quinn tried to explain the complexities of distributing an illegal book in terms he thought Miss Beach would understand. Smuggling, he wrote, requires "about the same amount of attention that would be involved, I should say, in having a dress fitted and made." As illuminating as Quinn's tailoring analogy might have been, Beach was already aware of the challenges. By August 1922 she had safely shipped copies of *Ulysses* to all destinations except New York, where, as she put it, "the jaws of the Sumner S.P.V. monster" were waiting (she mistook "Suppression" as "Prevention"). But she hadn't figured out how to ship the remaining copies, and she had been getting angry letters from New Yorkers since April.

One midtown bookshop was waiting for seventeen copies. The Sunwise Turn was a high-end shop below the Yale Club with an elaborate woodwork interior designed by Armory Show artists. It specialized in collector's items—old and rare books presented to customers in wrappings also designed by artists—and its business model depended upon fifty reliable patrons spending five hundred dollars on books every year. Supplying a marquee title like *Ulysses* was crucial both to the bookstore's survival and to its reputation. By May, the Sunwise Turn sent a letter reminding Shakespeare and Company that it had paid over three thousand francs in February and received neither a receipt nor the books. "We are rather disturbed." In case it helped, they included the names of individuals willing to act as middlemen to receive the merchandise. They were all women.

By the end of July, the Sunwise Turn sent two more letters and a telegram to Shakespeare and Company. They received no response. Mary Mowbray-Clarke, one of the shop's co-owners, was exasperated. "We cannot in any way of looking at it understand your treatment of us in regard to *Ulysses*." Dozens of copies had been in New York for months, but her bookshop was empty-handed. There were rumors that Sylvia Beach had pocketed the money from subscribers and sold the entire first edition to a middleman in London. The Sunwise Turn hoped the wild stories weren't true.

Sylvia Beach had known that publishing Joyce's book might involve illicit activity sooner or later, and she went so far as to contact Mitchell Kennerley, but for some reason (possibly his fee), she searched for other options. In August, she entrusted ten of the most expensive copies to a longtime friend in Illinois, where customs authorities were presumably less vigilant, and at the end of the month six copies for the Sunwise Turn bookshop arrived from Illinois. Mowbray-Clark said the twice-mailed packages arrived "like telephone books with papers falling off them and quite exposed to the eyes of the postman."

But the eyes of the postmen were no longer the primary problem: customs agents seized two of the ten copies. By the end of the summer, officials around the United States were looking for *Ulysses*, and there were still forty copies destined for New York. That's when Sylvia Beach decided to contact Hemingway's shadowy associate.

ERNEST HEMINGWAY WAS twenty-two years old when he arrived in Paris at the end of 1921. He didn't speak French, though his new wife, Hadley, gave him lessons on the steamship across the Atlantic, and he kept a rabbit's foot in his right pocket. He told everyone in Chicago that he was going to be a writer, and Paris was the best place to do it. Hemingway churned out articles for the *Toronto Star* and saved his best material for his fiction. He added up the prices in Paris. Their hotel room cost about a dollar a day (their rent would cost half that much). He knew a restaurant that served a steak and potatoes meal for 2.40 francs (about 20 cents), and he could find a bottle of wine for 60 *centimes*—a nickel. He calculated that one thousand dollars could sustain a person in Paris for a full year. For Hemingway, though, the bargain hunts were more of a sport than a necessity. The newspaper paid him decently, and Hadley had a trust fund of about three thousand dollars a year. The maid who cooked them dinner and their ski vacations in the Swiss Alps were not exactly bohemian, but Hemingway believed that hardship made him a better artist. He thought he understood Cézanne on an empty stomach and that abstaining from sex improved his writing.

In case the rabbit's foot wasn't enough, Hemingway had letters of introduction from Sherwood Anderson to help him get established with the right people in Paris. One letter was addressed to Miss Sylvia Beach. Within a week of arriving, Hemingway walked from the Jardin Luxembourg up the narrow rue Férou. He circled around the stone church and passed the statue of John the Baptist pointing skyward beside the wooden doors. When he turned right on rue de l'Odéon, he could see the signboard with the bard's picture halfway down the street. It was suspended above a newly painted storefront among shoemakers, a music shop and a nasal spray manufacturer. Shakespeare and Company had moved to 12 rue de l'Odéon the previous summer. The English bookstore and lending library was now across the street from its French counterpart, Monnier's La Maison des Amis des Livres. There was more foot traffic on rue de l'Odéon, and Sylvia Beach had more space for her growing library.

Walking into Shakespeare and Company felt like walking into someone's living room. There were odd rugs, mismatched pieces of furniture and goldfish. A small cluster of Larbaud's toy soldiers stood at arms in a cabinet by the front door, and the pictures of writers on the walls looked like snapshots lifted from the family album. It made Hemingway shy. So did Sylvia Beach's attractiveness. Her hair ran in waves down to the collar of her velvet jacket, and she wore a rigidly tailored skirt that allowed Hemingway to admire her lower legs.

Conversations with Hemingway opened up naturally, and before long he started talking about the war (a favorite subject) and what it was like to recover in an Italian hospital (another favorite subject). A bomb had exploded next to Hemingway while he was handing out chocolate in the trenches. It spewed more than two hundred pieces of shrapnel into the lower half of his body and left him with scars all over his right leg and foot. "Would you like to see it?" Hemingway took off his right shoe and sock and rolled up his pants to the knee. Miss Beach saw the barely healed marbled skin. She was quite impressed.

People think of 1922 as the year modernism came of age because it was the year *Ulysses* and T. S. Eliot's *The Waste Land* appeared. It was also the year Ernest Hemingway came of age. Posterity focuses on his fraught tutelage under Gertrude Stein, whom he met in February, but Shakespeare and Company did more to usher him into the literary world than Stein did. Hemingway met Ezra Pound by chance, also in February, at Beach's bookshop, and within a week Pound was reading his manuscripts and spreading the word about him around Paris and the States. Over the course of the year Pound sent six of Hemingway's prose vignettes to *The Little Review*, where they were published in the spring of 1923. Later that year, Beach encouraged Robert McAlmon to publish Hemingway's first book.

Hemingway met Joyce within weeks of meeting Pound, and before long the admiring young American began drinking with the great Irish novelist. Hemingway probably told stories about driving an ambulance during the war, and he listened skeptically as Joyce complained about his financial troubles. One night, Joyce became outraged by someone's egregious barroom offense, and when the scrawny novelist realized he was arguing with a man he could hardly *see*, he turned to his barrel-chested companion and shouted, "Deal with him, Hemingway! Deal with him!" Hemingway decided to deal with Joyce by carrying him home to Nora. "Well, here comes James Joyce the writer," she said in the doorway, "drunk again with Ernest Hemingway."

He met the pantheon of modernists just as *Ulysses* was published. Hemingway likely witnessed the scramble to fill orders at Shakespeare and Company, and the enthusiasm radiating through the Left Bank fueled his own ambitions. He ordered several copies of *Ulysses* and wrote to Sherwood Anderson, "Joyce has a most goddamn wonderful book." He purchased *Dubliners*, possibly during his first visit to Shakespeare and Company, and Joyce's short stories influenced him deeply. *Dubliners* taught him economy and how to leave the most important things unspoken. When *A Farewell to Arms* was published in 1929, Hemingway gave Joyce a copy with the censored expletives lovingly handwritten in. "Jim Joyce was the only alive writer that I ever respected," Hemingway said later. "He had his problems, but he could write better than anyone I knew."

Hemingway had a genius for learning. He didn't have a college degree, so he pursued his higher education through Shakespeare and Company, where he learned more about writing in a few months than most students learn in four years. His first selections from the library were D. H. Lawrence and Ivan Turgenev, and though borrowers had a two-book limit, Beach let him take more. He chose Tolstoy's *War and Peace* and Dostoyevsky's *The Gambler and Other Stories*. A few years earlier, Hemingway's favorite authors had been Rudyard Kipling and O. Henry. As a Shakespeare and Company member, he discovered Flaubert and Stendhal. Hemingway probably hadn't even heard of James Joyce and Ezra Pound before he left for Paris. Two months after he walked into Shakespeare and Company, Sylvia Beach made them his mentors.

Kindness made Hemingway an even better student. While Gertrude Stein offered him gnomic advice ("Begin over again and concentrate"), Sylvia Beach offered him food. As with so many others, her bookshop became his post office and primary source for advice and gossip. She listened to his problems and lent him money. "No one that I ever knew was nicer to me," he later claimed. Pound was similarly generous. Hemingway thought that he contained dangerous stores of energy ("He would live much longer if he did not eat so fast," Hemingway wrote), but what struck him most was Pound's kindness toward writers he believed in. "He defends them when they are attacked, he gets them into magazines and out of jail. He loans them money. He sells their pictures. He arranges concerts for them. He writes articles about them." The list went on. Pound was selfless and principled and angry like a saint. With his wild mane of hair and his staunch proclamations, he was a voice in the wilderness, a John the Baptist.

Pound taught Hemingway to distrust adjectives, and Joyce taught him how to be elliptical. He repaid Joyce by drinking with him and Pound by teaching him how to box. Wyndham Lewis recalled seeing Hemingway stripped down to the waist in Pound's studio, his pale torso gleaming with sweat. Hemingway blocked Pound's left jabs with a calm open glove, wasting as little energy as possible, moving instead of countering, nimbly avoiding the homemade furniture and Japanese paintings. The poet who taught W. B. Yeats how to fence in an English cottage was not afraid to learn how to box from a young Ernest Hemingway in a Left Bank studio. Pound needed to widen his stance and practice his left. He lunged, swung wildly and threw scattershot combinations— Hemingway had to shadowbox between rounds to keep up a sweat, which soon became a habit of his. He would bounce around on the sidewalks of Paris, jabbing and dodging, his lips moving as he goaded an invisible opponent.

Hemingway was younger and less educated than nearly everyone around him, and machismo was a way to compensate. Knowing he would never learn Latin or Greek (he would barely learn French), he cultivated streetside *afición*. Once, he took Sylvia Beach and Adrienne Monnier to a boxing match in a rough neighborhood on the city's outskirts. Hemingway led them through someone's backyard to get to the ring where two fighters kept slugging each other as the blood dripped down their chests. It was his way of giving back. He went to Switzerland for the slopes and to Spain for the bullfights. He went fishing, lugeing and bobsledding. As a journalist, he covered nightlife, political conferences and the grim aftermath of the Greco-Turkish war. He interviewed Mussolini twice. When he wasn't writing articles for the *Toronto Star*, he wrote short stories in cafés and talked about the war with disfigured men wearing Croix de Guerre ribbons. He drank. He changed his son's diapers. He gambled on horses and bicycle races. He seemed to be involved in everything.

IT OCCURRED TO SYLVIA BEACH that Hemingway might know something about smuggling. John Quinn mentioned the possibility of smuggling *Ulysses* in bulk from Canada to Detroit or Buffalo, far from Sumner's agents. Did Hemingway know anyone in Chicago who could smuggle contraband from Canada? He did.

"Give me twenty-four hours," he told her. When he returned, he said he had a friend back in Chicago with Canadian connections, and he was exactly the type of person who could help. Hemingway gave her the man's name and address so they could work out the details directly—he wanted his name kept out of the matter altogether. Beach wrote to the smuggler, Barnet Braverman, and said they had a mutual friend from Chicago. She had dozens of copies of a new novel by James Joyce that she wanted to move across the Canadian border. They were bound for important American readers like Alfred Knopf and Ben Huebsch, publishers who didn't have the nerve to publish and distribute the book themselves. Braverman would also be responsible for fulfilling the largest single order: twenty-five copies destined for the Washington Square Book Shop, where the book's criminal history began.

Braverman wasn't as easy to contact as Hemingway thought. Beach waited nearly two months before receiving a curt telegram ("Shoot books prepaid your responsibility") and a Canadian address. She did not respond. Braverman wrote a few weeks later to clarify his plans. He was now living in Detroit, where he regularly crossed the border into Windsor, Ontario, on business. She should ship the books in bulk to the Canadian address. Since storing them where he worked was out of the question, he would rent a small room in Windsor for a month and take the books across the river to Detroit one by one so that way the border agents on either side would be less likely to notice. The method was laborious, but Braverman knew people who could "expedite" the process. Once the books were in the United States, Braverman would bundle them in packages and send them by a private express company to avoid the Post Office. She would pay for the shipping, the customs duty and the rent on the room. He would offer his services for free.

Sylvia Beach waited over four months to respond, but after the first customs seizures in Chicago she decided that trusting a stranger to sneak *Ulysses* across the border was her best option. So she agreed. But if he got caught, she wrote back, he was on his own—she couldn't pay to defend him against state or federal charges. And his chances of being arrested was substantial, for while Braverman's plan minimized the risk of burned books (a border agent could only confiscate the copy he carried on any given day), it required him to break the law every time he crossed the border with a copy of *Ulysses*, possessed a copy for distribution in Michigan and shipped the book across state lines. He risked a five-thousand-dollar fine and five years in prison, but he would do it anyway. He found a room in Windsor for thirty-five dollars and told the landlord something vague about being involved in the publishing business.

Canadian customs agents were Braverman's first challenge. He wasn't worried about a seizure (it would take a couple of years before Canada banned the book, though it would maintain that ban until 1949), but he was worried about the steep import duty. The tariff on imported books was 25 percent of their retail price, which Sylvia Beach couldn't afford. The duty he owed for the shipment was three hundred dollars, but whatever retail price the inspecting officials estimated for the books, Braverman began talking his way out of it—never mind the size or the handmade paper, the books were more or less worthless.

Bargaining meant risking added scrutiny of the book itself, and though there wasn't a Canadian ban on *Ulysses*, censorship often began with routine inspections like this. But Braverman's gamble worked. Canadian customs agreed that the mighty tomes from Paris sold in the United States for sixty-five cents. Rather than hundreds of dollars, Braverman paid an import duty of $6.50. With the shipment from Shakespeare and Company in hand, he hauled the books away by truck and stacked them in the otherwise empty room, where the contraband would be stored before crossing the border.

A few days later, Braverman opened the door to the room in Windsor and saw the stacks of books he had agreed to smuggle. The sheer bulk of the contraband began to sink in when he was faced with the prospect of carrying just one of them. Why was *Ulysses*, which he had never read, worth the risk of being arrested day after day for over a month?

The century's changing tides drew people like Braverman to books like *Ulysses*. As the political protests of the nineteen-teens subsided into the cultural protests of the 1920s, prewar rebels found inspiration in Joyce's iconoclasm, blasphemy and sexual transgressions. *Ulysses* tapped into a feeling of ebbing revolt. Smuggling a work of art into a supposedly free country that refused to tolerate its sale or distribution was a cultural jab when a political coup no longer seemed possible, and the opportunity would have been irresistible to someone like Braverman. He wasn't a smuggler or a bootlegger or a criminal. He was a copywriter and salesman for an advertising agency. He was an artist in his spare time, and he was a radical.

BACK IN CHICAGO, where he had known Hemingway, Braverman was an editor of a magazine called *The Progressive Woman*. He delivered Socialist recruiting lectures and issued urgent pamphlets ("Suffragists, Watch Out for the Wolf!"). He denounced poverty and the wage slavery of women toiling in factories for as little as six dollars a week—"Womanhood," he wrote, "is the cheapest commodity in the industrial mart." He railed against the imprisonment and force-feeding of suffragist hunger strikers in England and condemned the assaults upon suffrage marchers at President Wilson's inauguration. The brutal attacks, he believed, were public manifestations of the abuse that wives and daughters faced in homes throughout the country. He denounced capitalism and the warped government it produced. "The United States Constitution," he wrote, "was framed and adopted by a horde of merchants, bankers, lawyers, smugglers and other cultured crooks, who had no use for popular institutions."

For Braverman, vice societies were paragons of capitalist hypocrisy. They were the agents of a system selectively punishing the vices of society's weakest members. Even when they had legitimate targets, they were fighting vices whose true cause was poverty. The country, according to Braverman, had three hundred thousand licensed prostitutes and more than a million unlicensed ones. If moralists really wanted people to lead virtuous lives, they'd focus less on the young women reading smut and more on helping the young women driven by hunger and exploitation to sell their bodies. "Behold the anti-vice crusaders! The dear things!" Braverman wrote. Comstock and Sumner couldn't see the economic basis of vice, either because their vision was so blinkered by capitalist ideology that they remained blithely unaware of it or because the wealthy financiers backing them—J. P. Morgan and Samuel Colgate, Vanderbilts and Carnegies—*told* them to ignore it. Businessmen wanted to stop lust and yet refused to pay their female employees living wages.

Braverman's articles sprang from the heady days of the 1910s. By 1922, with suffragists pacified by the Nineteenth Amendment, and the labor movement hobbled by the Red Raids, Braverman's life had become ordinary. He devolved from the editor of a radical magazine to a capitalist functionary—scripting slogans for an ad agency, no less. He shuttled back and forth between Curtis Company's two offices straddling the U.S.-Canadian border while the fervor of the 1910s slipped further into the distance. So when a letter arrived from a woman in Paris asking him to smuggle a book that capitalist society couldn't countenance, he told Miss Beach that he was eager to break the law of "the hideous U.S." He was ready, he said, to "put one over on the Republic and its Methodist smut hounds."

Braverman took a copy of *Ulysses* from the rented room, walked down to the wooden dock at the end of Ouellette Avenue and boarded the ferry for Detroit just as he did every weekday after work. The smokestacks on the Detroit skyline inched closer during the longest ten-minute ferry ride of his life. After being funneled through the customs pens, he stood in front of a uniformed agent who told Braverman to unwrap the package he was carrying. The guard glanced at the book, handed it back to Braverman and motioned him through. It was easy. But the next day, he would have to do it all again. And then the next day, and the next. The steady repetition was unnerving, and the low-grade anxiety increased as the same rotation of Detroit border guards glanced yet again at the conspicuously large book he carried. Wouldn't they get curious about James Joyce's *Ulysses*? Braverman thought they were beginning to eye him suspiciously, which made him more nervous, and nothing alerted border guards as much as nervousness.

The guards were especially vigilant in 1922, for these were the days of bootleggers smuggling whiskey and gin across the Detroit River. The newest Windsor-Detroit ferry, the *La Salle*, would have been a prime Prohibition-era bootlegging vessel. With a capacity of three thousand passengers, it was much larger than the older ferries, and a rumrunner could get lost in the crowd. The

La Salle could carry seventy-five cars belowdecks, which multiplied smugglers' opportunities. They built compartments for liquor inside fuel tanks. They constructed false bottoms to everything—car seats, animal cages and lunch boxes. People smuggled alcohol in hot water bottles strapped to their bodies or sewn inside the linings of coats.

Braverman started to feel a bout of bad luck coming on, and when the rent on the storage room in Windsor was good for only a few more days, he recruited a friend to help him smuggle the last few copies as quickly as possible. They stuffed two copies of *Ulysses* down their pants, cinched their belts tightly on unused notches and shuffled casually on and off the ferry's gangplanks. The late autumn weather made their bulky jackets plausible. The smuggling went faster, though Braverman and his friend were trading one risk for another. Guards couldn't inspect books they couldn't find, but if those jackets and baggy trousers could conceal a copy of *Ulysses*, then surely they could conceal a bottle or two of alcohol. And how could they explain it, exactly, if an agent searched one of them and found that the bulge in his waistband was a three-and-a-half-pound *book*?

Luckily, the border guards never stopped them. Braverman, with his shy demeanor and his hair brushed back from his boyish face, simply didn't look like a bootlegger. He didn't look like a radical, either. But he was. He was the first *Ulysses* booklegger, and he successfully smuggled every copy entrusted to him. The following year, he went to Paris and got his own copy of *Ulysses* signed by James Joyce.

20.

THE KING'S CHIMNEY

Joyce's life had become a shambles after *Ulysses*. In April 1922, Nora took the children to see her family in Galway. She didn't say when she would return, and they left Paris just as Ireland was descending into civil war. A 1921 treaty between the Irish and British Parliaments established Ireland as a Free State within the United Kingdom (the Irish Parliament would swear allegiance to the Crown). The treaty split the Irish Republican Army into factions, those who supported the Free State agreement and those who demanded full Irish sovereignty, and Nora and the children were caught in the middle of escalating violence. Free State troops commandeered their hotel room and mounted machine guns in the windows, forcing Nora, Giorgio and Lucia to dash through Galway and board the next train for Dublin.

Joyce felt helpless and abandoned in Paris. Nora seemed to be thinking of staying in Ireland, and he wrote desperate letters hoping to win her back. Was she leaving him? Did she need money? "O my dearest," he wrote, "if you would only turn to me even now and read that terrible book which has now broken the heart in my breast and take me to yourself alone to do with me what you will!" Nora felt that a part of Jim was moored to 1904 while she and their children pressed onward. Going to Ireland was her way of pulling him out of the terrible book that had colonized his life. Nora was reminding him that she was more than the voice of Molly Bloom.

Joyce did not fare well alone. He slept and ate poorly. He fainted in Shakespeare and Company. He had multiple tooth abscesses, and his iritis became worse than ever. Less than a week after Nora and the children returned (she would never leave him), Joyce developed glaucoma in his left eye. When the pain became unbearable, Joyce's oculist sent his assistant to Joyce's room in a small Left Bank residential hotel. The young man opened the door to find the famous Irish writer wrapped in a blanket and squatting on the floor in front of a stewpan containing the picked-over remains of a chicken. Nora was squatting across from him, and the entire place was in disarray. There were two rooms filled with mismatched furniture and half-empty bottles of wine. Clothes and toiletries were strewn over the tables, the mantelpiece and their chairs. Well-used trunks were gaping open, still half unpacked from the family's recent return. Joyce turned from the chicken carcass to the visitor.

The doctor's assistant told Joyce he needed surgery, and Joyce told the doctor never to send him again. A few days later, the doctor examined Joyce's left eye and confirmed that he needed an immediate iridectomy. The longer he waited, the worse his vision would be. The prospect was terrifying. Joyce's left eye was his "good" one—the one that hadn't been operated on, the one he needed to read and write. Even a successful iridectomy would impair his vision, and a failed operation could render his left eye blind. Joyce remained so traumatized by his eye surgery in Zurich five years earlier that he was determined to find a doctor with less zeal for the knife. He sent a panicked telegram to Miss Weaver. Could she possibly help? Would her doctor fly to Paris? He believed the operation would end his literary career. The telegram begged: "Urgent reply every minute important."

Sylvia Beach rushed over to find Nora renewing cold compresses on Joyce's eyes to reduce the swelling. She had been doing it for hours, she said. "When the pain is unbearable he gets up and walks the floor." So Beach decided to take Joyce to Dr. Louis Borsch, an American doctor who kept an inexpensive clinic on the corner of rue du Cherche-Midi and rue du Regard. The location, no doubt, was a good omen, but the clinic itself wasn't reassuring. It had a drab exterior, a waiting room filled with wooden benches and the back office was barely large enough for the portly doctor to turn around. Joyce was amused by his Yankee drawl. "Too bad ye got that kickup in your eye," he said, peering into the catastrophe. Nevertheless, Dr. Borsch thought he could diminish Joyce's stubborn case of iritis "by eliminating the poison from the system." Instead of surgery, he prescribed eyedrops (apparently cocaine), more cold compresses, a narcotic to help him sleep and a medication that would "purify the blood." Dr. Borsch urged Joyce to improve his general health and adopt "a more comfortable and wholesome mode of living," as Sylvia Beach described it to Miss Weaver.

IN 1922, Joyce decided to meet the other woman who had made *Ulysses* possible. Miss Weaver waited months for his illness to subside, and Dr. Borsch's treatment appeared to help. By August, Joyce believed he was well enough to make the trip across the channel, but like so many other recoveries, it ended with a sharp relapse. He doused his eye with countless eyedrops and fought off London doctors who were as determined to perform surgery as their Parisian counterparts. The doctors seemed to agree in all particulars. "Mr. Joyce's mode of life in Paris is very unhealthy," Miss Weaver's physician told her. He spent his nights in pain, sweating profusely and unable to sleep. Each morning at their hotel, Nora soaked cold compresses in a bucket of ice water and applied them to his eyes with cotton wads as big as small pillows. When the compresses were removed, Joyce stared at the brass knobs at the foot of his bed, their weak glimmer among the only things piercing the perpetual darkness.

But the writer and his patron finally met. Miss Weaver's flowers were freshly cut and arranged for Mr. Joyce's afternoon arrival at her flat. For seven years, Joyce had been an avid correspondent, a troubled figure in photos, a sensitive boy coming of age in *A Portrait* and the author of a city of voices in *Ulysses*. Now he was a man of full substance, of neat attire, impeccable manners and powerful spectacles. But what lay behind those spectacles jarred Miss Weaver, and it made her reluctant to look directly at her guest—not out of shyness but out of embarrassment. James Joyce's left eye had no pupil. The dark window at the center of his eye and the reticulations of his iris were swept over by a fog. The natural blue pigment soured to a bluish green. Simply listening to him speak challenged Miss Weaver's concentration, for even as he made jokes and pleasantries designed to put her at ease, Joyce looked back at her with something like a dull marble lodged in his head.

After years of imagining Joyce's affliction through his letters, she was now confronted with its awful presence. Whatever was causing Joyce's recurrent iritis had dilated his ocular blood vessels until they ruptured. The blood seeped into the intraocular fluid and mixed with dead cells and pus, all of which floated around inside his eye for months. The mixture of blood and exudate had persisted for so long that it started to "organize"—the viscous fluid was congealing into a solid membrane covering his pupil. To look at Mr. Joyce was to feel the dread of advancing blindness, to understand the delicacy of an eye and the terrible complexity of seeing.

MISS WEAVER DECIDED that the Egoist Press would publish the first U.K. edition of *Ulysses*. She was determined to correct Darantière's misprints and bolster Joyce's income—he would receive 90 percent of all profits after expenses. The edition would be two thousand copies, and like Shakespeare and Company, the Egoist Press would try to circumvent the authorities by selling directly to readers rather than bookshops. Sylvia Beach helped compile and distribute promotional materials, but there was only so much she could do from Paris. Miss Weaver approached only one London printer, the Pelican Press, who informally agreed to print *Ulysses* after seeing the first ten episodes. They changed their minds when they examined the rest.

Miss Weaver knew little about the legal risks she was taking. Her solicitor informed her that copies of a book deemed obscene could be seized anywhere (in a bookstore, in her office or in her home) if they were kept for sale or distribution, and, despite her inventive suggestion, distributing copies through an agent or dividing them among various distributors made no difference. A private edition's only legal advantage was that it would demonstrate to judges that the publisher wanted to limit the book's availability, or, in the words of the Hicklin Rule, that the publisher restricted the type of people "into whose hands" the book "may fall."

But this was not much of an advantage, for if the Shakespeare and Company edition was any indication, bookstores would start reselling the book anyway, and legal action against a single copy nabbed in a police raid would affect all copies. And "private" or not, *Ulysses* was now a known quantity. The full text was in print, outraged reviews were circulating throughout Britain, and the cloak of privacy was stripped away. Weaver and Beach weighed the possibility that a hostile reader would order a copy and send it to the police. The editor of *The Sunday Express*, for one, seemed determined to have "The Bible of the Outcasts" burned.

Miss Weaver found another solution. An old contributor to *The Egoist* named John Rodker was publishing limited-edition books under the name Ovid Press. She remembered Rodker from Ezra Pound's dinner meetings during the war—he had been imprisoned as a conscientious objector and joined the meetings after his hunger strike set him free. Rodker remained in Pound's orbit, and he was, clearly, willing to break the law for his principles. Miss Weaver asked Rodker if he would act as her Paris agent: the Egoist Press would publish and finance the edition, but it would be advertised, sold and distributed from Paris. Rodker would have to collect two thousand copies from Darantière in Dijon, send out circulars announcing the publication, collect orders and finally wrap and ship the copies to readers around the world. Miss Weaver would pay him two hundred pounds for his work. It was simple.

Rodker discovered his first problem immediately: the high prices of *Ulysses* attracted literary pirates. He heard rumors that someone was planning a counterfeit version of the original Shakespeare and Company edition. It would be printed on cheap paper, circulated to booksellers eager to peddle a rare commodity like *Ulysses*, legitimate or not, and the criminals would pocket the profits. John Quinn heard the same rumors in New York. He wrote to Miss Weaver to warn her that "a gang" was about to print a thousand copies in a press somewhere near the city and sell the pirated version for thirty dollars. Getting an injunction against the pirates would be expensive, he told Weaver, and ultimately futile. If an injunction were issued against one gang, they'd simply pass the printing plates and remaining copies to someone else in another state. They'd have to track down literary pirates all over the country, issuing injunction after injunction. It wouldn't end.

There was a more effective option, Quinn explained, but it made him cringe: he could ask John Sumner for help. The New York Society for the Suppression of Vice would happily track down and arrest anyone mailing advertisements for *Ulysses*. It was, of course, a violation of the Comstock Act, and Sumner might be able to stop the pirates before their copies hit the streets. He wrote to Miss Weaver, "It would be somewhat ironical, wouldn't it?—if I, who defended *Ulysses* in court against the charge brought by Sumner that it was obscene, should induce Sumner to suppress this new pirated edition because it was obscene." Ironic or not, Quinn wouldn't hesitate to use criminal law to stop pirates.

The worst part of the piracy was its timing. If it came out before the Egoist Press edition went on sale, buyers would evaporate. Rodker would have to sell the edition as quickly as possible, which meant that they no longer had time to correct the text's misprints. So the Egoist Press edition was really a second printing of the Shakespeare and Company edition with a list of errata appended. The rush also meant that Rodker needed someone to ship the copies while he received payments. As luck would have it, Miss Weaver found help from another erstwhile attendee of Ezra Pound's dinners. Iris Barry was twenty-two and already a former suffragette when she endured air raids to join the conversations. She was an avid *Egoist* reader growing up on a farm near Birmingham, and she moved to London in 1915, partly at Ezra Pound's urging. In 1922, Barry lost her job as a secretary on Bond Street, and Miss Weaver was giving her weekly baths and wholesome meals. When Miss Weaver and Rodker asked her to help with the first U.K. publication of James Joyce's *Ulysses*, she happily agreed.

Rodker arranged everything in less than a month. He borrowed the back room of a friend's bookshop to send out circulars and receive orders, and he rented a basement room in a shabby Left Bank hotel where Iris Barry could receive, store and ship copies of *Ulysses*. Rodker and Barry sailed for Paris, and on October 12, 1922, Darantière's shipment arrived. Rodker sent out word that *Ulysses* was available for two guineas each, about the same price as the cheapest Shakespeare and Company edition. The copies were sold out in four days. While Rodker handled the orders, Iris Barry sat in a small room with vaulted ceilings in the basement of the Hotel Verneuil. The table was covered with sheets of brown parcel paper and hundreds of mailing labels. All around her were piles of the blue inventory to be wrapped, tied and addressed, one book at a time. She carried them in fours or fives to the nearest post office.

With rumors of pirated editions and the jaws of Sumner's monster waiting for *Ulysses* in New York, the copies bound for the United States had to be shipped before officials realized another printing was circulating. Barry rushed the first lot of one hundred American orders into the mail, but the risk of detection by customs agents on the lookout for books with Paris postmarks increased with each book's passage. There were so many American orders that Miss Weaver refused some of them lest they be seized. She kept dozens with her in London.

The largest orders came from American middlemen planning to resell copies to bookstores clamoring for *Ulysses*. Those orders couldn't be refused, nor could they be shipped individually. Hundreds of copies certainly couldn't be shipped in bulk, where they would catch the eye of any customs officials who weren't bribed or incompetent. They would have to be smuggled—but the job was far too big for someone like Braverman. Rodker had a more ambitious plan. He shipped the books from Paris to London, where a wholesaler unstitched the bindings of each copy of *Ulysses* and pulled them apart. They tucked the dismembered sections of the books inside newspapers and stacked them for shipment. The first mate of an American merchant ship agreed to smuggle hundreds of copies disguised as a large consignment of British newspapers, filling, ostensibly, the New York area's sudden demand for rugby scores and parliamentary political cartoons. It worked, and by hiding them in newspapers, the U.K. *Ulysses* arrived on American shores duty-free.

While Rodker's first mate navigated copies through the North Atlantic and Iris Barry sent copies to individuals in the United States, France and beyond, Miss Weaver handled the London orders herself. Rodker sent copies to a private mailing agency, and when bookshops discreetly requested *Ulysses* from the Egoist Press, she withdrew them from the agency and delivered them herself. Miss Weaver would appear like any other reader in bookshops across London until she asked to see the shop's proprietor by name and it dawned upon the clerk that the nervous woman with the bow on her hat was the Egoist Press representative they had been expecting, and the package she clutched under her arm contained *that* book, the book they quickly hid behind the counter.

Miss Weaver kept some copies at her office despite her solicitor's advice. And while it meant putting herself in even more legal danger, she brought several copies to her apartment and hid them at the back of her large Victorian wardrobe—she wanted to protect as many books as possible from a potential police raid. They stayed there for months, and for months she waited for the constables to present themselves at her door and ransack her apartment while she would sit patiently and see if they would be brazen enough to rifle through a lady's belongings to confiscate a work of art.

Her family noticed her anxiety, though they said nothing. They had grown accustomed to her silence regarding her literary endeavors, especially with Joyce, and so much the better. The suffragist screeds and the birth control advocacy of *The Egoist* were tolerable to her siblings for their principled courage, yet her involvement with Joyce was another matter. Some family members had gone so far as to read parts of *Ulysses* only to be baffled that Harriet not only subsidized such filth but that she actually published it. Her brother-in-law reacted with a mixture of outrage and dismay. "How could she? How could she? An enigma! An enigma!"

THE SECOND EDITION seemed to be going well. Hundreds of disassembled copies hidden in newspapers slipped by New York customs agents, and wholesalers rebound them to be sold. But near the end of 1922, reports of missing copies began to accumulate, both from the Egoist Press edition and from the Shakespeare and Company edition still being smuggled through Canada. There was no official word from any government department on either side of the Atlantic. There were no notices of confiscations. No news of burnings. No packages sent back to Paris or London. No smugglers or first mates arrested. Not even a warning from the U.S. Post Office or customs. Every now and then, copies of *Ulysses* simply disappeared. There was only one unmistakable sign of trouble. In early November, after Miss Weaver began distributing *Ulysses* in twos and threes across London, she noticed a detective, alone, watching her outside her window. Miss Harriet Weaver was under police surveillance.

By December 1922, it was clear that U.S. authorities were seizing every copy of *Ulysses* they could find, though the details are hazy. Either the U.S. government never kept the records, or they disappeared. In any case, copies of *Ulysses* that had apparently vanished were in fact falling into the hands of law enforcement officials. A raid in Boston in November turned up some of the imported copies. Others were accumulating in New York's General Post Office Building on Thirty-fourth Street, where they awaited a decision from Washington. No one knew if it was John Sumner and the scathing press reviews that prodded officials to act or if they didn't need to be prodded at all. Either way, New York customs officials forwarded the matter to the solicitor of the Post Office Department for a ruling. When the solicitor leafed through the heavy book, pausing over the passages marked by the customs officials, he discovered that *Ulysses* didn't have to do with Greek mythology *at all*. It was about the Irish. The solicitor declared *Ulysses* "plainly obscene" and kept a copy in his office for his records.

When the solicitor's judgment was handed down, officials in Boston and at the General Post Office Building gathered up nearly five hundred copies of *Ulysses* they had been collecting through the fall, wheeled them down the basement's dim corridors and unloaded them in the furnace room. The piles of books sat before the furnace's black doors and a row of lower chambers, narrow like catacombs. The men opened the round cast-iron hatches and began tossing James Joyce's *Ulysses* into the chambers. Paper burns brighter than coal. Seven years of writing, months of revisions and typesetting, weeks of printing and hours of packaging and shipping were incinerated in seconds.

BURNING *ULYSSES* could not have been a difficult decision. A conviction against a portion of the book in New York would be enough to persuade even a lenient official that *Ulysses* was illegal throughout the country. It's unclear how Miss Weaver heard news of the seizure and destruction. Federal law required notification of a government seizure and an opportunity to challenge the decision in court, but if such notices were sent to any of the individuals or wholesalers waiting for *Ulysses*, none have ever been found. What we do know is that when the books were burned, Miss Weaver did not contact John Quinn or ask her own solicitor to intervene. She didn't remove the copies hidden in her apartment. She didn't lament or inquire after the burned books. Instead, she printed more. Within days, Miss Weaver ordered five hundred more copies from Darantière in Dijon—a third edition to replace the copies destroyed. Rodker would ship them to England, where they would smuggle the copies the same way they had before, by pulling them apart and shipping them to hostile American shores disguised as newspapers. Yet *Ulysses*, as everyone would soon discover, was no longer permissible on British shores, either.

The decision to ban *Ulysses* in the United Kingdom began in March 1922, when a concerned citizen sent the first book review to the Home Office. "Obscenity?" the London *Observer* asked. "Yes. This is undoubtedly an obscene book." The Home Office was the principal branch of His Majesty's government, and it was responsible for all law enforcement matters. Following the complaint, a Home Office official contacted the undersecretary of state and requested the name and address of any bookseller selling *Ulysses*—the detective observing Miss Weaver may have been carrying out the undersecretary's orders and following her as she delivered copies to London bookshops.

There was official silence regarding *Ulysses* until the end of November 1922, when the undersecretary obtained the sixteen-page *Quarterly Review* screed that compared *Ulysses* to a Fenian bomb blowing up the castle of English literature. Paraphrasing the review, the undersecretary called the book "unreadable, unquotable, and unreviewable." Two days later, he issued instructions: any copy of *Ulysses* found in the post should be detained. The decision was provisional—it was, after all, based on nothing more than a citizen's complaint and a couple of reviews (one of them favorable). The undersecretary did not so much as glance at the text itself. And how could he? *Ulysses* wasn't easy to obtain, and the price was prohibitively high. Given the nature of the case, the undersecretary requested the official opinion of the Director of Public Prosecutions, Sir Archibald Bodkin.

As the director of public prosecutions, Sir Archibald was the head of the Crown Prosecution Service. The office had been malleable when Sir Archibald first took the position in 1920, but by the time he left in 1930 he had established precedent for future practices. He prosecuted all capital crimes and advised central government departments, the police and all Crown prosecutors. He initiated and oversaw proceedings against an array of high crimes, including sedition, counterfeit, obstruction of justice, public corruption and obscenity. He gave instructions on twenty-three hundred cases every year.

The undersecretary's report on *Ulysses* may not have captured such a busy man's attention, but as it was making its way up the chain of command, officials seized a single copy of *Ulysses* at Croydon Airport in London. In December, a customs officer noticed an oversized book that a passenger was bringing back from Paris. He flipped through the final pages teeming with unpunctuated text, and his eyes fixated on page 704.

yes I think he made them a bit firmer sucking them like that so long he made me thirsty titties he calls them I had to laugh yes this one anyhow stiff the nipple gets for the least thing Ill get him to keep that up and Ill take those eggs beaten up with marsala fatten them out for him what are all those veins and things curious the way its made 2 the same in case of twins theyre supposed to represent beauty placed up there like those statues in the museum one of them pretending to hide it with her hand are they so beautiful of course compared with what a man looks like with his two bags full and his other thing hanging down out of him or sticking up at you like a hatrack no wonder they hide it with a cabbageleaf

The officer told the passenger that H.M. Customs and Excise was confiscating *Ulysses* as obscene under Section 42 of the Customs Consolidations Act of 1876. The owner objected to the confiscation and insisted that *Ulysses* was an important work of art by a reputable author. It was on sale in bookshops around London and reviewed by several esteemed periodicals, including *The Nation*, *The English Review* and the October issue of *The Quarterly Review*.

Given the citizen's protest, customs forwarded the book to the Home Office and requested a quick decision about its legality. The matter came before Assistant Undersecretary of State Sydney Harris, who was thorough enough to read page 705: "he made me spend the 2nd time tickling me behind with his finger I was coming for about 5 minutes with my legs round him I had to hug him after O Lord I wanted to shout out all sorts of things fuck or shit or anything at all[.]" Harris retrieved the growing Home Office file on *Ulysses*. Even if there were some doubt that such passages were obscene, they could be swept away by the fact that the citizen defended *Ulysses* by citing the very same *Quarterly Review* article that the Home Office was keeping as evidence that the book *was* obscene. Harris discussed the matter with the director of public prosecutions himself.

Sir Archibald was a ruthless barrister who came to prominence by prosecuting suffragettes before the war. "He's a beast," one of them said after a high-profile conviction. Suffragettes pelted him with rotten fruit in the courtroom, and when he received kidnapping and arson threats, Scotland Yard assigned officers to guard him and his chambers. But Sir Archibald was unfazed. He was a man of unwavering Victorian sensibilities (cars were anathema to him even in the 1950s), and he worked so tirelessly that his complexion became sallow and bags developed under his eyes. On the rare occasions when he told a bawdy joke, he drained away the humor by delivering the punch line with a disapproving glare.

Sir Archibald read the final chapter of *Ulysses*, and on December 29, 1922, he submitted his opinion about its legality under British law:

As might be supposed, I have not had the time nor, I may add, the inclination to read through this book. I have, however, read pages 690 to 732. I am entirely unable to appreciate how those pages are relevant to the rest of the book, or, indeed, what the book itself is about. I can discover no story, there is no introduction which might give a key to its purpose, and the pages above mentioned, written as they are as if composed by a more or less illiterate vulgar woman, form an entirely detached part of this production. In my opinion, there is more, and a great deal more than mere vulgarity or coarseness, there is a great deal of unmitigated filth and obscenity.

He declared that customs authorities had every right to confiscate and burn *Ulysses*. And in the event that there was a public protest against such burnings, he advised, "the answer will be that it is filthy and filthy books are not allowed to be imported into this country."

On January 1, 1923, Sir Archibald Bodkin's opinion became the official position of the United Kingdom, and Harris forwarded Bodkin's recommendation to the Home Secretary to make sure the decision was enforced. What if *Ulysses* started a trend? The Home Office was afraid that, in Harris's words, "other morbid writers with a love of notoriety will attempt to write in the same vein." They could not have books like this flooding British ports. They had to end it before it began.

In January, only days after Sir Archibald's decision, five hundred copies of *Ulysses* were on their way to London to be disassembled and smuggled to replace the books burned in New York. By the time the cargo ship carrying the books crossed the English Channel, customs officers at the port of Folkestone were waiting for it. H.M. Customs and Excise officers duly informed the Egoist Press that its property had been seized pursuant to Section 42 of the Customs Consolidation Act of 1876 because the Home Office deemed the material prima facie obscene. The Egoist Press had the opportunity to appeal the government's decision, but Miss Weaver couldn't bear the public scrutiny—and her solicitor almost certainly advised against it. Winning an appeal in court was doubtful, and even if the Egoist Press could recover its books, the chances that they could be successfully smuggled into the Port of New York were thinner than ever. When the window for the appeal passed, customs officials burned them in "the King's Chimney." Then they burned the records of the burning.

21.

THE PHARMACOPEIA

The 1920s were brutal to Joyce. For those who admired his work, the burnings in England and the United States solidified his status as the twentieth century's heretical victim, someone persecuted by righteous authorities for speaking the unvarnished truth. Other modernists suffered the fate of censored or bowdlerized books, but none had devoted themselves so singularly to such a doomed work of art. The burnings eliminated even the slight possibility of an American edition and assured that no other U.K. publisher would follow Harriet Weaver's lead. The stunning act of destroying an entire edition of a book, rather than merely halting its distribution or fining its publisher, sent a clear message to publishers, authors and booksellers. A book burning—even as an order executed in secrecy—was enough to throttle the book's circulation. A motivated reader could still find *Ulysses*, but the high prices and the relative scarcity meant that it would reach only a fraction of its potential audience.

The most brutal aspect of the burnings was that they deepened Joyce's isolation. Censorship may have enhanced his aura among his devotees, but the added fame made him reticent and cagey. He posed for photographs but never granted interviews and warily eased himself into conversations with a progressively tighter circle of friends—the days of boisterous dancing were ending. Joyce's social and literary isolation buttressed the more fundamental isolation he endured through the twenties: his rapidly deteriorating eyesight.

A painful procession of glaucoma, cataracts, nebulae and eye surgeries, which might have drawn people empathetically closer to him, became an ineffable ordeal that opened up a chasm between himself and everyone else. Encroaching blindness augmented the celebrity status that he dealt with so poorly. Reporters called regularly for updates on the status of Mr. Joyce's eyes, and he became famous for the postoperative black eye patches he wore like a broken-down pirate marooned in Paris. The spectacle of his own blindness became another way for him to conceal himself. Joyce donned his first eye patch in November 1922 not because of surgery but to hide the offensive nebula in his pupil. He was censored in more ways than one.

In April 1923, after months of sudden improvements and relapses, Joyce submitted himself to a long-overdue surgery. Over the next few years, he would become familiar with the surgical routine. Nurse Puard, Dr. Borsch's assistant, would pull his lower eyelid away from his eye, exposing the network of turgid blood vessels. She would douse it with cocaine, wait until the eye was numb and instill a couple of drops of scopolamine, a more potent relative of atropine. She would close his eye and wipe the eyelash dry with a cotton swab. In fifteen minutes, the muscle that contracts the pupil would dilate. In a couple of hours, his eyes would lose focus. When the patient was ready, Dr. Borsch's bulky fingers would grasp the shank of the lance knife and press the blade through Joyce's cornea. He would withdraw it quickly to prevent the iris from sticking to the metal and following the blade out through the wound. The incision would be about three to four millimeters.

Dr. Borsch asked for the back-toothed iris forceps and slid them into the incision. The tiny teeth bit into the iris near the edge of Joyce's occluded pupil, and the doctor tugged the inner circular margin outward. Nurse Puard gave him the iris scissors. He sidled the closed blades alongside the forceps and inserted them into the incision, trying not to let the moving instruments open it wider. With two snips, he cut away a small piece of the iris's inner edge and pulled it out. The space that remained was Joyce's new pupil. Dr. Borsch then inserted a hooked instrument into the posterior chamber and slowly, painstakingly, separated the iris wherever it was sticking to the lens behind it. Sometimes the tissue reattached immediately.

Iridectomies were the most difficult procedures to perform in any surgical field, and Joyce's case was more complicated than most. Dr. Borsch performed his first surgery on Joyce in April 1923, after he suffered his ninth attack of iritis in his left eye. In 1924, he performed two more surgeries: a complete iridectomy in June and a cataract extraction in November. In 1930, Joyce was scheduled for his twelfth surgery.

Decades of iritis triggered an array of secondary eye problems: glaucoma, synechiae, cataracts, conjunctivitis, episcleritis and blepharitis. His retina atrophied. His eyes hemorrhaged and lost vitreous fluid. In 1924, when Joyce told Sylvia Beach that he could feel his eyesight "slowly nearing extinction," he was not being dramatic. Most people who wear corrective lenses are familiar with prescriptions for plus or minus two or three diopters. In 1917, Joyce's prescription was +6.5. In 1932, it was +17. Joyce wasn't nearsighted. He was farsighted—reading and writing strained his eyes the most.

As severe as his hyperopia was, it was only a component of his failing eyesight. His bigger problem was that the shape of his hyperopic eyes increased the chances of closed-angle glaucoma, and each attack reduced his vision to a narrower, darker tunnel, and the nebulae forming from the hardening exudate made the people and objects at the end of that tunnel look like they were passing through a milky haze. Surgeries to assuage nebulae, cataractal and glaucomatic blindness (cutting away pieces of iris, making an artificial pupil, removing lenses) reduced his vision in other ways. No matter what surgery he endured, no matter how powerful his corrective lenses were, his vision was becoming hazy, spotted and dim. In 1930, Joyce's right eye had 1/30th its normal seeing power. His left eye was effectively blind: it was functioning between 1/800 to 1/1000 its capacity. Joyce reassured himself after surgery by trying to read the large print in children's books. Under the circumstances, it's remarkable he could see anything at all.

Joyce's life was a rhythm of pain and palliation, and everyone had a theory about the cause of his recurrent iritis. Miss Weaver, following her doctor's suggestion, blamed his "mode of life," especially his drinking. Sylvia Beach thought he needed good food, outdoor exercise and time away from his family. The newspapers reported that Joyce was going blind because of the strain of writing *Ulysses*. Joyce himself said he was going blind because of the weather. He blamed the climate, the rain and winds of every season in Paris, Nice, Zurich, London and Trieste—the weather all over Europe was conspiratorially bad.

There were as many treatments as there were suspected causes. Joyce endured steam baths, mud baths, sweating powders, cold compresses and hot compresses. He received a month of iodine injections. He had his temples massaged with a French tonic called synthol. One of Ezra Pound's friends gave him "endocrine treatment" by stimulating his thyroid. He received electrotherapy on multiple occasions—probably by having electrodes attached to his eyelids. They put multiple leeches around his eyes.

Joyce tried multiple medications—the variety of eyedrops alone was astounding. He took dionine to dissipate his nebulae as well as salicylic acid and boric acid to disinfect his eyes. He took cocaine to numb the pain from the disinfectants and the glaucoma. He took atropine and scopolamine to dilate his pupils and break up synechiae. He took pilocarpine to counteract the atropine and scopolamine, both of which induced delirium and hallucinations over the years. In 1924 he wrote to Miss Weaver that his room was haunted— objects around him kept slipping and tumbling about. He took scopolamine orally to calm his nerves, though excessive doses have the opposite effect, causing euphoria and anxiety. He reported at least one "attack of giddiness" in 1928, and one night, when Nora tried hailing a taxi home from a bistro, Joyce ran out into the empty street, threw up his arms and shouted, "No—I'm free, free!" before dancing down the shadowy road like a wildly handled puppet. In 1933, after a panic attack on a train and a night of hallucinations, he ran out into the snowy street early in the morning to inform neighboring friends that he was in danger. Joyce drank and took sleeping pills as a final refuge from the pharmacopeia.

In the early 1920s doctors agreed that the trouble with Joyce's eyes had something to do with his teeth. A common theory of infection at the time asserted that microbes migrate from one infected body part to another. The oral cavity was thought to be a common source of infection, and Joyce's mouth was indeed catastrophic. No amount of ophthalmic attention, presumably, would help his eyes unless a dentist stanched the flow of bacteria from his mouth. John Quinn was certain of it. As he explained to Miss Weaver, Joyce paid more attention to the weather than his teeth because "a great many Irish are wholly lacking in a scientific turn of mind." Quinn's opinion became the consensus (regarding the teeth, not the Irish), and in April 1923 a doctor extracted ten of Joyce's teeth, seven abscesses and a cyst. A few days later, he removed seven more teeth.

It's difficult to overestimate how a life of pain and weakening vision must have altered Joyce's understanding of consciousness. Pain collapses the world. It concentrates one's mind on one's own suffering body. And instead of visual distractions to carry him away from his agony, Joyce opened his eyes to a constant reminder of it, an obscured field of vision. His thoughts were the only life raft in the rising tide of pain, and the pressure pushing out from the inside of Joyce's eyes expanded the seconds. To read *Ulysses* is to feel time's dilation. We go so slowly through the characters' thoughts because even the most painstaking mental contours were something to hold on to. Joyce wrote an epic of the human body partly because it was so challenging for him to get beyond his own body. And yet he did.

Lying in bed with one or both eyes bandaged, Joyce conjured memories out of the medicinal haze. He habitually walked past the shop fronts on Dublin's O'Connell Street as they were in 1904. "I dream about my eye nearly every night performing feats of vision," he wrote to Miss Weaver. Even when he couldn't see—even when doctors told him that writing was making his vision worse—he began drawing large letters with a charcoal pencil on an oversized sheet of paper like a child. It was the beginning of *Finnegans Wake*. To convince himself that he wasn't going blind, he counted stripes on wallpaper and the lights along the Place de la Concorde. He memorized hundreds of lines of poetry. Sylvia Beach would bring Walter Scott's *Lady of the Lake* to his bedside, read a random line and look up as Joyce recited the next two pages without a mistake. Like superstitions, rote tasks made him feel in control of his life. But he wasn't in control. When Frank Budgen visited Joyce in Paris in 1923, he found his wartime friend pale and breathless. He was holding on to himself as if to keep his body from falling apart.

After his 1923 surgery, Joyce recovered in a small room above Dr. Borsch's clinic. It had rippled windows and warped walls meeting at unlikely angles. Cloves of garlic grew in a sponge on the windowsill. Nurse Puard gave him more scopolamine throughout the day and cooked his meals in the small kitchen across the hall. Nora stayed in the room next to Joyce's and helped put leeches around his eye. The nurse would hold one of the writhing bodies in the folds of a napkin and place its mouth on Joyce's canthus, the corner of skin where the eyelids meet. There were several leeches in the jar, and each of them would loll and hang off his face until they filled up with blood from the anterior chamber of his eye. Nora helped retrieve "the creatures," as she called them, when they fell on the floor around his bed. In the evening, through the night and well past dawn, James Joyce lay awake screaming.

22

GLAMOUR OF
THE CLANDESTINE

———

Despite confiscations and burnings in the United States and England, Sylvia Beach published eight more editions of *Ulysses*. Joyce's book was officially or unofficially outlawed in nearly every English-speaking country in the world, allowing Shakespeare and Company to sell only twenty-four thousand copies in nine years. Even for a literary book, this was small. When F. Scott Fitzgerald's *The Great Gatsby* sold nearly twenty-four thousand copies in its first year, it was a crushing disappointment.

Joyce's fans were few, but they were ardent. Shakespeare and Company became a pilgrimage destination for budding Joyceans, several of whom asked Miss Beach if they could move to Paris and work for her. One day on her way home she found a drunk young man sitting on the doorstep of her bookshop with his head buried in his folded arms. He was searching for James Joyce, and when he found Shakespeare and Company closed, he tried to find where Sylvia Beach lived. The concierges all along rue de l'Odéon had to force him out and bolt the doors behind him (he apparently urinated in a stairway). Beach sat down next to the young American and saw that he was crying. He had been kicked out of his midwestern high school when someone discovered a copy of *Ulysses* in his desk, and he felt ostracized from his town. He had come to Paris to be Joyce's assistant, but once he arrived, he was overwhelmed by the prospect of meeting him, and he drank to calm his nerves.

Ulysses had an intense attraction for certain people. Reading it said something about who you were. It was a mark of aesthetic, philosophical and sexual audacity. It initiated you into modernism's new era, and if it was a Bible of the outcasts, reading it made you part of an outcast community spanning the globe. Sylvia Beach filled orders from South America, India, the Balkans, South Africa and Borneo. A library in Peking ordered ten. For many people, including the American high school student, simply possessing *Ulysses* was a rebellion. Bringing it through customs was a crime. Printing, selling and distributing it was punishable by prison. Officials who aided the importation of even a single copy of *Ulysses* could receive a five-thousand-dollar fine and up to ten years in prison. Risk generated devotion—your relationship to a book changes when you have to hide it from the government.

Readers smuggled copies by binding Joyce's novel inside decoy covers of books like *Merry Tales for Little Folks*, *Shakespeare's Complete Works* or *The Holy Bible*. One was disguised as a biography of Ulysses S. Grant. Legal qualms discouraged Sylvia Beach from sending copies to the United States herself, but when her sister Holly in California wanted a copy for a friend, she reluctantly agreed. She wrote back, "Tell Mrs. Bullis to keep her mouth shut about where and how she got *Ulysses* if she gets it." She never got it. What she got instead a was a curt letter:

December 16, 1926

    Madam:

    One package addressed to you, containing one obscene book 'Ulysses,' has been seized from the mail for violation of section 305 [of the] Tariff Act, which prohibits the importation of all obscene or immoral literature. (Seizure No. 5217)

    If you will sign and return the enclosed Assent to Forfeiture no further action will be taken by this office.

                    Respectfully,

                    L. H. Schwaebe

                    COLLECTOR OF CUSTOMS

                    U.S. TREASURY DEPARTMENT

John Quinn thought for months about how to smuggle his fourteen copies into the country, and in May 1922 he decided that instead of hiding the books he would draw attention to them. A Paris art dealer wrapped each book individually, put them in a custom-made case, screwed it shut and placed the case in a larger shipment of artworks. The shipment's invoice, when it arrived in New York, included a vague entry, "14 books, 3400 francs," and Quinn requested that a customs inspector examine the shipment in his apartment. The inspector, whom Quinn knew personally (he seemed to know everyone personally), unsealed the cases to find wrapped books among several paintings: a pensive clown, a mother and child, three women painted as if they were chiseled from stone and a mountain landscape shading a village's geometry. Quinn's copies of *Ulysses* were smuggled with three Picassos and a Cézanne— the peculiar paintings were a diversion from the literary contraband. The ploy was one of John Quinn's last victories, for he succumbed to liver cancer two years later.

THE CRIMINAL AURA surrounding *Ulysses* was real. In England, the Home Office did everything in its power to stop the circulation of *Ulysses* short of a criminal prosecution, which it avoided only because a trial would give the book more publicity. Customs officials in British ports were told to confiscate all copies of *Ulysses* entering the country. The chief constables of major British cities were ordered to trace any copy sold in their districts, and the secretary of state issued warrants for copies going through the mail as late as 1933. The warrants were, in fact, instances of official restraint. A 1908 law gave the British government the authority to open suspicious packages without a warrant— all officials had to do was give the addressee the opportunity to watch.

Surveillance went beyond the post and ports. When a well-known book catalog called *The Clique* included *Ulysses* in its list, the Home Office told it to remove the title and issue a warning to subscribers in future editions. Sir Archibald Bodkin once requested that University College London strike Joyce's *name* from documents distributed by its School of Librarianship. In 1926 the town clerk of Stepney, a working-class district in London's East End, wrote to the Home Office requesting permission to place a copy of *Ulysses* in Stepney's library. The assistant commissioner of the London police assigned an inspector to investigate, and, after a covert inquiry, tracked down the name and address of the Joyce fanatic in Stepney who had initiated the request. It turned out he was "a red hot Socialist."

Britain's public media was similarly hostile. In 1931 a former British diplomat named Harold Nicolson planned a radio program for the BBC called *This Changing World,* which examined emerging twentieth-century literary techniques. The BBC's director general urged Nicolson to turn an upcoming broadcast about Joyce into a broadcast about John Galsworthy, who was not exactly an icon of the changing world. A few days later, the director of programs informed Nicolson that he could discuss Joyce only if he didn't mention *Ulysses*. To get around the BBC's ban, he planned to refer to a book *about* Joyce's novel. On the morning of the broadcast, the BBC chairman refused to allow Nicolson on the air. When he threatened to discontinue the series altogether, the chairman let him discuss Joyce briefly, though, as Nicolson informed his listeners, "I am not permitted by the BBC to mention the name of Mr. Joyce's most important work."

What's uncanny about censorship in a liberal society is that sooner or later the government's goal is not just to ban objectionable books. It is to act as if they don't exist. The bans themselves should, whenever possible, remain secret, which is to say that the ideal censorship is a recursion of silence. Harold Nicolson was no longer welcome in BBC studios.

The Home Office considered a young Cambridge University lecturer named F. R. Leavis one of the gravest threats to the silence of censorship. Leavis would become one of the twentieth century's most prominent literary critics. By midcentury he would spawn an entire school of scholars calling themselves Leavisites, but he was a newly minted PhD when he walked into Galloway & Porter in the summer of 1926 and asked the bookstore to obtain a copy of *Ulysses* for his new lecture course, "Modern Problems of Criticism." He wanted to place the copy on reserve at a university library for student reference. Leavis was certain the shop would have no problems obtaining the book from Paris. Porter thought otherwise. When Leavis left, the bookseller contacted the secretary of state to see if the Home Office would allow a copy into the country.

Five days later, Porter got a visit from a Cambridge police officer asking for the name of the individual making the request. When Chief Constable Pearson shared Leavis's name and asked the Home Office how to proceed, the undersecretary of state claimed the book was unsuitable for "boy and girl undergraduates" and suggested that the Home Office "take active steps to prevent the lectures from taking place."

He forwarded the matter to Assistant Undersecretary of State Harris, who remembered the *Ulysses* investigation a few years earlier. "This is an amazing proposition," he wrote in the file. "A lecturer at Cambridge who proposes to make the book a textbook for a mixed class of undergraduates must be a dangerous crank." To be safe, the Home Office again sought the advice of the director of public prosecutions, and Sir Archibald agreed: "If the last forty pages of this book can be called 'literature' there is a whole lot of it running to waste every day in the airing courts at Broadmoor" (that is, the Broadmoor Criminal Lunatic Asylum). Could a professor really be planning lectures on *Ulysses*? Surely, Sir Archibald wrote, the poor bookseller had been the victim of a hoax. He informed the chief constable of Cambridge that the ban would by no means be removed and, furthermore, that all lectures about Joyce must be stopped. Sir Archibald asked the Cambridge police to investigate and report back to the Home Office "as to who and what Dr. F. R. Leavis of Emmanuel College is."

A few days later, the vice chancellor of Cambridge University called Leavis into his office. Vice Chancellor Seward sat at his desk at the master's lodge of Downing College and handed Leavis a typescript several pages long. The document was an evaluation of Joyce's book along with information about Leavis himself. The Home Office knew where Dr. Frank Raymond Leavis lived and provided details about his rooms at the college. It included incriminating evidence: a copy of the course catalog announcing "Modern Problems of Criticism," a notice that the course "will be open to both men and women" and the bookseller's request to import *Ulysses* on his behalf. The Cambridge police were spying on Leavis, and they discovered that his request was not a hoax at all.

Sir Archibald wrote a delicate letter to the vice chancellor. "I don't pretend to be a scrutineer"—he crossed out *scrutineer*.

> *I don't pretend to be a critic of what is, as I suppose literature, but the book "Ulysses" which contains 732 pages is an extraordinary production of which, to use a colloquialism, I am unable to make head or tail, but there are many passages in it which are indecent and entirely unsuitable to bring to the specific attention of any person of either sex. The book concludes with reminiscences, as I suppose they may be called, of an Irish chamber-maid, in various part of which grossness and indecency appear.*

Sir Archibald assumed that the vice chancellor was unfamiliar with the book (he specialized in Jurassic flora, after all), so he offered to loan his well-marked copy seized at Croydon Airport.

Sir Archibald then threatened Cambridge University with "prompt criminal proceedings" if it were to find *Ulysses* available to anyone in Cambridge. Booksellers were warned once again not to sell Joyce's book, and the local police were on alert. But Sir Archibald wanted the vice chancellor to do more than stop the circulation of *Ulysses*. He wanted the university to cancel any lectures about the book—he was offended that the book's existence might even be *mentioned* to undergraduates, which would only tempt curious students to obtain it.

Leavis told the vice chancellor that he thought students should be free to read it if they chose, and the director of public prosecutions was mistaken if he thought he was gallantly protecting the purity of women's colleges at Cambridge. "I happen to know," Leavis said, "that there are copies circulating at both Girton and Newnham." Leavis was in fact doing both literature and morality a service—he wanted to eliminate "the glamour of the clandestine attending the cult" among the university's students, "for there *was* a cult," Leavis later insisted. He noted that he could have obtained a copy of *Ulysses* by contacting any number of shady book agents. "I'm glad you didn't do that," the vice chancellor said, a bit more ominously than Leavis would have wanted. "Letters get intercepted."

After Leavis left, the vice chancellor assured the director of public prosecutions that *Ulysses* would not be taught at Cambridge. Just in case, Seward asked a few questions about Dr. Leavis, and rumors spread to the English faculty. As well respected as F. R. Leavis would become, the rumors, he insisted, never left. Decades later, newer faculty members at Cambridge would ask about the cloud of "disfavor" surrounding Professor Leavis. They all received the same answer. "We don't like the books he gives to undergraduates."

23

MODERN CLASSICS

The people who published modernist writers were either magnanimous cultural gatekeepers with eccentric tastes or gamblers willing to pursue younger authors and risqué manuscripts. Horace Liveright was a gambler. Though *Ulysses* was too risky for him, Liveright published several daring books, including *Aphrodite*, George Moore's *A Story-Teller's Holiday* and D. H. Lawrence's *The Rainbow*. He exemplified the publishing industry's changes after the war. He was a high school dropout with a drinking problem, but he was brilliant and adventurous and he spotted talent early. Liveright began publishing Ezra Pound in 1920, and he brought out the first books of Hemingway, Faulkner and Dorothy Parker. Unlike everyone else, he advertised heavily, and his ads had testimonials from Hollywood stars and fonts that blared like billboards.

In the 1920s, publishing was close to the center of the nation's emerging celebrity culture, and Liveright had a hand in putting it there. He invented the book-launch party. Well-known authors could expect to draw crowds, and Boni & Liveright authors—like grumpy Theodore Dreiser and wild man Eugene O'Neill—blended seamlessly in an office that buzzed with actresses, showmen and bootleggers. The office's cocktail parties started in the early afternoon. Tommy Smith, the editor-in-chief, knew everyone in town—actors, philanthropists and brothel madams. He would mix Pernod with eye-watering bootleg liquor so strong that the rim of sugar on the glass would barely help you choke it down. Arthur Pell, the accountant, gave Horace Liveright false account statements and hoped that dire numbers would curb his lavish expenditures. Boni & Liveright was a company without brakes.

The vice president was twenty-four years old. Bennett Cerf was a wide-eyed newcomer, and the excitement of Boni & Liveright was exactly what he had hoped to find in the publishing world. After graduating from Columbia in 1919, he became a stockbroker on Wall Street, but he always wanted to be in publishing, and when a college friend, Richard Simon, left Boni & Liveright to start his own publishing house with Max Schuster, Simon claimed he could get Cerf's foot in the door.

Liveright didn't want Bennett Cerf for his business experience. He wanted him for his money. Cerf's mother, an heir to a tobacco fortune, died when he was sixteen and left him $125,000. On top of that, Cerf had made a small fortune speculating in the stock market, and Liveright needed more capital. The company wasn't keeping up with its royalty payments, and Liveright was financing a Broadway play he was producing (one of his bad gambles). When he met Cerf in 1923, he told the young man there was room for rapid advancement. "If you'd like to start with style, you could put a little money into the business." For a $25,000 loan, Bennett Cerf began his publishing career as the stylish vice president of Boni & Liveright.

To Cerf, Boni & Liveright meant the Modern Library, the imprint he associated with books like *Moby-Dick* and *The Scarlet Letter* that he had discovered in college. The Modern Library was Albert Boni's idea. He and Liveright wanted to put together an inexpensive series by cutting the costs of publication rights, and Boni's solution was to merge copyright-free classics with second-run editions of quality books whose sales had flagged and whose rights could be acquired for a bargain. Among the first twelve Modern Library books in 1917 (which included works by Rudyard Kipling, Friedrich Nietzsche, Oscar Wilde and Robert Louis Stevenson), only four of the writers were living, and most of the titles had no American copyright. They looked for titles with the potential to sell in small, steady numbers for years. As it turned out, there were plenty. After the war, their retail prices soared from sixty to ninety-five cents per copy, and yet the Modern Library remained one of readers' most economical options. By the mid-1920s, the series was the backbone of Boni & Liveright's profits.

When Cerf started his new job, Liveright was ignoring the Modern Library to focus on potential best sellers written by headline-producing authors. Zane Grey, Peter Kyne and Arthur Stuart-Menteth Hutchinson—you couldn't beat authors like that. The series became less interesting over time. When Liveright halfheartedly tried to acquire Joyce's *Portrait* after refusing to publish *Ulysses*, John Quinn balked. *A Portrait* was too modern. Being on the Modern Library's list, Quinn said, was a sign of a writer's decay, "a declension into the sunset preceding the dark night of literary extinction." Liveright was insulted. He reminded Quinn that the Modern Library included some outstanding contemporary authors: Max Beerbohm, Gustav Frenssen, Andreas Latzko and Arthur Schnitzler. That list made John Quinn's point exactly.

BENNETT CERF BECAME the imprint's de facto editor, and it wasn't long before he began thinking about owning it. He had his chance sooner than he expected. In May 1925, Cerf booked a trip to London and Paris for his twenty-sixth birthday. It was, as he wrote in his diary, "a trip I've dreamed of for years." Before he left, Horace Liveright met Cerf at a midtown speakeasy. Liveright had a few drinks beforehand, and he was nervously clenching his scotch. As Cerf recalled it, Liveright's father-in-law was breathing down his neck because he owed him portion of the seed money for the publishing house. Liveright had a few mistresses he liked to pamper, and he was apparently worried about what a disgruntled father-in-law might use as blackmail. "Oh, how I'd like to pay him off and get rid of him."

"One very easy way to pay him off," Cerf said, "is to sell me the Modern Library." Cerf expected Liveright to laugh and continue griping, but instead he asked, "What will you give me for it?" When the other executives found out that Liveright had made a deal to sell their primary source of steady income while half drunk at a speakeasy, they were livid. Liveright insisted that he was selling the list at its peak (it sold 275,000 copies in 1925), and Cerf had to fight an entire committee to keep his deal alive and sign the contract before his ship disembarked at one in the morning. In the end, Liveright prevailed, and the Modern Library belonged to Bennett Cerf.

They agreed on two hundred thousand dollars, the highest price ever paid for a reprint series. The only problem was that Cerf didn't have the money, and the contract required him to have it in three weeks, as soon as he returned from his trip. With time running out before his departure, Cerf called up a Columbia friend, Donald Klopfer, who hated working at his father's diamond-cutting business. Cerf offered to put up the remainder of his inheritance if Donald could find the other half of Liveright's price.

"Where the hell am I going to get a hundred thousand dollars?"

"That's your problem," Cerf said, "but it's got to be in cash."

Bennett Cerf and Donald Klopfer set up an office of six people in a loft building on Forty-fifth Street. Their desks faced each other, and they shared a secretary, as they would for years to come. Where Cerf was a charismatic deal maker, Klopfer was fastidious and patient—Cerf thought of him as "one of the nicest men that ever lived." They worked on the Modern Library nonstop for two years, personally visiting booksellers along the eastern seaboard, finding new buyers, redesigning the covers, the bindings, the colophon, everything. They added a new title to their catalog every month, including works by Ibsen and Joyce in 1926. While the catalog was more adventurous, the Modern Library as a whole became substantially *older*. The list doubled in ten years because it was growing in both directions.

But Cerf and Klopfer wanted more than backlist titles. They wanted a publishing house that would acquire new manuscripts just like Boni & Liveright. They were kicking around a modest version of their idea in front of Rockwell Kent, a celebrated commercial artist, when Cerf suddenly said he had a name for it. "We just said we were going to publish a few books on the side at random. Let's call it Random House."

Kent loved the name, and he drew the humble house colophon that would eventually adorn millions of books all over the world. In its first years, Random House tapped into the burgeoning market for expensive limited editions by reprinting deluxe versions of Modern Library books. Melville's *Moby-Dick* and Voltaire's *Candide* could be illustrated, printed on high-quality paper, expensively bound, numbered in lots of a thousand and signed by the translator or a well-known illustrator like Kent. The luxury editions would sell to book collectors at a dramatic markup—Sylvia Beach's strategy for the first edition of *Ulysses* became a new business model. What began as a way for dirty books to elude the police was, during the boom years of Wall Street, a mainstay of the publishing industry.

By 1929, Random House had issued dozens of deluxe limited editions. Their 1929 edition of Walt Whitman's *Leaves of Grass* sold out immediately at one hundred dollars per copy. Yet even then, Cerf and Klopfer were unaware of how advantageous their position was. When the stock market crashed, the Modern Library catalog of ninety-five-cent classics not only carried Random House through the Depression, it helped them increase their market share. They sold a million books in 1930 (four times their first year's sales) and turned a profit every year. The company that Cerf and Klopfer bought for two hundred thousand dollars was sold in 1965 for forty million.

THE MODERN LIBRARY dominated the market before the paperback revolution in the 1950s because it thrived on making prestige accessible. Cerf advertised it as "a collection of the most significant, interesting and thought-provoking books in modern literature." The pitch was tailored to the country's changing readership. College enrollment in the United States doubled every decade from 1890 to 1930, and students typically bought the inexpensive but durable Modern Library editions for their classes. But it wasn't just the number of college students. It was the way they read. When Cerf was at Columbia, the Great Books movement was incubating in the university's English department. Professors like John Erskine envisioned a two-year survey of the Western canon that, when it was instituted in 1920, the university described as a "Reading of Masterpieces of literature in poetry, history, philosophy and science." The reading list included works from Homer, Plato, Dante and Shakespeare. This sounds like typical fare, but having biology students read masterpieces outside of literature's disciplinary constraints (and there were plenty) was not something universities generally did before 1920.

Erskine's idea was to "treat the *Iliad*, the *Odyssey*, and other masterpieces as though they were recent publications"—they transcended centuries and bore directly upon contemporary lives. Masterpieces showed readers that the chaos of modern life was a part of the larger pattern of human civilization. The Great Books movement was, in other words, a syllabized version of *Ulysses*. Both within and beyond universities, people began thinking that certain books illuminated eternal features of the human condition. They didn't demand expertise—one didn't need to speak classical Greek or read all of Plato to benefit from *The Republic*—all they demanded was, as Erskine put it, "a comfortable chair and a good light." Bennett Cerf absorbed the ethos of reading great books as contemporary texts during his college years, and he was inspired by a freshman course on contemporary British authors (Rudyard Kipling, Arnold Bennett and H. G. Wells), which extended the great literary continuum to the present. The Modern Library catalog was, to some extent, an homage to Cerf's undergraduate education.

And so much the better. For the Modern Library provided a ready-made curriculum for a generation of upwardly mobile people who were either nostalgic for their college years or who wanted the cultivation that college offered— people like Bennett Cerf and Horace Liveright themselves. The Modern Library offered commodified prestige with the illusion of self-reliance. Readers could have the benefits of institutional culture without the institutions. They could rise above the masses by purchasing a dozen inexpensive books. Cerf changed the Modern Library's colophon from a cowled monk working at his desk to a lithe body leaping in the air with a torch held high. Reading classics wasn't about scholarship. It was about freedom and the promise that the individual's light could illuminate the world.

The prestige of reading great books appealed to a postwar population that was anxious about the future of Western civilization and liable to think of itself as the bearer of that civilization. American readers wanted to imagine contemporary American writers entering the Western canon just as the country was emerging onto the world stage. The Modern Library was where William

Faulkner, Dorothy Parker and Sherwood Anderson rubbed shoulders with Aeschylus, Milton and Cervantes. The catalog managed to make literature both cosmopolitan and patriotic.

None of this was planned. The Modern Library had begun as a gimmick. In 1915, Albert Boni sent a tiny copy of *Romeo and Juliet* bound in imitation leather to Whitman's Chocolates and suggested they include the tragic love story in each of their boxes. Whitman's placed an order for fifteen thousand copies. Tiny books were a novelty item, and when Boni realized he could sell the books without the chocolate he began retailing his Little Leather Library at Woolworth's for twenty-five cents (a set of thirty cost $2.98). He went into business with Liveright in 1917, and together they expanded the series, augmented the format, raised the price and began calling it the Modern Library. By 1930, the series was selling over a million books a year.

Bennett Cerf saw Boni's innovation through the prism of a Great Books program. What united the list wasn't the low cost of acquiring publishing rights. It was the books' shared modern spirit. "Most of the books have been written in the past thirty years," Cerf's catalog claimed, and the older ones "are so essentially modern, that the publishers feel they are properly embraced in the scope and aim of the series." Old or new, their books were "modern classics."

The concept was brilliant. Bennett Cerf used the word *modern* to evoke a way of thinking, a continuity with a global tradition. A reader could buy a modern classic decades after it was originally published, and it would still be up-to-date—it was always a good time to buy. Modernism's dicta—that writers respond to one another across nations and centuries, that artists renew ancient forms, that classics are being written as we speak—were folded into the modern classics brand. Bennett Cerf turned modernism into a marketing strategy. Pound, Joyce and Eliot didn't want to acquiesce to the mass market, but Bennett Cerf found ways to make the market acquiesce to them.

WHAT WAS SO STRANGE about publishing at the time was that the passage between prestige and prison was so narrow. Alfred Knopf faced criminal charges in court before he became more careful. Liveright and Huebsch were explicitly trying to avoid the disturbing prospect of prison when they refused to publish *Ulysses*. In New York, the penitentiary was on Welfare Island (formerly Blackwell's Island) with the Smallpox Hospital and a psychiatric institution. The corridors were designed to make prisoners feel powerless. Iron bars enclosing the catwalks along the cellblock tiers drew the prisoner's eye upward to a ceiling as distant as the nave of a cathedral. The cell doors had crosshatched metal slats and locks the size of mailboxes. In 1928 a man named Samuel Roth sat in one of those cells and plotted ways to continue building his publishing empire.

Roth shoveled coal in the South Prison House Gang, and in his unpublished memoirs he recalled how the other men laughed when they heard he was a publisher.

"You came here in a wagon, didn't you?"

"Is there any other way to get here?"

"You really don't know! You should've seen the way Mae West came here last year. You must be a very small publisher."

By anyone's estimate, Samuel Roth was the biggest literary pirate of the 1920s. He produced and distributed unauthorized editions of illegal and semilegal books, which, at the time, was a highly competitive business. He trafficked mostly in racy titles from Europe—*School Life in Paris*, *Only a Boy*, *The Russian Princess*. He printed them on cheap paper with cheaper bindings and sold them at inflated black market prices. When times were good (and the 1920s were very good) his system of pseudonyms and underground presses made him more than seven hundred dollars a week in Chicago alone. And it wasn't just smut. Samuel Roth ripped off everyone—George Bernard Shaw, Aldous Huxley and André Gide, to name a few. Roth was a pirate with excellent taste. He found his niche in the publishing world by combining his love for cutting-edge modernist literature and salacious pulp. When he stole a fragment of T. S. Eliot's *Sweeney Agonistes* he chose it at least partly for the appeal of Eliot's working title, *Wanna Go Home, Baby?*

Roth's biggest successes were counterfeit versions of *Lady Chatterley's Lover* and *Ulysses*, and he read Joyce eagerly in the pages of *The Little Review*.

He thought of *Dubliners* as an earnest character study and *A Portrait* as bizarre and unfinished with flashes of brilliance. But in *Ulysses* he saw, as he put it later, "a portrait of the metamorphoses of all men in one, of all nations in one, of all cities in one, and of all days in one Dublin day." He admired Joyce's novel so much he decided to steal it.

The best part about literary piracy was that in many cases it wasn't illegal. An English-language book didn't have American copyright protection unless it was printed on plates manufactured in the United States. All Roth needed to do was reprint British and European titles that hadn't yet found American publishers. Roth preferred to work in legal gray areas. Sometimes he obtained the author's permission to reprint their work, and on a few occasions he paid them nominal sums. But authorization didn't make the dirty books any less dirty, and he served time in at least five different prisons over twenty-five years.

Roth sold his first pornographic book in 1919. He opened up a small bookshop on Eighth Street called the New York Poetry Book Shop, which was a large room in an apartment building's basement with a window peeking out just above street level. Roth stayed open until midnight, and he never advertised. His bookshop was unremarkable for Greenwich Village, but with a few dozen reliable patrons, he figured he could eke out a living doing what he loved. He scoured Manhattan for hidden gems and secondhand books to build his inventory, and he eventually discovered a shop in a Park Avenue basement run by a lanky old man who was a connoisseur of contemporary poetry and pornography. Roth visited the old man's shop regularly until he found it padlocked. The old bookseller was serving ninety days on Welfare Island for selling a copy of John Cleland's *Fanny Hill* to an undercover agent, so Roth sent him two dollars a week for the duration of his sentence.

When the old man was released, he left the country and repaid Roth's generosity with a package from Paris containing several illicit books bound in paper with false titles on the covers. Roth got scared and stuffed them in a bookcase behind expensive first editions that no one ever ventured to purchase. He remained anxious about the stash until an editor on Christopher Street offered him five dollars for each one. When the editor said he'd pay the same price for similar books, Roth began asking the old man for more. After a few transactions, he made $130. This was how selling books could make a man rich.

When peddling armloads of banned books wasn't enough, Samuel Roth began printing them himself. He wanted to be a major presence in the publishing world, and he saw an opening in the risqué material that American publishers wouldn't touch—an entire market wasn't being served. But because he didn't have enough capital to break into the book industry, he began casting about for alternatives. Two business models were doing well at the time: deluxe limited editions of books that couldn't circulate openly and glossy magazines like *Vogue, Smart Set* and *Vanity Fair.* Roth decided to combine them. In the mid-1920s, he started a magazine called *Two Worlds Quarterly*, which spawned *Two Worlds Monthly* and *Casanova Jr's Tales.*

They were limited-edition magazines sent to subscribers via railroad express instead of the Post Office. Works by Lewis Carroll, Boccaccio and Chekhov appeared alongside tepid erotica. Evelyn Waugh woodcuts shared space with cartoonish drawings of buxom nudes beset by goblins or draped over the giant craniums of warlocks. Issues of some of Roth's magazines cost three to five dollars—more than the typical newsstand price of twenty-five or fifty cents but less than the ten to twelve dollars that Knopf and Liveright charged for private editions of *Painted Veils* or *A Story-Teller's Holiday.* Roth found a new price point. To bolster his empire, he launched his own glossy magazine complete with photographs and a fashionable Art Deco cover. He called it *Beau*, and it was the nation's first men's magazine.

Roth thought *Beau* would be his entrée into the legitimate publishing world, but it was expensive to produce, and he needed money to give it time to consolidate its position on the newsstands. He ran full-page ads in *Two Worlds* to find investors: "Mr. Roth Is Building the Most Powerful Magazine Group in America." When investors were not persuaded, Roth decided to peddle a reprint edition of Cheikh Nefzaoui's *The Perfumed Garden*, which described 237 positions of "the sweet recreation," as the translator phrased it. Roth knew he could find a thousand readers willing to pay thirty dollars a copy, and that would finance *Beau* for a year.

In 1927 two Post Office inspectors arrested Roth just days after he mailed his advertisements for *The Perfumed Garden*. Because it was his first offense, the judge fined him five hundred dollars and gave him two years' probation, but Roth's biggest problem was that he was now an entry in John Sumner's records. Anthony Comstock had taught Sumner about the economy of vice hunting: finding a smut peddler was a costly investment, but once found, he would yield multiple arrests. Four months after Roth's trial, Sumner walked into his bookshop with three detectives and a search warrant. The officers found a packet of obscene drawings they had been looking for and had no trouble uncovering indecent books when they searched the premises.

In court, Roth testified that the drawings had been planted by one of Sumner's men. The assistant DA needed to ask just one question: hadn't the defendant already pleaded guilty for advertising *The Perfumed Garden*? When Samuel Roth admitted he had, he was treated as a repeat offender violating federal probation. And that's when he was sentenced to three months in the prison workhouse on Welfare Island. By the end of 1928 what had seemed like a nascent publishing empire had evaporated. For by the time he was hauled off to Welfare Island, Samuel Roth was also the object of an unprecedented international protest.

ROTH HAD BEEN THINKING about *Ulysses* since the *Little Review* trial in 1921, and in 1922 he wrote a letter to Joyce about his plans for *Two Worlds*. "Among other things, we shall try to publish a novel complete in every issue," Roth wrote. He wanted to begin *Two Worlds* with one of Joyce's novels (hopefully *Ulysses*, though he didn't say it) and promised Joyce one hundred dollars and 15 percent of the titanic issue's sales.

Roth designed extravagant letterhead stationery with a descriptive header of his magazine's goal: to "serve established writers as the organ of their opinion and as a refuge from their persecutor." The complete description spilled down the sides of the page and managed to inflate Roth's already grand ambitions: "Every issue will contain a complete novel, a play, a short story, verse, and reviews of the books and plays of the period." Miss Weaver politely declined the offer on Joyce's behalf. She joked to Sylvia Beach that he must have been planning to use a font "the size of a needle's head."

But Roth wouldn't take no for an answer. He wrote to Ezra Pound in June 1922 both to acquire the rights to *Ulysses* (as Joyce's *Little Review* editor) and to secure Pound himself as a contributor. While Joyce virtually ignored Roth, Pound burst forth with a list of advice for the *Two Worlds* editor. He had some suitable poems, translations and an article for the magazine, and he suggested not only a potential art editor but also the artists *Two Worlds* should feature in the first five issues.

Little did Pound know, he was entering Roth's twilight world in which suggestions became verbal contracts. Writers offering advice found themselves listed as "contributing editors" of a magazine they had never seen. When Pound told Roth that he approved of any scheme that could circumvent the Comstock Act, Roth took this as permission to publish Joyce's work in full. To make his claim marginally more legitimate, Roth gave a check and four promissory notes totaling one thousand dollars to a lawyer and instructed him to hold them until Joyce officially gave *Two Worlds* permission to publish *Ulysses*. The eight hundred dollars in notes could be redeemed, cashed, Roth said, just as soon as he had enough money in his account. In 1925, four years after his first flash of inspiration, Roth published the first issue of *Two Worlds*. Ezra Pound threatened to sue when he saw his name on the cover, at which point Roth offered to pay him fifty dollars per issue. He would publish his poems or one of his characteristic screeds. "Make it as long as you like. Every word shall be held precious."

In July 1926, Roth started printing episodes of *Ulysses*—and he began cutting the offensive passages. He omitted references to urination, masturbation and gonorrhea. He changed "the grey sunken cunt of the world" to "the grey sunken crater." When a newspaper man shouts out, "He can kiss my royal Irish arse," *Two Worlds* politely substituted, "my royal Irish aunt." Roth did his best to appease the vice societies. Like so many other publishers before him, he tried to persuade John Sumner about his earnest intentions. He wanted to use the illicit aura of *Ulysses* to sell magazines, but he didn't want to go to jail.

His legal problems began to mount, however, when Hemingway told Sylvia Beach the details of Roth's piracy. One night in 1926, Roth met with Hemingway at a New York café while he was in town trying to sell a few short stories. Hemingway's rare silence (he showed up with a swollen jaw) gave Roth the chance to brag. *Two Worlds* had eight thousand subscribers, he said, and the backbone of the publication was James Joyce. Roth figured Joyce's name could lower Hemingway's price, but they never reached an agreement (Roth printed his short stories anyway).

At some point, the rumored number of *Two Worlds* subscribers went as high as fifty thousand, which suggested tens of thousands of dollars in lost profits, and yet Shakespeare and Company couldn't sue Roth for copyright violations, which came as a surprise. John Quinn told everyone that, as disastrous as *The Little Review* was, it had secured the American copyright over the portions of *Ulysses* printed in New York. Quinn was wrong in at least two different ways. Judges might simply refuse to enforce the copyright of obscene works, and even if a judge enforced copyright for *The Little Review*, that protection wouldn't extend to the serialized *Ulysses* episodes because individual portions of a magazine as a whole did. Beyond this, *Ulysses* had no copyright protection in 1926 because U.S. law required any English-language book to be printed on American-manufactured plates within (at most) six months of the initial publication. Since there was no American edition, *Ulysses* had fallen into the public domain while its reviews were still hitting the newstands. Samuel Roth could reprint, bowdlerize, alter and mutilate all he wished. As far as the U.S. government was concerned, nobody owned *Ulysses*.

Quinn was wrong about copyright, but he was right about literary pirates: legal action against them was futile. Pound told Joyce that he could either denounce Roth in print or "organize a gang of gunmen to scare Roth out of his pants. I don't imagine anything but physical terror works in a case of this sort (with a strong pull of avarice, bidding him to be BOLD)." Because Sylvia Beach couldn't sue for copyright violations (and because gunmen were not exactly her style), she had to be creative. After threatening a $500,000 lawsuit, she had the New York Supreme Court issue an injunction preventing Roth from using the name James Joyce in any of his ads or publications.

But that wasn't enough. Beach asked two of her friends (a novelist and a lawyer) to write up a formal protest against Roth's unauthorized version of *Ulysses*. If she couldn't stop the piracy through legal channels, she would ostracize Samuel Roth from the world of letters. Beach thought a public protest would ensure that no author gave him material, that no editor provided him advertising space and that no ethical book buyer patronized publishers who stole from the writers they loved. The protest declared that Samuel Roth was stealing James Joyce's property in the United States while publishing a bowdlerized and corrupted version of the text. He was both a thief and a butcher.

Shame was the protest's only weapon, and Beach wanted it to be as powerful as possible. She tracked down the addresses of writers all over Europe and mailed each of them a personal letter asking them to support the protest with their signature. The response was overwhelming. Many of the writers were victims of piracy themselves, and no one had launched a concerted international protest against the outright theft of writers' work. Beach gathered 167 signatures, a compendium of Europe's prominent writers. Yeats, Woolf and Hemingway. Thomas Mann, E. M. Forster, Luigi Pirandello, Mina Loy, H. G. Wells, Rebecca West, Jules Romains, W. Somerset Maugham. Even George Bernard Shaw agreed to sign. Joyce was especially pleased to see the signature of Albert Einstein. Beach sent the signed protest to nine hundred publications in the United States alone.

When the protest hit the papers in February 1927 (Beach made sure the first notices were published on Joyce's birthday), letters of support poured into Shakespeare and Company. Many of them were seething with anger. "The thought of such an outrageous business makes me ill," one fan wrote. "I cannot express my detestation of these people. . . . What the world needs today is a new *poison*, something to destroy the virus that has made these weaklings strong but oh how malignant!" *Two Worlds* subscribers were caught off guard. "If you are what I consider morally guilty of pirating *Ulysses*," one subscriber wrote, "so far as I should care you might suffer hanging in a noose." Roth tried to fight back in the press, but it was too late. Post Office inspectors, acting in what Roth called "a forceful advisory capacity," made sure that the express companies wouldn't touch his publications. The sales of *Two Worlds, Beau* and *Casanova Jr's Tales* plummeted, and booksellers removed them from the stands.

One gets the sense that with a bit more compunction and a bit less savvy, Samuel Roth could have spent the late 1920s developing his idiosyncratic mix of high modernism and sexploitation (a sort of arched middlebrow) instead of languishing in a prison cell ten bricks wide and fourteen and a half bricks long. His toilet was a white bucket sitting on a page of *The New York Times*. Roth had to explain his absence to his nine- and ten-year-old children. "My lovely and valiant babies," he wrote. "I am compelled, by mysterious reasons of state, to stay away from home a little longer." He wrote to his son that faithfulness to the best books was the only thing he would need in life: "learn to love them, read them to yourself over and over again, so that not only the stories but the paragraphs, sentences and even words become familiar to you."

The money could not have made piracy worth what he lost. Though there were moments of prosperity, the business was risky and erratic. Roth wanted an empire for reasons that went deeper than money. In 1913, when he was nineteen years old, Roth had spent his days reading in the New York Public Library and his nights sleeping in parks or tenement alleyways. At Columbia, he edited a poetry magazine called *The Lyric* and met a girl named Anna during the war. She lived with her family in Brooklyn, and Roth would go to her house at night, climb up to her room on the second floor and sit down beside her as she lay in bed. He read her Keats, Shelley and Swinburne. Sometimes he read his own poetry. Eventually, Anna told him that she had reservations about his four-dollar-a-week life. Roth remembered how she said that things could have been different if he had made forty dollars a week. She ended up marrying a dentist who made eighty dollars a week.

Roth ensconced himself in poetry's higher calling and saved what little money he had to publish the thin book of poems that Anna had rejected for dentistry. He called it *First Offering*. Since poetry would never pay the bills, selling books became the only thing that made him happy. Prominent writers and publishers visited Roth's bookshop, and he could claim to be acquainted with Max Eastman, Ben Huebsch, Thomas Seltzer and Mina Loy. Roth wasn't famous in New York's literary circles, but he had a presence. John Quinn heard of him as a "nut poet" and figured he was "either a fool or a wild man." Roth sent poetry and nonfiction manuscripts to Harcourt, Dutton and other reputable publishers, all of whom sent rejection letters. In 1921, Leonard Woolf wrote to inform Mr. Roth, regretfully, that Hogarth Press's publication list was already too full to accept additional contributions.

If only he knew that the Woolfs had also rejected *Ulysses*. Around the time he was trying to get published—and two days before the *Little Review* trial began—Roth wrote Joyce a fan letter. "Of all the writers in Europe today you have made the most intimate appeal to me." Before sending the letter off, he jotted down a belated question: "Why is not ULYSSES in book form yet?"

A READER COULD HAVE been proud to own a copy of *Ulysses* in 1929. The book's front matter indicated that it was the 1927 Shakespeare and Company printing. This was the ninth printing of Joyce's book, and it was still hard to come by. Most of the people who had a copy had gone to Paris to get it, but this one was behind the counter or hidden deep in the back room of a trusted bookstore like the Gotham Bookmart. It cost about ten dollars, more expensive than any other item on the average reader's shelf, but a bargain nonetheless. It had the famous solid blue cover, and it said DIJON.—DARANTIERE at the bottom of the last page, just where it should be.

But if you knew what to look for, you could tell something was wrong. The blue cover was just a shade darker than it should have been. The font seemed right, but the italicized words were noticeably different from Sylvia Beach's copies. The paper was smoother and slightly heavier. The margins were wider. It was about as thick as a Paris copy, but just a bit too narrow and long. The cover had no fold-overs for the bookbinder to insert the hardcover boards, and the binding looked like it would fall apart after one complete reading. The page listing James Joyce's other works was missing, and the page that noted his other publishers had the first of many typos: "Jonthan Cape." And then there was the spine: the author and title were printed clearly on the Shakespeare and Company edition, but this spine was blank.

Samuel Roth was no longer bothering with magazines. When he emerged from his first stint in prison in 1929, he entered the business of pirating books, and his counterfeit version of the 1927 printing of *Ulysses* wasn't bad. Roth oversaw the details and paid the Loewinger Brothers on Seventeenth Street to reset the type, which meant that if anyone's edition of *Ulysses* was going to have copyright in the United States, it would be his—it was the perfect revenge against "Sylvia Bitch," as he began calling her.

Prison and literary ostracism darkened Roth's perspective. Publishers seemed to be nothing but a syndicate of unscrupulous capitalists who didn't give a shit about literature. He, on the other hand, was brave. Where profiteers like Knopf and Liveright folded under the pressure of the New York Society for the Suppression of Vice, Roth saw himself as an unstoppable outlaw for artistic expression. No one else had the nerve to present books like *Ulysses* to the American public.

In the wake of his Welfare Island sentence and Sylvia Beach's protest, Roth took his business off the street, out of the press and far from any U.S. Post Office. He separated his business office from the warehouse holding his illegal inventory. His "publishing house" changed names and printers frequently, and he moved his family at a moment's notice. Selling pirated books in bulk meant that the bookshops assumed most of the risk, sweating each individual sale long after he disappeared—if he ever appeared at all. Enterprising book-leggers hired salesmen to walk door to door with briefcases or drive around to bookstores in a plain truck. The driver would walk into a shop, ask how many copies of *Aphrodite* or *Married Love* they wanted, rummage through the back of the truck and hand them over for half the retail price (cash only). The next time the truck came around, the driver would be different.

Samuel Roth had become especially elusive after he was released from prison, so when the NYSSV wanted to nab him again, they got to him through his brother. In October 1929, Max Roth was going door to door on lower Broadway with a briefcase packed with samples of obscene books, and he had the misfortune of trying to sell his wares to one of Sumner's vice society allies. When Max returned to the man's office at an appointed time the following afternoon, John Sumner, a police officer and a Post Office inspector were pretending to work in the adjacent office, and they casually ambled over in the middle of Max's sales pitch. Larry, the officer, purchased *Ulysses*, *Lady Chatterley's Lover* and *Fanny Hill* for sixty dollars, and as soon as money changed hands Max was promptly arrested. When they discovered that he was Samuel Roth's brother, the trail led to the Golden Hind Press on Fifth Avenue, where the vice hunters caught Samuel and one of his salesmen with three hundred dirty books.

But that wasn't all. Max happened to be carrying a large set of keys, and after Sumner found a lease in his name, they went to the Fifth Avenue address listed on the document and unlocked the door. It was a warehouse stocked with advertising materials, facilities for packaging and shipping inventory across the country and thousands of books—mostly *Lady Chatterley's Lover* and pirated copies of *Ulysses*. Because they didn't have a search warrant, a police officer stood guard at the warehouse overnight to secure the evidence.

Max Roth was sentenced to a prison term of six months to three years for his involvement in the nationwide Joyce piracy, and Samuel was back in jail less than a year after he left. When he was released six months later, a detective was waiting at the prison gate with another warrant for his arrest. Roth was extradited to Pennsylvania, where he was convicted for selling *Ulysses* yet again. After serving six months for Joyce's book in New York, he served three more in Philadelphia. And even then he didn't stop.

SAMUEL ROTH WAS modernism's doppelgänger. Like Margaret Anderson, he wanted a daring magazine devoted to art's supremacy. He insisted it was the artist's "right to have his creations printed and judged by the standards of literature alone and by none other." Like Ezra Pound, he wanted to bring far-flung writers together—the *Two Worlds* title referred to the connectedness of the Old World and the New.

And Roth was more than a bit like Bennett Cerf. Both were Columbia classmates in 1916, and neither was a traditional student. Roth had a one-year scholarship and never graduated. Cerf never received a high school degree but edged his way into the College from the School of Journalism, which didn't require the foreign language credits he didn't have. Both men left Columbia with an insider's respect for institutional culture and an outsider's desire to transform it, and they both claimed to be democratizing literature. Roth duplicated Cerf's Modern Library pitch when he insisted his magazines were "the only vehicle for the expression of the many artists who would otherwise reach only a very limited public."

And yet while the pirate was devoted to his wife and children, the esteemed publisher had slightly less regard for matrimony. For years, Bennett Cerf scheduled trysts in his little black books as "Deals"—"Deal at Midnight" (April 22), "Deal Maria" (December 8), "deal with Marian" (May 13). He had deals on April 29 and 30, May 5, 6, 13, 14, 28 and June 4. These were all weekends. He sent telegrams to various women—Rosamond ("you heavenly creature"), Francine ("Overwhelmed by your pulchritude Please rush rear view"), Marie ("Adoring and sex starved residents demand date of your return"). There were several telegrams to a woman named Marian. "Missing you darling" and "Cant wait" and "Thinking of you and missing you Love Bennett." Marian was Marian Klopfer, Donald Klopfer's wife.

Roth was not as sordid as that. He was candid with his desires. He wanted to be a staunch individualist, a literary crusader, and he wanted, like Joyce, to be loved. Roth wanted the prestige of James Joyce and Ezra Pound. He wanted their names listed beneath his own as the editor of *Two Worlds*. In a way, he did it for the letterhead. Unlike others craving prestige, however, Roth was willing to steal for it. Margaret Anderson drew inspiration from the dozens of contributors she published. Pound and Eliot recycled old poetry to make it new. Joyce accepted patronage, asked for favors and money and incorporated the work of scores of other writers to create his novels. And yet they all had a keen understanding of the debts they owed to others, both living and dead. Roth, on the other hand, thought individualism meant that everything permanent and universal belonged to him and that a cultural rebellion was an opportunity to build an empire. As much as he admired Joyce, he was a poor student of *Ulysses*.

24.

TREPONEMA

———

Joyce spent the years after *Ulysses* tunneling into a denser, more obscure novel. *Finnegans Wake* is written in the weltering language of dreams. Words spill out of definitions and syntax like a river breaking the banks, and puns are as destructive as they are playful. Joyce felt as if he had arrived at the end of the English language.

> All the world's in want and is writing a letters. A letters from a person to a place about a thing. And all the world's on wish to be carrying a letters. A letters to a king about a treasure from a cat. When men want to write a letters. Ten men, ton men, pen men, pun men, wont to rise a ladder. And den men, dun men, fen men, fun men, hen men, hun men wend to raze a leader.

This is one of the more lucid passages. *Finnegans Wake* kept Nora up at night. "Jim is writing at his book," she told a friend. "I go to bed and then that man sits in the next room and continues laughing about his own writing." She would get out of bed and pound on the door, "Now, Jim, stop writing or stop laughing."

Almost no one liked *Finnegans Wake*. When Ezra Pound first read a portion in 1926, he replied, "I make nothing of it whatever. Nothing so far as I make out, nothing short of divine vision or a new cure for the clapp can possibly be worth all the circumambient peripherization." The letter's deepest insult was Pound's salutation ("Dear Jim"). Even Miss Weaver disapproved. "I do not care much for the output from your Wholesale Safety Pun Factory," she confided, "nor for the darkness and the unintelligibilities of your deliberately-entangled language system. It seems to me you are wasting your genius." By the time Miss Weaver confessed her disapproval, Joyce had been wasting his genius for five years. "It is possible Pound is right," Joyce wrote in February 1927, "but I cannot go back." He would continue writing *Finnegans Wake* for twelve more years.

Joyce was being undone by his virtues. His concentration and single-mindedness deepened his isolation. His defiant egoism became self-absorption, and his writing lost the balance of concealment and revelation. For seventeen years, he kept the title of *Finnegans Wake* a secret, and his favorite game was having people try to guess what it was—writing became camouflage. His devotion to his work meant that everyone in his life became instruments for his literary purposes, and the instruments, in the end, became demoralizing crutches. Joyce was fully dependent upon Miss Weaver's patronage after *Ulysses*, and the censorship bans didn't help. In 1923, following Joyce's surgery, she gave him another capital gift of £12,000, bringing her total endowment to £20,500 (equivalent to more than £1 million today). The interest gave Joyce £850 per year after taxes (more than £40,000 today). But it was never enough. In 1927, Joyce began to divest small amounts from the principal, reducing his earnings each time. When the Depression hit, he began withdrawing more.

The qualities that made Joyce an excellent writer made him a ruthless human being, and Sylvia Beach may have suffered the most. There were letters to write, bills to pay, books to retrieve, requests for medications, advances needed on printings of *Ulysses* that were still months away. When the Roth piracy began, it wasn't enough that she organized an unprecedented global protest on his behalf. He wanted her to go to the United States to stop it herself. Beach endured his requests gracefully, but in the midst of the *Two Worlds* piracy, she got an unexpected bill for £200, and the dam finally broke. "The truth is that as my affection and admiration for you are unlimited," she wrote to Joyce, "so is the work you pile on my shoulders. When you are absent, every word I receive from you is an order. The reward for my unceasing labour on your behalf is to see you tie yourself into a bowknot and hear you complain." He gave her work mercilessly, as if he were testing how much she could handle. "Is it human?"

A few months later, in June 1927, Beach's mother was arrested in Paris for ignoring a petty shoplifting charge, and when she was released on bail, she overdosed on digitalis. For the rest of her life, Sylvia Beach concealed the suicide from her father and sisters. She withdrew herself from the suit against Roth, and she began to pull away from Joyce's affairs.

JOYCE'S LIFE WAS FALLING APART. One of the reasons why *Finnegans Wake* was taking so long was that he was consumed by his daughter's increasingly troubled life. In 1932, on Joyce's fiftieth birthday, Lucia threw a chair at Nora. A few months later, after a party celebrating her engagement to a man she didn't love (she was in love with Samuel Beckett, who began visiting Joyce in 1929), Lucia became catatonic. She was diagnosed with schizophrenia, and it was the beginning of a life of mental institutions. Joyce long insisted there was nothing wrong with her, that her mysterious pronouncements were clairvoyant, and that she was the greater genius of the family. "Whatever spark or gift I possess has been transmitted to Lucia, and it has kindled a fire in her brain." She was creating her own language, he said, and he understood most of it. Joyce's idea of therapy was to buy her a fur coat, which was as ineffectual as her doctors' therapies (one suggested she drink seawater). During her second stay at an institution in 1932, Joyce smuggled her out. When he didn't visit her, she sent him messages: "Tell him I am a crossword puzzle, and if he does not mind seeing a crossword puzzle, he is to come out [to see me]." When the truth was unavoidable, he blamed himself.

Lucia's illness strained Joyce's relationship with Nora. His excesses and spendthrift ways had become more difficult for her to handle over the years, and their quarrels became so serious that she would threaten to leave him. One friend remembers helping Nora pack up her belongings while Joyce implored her not to go, claiming he simply couldn't manage without her, and his dependence upon her deepened as the prospect of life without her became more real. In 1928, when Nora was hospitalized for a two-week radiation treatment for uterine cancer, Joyce insisted on staying in the adjoining room. When she had a hysterectomy a few months later, he set up a bed next to hers so that he could be by her side through her recovery. She bore the illness better than he did. Joyce wrote to Miss Weaver during Nora's treatments to tell her that listening to the nurses shouting in the emergency room and the storms howling outside kept him up at night and irritated his already fraying nerves.

By the time he reached his late forties, Joyce was already an old man. The ashplant cane that he had used for swagger as a young bachelor in Dublin became a blind man's cane in Paris. Strangers helped him cross the street, and he bumped into furniture as he navigated through his own apartment. Nora had to put the milk and sugar in his tea for him, and he held on to her arm when they walked through the streets. He wouldn't visit Miss Weaver in 1931 because he thought the tinted glasses he was wearing made him look like he was disguising himself for committing some monstrous crime. "I deserve all this," he wrote to Miss Weaver, "on account of my many iniquities."

Joyce was not being histrionic. He was trying to confess. One had to peer closely to see the nature of his iniquities, but it was visible. Nestled in the folds of Joyce's irises were soft granulomatous lesions less than a millimeter wide, and inside those lesions were colonies of pale bacteria shaped like corkscrews that were coiling and lurching into his iris's muscles and fibers. The bacterium that invaded Joyce's eyes was called *Treponema pallidum*. James Joyce was going blind because he had syphilis.

THE BACTERIUM that causes syphilis wreaks havoc wherever it goes. The first lesion appears on the skin and heals after a few weeks, but *Treponema pallidum* searches for homes as it circulates through the bloodstream. The bacteria can inhabit blood vessels and bones, muscles and nerves. They can overrun the heart, the liver, the spinal cord or the brain. The versatility of the *Treponema* means that syphilis can cause an array of medical problems depending upon which organs it infests. Unlike other venereal diseases, syphilis can induce anything from arthritis and jaundice to aneurysms and epilepsy. But what struck a special fear in anyone who visited a prostitute and later discovered an unsightly lesion was the prospect of contracting "General Paralysis of the Insane." If syphilitic bacteria invaded the central nervous system, the result was potentially a syndrome of psychoses, delusions and erratic mood swings combined with either full or partial paralysis. Joyce grew up terrified of what syphilis could do to a person. He whispered the word *paralysis* to himself at night as if the sound itself evoked the shiver of a ghost story.

Syphilis has a particular affinity for the eyes. Joyce suffered from many infections associated with syphilis—conjunctivitis, episcleritis, blepharitis— but the most common and devastating ocular manifestation of syphilis is iritis. His eye attacks were recurrent because syphilis advances in waves of bacterial growth and dormancy. A sudden eye attack would abate in a merciful period of health only to yield to another attack. The symptoms, duration and severity of the disease vary dramatically from one individual to another—Nora almost certainly contracted it from Joyce, but her case may have been negligibly mild. Only a third of syphilitics endure all three stages of the disease. Joyce, unfortunately, was one of them. He suffered his first recorded attack of iritis in 1907, when he was only twenty-five years old, and he endured twelve more attacks over the next fourteen years. By the late 1920s, his eyes had been ravaged by a twenty-year infection.

Today, syphilis is cured by a shot of penicillin, which became available as a medication in 1942, the year after Joyce died. Before penicillin, there were few good options for an advanced case of syphilis, and it didn't help that Joyce was a difficult patient. He didn't follow orders, he skipped appointments, and he searched for the doctors who gave him the answers he wanted. Dr. Borsch did his best to appease Joyce when he began seeing him in 1922. To gain his consent for a sphincterectomy in 1923, Borsch told him it was just a minor procedure, though it was essentially the same as an iridectomy.

The larger problem was that Joyce refused to take a drug called salvarsan, the only available medication that could attack syphilis effectively. He had good reasons not to take it. Salvarsan was the trade name for a modified form of arsenic called arsphenamine, which was essentially a low dose of poison. Some patients died from it, and others fell deaf or lapsed into comas. For Joyce, salvarsan's gravest threat was something else. As a writer who refused to dictate his prose, he was desperate to keep what little he had of his eyesight to continue working, and Dr. Borsch was obliged to tell his patient that one of salvarsan's side effects could leave him blind: the drug damages the optic nerve in about one in forty patients. After Joyce refused salvarsan, Dr. Borsch had to resort to treatments that attacked symptoms rather than their underlying cause, and Joyce's eyes became steadily worse.

By 1928, Dr. Borsch must have been at his wits' end. Joyce walked into his clinic perilously underweight: at five foot ten he weighed less than 125 pounds. Seeing Joyce's weight loss, his bevy of eye infections, his uncommon fatigue and the "large boil," as he described it, on his right shoulder, Dr. Borsch desperately needed an alternative to salvarsan, an antisyphilitic treatment that would curtail the *Treponema* infestation destroying his patient's body without endangering his eyes.

He happened to know of one: an obscure French drug called galyl. Borsch probably remembered using galyl when he was a French military doctor during the war—the French army administered thousands of galyl shots to syphilitic soldiers because it was a patriotic substitute for the German-made salvarsan. Galyl was another modified form of arsenic—not arsphenamine but phospharsenamine, a chemical combination of arsenic and phosphorus. Separately, each element is highly poisonous. Together, they're less toxic than salvarsan. The more Dr. Borsch thought about it, the more he must have realized that galyl was Joyce's best option. There were no indications that the drug would harm his optic nerve, and one of galyl's side effects was fortunate: it improved a patient's appetite. It would help Joyce put on much-needed weight.

Because it was weaker than salvarsan, doctors recommended several injections of galyl. So in September and October 1928, Joyce walked up the miserable back stairwell of Dr. Borsch's eye clinic and rolled up his sleeve. The doctor unsealed a glass ampule containing a greenish-gray powder, mixed less than a half-gram of galyl with sodium carbonate and water and injected it into Joyce's bloodstream every other day for three weeks. It didn't help. Doctors rarely used galyl after World War I because the drug simply wasn't effective. The only benefit was that Joyce became ravenous after the injections—he began eating toffee, cream sweets and Turkish delight. His decade-long case of syphilis, unfortunately, continued.

Some people must have guessed the reason for Joyce's eye problems. Before penicillin, syphilis was the most common cause of recurrent iritis. John Quinn and Ezra Pound suspected it, but they said nothing. Dr. Borsch, however, didn't suspect. He knew. What were the chances that a man *without* syphilis would develop iritis at repeated intervals for decades? Slim. What were the chances that Dr. Borsch would misidentify syphilis—that he would, after peering into James Joyce's eyes with his ophthalmoscope, not know a syphilitic lesion when he saw one? Virtually none. Nearly everything about syphilitic lesions is distinctive—the way they look, the substances they contain, the high amount of exudate they produce and their location on the iris. Dr. Borsch knew exactly what to look for.

By 1928, when he treated Joyce for syphilis, Dr. Borsch had been a clinician for twenty years in Paris, where the disease was widespread (a single Parisian hospital treated ten thousand cases in 1920 alone, and the numbers only increased through the decade). Beyond that, diagnosing syphilis simply wasn't difficult, especially for someone like him. Dr. Borsch had received two medical degrees—the second from Paris's Faculté de Médecine, which was regarded as providing the best ophthalmological training in the world. If, in the end, he was at all uncertain, Dr. Borsch could have administered a serology test, though the results of any tests Joyce may have taken are gone. In fact, nearly all of Joyce's medical records have been either lost or destroyed.

Joyce and Nora kept it a secret, but he wanted people to discover the truth, like guessing the title of *Finnegans Wake*. His complaints to Miss Weaver and Sylvia Beach—the array of symptoms he described in detail, the impending blindness, the boils, abscesses, nebulae, aches and pains, the eye attacks and the surgery he sketched the first day he visited Shakespeare and Company—seemed like appeals for sympathy, and to some degree they were. He needed their help, after all, and sympathy helped to ensure it. Joyce's grievances were his way of scattering clues.

"I deserve all this on account of my many iniquities"—it was the truth masquerading as hyperbole. If you had run out of patience with Joyce, it sounded melodramatic, but he was prodding Miss Weaver to piece together the details from years of letters. He dropped another hint when he told her that he was getting three weeks of arsenic and phosphorus injections. Galyl, after all, is the *only* drug that fits that description, and syphilis is the only disease galyl treats. *Phosphorus* would have meant nothing to her, but *arsenic* would have been revealing to anyone who was reasonably knowledgeable about current treatments for venereal disease. Miss Weaver, alas, was too sheltered for that. While Joyce was divulging the intricacies of his case, she was looking up *glaucoma* in *Black's Medical Dictionary* and reading pamphlets about the effects of drinking alcohol.

Joyce finally mentioned the word in 1930. "A young French ophthalmologist," he wrote to Miss Weaver, "said the only possible solution of the case was that my eye trouble proceeded from congenital syphilis, which being curable, he said the proper thing for me was to undergo a cure of I have forgotten what"—a rare moment of forgetfulness for Joyce. He then wrote that Dr. Borsch's assistant "dissuaded me strongly from undergoing it" and that the assistant and the doctor "had discussed the possibility and that Borsch had excluded it categorically on account of the nature of the attacks, the way in which they were cured and the general reaction of the eye[.]"

The crucial question for Miss Weaver, who could not have been reading casually at this point, was: what possibility did the doctors discuss and exclude? Or, to put a finer point on it—to make the letter a bit more of a grammatical puzzle—what is the antecedent of *it* in that sentence involving Dr. Borsch? Did the doctors categorically exclude the diagnosis or the treatment— "congenital syphilis" or "a cure"? Miss Weaver might have dismissed the graver option as an embarrassing misreading, for as soon as Joyce revealed the innocent version of his diagnosis (his syphilis was acquired, not congenital— the pathologies are entirely different), he buried it with a joke ridiculing the supposed French preoccupation with syphilis.

But it was not a joke. Lying on any number of sickbeds, sometimes with both eyes bandaged, Joyce had to contend with the memories of a lifetime of pain, surgery, medication, eyedrops, electrotherapy and leeches. The abscesses that ravaged his mouth and the large "boil" on his shoulder were probably syphilitic. Syphilis "disabled" his right arm in 1907, when Stannie rubbed his brother's body with reeking lotions mixed with salt, presumably to treat syphilitic lesions. Joyce didn't have neurosyphilis, but his treatments and the disease's psychological toll likely caused Joyce's periodic fainting spells, his insomnia and his "nervous collapses."

Throughout all of this, Joyce must have wondered: why me? Nora was apparently spared. Perhaps he was so malnourished in Dublin and Trieste that colonies of *Treponema pallidum* had nearly free rein over his weakened body after he became infected, likely by a woman in Nighttown. Joyce knew he contracted gonorrhea in 1904, and he may have acquired syphilis simultaneously, in which case he probably mistook his disappearing symptoms as a cure when it was really an early syphilitic dormant period. He met Nora that summer, left Ireland with her in the fall, and when his symptoms recurred—and worsened—reality must have set in. No matter when he contracted it, the truth was clear by the time of his extended illness in 1907. In Dublin, Joyce preferred to think of diseases like syphilis as "venereal ill-luck" rather than God's judgment, but when he looked back on his life in the 1930s, it must have been difficult to imagine that decades of pain and blindness could derive from a single unfortunate night with the wrong prostitute, that the life of an artist who could "pierce the significant heart of everything" was at the mercy of bacteria. Even God's judgment might have seemed more plausible.

However odious Catholicism seemed to Joyce, it had enviable explanatory power. Syphilis could have been God's punishment for iniquities that went beyond excursions into Nighttown. It could have been punishment for refusing to marry Nora, for infecting her with syphilis, for his unspeakable sexual proclivities, for blasphemy, for celebrating heretics as heroes and for refusing to pray at his mother's deathbed. And it would have been appropriate for his punishment to deepen with his intransigence, his lifelong refusal to repent, his eagerness not only to speak against God but to emblazon his blasphemies and obscenities in *Ulysses*. The countless hours of pain and the slow, encroaching blindness could have had at least some overarching moral significance.

But Joyce did not accept a punishing God, and rejecting the possibility of divine wrath must have forced him to face a more crushing reality: that his disease had merely happened. If such monumental suffering were not part of the moral order of the universe, it was inanely banal. Damnation was the only alternative to the pointlessness of bacteria. Joyce spent his life coming to terms with that pointlessness, reconciling egoism with the empire of microbes—a lesson, perhaps, too deep for epiphanies. While he would never accept an angry God, he would never entirely lose that God, either, for the foibles and ugly truths about Stephen Dedalus and Leopold Bloom were, to some degree, personal confessions in fantastic guises, words of contrition written with the hope of finding absolution. The individualism that defined Joyce's career never escaped the shadow of Catholicism, the most rigid, hierarchical power structure he knew. After years of writing *Ulysses*, the word that Joyce rushed to Darantière in a telegram just days before publication was *atonement*.

25.

SEARCH AND SEIZURE

The First Amendment could not protect *Ulysses*, nor could it protect any other book the U.S. government had burned before it. Freedom of speech, the right that Americans consider fundamental to democracy, did not emerge as a freedom in any real sense until well into the twentieth century. When the Bill of Rights was passed, the First Amendment was understood to protect citizens from "prior restraint"—it prohibited the federal government from interfering with a publication before it was printed. The government therefore retained the authority to halt the circulation of any words that had a "bad tendency" upon general readers, and a troublesome idea (including a statement of fact) could be outlawed if it was printed or spoken in public. Even if the speech wasn't troublesome, a state like New York or Ohio could ban it because judges believed that the First Amendment pertained only to the federal government. The idea that the Constitution protects free speech rights from both federal and state interference didn't start to develop until 1925.

First Amendment law began to shift in response to the Espionage Act. In a pair of 1919 Supreme Court decisions regarding pamphlets protesting the war, Justice Oliver Wendell Holmes indirectly expanded the First Amendment's scope. That is, he whittled down unprotected speech from utterances that have a vague "bad tendency" to speech that amounts to a "clear and present danger" to the public. Holmes's more forceful opinion came out as a dissent in *Abrams v. United States*.

When men have realized that time has upset many fighting faiths, they may come to believe even more than they believe the very foundations of their own conduct that the ultimate good desired is better reached by free trade in ideas—that the best test of truth is the power of the thought to get itself accepted in the competition of the market, and that truth is the only ground upon which their wishes safely can be carried out.

Free speech was a constitutional freedom because it created the conditions for discovering truth—namely, a free marketplace of ideas. But Holmes didn't think the marketplace included all ideas. The trade that concerned the First Amendment was overtly political speech involving society's ultimate good. Free speech was the best way for a society to find stability when turbulent times upset fighting faiths, and yet free speech was not itself a fighting faith. Rather, it was a way to cope with political doubt. To invoke the First Amendment to defend a novel like *Ulysses*—even if it *wasn't* obscene—would have been absurd.

One of the only people who thought *Ulysses* could be legalized in the United States was a civil liberties lawyer named Morris Ernst. Without the help of the First Amendment, however, Ernst believed that he would have to do more than convince the federal government that *Ulysses* had some nominal value in the marketplace of ideas. He would have to convince the government to declare *Ulysses* a modern classic.

Ernst was the son of a Jewish Czech immigrant who arrived in the United States with a label around his neck—the address of a relative. The Ernst family had erratic fortunes. Morris spent part of his childhood on the Lower East Side in the 1890s, when the neighborhood was at its roughest, before the family moved to Harlem and then the Upper East Side. Ernst prepared for college at Horace Mann during prosperous years, and he attended Williams after flunking Harvard's entrance exams (he kept the rejection letter for inspiration). After graduation, he took night classes at New York Law School on a whim while selling furniture to make ends meet. Ernst started a small law firm, also on a whim, with two friends, and the partnership flourished for decades.

Ernst was more intuitive than bookish. The other partners did most of the legal research while Ernst was their brilliant litigator. He was quick on his feet, persuasive and driven by idealism. Justice Brandeis bequeathed his Supreme Court lamp to Ernst, and he imagined that it spoke to him as he worked by its light. In the 1920s, he became the co-general counsel of the American Civil Liberties Union and took on civil liberties cases pro bono. When he received an invitation to join the American Bar Association, Ernst wanted to know if they admitted African American lawyers. The Association wrote back and apologized for not realizing that Mr. Ernst was a Negro.

Ernst's topsy-turvy formative years shaped his legal philosophy. He believed that the unruly mixture of people and ideas in a Holmesian marketplace was the country's greatest asset. Yet while Holmes thought of free speech as a source of stability, Ernst thought of it as a way to keep the culture roiling. Censorship was a tactic used by entrenched powers to quell democracy's inherent turbulence, and groups like the New York Society for the Suppression of Vice, Ernst thought, were their moral instruments. Censorship was what happens when power brokers who benefit from the status quo team up with moralists who believe society is perpetually on the brink of collapse.

To fight for the freedom of books was to fight for the principle of self-governance that had inspired the American Revolution. For Ernst, there was no strict separation between political and sexual ideas—burning books sent a chill across the entire culture. Censorship, he wrote, had "a pervading influence on the subconscious recesses of individual minds." It altered the way the country approached science, public health, psychology and history. Only a blinkered Victorian mentality, Ernst thought, could think that the Roman Empire fell because of its moral decadence.

The worst part about the censorship regime was that it was maddeningly arbitrary. Books that circulated for years might be banned without warning. Customs officials might declare a book legal only to have the Post Office issue its own ban. A judge or jury could acquit a book one day and condemn it the next, and the wording of the statutes themselves stoked confusion. The New York law described criminal literature with what Ernst called the "six deadly adjectives": *obscene, lewd, lascivious, filthy, indecent* and *disgusting—*

lawmakers kept adding words when they updated the law. Multiplying the number of adjectives was a way of papering over the elusiveness of any given designation. What was the difference between *obscene* and *lascivious*? If a judge seemed reluctant to find something *lewd,* a prosecutor could argue that it was *disgusting*—and every one of those adjectives was subjective. Unpredictable standards amplified the power of obscenity laws far beyond the way they were enforced because writers and publishers who couldn't risk prosecution stayed well within objectionable bounds. The marketplace of ideas was being crushed under the tyranny of uncertainty.

Ernst started fighting that tyranny by defending birth control advocates. In 1928, he defended an educational manual by Mary Ware Dennett called *The Sex Side of Life*, which had a remarkable nationwide demand. Dennett got mail orders from schools, public health departments and the YMCA. *The Sex Side of Life* had been in circulation for nearly a decade before the Post Office banned it under the Comstock Act in 1926. Dennett suspected that the ban was retribution for her outspoken criticism of the postal authority, and she approached the ACLU's co-general counsel, Arthur Garfield Hays, to intervene. Hays was eager to expand the judiciary's First Amendment readings, but World War I–era decisions made it clear that the courts wouldn't overturn a postal ban.

Two years later, the only other ACLU board member willing to fight for "nonpolitical" speech took up Dennett's cause pro bono. Morris Ernst wanted people to see Mary Ware Dennett as a victim of bullying censors, and the government made his job easier. Shortly after Ernst took the case, a Post Office inspector sent Dennett a decoy letter requesting *The Sex Side of Life*. When it arrived in the mail, the government brought criminal obscenity charges against her. An outcry followed her conviction in federal court, and by the time Ernst won the case in a 1930 appeal, the public had been so roused that the ACLU opened a new front in the fight for free speech, and Morris Ernst was one of its leaders.

The following year, Ernst won two more federal obscenity cases on behalf of two works by Dr. Marie Stopes: a marital aid called *Married Love* and a physicians' pamphlet called *Contraception*. He was on a roll. The only problem was that he was not winning constitutional freedoms. Every time Ernst claimed that the First Amendment protected an individual's right to circulate sexually related material, the judges flatly rejected his argument. Not only did books about pregnancy and reproductive systems have nothing to do with the First Amendment, but Ernst's constitutional argument implicitly undermined federal and state Comstock Acts, which were sacrosanct after decades on the books.

So Ernst had to open up the marketplace of ideas another way. Instead of expanding the First Amendment, he eroded censorship by whittling down the legal meaning of the word *obscene*. And yet these early victories weren't enough. While they were important, they affirmed what the country had already come to believe: that sex education wasn't obscene. Ernst was chipping away at the nation's censorship regime, but what he was really looking for was a way to take a sledgehammer to it.

In August 1931, just weeks after his victory in the *Contraception* case, Ernst found his opportunity. Alexander Lindey, an associate at Ernst's law firm, approached Sylvia Beach's sister Holly when he heard that James Joyce was looking for an American publisher for *Ulysses*. Ernst and Lindey had excellent timing. Joyce was desperate for money, and Sylvia Beach heard rumors that Samuel Roth was about to sell another edition of Joyce's novel. This time, she heard, the printing would be twenty thousand copies. Unauthorized books would flood the market, and the prospect of income stolen by a pirate was infuriating.

Nevertheless, while *Ulysses* was still illegal a full decade after the *Little Review* trial, several U.S. publishers were willing to defend the book in court, and Morris Ernst's firm was eager to be involved. Lindey could barely contain himself in a note he wrote to Ernst, "This would be the grandest obscenity case in the history of law and literature, and I am ready to do anything in the world to get it started."

BUT STARTING THE CASE wasn't easy. Ernst wouldn't take it pro bono, and the prospective publishers willing to pay his fees found themselves hampered by, of all people, Sylvia Beach. In 1930, Joyce gave Beach world rights for *Ulysses* in order to free himself from the legal fees associated with fighting Samuel Roth's piracy. As publishers began to pursue *Ulysses*, however, they blithely ignored her contract. Their offers kept referring to Sylvia Beach as Joyce's "representative" rather than the publisher and owner of *Ulysses*, and no one offered her any payment for the rights.

Beach became indignant, and after asking Hemingway for his advice, her response bears his brash imprint. She wanted Joyce to receive 20 percent of the book's retail price and a five-thousand-dollar advance. And for the right to publish *Ulysses*, she demanded twenty-five thousand dollars. It was, she said, "a modest estimate of the value that *Ulysses* represents to me." It was also absurd. A publisher couldn't afford to pay half that amount for a foreign title, let alone for a decade-old book that was a legal nightmare. The Curtis Brown Company, one of the most serious bidders, made a counteroffer of 10 percent royalties—15 if Joyce wrote a preface. Instead of a five-thousand-dollar advance, they offered one thousand, and they ignored Sylvia Beach's request for payment altogether.

Once word got out about her demands, the offers stopped. Ernst met with the most likely publisher, Ben Huebsch, in October 1931 to push the case forward. He insisted on a retainer of one thousand dollars and warned Huebsch that legal expenses could run as high as eight thousand dollars if the case went to the Supreme Court. By December, when it was clear that Sylvia Beach was standing by her demands, Huebsch gave up on *Ulysses*. Instead of counteroffers for the rights, American publishers offered her nothing, and Joyce found himself shackled to the contract he had demanded.

There was, however, one last publisher willing to step into the fray: Random House. As soon as Huebsch stepped aside, Bennett Cerf contacted Morris Ernst to talk about a possible court case. Cerf figured that if he could publish the first legal edition of *Ulysses* in the United States, it would be a coup for Random House—its "first really important trade publication," as he later put it. Ever since the government started burning the editions arriving from Paris, the buzz about *Ulysses* continued. Joyce's book was everything Cerf wanted: a guaranteed commercial success with great literary esteem. And a highly publicized trial would do more than boost his sales figures with a headline-generating book. It would promote Random House's brand and help the six-year-old company consolidate its place in the industry.

Shakespeare and Company was the only problem. Bennett Cerf wrote to Ernst, "I don't know just what we can do if Sylvia Beach maintains her preposterous stand." Cerf likely would have paid her a modest fee for royalties, but when he heard about her figures from Huebsch, who had been negotiating for months, he concluded that dealing with her was impossible, so he never tried.

As it turned out, Cerf didn't have to. Ben Huebsch's withdrawal turned Joyce's desperation into indignation. He wanted Beach to receive money, but her exorbitant claims effectively made *Ulysses* captive to publishers' sexism, and after six months of waiting for something to change, Joyce felt justified in trying to reclaim the book. But he couldn't do it himself. One of Joyce's old friends from Dublin, Padraic Colum, began visiting Shakespeare and Company and encouraging Miss Beach to give up her publishing rights. She recounted the details of the conversation in her memoirs.

"What right do ya have to *Ulysses*?" he asked.

"But what about our contract?" she asked. "Is that imaginary?"

"That's no contract. It doesn't exist, your contract."

She informed him that it most certainly *did* exist.

Colum finally told her, "You're standing in the way of Joyce's interests."

After a decade of devotion, the accusation left her speechless. When Colum walked out of the shop, she picked up the phone and called Joyce to tell him that he was free to do whatever he wished with his big blue book. She relinquished all claims on it. Sylvia Beach exited the life of *Ulysses* the same way she had entered it: swiftly, informally and at James Joyce's coy behest.

RANDOM HOUSE SIGNED a contract with Joyce in March 1932. Joyce would receive a one-thousand-dollar advance and 15 percent royalties on sales. By then the crucial relationship for the future of *Ulysses* was the one between the book's prospective publisher and its lawyer. In some ways, the partnership between Bennett Cerf and Morris Ernst was natural. They were both ambitious risk takers, and they both understood the importance of publicity. Yet there was tension between them. Ernst suspected that Cerf harbored unfriendly feelings toward him, probably because Ernst's proposal was a bit too shrewd. To dispel Cerf's qualms about the costs of an obscenity trial, Ernst offered to defend *Ulysses* for free if Random House would pay him a percentage of the book's royalties. He wanted 5 percent of all trade edition sales and 2 percent of reprint editions. It would be a gamble for both of them: Ernst would pay substantially if they lost. Random House would pay substantially if they won. It was a deal.

Ernst had his work cut out for him. The federal government had to seize copies of *Ulysses* before he could challenge the government's position, and despite his recent victories, time only seemed to strengthen the Comstock Act—the Supreme Court repeatedly affirmed the government's authority to control material distributed through the mail system and across state lines. The ban on *Ulysses* had been in place for over a decade, and nothing remotely like it had ever been permissible by the Post Office.

So Ernst decided not to challenge the Comstock Act at all. Rather than mailing copies of *Ulysses* around the United States, Random House could simply do what Joyce's readers had been doing since 1922: they could break federal law by importing *Ulysses* from another country. Instead of violating the Comstock Act, Random House would violate the Tariff Act, which banned the importation of obscenity. Cerf and Klopfer would not have to print an edition of *Ulysses* and risk having the books destroyed. All they would need to do was import a single copy from Paris and wait for the government to seize it. Their goal was to have a federal court legalize Joyce's book, and one copy would test its legality as much as one thousand.

The Tariff Act strategy mitigated several problems, the most important of which was that no one at Random House would go to jail. The law provided for an in rem proceeding, which meant that the book itself would be on trial rather than the importer. There were technical advantages, too. While the Comstock Act banned anything "obscene, lewd, lascivious, filthy, indecent or disgusting," the Tariff Act outlawed only the importation of "obscene" material. Instead of six deadly adjectives, Ernst would have to defend against only one.

The plan was, nevertheless, a long shot. Even if *Ulysses* were deemed legal under the Tariff Act, the Post Office could still bring charges under the Comstock Act, and the government had a long history of prosecuting the same book under two separate laws. Ernst was gambling that a court decision legalizing *Ulysses* would free Joyce's book from all federal and state obscenity charges. It would not be enough to win. Their victory would have to be resounding.

THE CORNERSTONE OF Ernst's argument was that *Ulysses* was a "modern classic," and a classic couldn't be obscene. Instead of defending Joyce's lewd passages, Ernst wanted to change the terms of the debate—he was going to transform an obscenity trial into a trial about literary value. But to do this he had to get the opinions of literary critics admitted as evidence, which was nearly impossible. The consensus in American courts remained that a book's literary merit had no bearing on the question of its obscenity. A book should be judged in the courtroom just as it would be in the marketplace—on its own.

Ernst believed that a book couldn't be separated from expert opinions about its value, but the courts wouldn't listen, and Ernst had learned this the hard way. During his first obscenity trial in 1927, the judge had barred all the witnesses he brought to defend the accused novel. Ernst was reduced to reading the names of the would-be defenders in front of the jury, and he lost the case. He tried again the following year. He lined up dozens of professors, doctors and social workers to testify in defense of *The Sex Side of Life*. Once again, the judge rejected them all.

At some point it occurred to him: why not put literary opinions *in* the book? If praise were physically inseparable from the government's seized copy of *Ulysses*, it would be incorporated into Exhibit A of Random House's customs-seizure dispute. Critical praise would sneak its way into the courtroom. Even if the judge didn't read the opinions, Ernst could base arguments on them instead of having them dismissed outright. He could engineer the content of the federal trial before it began. And so Bennett Cerf relayed detailed instructions to Joyce's assistant in Paris, Paul Léon: purchase a copy of the latest edition of *Ulysses*, find praise for the book written by prominent critics, and paste the reviews inside the book's front cover.

The package containing an illegal copy of *Ulysses* was due to arrive on the SS *Bremen* on May 3, 1932. The day before the book's arrival, Ernst's firm sent a letter to the New York City Customs House informing them of an illicit package arriving from France. They should inspect it very carefully as they might want to decide if the contents violated the Tariff Act. But perhaps a letter wasn't enough. Cerf was worried that if *Ulysses* wasn't seized within the next two weeks, the case wouldn't come up before the summer and another publishing season would be wasted. The day before the *Bremen* was scheduled to dock in the Port of New York, Alexander Lindey called Mr. Handler in the customs legal department to let them know exactly what was on the *Bremen*. Handler thanked him for the information and assured him they would be on the lookout.

But the *Bremen* was huge. All the passengers were disembarking at once, and, as Cerf recounted in his memoirs, the customs agents were so overworked that they weren't bothering with inspections. They were dispatching packages and passengers as soon as possible, stamping everything on sight—trunks, cases, duffel bags—telling delighted travelers, "Get out. Go on out." Like nearly everything else that day, *Ulysses* passed through customs and arrived, safe and sound, at the Random House office on Fifty-seventh Street.

Ernst was furious when Cerf told him. They had planned for a federal trial pitting *Ulysses* against the Tariff Act for months, so Ernst went *back* to the New York Customs office with the unopened package. He was at a loss as he walked down to the port. How could Handler have let this happen? And how, exactly, did you force a customs agent to search your property?

Ernst walked up to one of the agents and insisted that the official in charge inspect the parcel he was carrying. The inspector didn't quite hear him. Ernst raised his voice, "I think there's something in there that's contraband, and I insist that it be searched."

Well, this was a new one. The package clearly listed the *Bremen*, which had arrived days ago. The inspector looked askance at Ernst, who stood there and waited as he opened the parcel to see what it contained.

"Aha!" Ernst exclaimed, thinking the gears of the state were now in motion. A copy of *Ulysses* by James Joyce! Thank goodness we checked! But the customs inspector was unimpressed.

"Oh, for God's sake, everybody brings that in. We don't pay attention to it."

Ernst became frantic. "I *demand* that you seize this book!"

This was too much. The inspector waved over his supervisor. "This fellow wants me to seize this book." The supervisor looked over at the sweating man in his slightly wrinkled suit and glanced down at the book in question. It was bulging with papers. There were pamphlets and articles in English, French and German. There were circulars and the international Roth protest with columns of signatures. Pages were brusquely folded in or sticking out from the sides, and all of it was attached inside the front and back covers with multiple strips of Scotch tape, like some hasty vacation scrapbook. The supervising inspector decided to seize the man's book, papers and all.

Bennett Cerf and Morris Ernst had their federal court case.

THE ASSISTANT CUSTOMS COLLECTOR knew that he didn't want to read the confiscated book when it came across his desk a few days later. Luckily, he didn't have to. When he looked through Treasury Department records for relevant information, he found that in 1928 customs officials in Minneapolis had seized a shipment of forty-three books, including *The Vice of Women, Aphrodite* and seven copies of James Joyce's *Ulysses*. The Custom Court's ruling was unambiguous: "Only a casual glance through the books in evidence is sufficient to satisfy us that they are filled with obscenity of the rottenest and vilest character." The matter had been decided for him. The collector duly forwarded the obscene book to the United States Attorney for the Southern District of New York so that the federal government could begin proceedings for the book's "forfeiture, confiscation and destruction" in accordance with Section 305(a) of the Tariff Act of 1930. Once it was deemed obscene, the law stated, "it shall be ordered destroyed and shall be destroyed."

Sam Coleman wasn't yearning to read the book, either. He was the chief assistant DA in the U.S. Attorney's office for the Southern District of New

York. Sam was intelligent, even-tempered and, at thirty-eight, one of the younger prosecutors in the office. It was up to him to decide if the government was going to take James Joyce's *Ulysses* to court or drop the case altogether. After a month, Coleman had read less than half of it. When he told Ernst and Lindey that he was having a difficult time, they offered to send scholarly books that could help, but Coleman preferred to trudge through *Ulysses* on his own. Nearly six weeks later, he came to the final chapter.

they want everything in their mouth all the pleasure those men get out of a woman I can feel his mouth O Lord I must stretch myself I wished he was here or somebody to let myself go with and come again like that I feel all fire inside me or if I could dream it when he made me spend the 2nd time tickling me behind with his finger I was coming for about 5 minutes with my legs round him I had to hug him after O Lord I wanted to shout out all sorts of things fuck or shit or anything at all only not to look ugly or those lines from the strain who knows the way hed take it you want to feel your way with a man theyre not all like him thank God some of them want you to be so nice about it I noticed the contrast he does it and doesnt talk I gave my eyes that look with my hair a bit loose from the tumbling and my tongue between my lips up to him the savage brute Thursday Friday one Saturday two Sunday three O Lord I cant wait till Monday

Molly Bloom was having an affair. Coleman called up Lindey and told him that he thought *Ulysses* was "a literary masterpiece." He passed the book around his office and joked that it was "the only way my staff could get a literary education." He also concluded that *Ulysses* was obscene under federal law. Because of the book's literary importance, he thought prosecution was too big a decision for him to make alone. He wanted his superior, U.S. District Attorney George Medalie, to make the final decision.

At the time, Medalie was preparing to be the Republican nominee for the U.S. Senate in New York. He burnished his reputation among voters by pursuing racketeers and smugglers. But initiating obscenity proceedings against a celebrated book before an election was a tougher call, and Ernst's involvement made him even more cautious. The ACLU lawyer had made Medalie's office look foolish the previous year when he defended Dr. Stopes's *Contraception* against federal censorship. Eager to avoid another embarrassment, Medalie decided to stall until after the election. Random House had been sending out questionnaires and collecting hundreds of opinions about the merits of *Ulysses* from libraries, bookstores, writers, journalists and professors, and Medalie said he needed to see them all before he could decide. In mid-November, after Medalie lost the Senate race in a nationwide Democratic landslide, the DA's office informed Morris Ernst that the U.S. government was taking *Ulysses* to court. Medalie agreed with Sam Coleman: *Ulysses* was important, but the government was going to bring legal action against it anyway.

Bennett Cerf wanted a trial as soon as possible. He sent out nine hundred questionnaires in an attempt to gauge public opinion about *Ulysses*, and the mailings to libraries and bookstores conveniently doubled as a publicity campaign. As word spread about an impending *Ulysses* obscenity trial, Random House was flooded with questions about the publication date. Even movie studios perked up—Warner Brothers contacted Joyce about acquiring the film rights to *Ulysses*. The anticipation was exactly what Cerf wanted. When the confiscated copy of *Ulysses* was sailing over on the *Bremen* in early May, Cerf had expected to go to press with their edition at some point that summer. But by November 1932 they still didn't have a trial date, and Ernst's predictions were frustratingly vague. The case would go to court "some time between now and March," he said. Cerf warned Ernst that public interest would wane by then.

But if they didn't win the case, there wouldn't be any sales at all. Ernst didn't want to rush the DA's office because, for the moment, Sam Coleman was sympathetic to their cause, and he wanted to keep it that way. If Ernst pressed them for an early trial, Coleman might insist on exercising the government's right to read entire chapters to the jury. Ernst didn't want a jury to read a single word of *Ulysses*. In fact, he didn't want a jury at all. In his experience, jury rooms encouraged the performance of purity. A man who used dirty words freely in the street would pretend to be offended by them as soon as he was impaneled with a group of twelve strangers. Perceptions of other people's virtues affected obscenity juries through and through. Because jurors were instructed to judge the book's effect on the average person, not on themselves, they were left to imagine the book's influence on a hypothetical person who was always somehow more corruptible than anyone in the jury box.

Ernst wanted a judge to decide the case, and he was determined to find a favorable one. The quest for the perfect judge became a months-long series of delays as they dodged hostile judges on the ever-changing calendar for the Southern District Court of New York. Judge Bondy was too conservative. Judge Caffey wasn't any good either. Adverse judges were presiding throughout January and February, and Ernst was willing to wait for someone favorable—Judge Patterson, perhaps, or Judge Knox.

But the man Ernst really wanted was Judge Woolsey, who had a track record of liberal obscenity rulings. In fact, it was Woolsey who had legalized Dr. Marie Stopes's *Married Love* and *Contraception*. After the first decision, Ernst, eager to make a new friend, gave Judge Woolsey a signed copy of his book about obscenity law—it was a book-length brief disguised as a gift, though if the judge read it he was not entirely persuaded. Woolsey flatly rejected Ernst's First Amendment arguments—twice—but he was a man of culture, a reader, someone who valued literature and loved words. When he considered the meaning of *obscenity* in his *Married Love* decision, Ernst noticed that he didn't bother with the Hicklin Rule. The judge went straight for his *Oxford English Dictionary*.

But the judicial calendar wasn't cooperating. In March 1933 the DA's office told Ernst that Woolsey and Knox were both "out of the question for months." The judges presiding through April and May were generally unfavorable, and at the end of May, Judge Coxe declined to hear the case for unspecified "technical reasons." Stalling through months of bad luck required more than patience. It required Sam Coleman's cooperation. This wasn't the first time they had faced each other in the courtroom. Coleman had presented the government's case when Ernst defended *Enduring Passion*, Stopes's sequel to *Married Love*, and Coleman seemed satisfied with Ernst's victory. By 1933, Coleman and Ernst had almost become friends, and Ernst was about to test that friendship.

One day in early June, Coleman came across a *New York Times* headline, "Ban upon 'Ulysses' to Be Fought Again." It rehashed basic information about the case, Random House and Bennett Cerf—all of the promotional material disguised as news that Coleman expected Random House to plant before the trial. But deep in the article he found a nugget of genuine news: "It was learned yesterday that [Cerf] had won a preliminary victory by obtaining the admittance of one copy of the book. This was made possible by an exception in the 1930 Tariff Act."

Coleman was furious. The law contained a provision allowing the importation of banned books if the U.S. Treasury Department recognized the book as a classic. The classics exemption tucked into the Tariff Act was part of the reason why Ernst was focusing on the literary value of *Ulysses*. Ernst was convinced that literary praise mattered in obscenity decisions because the newly revised Tariff Act said it did. And how did Ernst know about the new revision? Because he had written it himself, it helps to have connections.

Back in February, Ernst and Lindey shipped a second copy of *Ulysses* to New York and petitioned the secretary of the Treasury to admit it under the exemption. "We have come to realize that there can be *modern* classics as well as ancient ones. If there is any book in any language today genuinely entitled to be called a 'modern classic' it is *Ulysses*." The secretary of the Treasury agreed, which added a government voice to the laudatory opinions stuffed inside the books' covers. Coleman felt ambushed. Ernst and Lindey filed the petition behind his back while his office spent months helping the defense team stall their way past judge after judge. Without stepping foot in a courtroom, Ernst managed to make the DA's office look foolish again.

Three days later, Coleman's office called Ernst's office to say he wanted another adjournment until late June, and he was evasive about the reasons why. Ernst and Lindey found that Judge Coleman (no relation to Sam) was presiding then, but neither of them knew who he was, and whoever heard the preliminary motion would preside over the trial. When they asked around, they discovered that Judge Coleman was a "strait-laced Catholic" and probably the single worst judge the defense team could face.

When Lindey reported to the federal courthouse, he found an impatient Judge Coleman waiting to hear preliminary motions for a case that had been bouncing around their calendar for months, and he flatly refused to grant a two-week adjournment. Judge Coxe would be presiding then, Judge Coleman explained, and after declining for "technical reasons" two months earlier, Coxe had specifically told the other judges that he didn't want the *Ulysses* case. The DA's office politely suggested the following week. The judge looked at the calendar and said he didn't want to do that, either. Judge Patterson would be presiding that week, and the case would be a burden for him—Patterson was recovering from pneumonia, and one of his children was very ill. So Judge Coleman took it upon himself to postpone the hearing until the next open date, August 22. And who would be presiding then, Lindey asked? Judge Woolsey.

After eight months of delays, Morris Ernst had his man. The government agreed to waive its right to a jury, so the government's case against the legality of *Ulysses* in the United States would be decided upon direct arguments before the judge. Woolsey would determine the fate of *Ulysses* himself.

With another crucial moment approaching, it was again time to search for omens. Sylvia Beach had recently heard that the Pope had inadvertently blessed a copy of *Ulysses* concealed beneath a prayer book. It wasn't clear if that was a good omen or a bad one. Random House was getting bad omens. Cerf and Klopfer heard rumors that "a notorious pirate" on Fifth Avenue was about to exploit the publicity of the trial to produce a quick and cheap edition that would be on the streets the day *Ulysses* was legalized, if not before. Cerf asked Ernst, "Can we write him some kind of a letter threatening to clap an injunction upon him, and seize any copies of *Ulysses* that he prints as soon as they come off the press?" And if the threat of piracy wasn't unsettling enough, Random House began to receive suspicious letters.

Gentlemen: —

Please send me under personal cover your list of books like 'the Decameron' and other obscene books which you publish. I am interested in the best and most obscene which you have. Kindly address me under personal cover.

Yours truly
Claude J. Black

It was like an inartful version of one of Comstock's decoy letters. It read so much like a smut hound's trap, in fact, that it couldn't be a smut hound. Was it a joke? A legal ambush? To respond with a list of titles fulfilling Mr. Black's request would be tantamount to admitting that Random House was a publisher of obscene materials, which would strengthen the government's case against *Ulysses*. It may have seemed paranoid, but it was difficult to escape the impression that someone was trying to set them up. Bennett Cerf wrote back immediately.

> *Dear Mr. Black:*
> *We have in hand your inquiry for a list of obscene books. May we recommend the following titles:*
>
> *Thus Spake Zarathustra* by Nietzsche
> *Autobiography of Benjamin Franklin*
> *The Education of Henry Adams*
> *Alice in Wonderland* by Lewis Carroll
> *Pickwick Papers* by Charles Dickens
>
> > *Sincerely yours*
> > *Bennett A. Cerf*

Whoever it was, the joke either didn't register, or it didn't deter him. He wrote back thanking Random House for their list of obscene books and asked if they could send one for his inspection. This time, Cerf responded without humor. "There is a growing suspicion in the minds of the board of directors of the Modern Library that we are being kidded by an expert. If this correspondence is to go any further, you will have to send us a picture of yourself with your next letter." Mr. Black wrote back that he did not have a picture to send them. Collecting obscenity was simply a hobby of his, and he wanted to keep it secret. "Also I can assure you they are for me personally and no one else is involved." Random House stopped answering Mr. Black's letters.

26

THE UNITED STATES OF AMERICA V. ONE BOOK CALLED "ULYSSES"

J udge Woolsey liked to lumber up to his library on the hill behind his summer home while huffing a cigar or a pipe. In 1933 he stayed long enough in Petersham, Massachusetts, to see the leaves beginning to turn at the end of a particularly lively season. Woolsey played tennis with his wife for recreation (he wore a tie to their matches), and lawyers scattered over the fields picking blueberries during lunch recesses. The judge's hilltop library doubled as a courtroom—there was a bench at the far end of the spacious hall and tables for counsel.

In the hot months, Woolsey liked to get out of Manhattan and convene his federal cases in Petersham, where he could hear the summer birds during arguments and where his gavel, carved from the original hull of the USS *Constitution*, could remain mostly ornamental. The library used to be the town hall of Prescott. The Woolseys transported the entire building to Petersham, set it down at the top of the hill behind their house and refurbished it with colonial paneling. When the judge was not hearing cases or writing decisions, he read in one of the upholstered armchairs by the fireplace. The wide floorboards creaked under his heavy legs, and he plumped himself down.

Judge Woolsey probably wanted a drink. It had been over a decade since he had one because he considered it hypocritical to put men behind bars for selling liquor if he was going to drink it. A century-old bottle of sherry had tempted him in his Manhattan apartment since Prohibition began, but even a convicted bootlegger might not have begrudged the man a glass after the year he had endured. Woolsey had presided over a fraud trial of a corporation that had scammed hundreds of Catholic priests out of three million dollars, purportedly to finance morally uplifting Hollywood talkies. It turned into the longest criminal court case in U.S. history. The testimony of ninety-eight witnesses produced a fifteen-thousand-page transcript. The trial began before Christmas 1932 and didn't end until after the Fourth of July, and when it was over, Judge Woolsey told the jurors they should form an alumni association.

His trip to Petersham in the fall of 1933 was supposed to be his vacation, and he planned to spend a few leisurely weeks preparing to hear arguments regarding *Ulysses*. By then, Woolsey was comfortable with obscenity cases, so it would be rather enjoyable to apply the law to a book that was presumed to be a modern classic. Sitting in his library, with his legs crossed and an open novel resting on his outmoded knickerbockers, several pleasures in life would coalesce. But that was before he knew what he was getting into. Reading *Ulysses*, he said later, was "just about the hardest two months of my life." After several weeks, he had barely gotten through the first few chapters, and he postponed the case for another month. Morris Ernst sent him a trove of supplementary materials to help him make sense of it, including Paul Jordan Smith's *The Key to the Ulysses of James Joyce* and Herbert Gorman's *James Joyce: His First Forty Years*. Ernst planned to send Stuart Gilbert's book, *James Joyce's Ulysses*, but Judge Woolsey already owned a copy.

Woolsey owned thousands of books. There were, of course, entire walls filled with legal titles—*Patent Essentials, Maritime Cases, The Law of Unfair Competition and Trade-Marks*—but he also devoured poetry and fiction. Browning and Tennyson, Thackeray and Fielding. He had a limited edition of *The Odyssey of Homer* signed by the translator and illustrator. He acquired every first edition of Samuel Johnson he could find, and he loved Anthony Trollope's novels. *Phineas Finn. Kept in the Dark. Can You Forgive Her?* The judge planned to read them all.

Woolsey was a promiscuous connoisseur. He collected colonial furniture and pewter, old clocks and maps, pipes and blended tobaccos. Filling his life with the trappings of culture was a way of living up to his name, like stuffing your grandfather's shoes in order to walk in them. John Munro Woolsey's first New World ancestor had arrived in New Amsterdam in 1623 and ran an alehouse on the East River. Woolseys had attended Yale since 1705, and the judge was no exception. He was the descendant of a Yale founder, Yale presidents and Jonathan Edwards, the preacher who reminded sinners of their depravity. "The God that holds you over the pit of hell, much as one holds a spider, or some loathsome insect over the fire, abhors you."

Woolsey had received a growing pile of letters ever since the newspapers reported that he was presiding over the case. One man said *Ulysses* "seared his soul." Another called Joyce's book "the most precious thing in [my] life." Legally, the judge could ignore it all—the letters, the books about *Ulysses* and the opinions pasted into the seized copy's covers. In fact, he wasn't even obliged to read *Ulysses* itself beyond the passages that the DA had marked as obscene. Judges were free to limit their evaluations to a book's objectionable portions instead of bothering with the whole text. Judging excerpts wasn't laziness. It was the logical consequence of the legal definition of obscenity. The Hicklin Rule was formulated to protect the people most susceptible to a text's corrupting influence and, as even the liberal Learned Hand pointed out, "it would be just those who would be most likely to concern themselves with those parts alone, forgetting their setting and their relevancy to the book as a whole." Judges and juries read books the way children did.

Yet judges and juries didn't need the Hicklin Rule to have their readings blinkered by an obscenity charge. The very nature of obscenity encourages a piecemeal approach to books. Obscenity offends. It reads as a singular, jarring moment, something ripped out of the larger context of the book—blinding us to mitigating contexts is what offenses do. The word *cunt* or *fuck* stands out in relief against a page. Offended readers don't contemplate their function in the narrative's grand scheme or the role they play in the development of the characters. They become fixated on the words themselves. Judges of obscenity are the closest of close readers.

Woolsey was determined to read *Ulysses* cover to cover. It began like any other novel: "Stately, plump Buck Mulligan came from the stairhead bearing a bowl of lather on which a mirror and a razor lay crossed." An Englishman is visiting two Irishmen in an abandoned military tower on the shore overlooking the Irish Sea. The stage is suitably set. The first chapter has punchy dialogue mixed with a few mental impressions. There are dashes instead of quotation marks, though one gets used to that easily enough. But then the story begins to slip away from you. Instead of a voice breaking in to limn the characters and provide background and perspective, it inches forward with clipped impressions mixing seamlessly with details from the city of Dublin—streetside advertisements, a blind stripling tapping a cane, hungry seagulls by the river. Nothing is cordoned off from anything else. You begin to miss quotation marks.

Hundreds of characters pass through the pages. Who are you supposed to pay attention to? What is important? What isn't? There is a funeral with a stranger in a macintosh whose name nobody knew. There are idle conversations, acrobatic theories about Hamlet and arcane political disputes. Most readers stop around page eighty, but it gets easier once you settle in and allow yourself not to know everything. There is a chapter in a newspaper office riven with headlines. Another chapter parodies dozens of writers, including Samuel Johnson, which Woolsey must have enjoyed. Then the bizarre drama in the brothel bursts forth. How many ways are there to tell a story? An entire chapter is a volley of questions and answers passed between two bodiless spectators as if they were conducting a deposition or an inquest. Leopold Bloom and Stephen Dedalus walk out into Bloom's tiny backyard in the middle of the night.

What did each do at the door of egress?

Bloom set the candlestick on the floor. Stephen put the hat on his head.

For what creature was the door of egress a door of ingress?

For a cat.

What spectacle confronted them when they, first the host, then the guest, emerged silently, doubly dark, from obscurity by a passage from the rere of the house into the penumbra of the garden?

The heaventree of stars hung with humid nightblue fruit.

This wasn't Trollope. When the judge turned to the final chapter, he found an unbroken block of text. Molly Bloom's voice was unfastened from all punctuation. The thoughts were presumably liquid, but the absence of commas and periods had the opposite effect. It slowed Judge Woolsey down and forced him to focus on words he would otherwise glide past. The text compels readers to imagine the shapes of her phrases, to supply her pauses and breaths, to mouth her words.

yes when I lit the lamp because he must have come 3 or 4 times with that tremendous big red brute of a thing he has I thought the vein or whatever the dickens they call it was going to burst though his nose is not so big after I took off all my things with the blinds down after my hours dressing and perfuming and combing it like iron or some kind of a thick crowbar standing all the time he must have eaten oysters I think a few dozen he was in great singing voice no I never in all my life felt anyone had one the size of that to make you feel full up he must have eaten a whole sheep after whats the idea making us like that with a big hole in the middle of us or like a Stallion driving it up into you because thats all they want out of you with that determined vicious look in his eye I had to halfshut my eyes still he hasnt such a tremendous amount of spunk in him when I made him pull out and do it on me considering how big it is so much the better in case any of it wasnt washed out properly the last time I let him finish it in me

The obscenity came when you weren't expecting it and departed briskly. You stopped, as if you didn't quite catch it, and went back to read it again. The judge took pride in acknowledging the perspectives and desires of women. That was why, in his opinion, *Married Love* was an important marital guide. But even after reading Dr. Stopes, a woman's perspective was rather abstractly important, a matter of fairness, something to consider for the sake of a healthy marriage. Molly Bloom's thoughts were not abstract, nor, it seemed, was her marriage healthy.

> Ill put on my best shift and drawers let him have a good eyeful out of that to make his micky stand for him Ill let him know if thats what he wanted that his wife is fucked yes and damn well fucked too up to my neck nearly not by him 5 or 6 times handrunning theres the mark of his spunk on the clean sheet I wouldnt bother to even iron it out that ought to satisfy him if you dont believe me feel my belly unless I made him stand there and put him into me Ive a mind to tell him every scrap and make him do it out in front of me serve him right its all his own fault if I am an adulteress

There were dark X's like targets all along the margins. Passages like this were only a fraction of the book, but when you finally finished *Ulysses* and thought about it as a whole, as Woolsey intended to do, it was her voice that stayed with you. He read the marked passages several times. If they weren't obscene, what was obscene? Parts of *Ulysses*, he felt, were artful, even brilliant. Others were inscrutable or downright boring. He knew how to judge something like *Married Love* (not guilty) or *Fanny Hill* (guilty), but this was a conundrum. Most of the book had nothing to do with sex, but when it did it was far worse than anything he had encountered in print.

Judge Woolsey skimmed through the supplementary books and the reviews taped into the covers of *Ulysses*. He was determined to be thorough both because he cared about literature and because he didn't want to be duped. It would have been a nightmare, he said later, to discover, through some journalistic exposé, that James Joyce was indeed a pornographer, that *Ulysses* was little more than smut cloaked in opaque prose. Woolsey risked throwing his weight—his judgment, his name—behind something that might be a pornographic hoax or else banning a work of genius in a country that prided itself on fighting for freedom. He was beleaguered by two grim prospects: the dishonor of Woolseys preceding him and the derision of generations to come. He needed something stronger than sherry.

ON NOVEMBER 25, 1933, the small oval courtroom on the sixth floor of the Bar Association Building on Forty-fourth Street was filled to capacity. If Judge Woolsey had convened the hearing on a Saturday morning to avoid a crowd, he was disappointed. Nevertheless, a weekend morning allowed them to take their time. Woolsey had been convening cases at the Bar Building for weeks (he was, for a judge, surprisingly dissatisfied with courtrooms), and the well-appointed space suited his taste. A white-haired African American bailiff welcomed the judge at the door (he was also Woolsey's chauffeur), and the crowd began to hush as he made his way toward the bench. A gold ring around his cravat was visible over his black robe's neckline. No witnesses would be called, and each side would put forth arguments on competing motions. When the judge sat down, he looked over the documents pertaining to the case: *The United States of America v. One Book Called "Ulysses."*

Sam Coleman was unusually flustered, and he approached Ernst just before they were called to order.

"The government can't win this case," Coleman said.

"Why?"

"The only way to win the case is to refer to the great number of vulgar four-letter words used by Joyce. This will shock the judge and he will suppress the book. But I can't do it."

"Why?"

"Because there is a lady in the courtroom."

Ernst turned around, and among the reporters near the front row he saw his wife, Maggie. She had taken the day off from school to hear the arguments her husband had been rehearsing for months. Ernst told Coleman he didn't need to worry about offending his wife's sensibilities. She saw the "Anglo-Saxon" expressions scribbled by her students on the school's bathroom walls every day. In fact, Maggie had helped him parse the etymology of the words Coleman wouldn't speak in her presence.

When the proceedings began, Judge Woolsey made it clear that he was skeptical about *Ulysses*. "Suppose that a girl of eighteen or twenty read the soliloquy of Molly Bloom," he asked Ernst, "wouldn't it be apt to corrupt her?"

"I don't think that is the standard we should go by," Ernst replied. "The law does not require that adult literature be reduced to mush for infants."

Ernst's argument depended upon discarding the Hicklin Rule. He wanted a definition of obscenity that protected Molly Bloom from phantom young readers rather than the other way around. To do so, he plucked Judge Learned Hand's 1913 definition from obscurity: the word *obscene* should indicate "the present critical point in the compromise between candor and shame at which the community may have arrived here and now." Judge Hand had made obscenity a "living standard," as Ernst put it, a judgment that communities revise continually. Even if *Ulysses* had been obscene in 1922, it could still be legal in 1933. After all, Ernst noted, the signs of changing standards were all around them. Women once wore sleeves and long skirts at the beach. Twenty years ago, they began baring their knees—and he hardly needed to explain to the court how the so-called sunsuits of the 1930s left little to the imagination.

In case Woolsey didn't like these mutable standards, Ernst also invoked steadfast principles. Judge Hand's declaration that "truth and beauty are too precious" to be sacrificed to unsophisticated readers suggested a government interest in literary merit. If *Ulysses* was what the Treasury Department said it was—if it was a modern classic, if it rendered truth and beauty—then it was worthy of protection in the marketplace of ideas. Ernst didn't dare bring up the First Amendment, but the crux of his argument echoed Oliver Wendell Holmes: books leading society toward the truth are essential.

Yet it would be enough if Woolsey accepted that literature couldn't be obscene. Ernst cited the definition of *classic* in *Webster's Collegiate Dictionary* and reasoned that obscenity, which depraves and corrupts, cannot also be a work "of acknowledged excellence." The judge was forced to choose.

Judge Woolsey had been listening patiently. "Mr. Coleman," he asked the prosecutor, "what do you think constitutes obscenity?"

"I should say a thing is obscene by the ordinary language used and by what it does to the average reader." Obscenity could be measured by community standards rather than corruptible children, if Morris Ernst wished. In fact, Coleman made Ernst's argument for him—he praised *Ulysses*. The style was "new and startling." *Ulysses* offered "a new system of presenting people to themselves." Joyce's book was as scientific as it was poetic. "We know that it is an encyclopedia," the government said in its brief, "thorough and classified, of the very substance of two beings, both physical and psychological, external and internal. We realize that it is a deep character study, that even the remotest characters in the book are limned with unmistakable distinctness upon its huge canvas." The government defended *Ulysses* more eloquently than the defense.

Sam Coleman wasn't a fool. He knew how much Ernst's argument depended upon establishing the literary merit of Joyce's book. He knew Ernst and Lindey would come trotting into court with piles of statements gathered from professors, clergymen, librarians and writers from around the country. They would juxtapose tributes to *Ulysses* from Paris art dealers ("almost perfect") and well-known writers ("majestic genius") with words of praise from female librarians in Texas ("superb") and North Dakota ("classically exquisite"). He knew Ernst would piece together a "whole book" standard from an esoteric case history. He also knew that Ernst would take advantage of his admittedly ingenious tactics, from the seized copy loaded down with critical praise to the U.S. Treasury's designation of the book as a "classic." Section III, Subheading A of Ernst's legal brief trumpeted the Treasury secretary's approval: "THE FEDERAL GOVERNMENT HAS OFFICIALLY PAID TRIBUTE TO THE GREATNESS OF ULYSSES." Ernst had outdone himself, and Judge Woolsey would be sympathetic. So instead of disputing the literary merit of *Ulysses*, the government simply agreed.

"No one would dare attack the literary value of the book," Coleman said. But after praising *Ulysses* he began to zero in on the book's unprintable words—he alluded to them indirectly, of course, for the sake of the lady present. Not even the most liberal judge thought an author's artistry could legalize *unlimited* filth. All the government had to do was point out what Judge

Woolsey already knew: that the filth in *Ulysses* went far beyond what any American court had ever allowed.

Sam Coleman and his assistant, Nicholas Atlas, pored over all of the books recently exonerated of obscenity charges and found their language far less colorful than Molly Bloom's. Neither *Mademoiselle de Maupin* nor *Casanova's Homecoming* contained bawdy words. *Female* wasn't bad, either. "An occasional word is offensive to the general taste," they found, but it wasn't obscene by current standards. *Woman and Puppet* didn't have a single dirty word. Clement Wood's *Flesh* was the most obscene book they examined, and yet it didn't have any dirty words either. *Ulysses*, on the other hand, was teeming with both obscenity and, they added, "endless blasphemy." No other book contained what *Ulysses* contained.

Obscenity could be a "living standard" if Morris Ernst and Judge Woolsey felt so inclined. Coleman's rebuttal was that the nation's standards—shocking sunsuits notwithstanding—hadn't changed enough to legalize Molly Bloom's thoughts. The text made his case for him: "Ill tighten my bottom well and let out a few smutty words smellrump or lick my shit or the first mad thing comes into my head[.]" To answer the judge's earlier question, Coleman said, "I do not think that obscenity necessarily should be limited to exciting sexual feeling." A book could be banned if its language were coarse or disgusting, and if the judge went back to his *Oxford English Dictionary,* he would find that it agreed. The case against *Ulysses* wasn't just about isolated obscenities. Coleman granted that the book was a modern classic, a cohesive work of art to be judged as a whole, so that he could turn Ernst's argument on its head. *Ulysses* had to be banned, he said, precisely *because* it was so skillfully integrated: it was both obscene and a masterpiece through and through.

THE GOVERNMENT'S STRATEGY WAS, for Ernst, both frustrating and exhilarating. Coleman sidestepped the brunt of his case with the same argument he had made on the phone the previous year. Though Coleman wouldn't say the dirty words in front of the lady in the courtroom, he mounted more of a case than Ernst anticipated, possibly because Coleman resented his

Treasury Department gambit. The DA's office had began dragging its feet in the final months—Ernst had to contact Woolsey personally to get a court date. Now that Random House had its hearing, Ernst was forced to address the government's argument about "bawdy words," and he wasn't going to tiptoe around it.

"Judge, as to the word *fuck*, one etymological dictionary gives a possible derivation from 'to plant,' an Anglo-Saxon agricultural usage—the farmer fucked the seed into the soil." Ernst wanted to demystify the word by saying it out loud, and he wanted to make it less threatening by giving it a history (even if that history was wrong). Ernst said he rather liked the word. He was careful about when he used it—it didn't win him many friends, he admitted—but that single syllable was freighted with power and honesty. "This, your honor, has more integrity than a euphemism used every day in every modern novel to describe precisely the same event."

"For example, Mr. Ernst?"

"Oh—'They slept together.' It means the same thing."

Woolsey found the turn of phrase amusing. "Counselor, that isn't even usually the truth!"

Ernst made his case to Judge Woolsey for nearly an hour, largely by extolling Joyce's merits. James Joyce, he argued, "led a monastic existence" away from fans and reporters like "an austere Olympian." His text was painstakingly structured. Not only did each chapter have its own distinctive style and correspondence with Homer's *Odyssey*, it had its own color, its own symbol, and its own bodily organ. The novel didn't pander to base instincts—the first sexually suggestive scene was several chapters into the book, by which point any reader looking for smut would have stopped reading. *Ulysses* as a whole didn't even resemble pornography, he argued. It didn't have a suggestive title. The book was too long. There wasn't a single illustration. And Random House wasn't in the pornography business—it published Nathaniel Hawthorne, Emily Brontë and Robert Frost. And if all of that wasn't enough, Ernst produced a map of the United States with a red pin marking every city where a librarian expressed interest in obtaining *Ulysses*. The "community" that accepted *Ulysses* was nothing less than the entire nation. The argument was, in the end, about a gut reaction. People knew pornography when they saw it, and this wasn't it.

Ulysses, after all, was bewildering. For every filthy word, how many inscrutable ones were there? Ernst and Lindey listed dozens of puzzling words in the book. *Quadrireme. Entelechy. Epicene. Hebdomadary.* For all they knew, some of *those* were obscene—and that was the point. If they were dirty, it wouldn't matter. Obscenity, by definition, must deprave and corrupt. "It is axiomatic that only what is understandable can corrupt," Ernst argued. "The worst Chinese obscenity is innocuous to anyone not acquainted with the language." *Ulysses* was high art to the sophisticates who could understand it and gibberish to the morally vulnerable. They quoted incomprehensible passages (including Stephen's "ineluctable modality") to bewilder Judge Woolsey. If John Quinn had been alive to hear it, he would have been proud.

At first, Woolsey agreed with Ernst. He described what it had been like to read *Ulysses* in Petersham. "Some of it was so obscure and unintelligible that it was difficult to understand it at all. It was like walking around without your feet on the ground." He sat back and, taking advantage of the setting, lit a cigarette lodged in a long, ivory holder. "This isn't an easy case to decide," he said. "I think things ought to take their chances in the marketplace. My own feeling is against censorship. I know that as soon as you suppress anything the bootlegger goes to work. Still . . ."

He broke off for a moment, remembering some of the passages the DA underlined—*Ill let him know if thats what he wanted that his wife is fucked yes and damn well fucked too up in my neck nearly not by him 5 or 6 times*—"Still, there is that soliloquy in the last chapter. I don't know about that."

The judge was curious about Mr. Ernst's grasp of the novel. "Did you really read this entire book? It's tough going, isn't it?"

Ernst had tried to read it ten years ago, but he couldn't get through it until the previous summer, when, in preparation for the case, he had an epiphany about Joyce's technique. Ernst described it not as a stream of consciousness but as a *double* stream of consciousness that shaped our mental lives every day without our fully realizing it.

"Your honor, while arguing to win this case I thought I was intent only on this book, but frankly, while pleading before you, I've also been thinking about that ring around your tie, how your gown does not fit too well on your shoulders and the picture of John Marshall behind your bench."

The judge smiled and rapped lightly on the bench in front of him. "I've been worried about the last part of the book, and I have listened as intently as I know how, but I must confess that while listening to you I've been thinking about the Hepplewhite chair behind you."

Ernst smiled. "That, Judge, is the essence of *Ulysses*."

As the thin, bespectacled lawyer continued, talking about "a weird epitome of what is going on in a human mind," Woolsey began to wonder if that simultaneity really was the source of the book's peculiar power. For in the same way that a pair of hornrimmed glasses reminds Leopold Bloom of his father who poisoned himself when Leopold was still a boy, the arching curve of the Hepplewhite chair might have reminded Woolsey of his mother sitting at home in South Carolina, where the rickety cotton pickers' shacks were visible through the windows. A few years after they left that house, John Woolsey's mother, having left his father, threw herself from a window in Brooklyn.

Something about *Ulysses*, Woolsey said, left him "bothered, stirred and troubled." Even now, some of the passages moved him in unexpected ways. Molly Bloom's final words—the novel's final words—stayed with him.

O that awful deepdown torrent O and the sea the sea crimson sometimes like fire and the glorious sunsets and the figtrees in the Alameda gardens yes and all the queer little streets and the pink and blue and yellow houses and the rosegardens and the jessamine and geraniums and cactuses and Gibraltar as a girl where I was a Flower of the mountain yes when I put the rose in my hair like the Andalusian girls used or shall I wear a red yes and how he kissed me under the Moorish wall and I thought well as well him as another and then I asked him with my eyes to ask again yes and then he asked me would I yes to say yes my mountain flower and first I put my arms around him yes and drew him down

to me so he could feel my breasts all perfume yes and his heart was
going like mad and yes I said yes I will Yes.

Judge Woolsey interrupted the counselor again. "There are passages of
moving literary beauty, passages of worth and power. I tell you," he continued.
"Reading parts of that book almost drove me frantic. That last part, that soliloquy, it may represent the moods of a woman of that sort. That is what dis-
turbs me. I seem to understand it."

BY THE TIME JUDGE WOOLSEY began to consider the legality of *Ulysses*,
there were a few federal rulings, scattershot and little known, that could have
laid the groundwork for a lenient judgment. Learned Hand's 1913 ruling was
the most ambitious, but not a single federal opinion had cited it in the inter-
vening twenty years. It was easy for Hand to reject the Hicklin Rule and defend truth and beauty when the stakes were so low. He didn't have to apply his
standard to a particular book, and he certainly didn't have to decide whether
Molly Bloom's nighttime thoughts struck the proper "compromise between
candor and shame"—the very notion of a compromise must have seemed
quaint to Woolsey. In *Ulysses*, the relationship between candor and shame felt
more like a battle. Since the government acknowledged the book's literary
merit only to contend that it did nothing to mitigate its filth, Woolsey had to
pit the virtue of literature against the vice of obscenity and declare a victor. He
had no intention of categorically legalizing Molly's coarse language. If *Ulysses*
was going to be permissible in the United States, he would have to assert that
the novel was transcendent, that it turned filth into art.

After the *Ulysses* hearing, Judge Woolsey walked to the Century Association around the corner, where he had his customary Saturday lunch. He might
have felt alone as he left the Bar Building. The types of cases he knew best—
patent, copyright and admiralty law—had clearer precedents. And yet even
with decades of obscenity case law, it was difficult to escape the notion that a
judge had to make it up as he went along. How could a person know whether a

book stirred sexual impulses in the average person? Would he have to commission a poll?

It occurred to Woolsey that he might ask the Centurions what they thought about Joyce's book, so he approached two members of the Century Association's Literature Committee: Charles E. Merrill, Jr., a publisher, and Henry Seidel Canby, a former Yale English professor and a founding editor of the *Saturday Review of Literature*. It was not an "average" community, perhaps, but it would provide some semblance of objectivity. Woolsey wanted them to be as objective as possible, so he took each of them aside separately, into an alcove of the club's reading room perhaps. Did James Joyce's *Ulysses* incite sexual or lustful thoughts in them? (He was asking, of course, for legal purposes.)

Canby was no fan of literary modernism, and he remained one of the only nationally renowned critics who used the phrase "puritanic censorship" approvingly. In the 1920s, Canby had written that Joyce's "obsession with inflamed or perverted sex" made *Ulysses* incoherent. The fact that Joyce finished his book, he noted in another essay, was the only real indication that he was sane. And yet Canby, like so many others, had changed his mind about Joyce's novel. Both he and Merrill independently told Woolsey that the overarching effect of *Ulysses* wasn't sexual at all—if anything, it was "somewhat tragic" and a "powerful commentary on the inner lives of men and women."

At eight o'clock on Thanksgiving morning, Judge Woolsey was still thinking about the *Ulysses* case as he shaved. There was a vanity to his decisions. Like Joyce, he drafted in longhand and revised repeatedly. By the time he began sketching his *Ulysses* verdict he was trying to establish his own legal tradition. Woolsey wasn't going to cite Judge Hand's definition of obscenity (the two judges didn't get along), and he made only passing references to a handful of other decisions. "The practice followed in this case," Woolsey stated in his overview, "is in accordance with the suggestion made by me in the case of *United States v. One Book, Entitled 'Contraception.'*" And Woolsey's *Contraception* decree declared that Dr. Stopes's birth control manual "does not fall within the test of obscenity or immorality laid down by me in the case of *United States v. One Obscene Book, Entitled 'Married Love.'*" It was Woolsey all the way through.

The clocks in Judge Woolsey's Lexington Avenue apartment (wall-mounted timepieces, nine-foot mahogany monuments) chimed on the hour with precision. The rugs and upholstery throughout the corner duplex softened the peals, and the bathroom door muffled them a bit more. When Woolsey glanced above his lathered face in the mirror, he could see the reflection of the clear blue sky. He often thought about a dreary Thanksgiving in New Hampshire decades earlier. The rain had kept him inside his friend's house all day, and they explored the attic after dinner. Among the boxes of castoffs archived in crumpled newspaper, he found an old poetry anthology. Fipping through the pages, he came across a stanza from an eighteenth-century poem that inspired him enough to jot down a paraphrase. "I fear, Sir, that you may consider these protestations unmaidenly, but by the laws of Nature we are bound to love, although the Rules of Modesty oftentimes compel us to conceal it."

Woolsey imagined the woman in the poem struggling against Rules of Modesty she had no part in creating, against customs whose power derived primarily from habit. It was, to Woolsey, an epiphany about the law itself, an insight he recited repeatedly over the years, an insight that was more compelling because he had rescued it from an attic: the law was really just a collection of rules pitted against the immutable laws of Nature, and the rules would have to bend lest they snap. Perhaps the law needed sincere, immodest women to bend the rules. He scraped away the unmaidenly stubble from his face and glanced from the lathered razor back to the blue sky. It was a kaleidoscope of impressions.

Judge Woolsey rushed to his desk, grabbed his pen and began writing his decision with a dripping razor in his left hand.

Joyce has attempted—it seems to me, with astonishing success—to show how the screen of consciousness with its ever-shifting kaleidoscopic impressions carries, as it were on a plastic palimpsest, not only what is in the focus of each man's observation of the actual things about him, but also in a penumbral zone residua of past impressions, some recent and some drawn up by association from the domain of the subconscious.

The decision stemmed from Joyce's sincerity. Judge Woolsey peered into the text and imagined James Joyce, a half-blind artist, compelled by nature to say everything, and everything, including decorum, was subservient to his design. Joyce had been attacked and misunderstood, Woolsey wrote, because he "has been loyal to his technique" and "has honestly attempted to tell fully what his characters think about," no matter the consequences. Some of those thoughts were sexual, but, he pointed out, "it must always be remembered that his locale was Celtic and his season spring."

Woolsey did more than legalize Joyce's book. He became an advocate. "*Ulysses* is an amazing tour de force when one considers the success which has been in the main achieved with such a difficult objective as Joyce set for himself." He acknowledged the persuasiveness of Sam Coleman's argument before casting it aside.

In many places it seems to me to be disgusting, but although it contains, as I have mentioned above, many words usually considered dirty, I have not found anything that I consider to be dirt for dirt's sake. Each word of the book contributes like a bit of mosaic to the detail of the picture which Joyce is seeking to construct for his readers . . . when such a great artist in words, as Joyce undoubtedly is, seeks to draw a true picture of the lower middle class in a European city, ought it to be impossible for the American public legally to see that picture?

"*Ulysses*," he concluded, "may, therefore, be admitted into the United States."

THE KEY PHRASE in the decision's heading—"the government's motion for a decree of forfeiture and destruction is denied"—did not quite capture how sweepingly successful Ernst's argument was. Legal protection for literary value was more than granted. It was urged.

Time magazine declared Woolsey's opinion "historic for its authority, its eloquence, its future influence on U.S. book publishing." When the book was published, the magazine put Joyce on the cover, eye patch and all.

> Watchers of the U.S. skies last week reported no comet or other celestial portent. In Manhattan no showers of ticker-tape blossomed from Broadway office windows, no welcoming committee packed the steps of City Hall. . . . Yet many a wide-awake modern-minded citizen knew he had seen literary history pass another milestone. For last week a much-enduring traveler, world-famed but long an outcast, landed safe and sound on U.S. shores. His name was *Ulysses*.

In Paris, the Joyces' telephone was ringing constantly with the news. "Thus one half of the English speaking world surrenders," Joyce said. "The other half will follow." As calls of congratulations kept coming in, Lucia cut the telephone wires.

At 10:15 in the morning on December 7, 1933, just minutes after the decision was filed, Donald Klopfer called up Ernst Reichl and said, "Go ahead." Random House had commissioned Reichl to design the Random House edition of *Ulysses,* while Judge Woolsey was still reading the book in Petersham, so that production could begin the moment it was legalized. Reichl, a PhD in art history, had designed everything himself—the binding, the cover, the jacket, the interior—to ensure that every aspect of *Ulysses* would be cohesive. It had taken him two months to test a variety of fonts and formats before he produced a sample copy set in Baskerville.

It was just what Random House wanted: bold, clean and jarringly modern. "Stately, plump Buck Mulligan" began with a monumental *S* on a page all to itself. Five minutes after Reichl got the call from Random House, his team began printing the first chapters. They included the full text of Judge Woolsey's decision so that if the government brought charges again, Woolsey's praise would be entered into evidence. It remained in the Random House edition for decades, making it possibly the most widely read legal decision in U.S. history.

Ulysses was bound and delivered to the publisher five weeks later. Random

House planned an initial printing of ten thousand copies, but by the time publication day arrived (January 25, 1934) advance sales topped twelve thousand—"a really phenomenal figure for a $3.50 book in times like these," Cerf said, a figure they had thought was months away. By April, sales climbed to thirty-three thousand copies, and Cerf went to Paris and gave Joyce a check for $7,500. *Ulysses* sold more in three months than it had in twelve years. In 1950, it was the Modern Library's fifth highest-selling book. There was only one problem. The book that Random House gave Reichl to print wasn't the latest Shakespeare and Company edition. It was Samuel Roth's edition. The first legal edition of *Ulysses* in the United States was the corrupted text of a literary pirate.

27.

THE TABLES OF THE LAW

The Home Office in London kept a close eye on the developments overseas. For years, British citizens had been requesting permission to import personal copies of *Ulysses* from France, and after the Woolsey decision the requests were difficult to refuse. In January 1934, T. S. Eliot, by then a director at Faber and Faber, approached the Home Office about publishing a British edition of *Ulysses*, at which point officials decided "to arrest developments" as long as possible.

That same month, a literary critic named Desmond MacCarthy—the man who had ridiculed *Ulysses* in Virginia Woolf's drawing room nearly twenty years before—requested a copy for a lecture he was giving on Joyce at the Royal Institute. The Home Office granted MacCarthy's request but worried that people attending the lecture would ask how he obtained his copy, which would lead to more requests. Officials were bound to get questions about how the Home Office made its decisions, including, as one official put it, "whether we regarded the book as obscene or not according to its recipient"—which was exactly how they regarded it.

But the Home Office wanted to apply a uniform principle for *Ulysses,* and it hoped the U.S. rulings would help. British officials examined Woolsey's decision thoroughly and waited to see if the U.S. government would file an appeal. Sure enough, it did. One week after Woolsey's decision, Franklin D. Roosevelt unexpectedly replaced George Medalie with a man named Martin Conboy, a close friend of the president's. Conboy was both a graduate and a regent of Georgetown University as well as an erstwhile president of the Catholic Club of New York. Pope Pius XI made him a knight commander of the order of St. Gregory the Great. Conboy also happened to be a former lawyer for the New York Society for the Suppression of Vice, and he convinced Roosevelt's new attorney general to take the case to the U.S. Court of Appeals for the Second Circuit, one step before the Supreme Court. In May 1934 the *Ulysses* case appeared before Judge Martin Manton, Judge Learned Hand and Judge Augustus Hand (Learned's cousin).

Where Sam Coleman had finessed the government's case, Conboy was blunt. "This is an obscene book," he told the judges. "It begins with blasphemy, runs the whole gamut of sexual perversion, and ends in inexpressible filth and obscenity." He noted that Morris Ernst's book about obscenity, *To the Pure*, was as appalling as Joyce's—Ernst argued that obscenity didn't even *exist*. It was absurd enough to disqualify the defense counsel altogether. Conboy asserted the lasting importance of the Hicklin Rule and argued that literary merit, Random House's motives and James Joyce's genius were all irrelevant. Joyce's honesty and sincerity and the detailed accuracy of his Dublin mosaic were also irrelevant. "A book that is obscene is not rendered less so by reason of the fact that the matter complained of is in fact truthful." Judge Woolsey's opinion was incontestably wrong. "No reasonable man," Conboy argued, "applying the proper rule of law could come to any conclusion other than that *Ulysses* is obscene."

Conboy compiled a list of fifty-three "unchaste and lustful" pages and read all of them in the courtroom, stammering and red-faced. The judges followed along in their own copies, heads down and pencils poised. After ten minutes, a woman gasped and walked out. The other woman in the courtroom was determined to stay.

"Are you going to read the whole book?" Learned Hand asked.

"Well, I'll give you a generous sampling." After lunch, he read for another forty minutes. He continued to read the following day.

It was the most publicized obscenity case in U.S. history. Augustus and Learned Hand were annoyed that Woolsey's decision exacerbated the media circus. Woolsey thought of himself as "literary," Learned Hand said later, and "that's a very dangerous thing for a judge to be." The Hands wanted their decision to be bland and unquotable (to "give the book a minimum of advertising"), but the case made quotability inevitable. In preliminary memos, the judges unanimously agreed that Molly Bloom's monologue was "erotic." Learned Hand went so far as to say that several passages "could excite lustful feelings" in both young people and normal adults—it seemed to violate even his own liberal ruling in 1913. Judge Manton railed against *Ulysses*. "Who can doubt the obscenity of this book," he wrote, "after a reading of the pages referred to, which are too indecent to add as a footnote to this opinion?" Manton argued that literature exists "to refresh the weary, to console the sad, to hearten the dull and downcast, to increase man's interest in the world, his joy of living." *Ulysses* had none of literature's ennobling moral aims. Masterpieces, Judge Manton reminded the court, are never produced by "men who have no Master." (A few years later, Manton would go to prison for taking bribes.)

Manton's opinion was a dissent. Learned and Augustus Hand joined together to legalize *Ulysses* in the United States. Though they balked at Woolsey's style, they agreed with his substance. "I cannot say that *Ulysses* deals in smut for smut's sake," Augustus wrote in a preliminary memo, and Learned Hand agreed, but they could come to that conclusion only by stepping away from the obscene passages. Learned wanted to terminate the policy of evaluating excerpts. Judges, he thought, should weigh the danger of debauching readers' minds against the freedom of artistic expression, which could only be determined by judging an entire book. He believed that the "relevance" of filth, not its mere presence, should be the legal standard for obscenity.

The Circuit Court declared portions of *Ulysses* "coarse, blasphemous, and obscene," but it was more than that. "The erotic passages are submerged in the book as a whole and have little resultant effect." Augustus Hand's opinion for the court offered a cautious restatement of Woolsey's praise: Joyce was "an excellent craftsman of a sort." He predicted that "*Ulysses* will not last as a

THE TABLES OF THE LAW

substantial contribution to literature," though "it has become a sort of contemporary classic." Joyce's novel was sincere and artful. It captured men and women who were at turns "bewildered and keenly apprehensive, sordid and aspiring, ugly and beautiful, hateful and loving." The Hands and Manton agreed about one thing: the reader of *Ulysses* was left not with consolation but with a panorama of humanity's "confusion, misery and degradation." And yet while corrupting an innocent mind was forbidden, misery and degradation were perfectly legal.

In London, the director of public prosecutions (Sir Archibald's successor, Edward Atkinson) read the Circuit Court decision and a *New York Tribune* article covering it. He was interested, he said, both in the arguments and "the admirable way in which they are expressed." When Martin Conboy decided not to appeal the case to the Supreme Court, one half of the English-speaking world surrendered at last. The other half did nothing until the fall of 1936, when Scotland Yard informed the British secretary of state that a gentleman named Stephen Winkworth had received a letter from a London bookseller announcing a forthcoming U.K. edition of *Ulysses*.

Winkworth was aghast. He forwarded the circular to London's police commissioner and wanted to know "whether you are able to make your prohibition effective." Stories about the edition began appearing in the press, and angry letters to customs officials followed. "If I can purchase a copy of this book anywhere in London," one man wrote, "on what grounds do you tell me that it is forbidden in this country . . . Surely, there is a fallacy somewhere?" The press indicated that the publisher, John Lane, had consulted the Home Office, but no one had any record of it. The new edition was an unwanted surprise, and the government no longer had the privilege of stalling.

Undersecretary of State Henderson conferred with Director Atkinson and anticipated defense attorneys' arguments. The "Penelope" episode would be defended as "Freud in novel form," and, following Morris Ernst, they would argue that the Hicklin Rule was untenable, that the nation's reading standards couldn't be dictated by children. John Lane's expensive edition had a good case because it was unlikely to fall into the hands of corruptible readers, and

Henderson warned the director that "if this limited edition goes well, it will be followed by a cheaper edition." The government would either have to accept the widespread circulation of *Ulysses* or prosecute the publisher immediately.

So on November 6, 1936, the undersecretary of state met with the director of public prosecutions and the attorney general. At the meeting, the attorney general declared the Hicklin Rule "inadequate." Obscenity was not as simple as identifying a book's tendency to deprave and corrupt. The government must consider intent and context—the character of a book was all contingent. The principle was that there was no principle. So the officials decided "to take no further action" regarding *Ulysses*, and they duly informed customs and postal officials to also do nothing. That's how the fifteen-year battle ended. Not with a whimper, but with a shrug.

"Is there one who understands me?" The question James Joyce had asked Nora Barnacle before they left Ireland together was more difficult to answer in his old age. One afternoon in the fall of 1930, Joyce was walking quietly in Paris with the help of his assistant, Paul Léon, when a young woman on the Boulevard Raspail summoned the courage to approach the Irish writer and compliment him on his work. By then, Joyce's eyesight was abysmal. He had cataracts in both eyes. A Swiss surgeon had recently opened up an artificial pupil in his left eye, and he was expecting more operations. For months, he could not fully see what he was writing. Joyce turned from the woman and looked up at the sky—the sun's light was barely visible—and then at the boulevard's trees with cages around their growing trunks. "You would do better," he told her, "to admire the sky or even those poor trees." Transparency had its own beauty.

Joyce's belated victory revealed more about us than it did about Joyce. The legalization of *Ulysses* announced the transformation of a culture. A book that the American and British governments had burned en masse a few years earlier was now a modern classic, part of the heritage of Western civilization. Official approval of *Ulysses*, in prominent federal decisions and behind closed doors, indicated that the culture of the 1910s and 1920s—a culture of experimentation and radicalism, Dada and warfare, little magazines and birth control—was not an aberration. It had taken root. Or, more accurately, it indicated that rootedness itself was a fiction.

For beyond the fact that *Ulysses* had turned so quickly from contraband to classic was the more unsettling idea that no obscenity was fundamental. Everything could be transformed by a context. By sanctioning *Ulysses*, British and American authorities had, to some small but important degree, become philosophical anarchists. They accepted that there were no immutable abstractions in culture, no permanent values, no indelible markers between "classic" and "filth," tradition and depravity. There was no absolute authority, no singular vision for our society, no monolithic ideas towering over us. For the most elaborate designs and the most dangerous books are subsumed by a torrent of details, mistakes and revisions, insertions in notebooks, blind spots in the vision, bacteria in the veins, fleeting moments between people in tiny backyards peering out into the universe at night, and the universe is humid nightblue fruit, and the word that shakes it all down is *yes*.

EPILOGUE

*"Say! What was the most revolting piece of obscenity
in all your career of crime? Go the whole hog.
Puke it out! Be candid for once."*

—ULYSSES

Obscenity is as illegal today as it was in 1873. What changed is the way we define it. The legal transformation began in earnest the moment Judge Woolsey (and the Circuit Court following him) measured vices against virtues, when they shifted from hunting for corruption to weighing corruption against beauty. Once art became a state interest, the scales of justice gradually tilted toward art's favor so that by the mid-twentieth century the U.S. Supreme Court defined obscenity as "prurient" material deemed "utterly without redeeming social importance"—an ounce of virtue can legalize a pound of vice.

In the world before *Ulysses*, a filthy word or a salacious episode seemed like a contaminant—no matter how small it was, it could poison the whole. Joyce's book altered our understanding of obscenity partly by exploring the sustaining qualities of filth, but it also altered obscenity by altering our understanding of ourselves. We are not, according to *Ulysses*, blank slates corrupted by the world. We are born into patterns and stories thousands of years old, and indecency seems less dangerous when people seem less pristine. After *Ulysses*, books seemed less likely to "deprave and corrupt" us. If anything, they convinced us that the most dangerous fiction was our innocence.

The dramatic reduction of obscenity as a legal category—the expansion of the types of speech protected by the First Amendment—involves more than the freedom to print dirty words. It confirms the power of all words to hash out the truth. Obscenity rulings presented themselves as sensible bans on worthless speech, as judgments beyond the realm of debate. When Judge Manton refused to quote *Ulysses* in his dissenting opinion, he was not being bombastic. His decree absolved him from naming the content he wanted to banish—silence is both the way we judge obscenity and the way we solve it. To legalize what was once patently unspeakable, however, is to replace silence with both debate and debatability. It is to invite deep—even systemic—uncertainty. For to change moral standards is to upset what we assumed was natural (nothing serves systems of power more than the conviction that things cannot change), and few modes of expression seem more natural—more instinctive and indisputable, less amenable to logic or academic study—than what we find offensive or obscene. If obscenity can change, anything can change. The advent of *Ulysses* showed us how arbitrary even the presumably natural categories can be. Edith Wharton called Joyce's book "a turgid welter of pornography" despite the fact that only a small sliver of the text is offensive to anyone. While many readers see the unprecedented complexity of Joyce's characters as the book's hallmark, E. M. Forster saw in *Ulysses* "a dogged attempt to cover the universe with mud . . . a simplification of the human character in the interests of Hell."

Younger writers like Hart Crane took it as a revelation. "I feel like shouting EUREKA! . . . Easily the epic of the age." The truths contained within it were so jarring that he thought "some fanatic will kill Joyce sometime soon for the wonderful things said in *Ulysses*." Whether or not he wrote in the interests of Hell, Joyce paved the way for authors that followed. Vladimir Nabokov's *Lolita*, for example, would not have been possible without *Ulysses*. "Oh, yes," Nabokov said, "let people compare me to Joyce by all means, but my English is pat ball to Joyce's champion game." Henry Miller, whose *Tropic of Cancer* was part of the 1960s legal battles that ended U.S. prosecutions against literary obscenity, compared the end of *Ulysses* to the end of the Book of Revelation. "And there shall be no more curse!" Miller wrote. "Henceforth no sin, no guilt, no fear, no repression, no longing, no pain of separation. The end is accomplished—man returns to the womb."

IN ONLY A FEW DECADES, *Ulysses* transformed from an insurgency to an institution. The academic Joyce industry boomed in the 1960s and has only increased with time. There are roughly three hundred books and more than three thousand scholarly articles devoted, partly or entirely, to *Ulysses*, and about fifty of those books have been written in the past ten years. The mountain of research is at turns enlightening and obsessive—in 1989 two Joyceans attempted to reconstruct the contents of a *Ulysses* manuscript notebook that no one can find. Even the literal content of the published text has been a site of controversy. Joyce's endless revisions, his idiosyncratic writing and the error-filled 1922 edition have led scholars to fight—with a ferocity only PhDs can muster—over which edition of *Ulysses* is definitive. Battles over competing editions led to heated debates about prepositions, transposed letters and missing accent marks. In the 1980s the disputes snowballed into accusations of stolen and unacknowledged work followed by aspersions cast about qualifications and broken editorial protocols, all of which culminated in conference panel betrayals and smear campaigns. To this day, Random House publishes two rival editions of *Ulysses* in an effort to bypass the academic melee. Many Joyceans are dissatisfied with both.

And yet what's remarkable about Joyce's novel is that it surpasses all of the disputes and dissections. It is, as Nabokov said, "a divine work of art and will live on despite the academic nonentities who turn it into a collection of symbols or Greek myths." After ninety years in print, *Ulysses* sells roughly one hundred thousand copies a year. It has been translated into more than twenty languages, including Arabic, Norwegian, Catalan and Malayalam. There are two Chinese translations. Groups of readers gather in houses and pubs to read and discuss *Ulysses* together, and as unusual as that is for a decades-old book, the life of *Ulysses* is even more vibrant than that.

Every year, on June 16, people around the world gather to celebrate Bloomsday. They dress like Stephen, Molly and Leopold Boom. They eat kidneys for breakfast and gorgonzola sandwiches with burgundy for lunch. They reenact scenes, sing songs featured in *Ulysses* (there are hundreds) and carouse in makeshift Nighttowns. Revelers savor Joyce-inspired art, poetry, dance, film and drama—Melbourne held a mock trial of Joyce in 2002. There have been Bloomsday celebrations in Tokyo, Mexico City and Buenos Aires. Santa Maria, Brazil, has been celebrating for twenty years straight. Two hundred cities in sixty countries have celebrated Joyce's novel. There is no other literary event like it. One day each year, fiction creeps into reality as people around the world reenact events that never happened.

One Leopold Bloom, wearing his bowler and black mourning suit, remembers New Yorkers greeting him on the 1 train going uptown. "Yo, Bloom, Happy Bloomsday." Since 1982, actors have gathered in New York's Symphony Space to perform readings that can last as long as sixteen hours (the backstage celebration, fueled with beer donated by the city's oldest Irish pub, lasts just as long). Before Molly takes the stage at roughly eleven at night, an organizer warns the audience listening on public radio stations across the country that they should gird themselves for explicit language. Then a single actress takes the stage and reads the "Penelope" episode until nearly two in the morning as drowsy spectators—cab drivers, travel agents, people who have never read *Ulysses* and people who have studied it for years—listen to the river of Molly Bloom's thoughts in the darkened auditorium.

Bloomsday's Mecca is, of course, Dublin. The first Bloomsday celebration, in 1954, involved five men who assigned themselves roles and planned to track the novel's events around the city in two horsedrawn carriages. The commemoration was abandoned halfway through when the group somehow ended up in a pub *not* featured in *Ulysses*. By the 1970s the crowds of people following Bloom's footsteps began to stop traffic. In 2004 the James Joyce Centre served breakfast to ten thousand people. Gentlemen in hats and striped blazers, women in frilly collars and ankle-length dresses, crowded onto the stairs winding up to the Sandycove Tower's parapet so they could hear the early morning exchanges between Stephen Dedalus and Buck Mulligan. One year, celebrants re-created Paddy Dignam's funeral in the "Hades" episode with a horsedrawn hearse and a corpse played by one of Joyce's grandnephews. On the way to Glasnevin Cemetery, he popped out of the casket to check their progress and terrified onlooking schoolchildren. Amid the hilarity, the hearse clipped a curb as it rounded the cemetery's corner and cast everyone out, the living and the dead.

It's tempting to think of *Ulysses* as a book about how feeble life has become in the modern era. The warrior King of Ithaca is reduced to a lonely, cuckolded ad salesman, and the defiant genius who penned the novel was reduced to a rueful figure tapping his cane down foreign city streets. Even the censorship of the book demonstrates how an arduous work of art can be scuttled by the cursory glance of a government functionary—the writing takes place over the course of years, and the ban takes place before lunch. Censoring a book is easy. It merely requires increasing the risk of publication enough to make it too much of a gamble for a publisher, and publishing a book is already almost quixotic. One of the paradoxes of the printed word is that whatever strength and durability it has is inseparable from this inherent weakness. Even a book like *Ulysses,* we consider essential to our cultural heritage book, might never have happened—might have ended in a New York police court or with the outbreak of a world war—if it were not for a handful of awestruck people. Joyce's novel, with its intricacies and schoolboy adventures, with each measured and careful page, gave them what it gives us: a way to sally forth into the greater world, to walk out into the garden, to see the heaventree of stars as if for the first time and affirm, against the incalculable odds, our own diminutive existence. It is the fragility of our affirmations—no matter how indecorous they may be—that makes them so powerful.

When Joyce was a little boy and dessert time was announced, he would make his way down the staircase, holding his nursemaid's hand, and call out to his parents with every accomplished step, "Here's me! Here's me!"

ACKNOWLEDGMENTS

Perhaps the only way in which I resemble Joyce is that I have collected many debts. I am grateful to Suzanne Gluck, my agent, for her support, energy and confidence as well as her unfailingly good advice over the years. I owe a tremendous debt to my editor, Ginny Smith, for her instinct and her careful attention to my writing in draft after interminable draft. This book owes so much to her. Nick Trautwein's faith in the early stages was inspiring and helped me to see this book's possibilities, and this project would not have happened without Matthew Pearl's encouragement, advocacy and support from the very beginning. Our conversations over coffee and more colorful drinks buoyed me through the challenges. I owe a debt of gratitude to everyone at Penguin Press, including Kaitlyn Flynn, Sofia Groopman, Patricia Nicolescu and, for their legal advice, Marlene Glazer, Emily Condlin and Karen Mayer. I would also like to thank the staff at William Morris Endeavor, including the ever-helpful Eve Attermann and Caroline Donofrio.

Several people have been kind enough to read drafts, and I'm grateful for their comments and advice as the manuscript took shape. Bob Kiely, J. D. Connor and Alan Friedman read either drafts or excerpts and were all encouraging. Eric Idsvoog and Michelle Syba as well as Samantha Frank at William Morris subjected themselves to more than one complete draft. Louis Menand gave me invaluable comments and suggestions on the manuscript long after he thought his days advising me were over.

ACKNOWLEDGMENTS

I am grateful for the expertise of the countless librarians, archivists and curators who helped during the research process, but there are several whose names deserve special recognition. Thomas Lannon and Tal Nadan helped with several questions regarding the extensive John Quinn collection at the New York Public Library, and they both went to great lengths to help track down elusive items. Alison Greenlee and Nicholas Geiger at the University of Tulsa guided me through the Ellmann Collection, and I could not have used it without them. James Maynard at the University of Buffalo helped answer my questions over several days and responded to my belated requests and questions. Simone Munson helped me navigate the John Saxton Sumner papers at the Wisconsin Historical Society in Madison, and she went through the trouble of duplicating hundreds of pages for my use. Liam Kelly at the National Transport Museum of Ireland provided photographs and information about 1904 Dublin trams, and Richard Tuske supplied me with details about the Byrne Room in the old New York City Bar Association building. I received extraordinary assistance from Gabriel Swift at Princeton; Mandy Wise at University College London; Zoe Stansell at the British Library; William Creech at the National Archives and Records Administration in Washington, D.C., and Alex Johnston at the University of Delaware. Julia Whelan at the Countway Library of Medicine at the Harvard Medical School and Jack Eckert at the Center of the History of Medicine helped me navigate the esoteric world of pharmacopeias and early twentieth-century medications. Asim Ahmed advised me about my questions regarding epidemiology and infectious diseases, and Allan Brandt and Ariel Otero provided medical commentary on an early draft of my evaluation of Joyce's medical history.

The Fuerbringer Summer Faculty Grant helped support my research in various archives during three summers, and during the fall and spring the History & Literature faculty at Harvard provided research ideas, conversation and much-needed happy-hour drinks. I have presented some of this work to the Hist & Lit faculty colloquium, and I'm grateful for the feedback and guidance I received. Robert Spoo offered his expertise on Joyce, Samuel Roth on the intricacies of copyright law. Judge John Woolsey would not be alive in these pages were it not for the help of Anna Henchman and Steven Biel, who

ACKNOWLEDGMENTS

put me in touch with members of the Woolsey family, including Mary Woolsey. Peggy Brooks kindly spent an afternoon discussing her memories of the judge and provided me with documents and information I could not have obtained elsewhere. The most generous assistance with the life of Woolsey came from the judge's grandson. John Woolsey III shared countless family documents with me over the years, and (as if that were not enough) he graciously invited me to Petersham to spend the day visiting the judge's library. We celebrated Bloomsday Eve 2010 eating sandwiches on the hillside where the legalization of *Ulysses* in the United States began.

I've had the great fortune of working with three wonderful and dedicated research assistants over the years: Emma Wood, Rachel Wong and Caroline Trusty. They helped with various aspects of the project and tracked down answers to my ever-growing list of questions about everything from census records and currency conversions to the weather on particular days nearly a century ago. I want to give special thanks to Mathilda Hills and Jackson R. Byer, for their thoughts and help regarding Margaret Anderson; to Julie Ahrens and the Stanford Fair Use Project, for their counsel about copyright; to Miriam Otero, for transcribing archival letters filled with crabbed handwriting; to Lisa E. Smith, for her energetic pursuit of an unpublished document; to Louis Hyman and Katherine Howe, for their friendship and their generous hospitality in New York; to Amy Maguire, for her support and understanding during the most hectic months; to the wonderful baristas of Cambridge, for keeping me caffeinated; to the members of an intrepid *Ulysses* book club (Katrin Holzhaus, Eric Idsvoog, Ana Ivkovic and Sean Smith), for untangling some of the mysteries of June 16, 1904; to many other friends—too numerous to name—for keeping me sane; to my students, for keeping me on my toes, for inspiring me, and for reminding me that history and literature are worth everything you put into them; to my mother, for being my mother, and to my dad. I still have your copy of *Dubliners*.

NOTES

ABBREVIATIONS OF ARCHIVES

BL: Harriet Shaw Weaver Papers, British Library, London

BNA: National Archives, London

Buffalo: James Joyce Collection, Poetry Collection of the University Libraries, University at Buffalo, State University of New York

Cerf Papers: Bennett Cerf Papers, Rare Book and Manuscript Library, Columbia University

Cornell: James Joyce Collection, #4609. Division of Rare and Manuscript Collections, Cornell University Library

Delaware: Florence Reynolds Collection Related to Jane Heap and *The Little Review*, Special Collections, University of Delaware Library, Newark, Delaware

Ernst Papers: Morris Ernst Collection, Harry Ransom Humanities Research Center, University of Texas at Austin

HRC: Harry Ransom Humanities Research Center, University of Texas at Austin

NARA: National Archives and Records Administration, Washington, D.C.

NLI: James Joyce Papers, National Library of Ireland, Dublin

NYPL: John Quinn Papers, Manuscripts and Archives Division, New York Public Library, Astor, Lenox, and Tilden Foundations

Roth Papers: Samuel Roth Collection, Rare Book and Manuscript Library, Columbia University

SBP: Sylvia Beach Papers, Firestone Library, Princeton University

SIU: Gorman Papers, Harley Croessmann Collection, Special Collections Research Center, Morris Library, Southern Illinois University–Carbondale

Tulsa: Richard Ellmann Collection, University of Tulsa

UCL: James Joyce Collection, Lidderdale Papers, University College, London

UWM: *Little Review* Records, University of Wisconsin–Milwaukee

WHS: John Saxton Sumner Papers, Wisconsin Historical Society, Madison

Yale Anderson: Elizabeth Jenks Clark Collection of Margaret Anderson, Beinecke Rare Book and Manuscript Library, Yale University

Yale Pound: Ezra Pound Papers, Yale Collection of American Literature, Beinecke Rare Book and Manuscript Library, Yale University

Yale Joyce: James Joyce Papers, Beinecke Rare Book and Manuscript Library, Yale University

ABBREVIATIONS OF BOOKS AND PERIODICALS

DMW: Jane Lidderdale and Mary Nicholson, *Dear Miss Weaver: Harriet Shaw Weaver, 1876–1961*

Ell: Richard Ellmann, *James Joyce*, revised edition (New York: Oxford UP, 1982)

EP/JJ: *Pound/Joyce: The Letters of Ezra Pound to James Joyce*

EP/JQ: *Letters of Ezra Pound to John Quinn*

JJ/SB: *James Joyce's Letters to Sylvia Beach, 1921–1940*

JJQ: *James Joyce Quarterly*

LI, LII, LIII: *The Letters of James Joyce*, vols. 1, 2 and 3

LR: *The Little Review*

LSB: *The Letters of Sylvia Beach*

MBK: Stanislaus Joyce, *My Brother's Keeper: James Joyce's Early Years*

MNY: B. L. Reid, *The Man from New York: John Quinn and His Friends*

NYT: *New York Times*

SBLG: Noël Riley Fitch, *Sylvia Beach and the Lost Generation: A History of Literary Paris in the Twenties and Thirties*

SC: Sylvia Beach, *Shakespeare and Company*

SL: *Selected Letters of James Joyce*

TWQ: *Two Worlds Quarterly*

TYW: Margaret C. Anderson, *My Thirty Years' War: An Autobiography by Margaret Anderson*

UvU: *United States of America v. One Book Entitled Ulysses by James Joyce: Documents and Commentary: A 50-Year Retrospective*

ABBREVIATIONS OF NAMES

EH: Ernest Hemingway
EP: Ezra Pound
JJ: James Joyce
JQ: John Quinn
MCA: Margaret Anderson
NB: Nora Barnacle
SB: Sylvia Beach
SJ: Stanislaus Joyce
VW: Virginia Woolf

INTRODUCTION

3 **"*Ulysses* lay stacked"**: Cyril Connolly, *Enemies of Promise*, p. 75, qtd. in *SBLG*, p. 14.

4 **"tyrants willing to be"**: JJ, *Ulysses*, ed. Hans Walter Gabler (New York: Vintage Books, 1993), p. 24 (2: 171–2).

4 **societies for the "suppression"**: R. J. Morris, "Voluntary Societies and British Urban Elites, 1780–1850: An Analysis," *Historical Journal* 26, no. 1 (1983), pp. 95–118.

4 **helped write**: M.J.D. Roberts, "Morals, Art, and the Law: The Passing of the Obscene Publications Act, 1857," *Victorian Studies* 28, no. 4 (1985), p. 621.

4 **ebb and flow**: Colin Manchester, "Lord Campbell's Act: England's First Obscenity Statue," *Journal of Legal History* 9, no. 2 (1988), pp. 223–41.

5 **"Lust defiles"**: Anthony Comstock, *Frauds Exposed; Or, How the People Are Deceived and Robbed, and Youth Corrupted* (New York: J. H. Brown, 1880), p. 416.

5 **"obscene, lewd"**: 17 Stat. 598 (1873). Current version at 18 U.S.C. § 1461 (1988).

6 **concealed the scar**: Anna Louise Bates, *Weeder in the Garden of the Lord: Anthony Comstock's Life and Career* (Lanham, Md.: University Press of America, 1995), p. 56.

6 **"You must hunt"**: Comstock qtd. Timothy Gilfoyle, *City of Eros: New York City, Prostitution, and the Commercialization of Sex, 1790–1920* (New York: Norton, 1992), p. 188.

6 "If we can't write": EP, "Meditatio," *Egoist* 3, no. 3 (March 1, 1916), pp. 37–38, reprinted in *EP/JJ*, p. 73.

7 "an assembly": EP to W. H. Taft, Dec. 1, 1928, Yale Pound, Box 53 Folder 2418.

7 a million times: Helen Nutting Diary, Tulsa, Series 1 Box 176.

8 "willful women": JQ to EP, June 2, 1917, NYPL.

8 "stupid charlatans": Ibid., Oct. 16, 1920.

8 squabbles: See, e.g., "An International Episode," *LR* 5, no. 7 (Nov. 1918), pp. 34–7.

8 "skoom": *LR* 7, no. 3 (Sept.-Dec. 1920), p. 73.

8 chocolates and typewriters: E.g., *LR* 5, no. 3 (July 1918), p. 66, and *LR* 6, no. 3 (July 1919), p. 2.

8 "beyond doubt": Israel Solon, "The December Number," *LR* 6, no. 9 (Jan. 1920), p. 30.

8 "freak magazine" and "throwing chunks": *LR* 5, no. 3 (July 1918), p. 64.

8 "slings 'obscenities' " and "vulgar!": Elsa von Freytag-Loringhoven, "The Modest Woman," *LR* 7, no. 2 (July–Aug. 1920), p. 40.

8 "There is hell": JJ to Frank Budgen, Nov. 1922 (n.d.), *LIII*, p. 30.

9 "Each month he's worse" and "has no concern": *LR* 5, no. 2 (June 1918), p. 54.

9 "utter amazement" and "the most remote": Simone de Beauvoir, *"The Useless Mouths" and Other Literary Writings* (Urbana: University of Illinois Press, 2011), p. 316.

9 "slit open": JJ to SB, April 25, 1924, *JJ/SB*, p. 38.

10 "hurt like hell": EH to JJ, Jan. 30, 1928, in Ernest Hemingway, *Selected Letters, 1917–1961* (New York: Scribner, 1981), p. 271.

10 trace phrases blindly: Myron Nutting to Ellmann, April 26, 1955, Tulsa, Series 1 Box 176.

10 "You are an": Burton Rascoe, *A Bookman's Daybook* (New York: H. Liveright, 1929), p. 27.

10 "full of the filthiest": Paul Claudel to Adrienne Monnier, Dec. 28, 1931, Berg Collection, NYPL (translated from French).

10 "the excrementitious": Rebecca West, "The Strange Case of James Joyce," *Bookman*, Sept. 1928, pp. 9–23.

12 belatedly acknowledged: Maria Jolas, "The Joyce I Knew and the Women Around Him," *Crane Bag* 4, no. 1 (1980), p. 86.

13 several scholars: See, also Joseph Kelly, *Our Joyce: From Outcast to Icon* (Austin: University of Texas Press, 1998); Paul Vanderham, *James Joyce and Censorship: The Trials of Ulysses* (New York: New York University Press, 1998); and Bruce Arnold, *The Scandal of Ulysses* (New York: St. Martin's Press, 1991).

14 devotes two pages: Ell, pp. 502–3.

14 only one page: Ibid., pp. 666–7 (i.e., two half pages).

14 immediately after: See Richards to JJ, Sept. 24, 1906, Cornell, Series IV Box 13; JJ to SJ, Sept. 30, 1906, *LII*, p. 168.

14 "the epic of the human body": Frank Budgen, *James Joyce and the Making of Ulysses* (Bloomington: Indiana University Press, 1964), p. 21.

1. NIGHTTOWN

17 "Now, my darling": JJ to NB, Sept. 7, 1909, *SL*, p. 169.

19 second city and fifth largest: Joseph O'Brien, *Dear, Dirty Dublin: A City in Distress, 1899–1916* (Berkeley: University of California Press, 1982), pp. 3–4.

19 a new law: K. T. Hoppen, *Ireland Since 1800: Conflict and Conformity* (New York: Longman, 1998), pp. 11–16.

19 less than £20: O'Brien, *Dear, Dirty Dublin*, p. 6.

20 Slaughterhouses were scattered: Jacinta Prunty, *Dublin Slums, 1800–1925: A Study in Urban Geography* (Dublin: Irish Academic Press, 1998), pp. 25, 56.

20 dozens of people: Ibid., p. 32.

20 dysentery, typhoid and cholera: Ibid., pp. 36, 76.

20 washed the waste: O'Brien, *Dear, Dirty Dublin*, p. 18.

20 heaped in tiny backyards: Prunty, *Dublin Slums*, pp. 25, 28, 80; O'Brien, Dear, Dirty Dublin, p. 8.

20 more likely to die: Prunty, *Dublin Slums,* pp. 46, 66.

20 dug up from graveyards: Ibid., p. 25.

20 "surrender to the trolls": JJ, "Day of the Rabblement," in *Critical Writings,* ed. Ellsworth Mason and Richard Ellmann (London: Faber and Faber, 1959), p. 71.

21 "To live": Henrik Ibsen qtd. in Michael Leverson Meyer, *Ibsen: A Biography* (New York: Doubleday, 1971), p. 274.

21 write to him: JJ to Ibsen, March 1901, *SL*, p. 7.

21 eighty-five copies: Ell, pp. 88–89; *MBK*, pp. 144–5.

21 One night in 1902: Ell, pp. 98–100.

21 recited Ibsen: Russell to Lady Gregory, quoted in Ulick O'Connor, *Celtic Dawn: A Portrait of the Irish Literary Renaissance* (London: Hamish Hamilton, 1984), p. 208.

21 "He is an extremely": Russell qtd. in Ell, p. 100.

21–22 "I do so" and "shows how rapidly": JJ qtd. in Russell's unpublished account, Ell, p. 103.

21–22 "a very delicate": Yeats qtd. in Ell, p. 104.

22 "I am twenty": JJ qtd. in Yeats account, Ell, pp. 103, 103n.

22 "We have met": Russell unpublished account, Ell, p. 103.

22 new set of teeth: JJ to Mary Joyce, Dec. 15, 1902, *LII*, p. 21.

22 fees up front and quit: Herbert Gorman, *James Joyce: His First Forty Years* (New York: Farrar and Rinehart, 1939), p. 90.

22 two students: JJ to Mary Joyce, March 8, 1903, *LII*, p. 34.

22 by the hours: Ibid., Feb. 21, 1903, p. 29.

22 he vomited: Ibid., Feb. 26, 1903, p. 31.

22 a cruel toothache: Gorman, *James Joyce*, p. 91; *MBK*, p. 214.

22 wooden clogs: Gorman, *James Joyce*, p. 92.

22 conceal the stains: Ell, p. 123.

23 "How are yr": Mary Joyce to JJ, March 19, 1903, *LII*, p. 36.

23 candles burned down: JJ to Mary Joyce, Feb. 26, 1903, *LII*, p. 31.

23 sweeping definitions: Gorman, *James Joyce*, p. 88; Michael Groden, "The National Library of Ireland's New Joyce Manuscripts: A Statement and Document Descriptions," *JJQ* 39, no.1 (Fall 2001), pp. 34–37.

23 "chattering, crushing": JJ, "Epiphany 33," in *Poems and Shorter Writings: Including Epiphanies, Giacomo Joyce, and "A Portrait of the Artist,"* ed. Richard Ellman, A. Walton Litz, and John Whittier-Ferguson (London: Faber and Faber, 1991), p. 193.

23 "the soul of": James Joyce, *Stephen Hero* (New York: New Directions, 1963), p. 213.

23 "to pierce": Ibid., p. 33.

23 Notre Dame: Ell, p. 128.

24 "MOTHER DYING": *MBK*, p. 229; Gorman, *James Joyce*. p. 108.

24 diagnosed her with cirrhosis: Ell, p. 129.

24 confession and darkened room: SJ and George Harris Healey, *The Complete Dublin Diary of Stanislaus Joyce* (Dublin: Anna Livia Press, 1994), pp. 8–9.

24 mind deteriorated: *MBK*, p. 233.

24 already died: Ell, pp. 21, 92.

24 under the sofa: May Joyce to JJ, Sept. 1, 1916, *LII*, p. 383.

24 family portraits: Mary Maguire Colum and Padraic Colum. *Our Friend James Joyce* (Garden City, N.Y.: Doubleday, 1958). p. 52.

24 false receipt: SJ and Healey, *Complete Dublin Diary*, p. 123.

24 eleven addresses: *LII*, p. lv.

25 uncle John and remained standing: *MBK*, p. 234.

25 draped with a sheet: *Ulysses*, p. 156 (9: 221); Don Gifford, *Ulysses Annotated: Notes for James Joyce's Ulysses* (Berkeley: University of California Press, 1988), p. 206.

25 departing ghost: Ell, p. 136.

25   cried alone: *Ulysses*, p. 156 (9: 224).

25   closed on him: Colum and Colum, *Our Friend Joyce*, p. 51.

25   First it was sack: Ell, pp. 131–2.

25   Three generations and two Dublin homes: Ulick O'Connor, *Oliver St. John Gogarty* (London: Jonathan Cape, 1964), pp. 11–13.

25   gold buttons: Gogarty, *Mourning Became Mrs. Spendlove*, p. 52.

25–26   one-sided fight and Alfred H. Hunter: Ell, p. 161.

26   eighteenth-century houses and Painted facades: Ibid., p. 367.

26   more here than in Paris and police had given up: O'Brien, *Dear, Dirty Dublin*, p. 191.

26   "arse over tip": Gogarty to JJ, [n.d.] 1904, Cornell, Series IV Box 8.

26   economical houses and lead pipe: Ell, pp. 367–8.

26   paid with the money: Colum and Colum, *Our Friend Joyce*, p. 53.

26   "He has the fuckin'est": SJ and Healey, *Complete Dublin Diary*, p. 27.

26   father's gravelly voice: Ibid., p. 170.

26   "Ye dirty pissabed": Ibid., p. 28.

26   launch it blindly and guarding their sisters: Ibid., p. 24.

26   "I'll break your heart": Ibid., p. 176.

26–27   den of syphilis and the continent's manias: Ibid., pp. 51–52.

27   was a "syphilisation": *Ulysses*, p. 266 (12: 1197).

27   rejected it as incomprehensible: Ell, p. 147.

27   eleven chapters: SJ and Healey, *Complete Dublin Diary*, p. 19.

27   "Thy love": JJ, "A Portrait of the Artist," in *Poems and Shorter Writings*, p. 216.

2. NORA BARNACLE

28   He declined and *The Goblin:* Ell, pp. 140–1; Colum and Colum, *Our Friend Joyce*, p. 56.

28   anthology of poetry: Padraic Colum in Ulick O'Connor, ed., *The Joyce We Knew* (Cork: Mercer Press, 1967), p. 70.

28   joint-stock company: Ell, p. 164; Gogarty, *Mourning Became Mrs. Spendlove*, p. 46.

28   Nassau Street: David Pierce, *Joyce's Ireland* (New Haven, Conn.: Yale University Press, 1992), p. 52.

28   brass handles: Liam Kelly, National Transport Museum of Ireland, May 18, 2011, email and photographs.

28   dirty canvas shoes: Brenda Maddox, *Nora: A Biography of Nora Joyce* (London: Hamish Hamilton, 1988), p. 5.

28   like a little boy: Ibid., p. 25.

29   low, resonant voice: JJ to NB, ca. Sept. 1, 1904, *LII*, p. 51.

29   "*Bear*nacle": Ibid., p. 9. My italics.

29   fifteen thousand: Enhanced British Parliamentary Papers on Ireland, http://eppi.dippam.ac.uk/documents/21962/eppi_pages/616790.

29   originated in Galway: Ell, p. 11.

29   waited tables and helped tend: Ibid., p. 26.

29   "I may be blind": JJ to NB, June 15, 1904, *LII*, p. 42.

29   her grandmother and convent, Uncle Tommy: Maddox, *Nora: A Biography*, p. 12.

29   blackthorn stick and stole vegetables: Ell, p. 158.

29   foul language: Maddox, *Nora: A Biography*, p. 19.

30   Michael Feeney: Ibid., p. 15.

30   Sonny Bodkin: Ell, p. 158.

30   "man killer": Maddox, *Nora: A Biography*, p. 18.

30   young priest once invited: JJ to SJ, Dec. 3, 1904, *LII*, p. 72.

30   trousers, neckties and "My love" and "Good night": Mary O'Holleran qtd. in Ell, p. 158.

30   balsam and rose: Maddox, *Nora: A Biography*, p. 20.

30   shirttails and fingers: JJ to NB, Dec. 3, 1909, *SL*, p. 182.

30 "What is it, dear?": Ibid., Aug. 7, 1909, p. 159.

31 "How am I": Ibid., Aug. 15, 1904, p. 47.

31 small birds: Ibid., Sept. 1, 1904, p. 50.

31 frustrated and suspicious: Ibid., Late July(?), 1904, p. 44.

31 unbuttoned and well behaved: Ibid., July 12(?), 1904, p. 43.

31 "common": SJ and Healey, *Complete Dublin Diary*, p. 57.

31 "Oh, she'll never": Ell, p. 156.

31 he had met her first: Maddox, *Nora: A Biography*, p. 25.

31 "Their least word": JJ to NB, Aug. 29, 1904, *LII*, p. 49.

32 "How could I": Ibid., p. 48.

32 study his letter: NB to JJ, Sept. 12, 1904, *LII*, p. 52.

32 He had *thirteen* letters: JJ to NB, Sept. 1, 1904, *LII*, p. 51.

32 Joyce was evicted: SJ and Healey, *Complete Dublin Diary*, p. 86.

32 Martello towers: Colum and Colum, *Our Friend Joyce*, p. 61; Oliver Gogarty, *It Isn't This Time of Year at All!* (Garden City, N.Y.: Doubleday, 1954), p. 86; Ell, pp. 171–2.

33 "Blessed Michael, the ass": Gogarty, *It Isn't This Time of Year*, pp. 87–88.

33 firing a pistol: Ibid., p. 96; Oliver Gogarty, *Mourning Became Mrs. Spendlove* (New York: Creative Age Press, 1948), pp. 56–57.

33 middle of the night: JJ to James Starkey, Sept. 15, 1904, *LII*, p. 42.

33 "Is there one": Ell, p. 176.

33 only Protestant: Maddox, *Nora: A Biography*, p. 20.

34 followed her home: Ell, p. 159.

34 began beating: JJ to SJ, Dec. 3, 1904, *LII*, p. 72–73.

34 She was nineteen: Ibid.

3. THE VORTEX

35 how to fence: Humphrey Carpenter, *A Serious Character: The Life of Ezra Pound* (London, Boston: Faber and Faber, 1988), p. 222.

35 slash the air: Qtd. in John Tytell, *Ezra Pound: The Solitary Volcano* (New York: Anchor Press, 1987), p. 96.

35 "Wild and haunting": Betsy Erkkila, *Ezra Pound: The Contemporary Reviews* (Cambridge: Cambridge University Press, 2011), p. 3.

35 velvet jacket: Charles Norman, *The Case of Ezra Pound* (New York: Bodley Press, 1948), p. 19.

35 billiard-green felt trousers: Tytell, *Pound,* p. 93.

35 ate them and "Would anyone mind": EP qtd. in Ernest Rhys, *Everyman Remembers* (Toronto: J.M. Dent, 1931), p. 244.

36 needed the admiration and no poetry and rumors: James Longenbach, *Stone Cottage: Pound, Yeats, and Modernism* (New York: Oxford University Press, 1988), p. 14.

36 deepened Yeats's concentration: Anthony Moody, *Ezra Pound: Poet: A Portrait of the Man and His Work* (Oxford: Oxford University Press, 2007), p. 240.

36 humming and chanting: Longenbach, *Stone Cottage,* p. 8.

36 Yeats from Wordsworth: Carpenter, *Serious,* p. 222.

36 "Have you ever": EP to Harriet Monroe qtd. in Moody, *Pound,* p. 215.

36 edited one of Yeats's poems: Ibid., pp. 200–1.

36 "more salt": Yeats qtd. in Marjorie Elizabeth Howes, "Introduction," *The Cambridge Companion to W. B. Yeats* (Cambridge: Cambridge University Press, 2006), p. 6

36 "Romantic Ireland's": Yeats, "September 1913," qtd. ibid., p. 19.

36 "Bad art": EP, "The Serious Artist," in Ezra Pound, *Early Writings: Poems and Prose,* ed. Ira B. Nadel (New York: Penguin Books, 2005), p. 235.

37 Paris metro: EP, "How I Began" and "Vorticism," ibid., pp. 214–5, 286.

37 "The apparition": EP, "In a Station of the Metro," *Poetry* 2, no. 1 (April 1913), p. 12.

37 "Use no superfluous": EP, "A Few Don'ts by an Imagiste," ibid., p. 254.

37 hand-me-down: EP, "Hell" in *Literary Essays of Ezra Pound* (New York: New Directions, 1968), p. 205.

37 "The artist": EP, "How I Began," *Early Writings*, p. 211.

38 "Dear Sir": EP to JJ, Dec. 15, 1913, *EP/JJ*, pp. 17–18. First ellipsis EP's; the second is mine.

38 "My Dear Mr Santa": EP to Santa Claus, 1891, Yale Pound, Box 46 Folder 2026.

38 the largest city: Stephen Inwood, *City of Cities: The Birth of Modern London* (London: Macmillan, 2005), pp. 1–9.

38 Forty percent: Jerry White, *London in the Twentieth Century: A City and Its People* (London, New York: Viking, 2001), p. 177.

39 the most turbulent: George Dangerfield, *The Strange Death of Liberal England, 1910–1914* (New Brunswick, N.J.: Transaction Publishers, 2011).

39 Food lay rotting: Tytell, *Pound*, p. 65.

39 coal supply: White, *London*, pp. 73–74.

39 thirty-eight million workdays: Les Garner, *A Brave and Beautiful Spirit: Dora Marsden, 1882–1960* (Brookfield, Vt.: Avebury, 1990), p. 78.

39 Windows were smashed: Jean Baker, *Votes for Women: The Struggle for Suffrage Revisited* (Oxford, New York: Oxford University Press, 2002), p. 118.

39 steel spike: Richard Lloyd George, *My Father, Lloyd George* (New York: Crown Publishers, 1960), p. 122.

39 Churchill was horsewhipped: "Attacked by Suffragette," *Troy Northern Budget*, Nov. 14, 1909, p. 1.

39 Empty houses and Bombs exploded: See, e.g., Laura Mayhall, *The Militant Suffrage Movement: Citizenship and Resistance in Britain, 1860–1930* (Oxford: Oxford University Press, 2003), p. 107; Inwood, *City of Cities*, p. 158; William Wees, *Vorticism and the English Avant-Garde* (Toronto: University of Toronto Press, 1972), p. 18; "Suffragettes on the Warpath Again," *NYT*, Jan. 29, 1913, p. 1; "Bomb Outrage by Suffragettes," *Daily Express*, Feb. 20, 1913, p. 1; "Gunpowder Bomb," *Evening Post*, May 6, 1914, p. 7.

39 first camera: "Spy Pictures of Suffragettes Revealed," *BBC News Online*, Oct. 3, 2003. http://news.bbc.co.uk/2/hi/uk_news/magazine/3153024.stm.

40 more than a third: White, *London*, p. 154; Inwood, *City of Cities*, p. 458.

40 storm Parliament: Garner, *Spirit*, p. 43; Wees, *Vorticism*, p. 17.

40 nasal membrane: "Miss Emerson's Injury Permanent, Say Doctors" *New York Tribune*, April 10, 1913, p. 3.

40 seized suffrage headquarters: Inwood, *City of Cities*, p. 159.

40 plotted to assassinate: "Suffragette 'plot to Assassinate Asquith,'" *Telegraph*, Sept. 29, 2006; Inwood, *City of Cities*, p. 157.

40 "Admirably indecent" and One man laughed: Tytell, *Pound*, pp. 65–66.

40 hadn't absorbed Impressionism: Wees, *Vorticism*, p. 21.

40 from the 1890s: Roger Fry and Desmond McCarthy, "Manet and the Post-Impressionists," Exhibition Catalogue (London: Grafton Galleries, 1910); White, *London*, p. 341; Wees, *Vorticism*, p. 22.

41 "To revert in the name": Charles Ricketts, "Post-Impressionism at the Grafton Gallery," qtd. in Wees, *Vorticism*, p. 26.

41 nightclubs and cabarets: White, *London*, p. 329.

41 Cave of the Golden Calf: "The English Cabaret," *NY Tribune*, Aug. 11, 1912, p. B3; "The Cabaret Theatre Club" *The Times [of London]*, June 27, 1912, p. 10; Wees, *Vorticism*, p. 50; Richard Cork, *Art Beyond the Gallery in Early 20th Century England* (New Haven, Conn.: Yale University Press, 1985), pp. 61–105.

41 veins swelled and machine-gun fire: "The Aims of Futurism," *Times*, March 21, 1912 p. 2; Tytell, *Pound*, p. 106.

41 "Set fire to the shelves": F. T. Marinetti, "The Founding and the Manifesto of Futurism," in *Modernism: An Anthology*, ed. Lawrence Rainey (Malden: Blackwell Publishing, 2005), p. 5.

41 Freda Graham: "Militant Slashes Herkomer Canvas," *New York Tribune*, May 13, 1914, p. 6.

42 **Venetian paintings:** "'Wild Women' Damage Paintings" *NYT*, May 23, 1914, p. 2; "Heavy Sentences for Suffragettes," *New York Tribune*, May 27, 1914, p. 5.

42 **portrait of Henry James:** "Militant Ruins Sargent Portrait," *New York Tribune*, May 5, 1914, p. 7.

42 **assaulting a police officer:** Garner, *Spirit*, pp. 31–32; *Daily Mirror*, April 1, 1909.

42 **two more months:** Garner, *Spirit*, p. 35; *Votes for Women*, Sept. 10, 1909.

42 **tore off and straitjacket:** Elizabeth Crawford, *Women's Suffragette Movement: A Reference Guide, 1866–1928* (New York: Routledge, 2001), p. 379.

42 **Southport in 1909 and "But it does not":** Garner, *Spirit,* pp. 39–40; "Budget Battle Rages in Britain," *San Francisco Chronicle*, Dec. 5, 1909, p. 32. My exclamation point.

42 **rain and freezing temperatures:** Daily Weather Reports for Dec. 1909, National Meteorological Library, Exeter.

43 **signs on boats:** Garner, *Spirit*, p. 43.

43 **"a vast revolution":** Marsden qtd. in ibid: pp. 56–57.

43 **"centre of the Universe":** Marsden qtd. in Andrew Thacker, "Dora Marsden and *The Egoist:* 'Our War Is with Words,'" *Twentieth Century Literature* 36, no. 2 (1993), p. 186.

43 **"destroy Causes":** Marsden, *Freewoman*, July 1, 1913, p. 25, qtd. in Mark Morrisson, "Marketing British Modernism: *The Egoist* and Counter-Public Spheres," *Twentieth Century Literature* 43 (Winter 1997), p. 456.

43 **"should be banished":** Marsden, "Intellect and Culture," *New Freewoman*, Jan. 7, 1913, p. 24, qtd. in Thacker, "Marsden and *Egoist*," p. 186.

43 **"Our war is with":** Marsden, *Egoist*, Jan. 1, 1915, p. 1, qtd. in Thacker, Marsden and *Egoist*, p. 188.

43 **"poets and creative":** Marsden, "The Growing Ego," *Freewoman*, Aug. 8, 1912, pp. 221–2.

43 **"I suppose I'm":** EP to Marsden (n.d). qtd. in "Bruce Clarke, "Dora Marsden and Ezra Pound: *The New Freewoman*' and 'The Serious Artist,' " *Contemporary Literature* 33, no. 1 (Spring 1992), p. 100.

43 **"presents the image":** EP, "The Serious Artist," *Early Writings*, p. 239.

44 **Marsden changed:** Bruce Clarke, *Dora Marsden and Early Modernism: Gender, Individualism, and Science* (Ann Arbor: University of Michigan Press, 1996), pp. 129–30.

44 **"a VORTEX":** EP, "Vorticism," *Early Writings*, p. 289.

44 **"WE ONLY WANT":** *Blast* 1, June 28, 1914, p. 31.

44 **"TO THE INDIVIDUAL":** Ibid., p. 7 (unnumbered).

44 **"WE ADMIRE YOUR ENERGY":** Ibid., p. 151.

45 **"He attacks Mother":** Ibid., p. 25.

45 **"great enemy":** Ibid., p. 27.

45 **one-thousand-page:** JJ to Grant Richards, March 13, 1906, *LII*, p. 132.

45 **into the fire:** Ell, p. 314.

45 **"I'm not supposed":** EP to JJ, Jan. 17 and 19, 1914. *EP/JJ*, p. 24.

4. TRIESTE

46 **Everyone thought the same:** Stephen Van Evera, "The Cult of the Offensive and the Origins of the First World War," *International Security* 9, no. 1 (Summer 1984), pp. 58–107.

46 **fifty million people:** See *LSB*, p. 49n.

47 **Nora watched Joyce:** Ell, p. 179.

47 **"I saw a life":** John Joyce to JJ, April 24, 1907, *LII*, p. 221.

47 **only merchant seaport:** John McCourt, *The Years of Bloom: James Joyce in Trieste, 1904–1920* (Madison University of Wisconsin Press, 2000), p. 28.

47 **second-largest port:** Ibid., p. 29.

47 **2.5 million tons:** Karl Baedeker, *Austria-Hungary, Including Dalmatia and Bosnia; Handbook for Travelers* (New York: C. Scribner's Sons, 1905), p. 205.

47 population grew: McCourt, *Years,* p. 33.

47 ostrich feathers: Peter Hartshorn, *James Joyce and Trieste* (Westport, Conn.: Greenwood Press, 1997), p. 25.

47–48 laugh at Nora's and forced to leave: JJ to SJ, July 12, 1905, *LII,* p. 93–94.

48 twenty crowns: Ell, p. 262.

48 "Will all that paper": JJ to SJ, Jan. 19, 1905, *LII,* p. 78.

48 eighty-five crowns and lower end: McCourt, *Years,* p. 33.

48 with electric lighting: Ibid., p. 63.

48 too steep and narrow: Baedeker, *Austria-Hungary,* p. 206.

48 sang songs: Mario Nordio, "My First English Teacher," *JJQ* 9, no. 3 (Spring 1972), p. 324.

49 in the gutter: Alessandro Francini Bruni, "Recollections of Joyce," in Willard Potts, ed., *Portraits of the Artist in Exile: Recollections of James Joyce by Europeans* (Seattle: University of Washington Press, 1979), p. 40.

49 drag his older brother back: Ell, p. 213.

49 Dante-esque Italian: Francini Bruni, "Recollections," p. 40.

49 "Do you want" and "Faith I tell": Ell, pp. 267–8.

49 advances on his wages: JJ to SJ, July 12, 1905, *LII,* p. 94.

49 "It's no use": Ell, p. 215.

49 "Ireland is" and "The tax collector": Alessandro Francini Bruni, "Joyce Stripped Naked in the Piazza," in Potts, *Portraits of the Artist in Exile,* p. 27. Ellipsis in original.

50 "I will not serve": JJ, *A Portrait of the Artist as a Young Man,* ed. Chester G. Anderson (New York: Viking, 1968), pp. 246–7.

50 an anarchist and his stomach: SJ, Trieste Diary, April 11, 1907, Tulsa, Series 1 Box 142. For more on Joyce's anachronism, see Dominic Manganiello, *Joyce's Politics* (London, Boston: Routledge & Kegan Paul, 1980), and "The Politics of the Unpolitical in Joyce's Fictions," *JJQ* 29, no. 2 (Winter 1992), pp. 241–58. See also David Kadlec, *Mosaic Modernism: Anarchism, Pragmatism, Culture* (Baltimore: Johns Hopkins University Press, 2000), pp. 90–121.

51 Parliament empowered: Metropolitan Police Act 1839 2&3 Vict. c. 47.

51 "profane, indecent, or obscene": Ibid.

51 By 1878, the British: Stefan, Petrow, *Policing Morals: The Metropolitan Police and the Home Office, 1870–1914* (New York: Clarendon Press; Oxford University Press, 1994), pp. 31–32.

52 137 students: Hartshorn, *James Joyce and Trieste,* p. 5.

52 Trieste was empty and pieces of string: Ibid., p. 109.

52 books crammed and chairs: McCourt, *Years,* p. 209; Ell, p. 381.

52 "Stately, plump": *Ulysses,* p. 3 (1: 1).

53 finished the first chapter: JJ to SJ, June 16, 1915, *SL,* p. 209.

53 air raids: Ell, p. 383; Hartshorn, *James Joyce and Trieste,* p. 108.

53 "*Avanti, Cagoia*": Gorman, *James Joyce,* p. 229; Philip Nicholas Furbank, *Italo Svevo: The Man and the Writer* (Berkeley: University of California Press, 1966), p. 101.

53 list of enemy aliens and arrested: Franz Stanzel, "The Austrian Subtext of James Joyce's *Ulysses,*" *Anglistik* 16, no. 2 (2005), p. 71; Stanzel, "Austria's Surveillance of Joyce in Pola, Trieste, and Zurich," *JJQ* 38, no 3/4 (Spring/Summer 2001), pp. 363–4.

53 Austrian mobs: McCourt, *Years,* p. 246; Hartshorn, *James Joyce and Trieste,* p. 108.

53 state of siege and last open bakery: Furbank, *Italo Svevo,* p. 101.

53 "Whoever has": JJ qtd. in McCourt, *Years,* p. 243.

53 only 499 copies: Grant Richards to JJ, April 29, 1915, Cornell, Series IV Box 13.

54 twenty-six copies: Ell, p. 400.

54 a short story: JJ to SJ, Sept. 30, 1906, *LII,* p. 168.

54 gathering his ideas: Rodney Wilson Owen, *James Joyce and the Beginnings of Ulysses* (Ann Arbor: UMI Research Press, 1983), pp. 63–69.

54 "the soul": JJ, *Stephen Hero,* p. 213.

54 "intense instant": *Ulysses*, p. 160 (9: 381, 383–5).
55 "Ineluctable modality": Ibid., p. 31 (3: 1–4).

5. SMITHY OF SOULS

57 Newsstand sales: Garner, *Spirit*, p. 116.
57 "unsuitable to be exposed": Ibid., p. 77; Thacker, "Marsden and *Egoist*," pp. 183–4.
57 publisher withdrew: Garner, *Spirit,* pp. 97–98.
57 two hundred pounds: *DMW*, p. 57.
57 "edited on a mountaintop": Weaver qtd. *DMW*, pp. 53–54.
58 leasing a new office and London printers: Ibid., pp. 87, 108.
58 three-room flat and flowers: Ibid., p. 89.
58 stage production: Ibid., p. 43.
58 resigned: Ibid., pp. 86, 91.
58 *Egoist* print run: Morrisson, "Marketing British Modernism," p. 466n.
58 reduced issues and £37: *DMW*, pp. 99–100.
58 wholesale prices: Paul Johnson, *Modern Times: A History of the World from the 1920s to the 1990s* (London: Phoenix, 1992), p. 35.
58 In 1915, zeppelins: Ian Castle, *London 1914–1917: The Zeppelin Menace* (Oxford: Osprey, 2008), pp. 35–39.
59 "indescribably beautiful": Captain Breithaupt qtd. ibid., p. 44.
59 "Can't you?": Marsden qtd. in *DMW*, p. 107.
59 Pound suggested: Ibid., p. 98.
59 manager refused: Ibid., p. 92.
59 they cut two sentences: Weaver to JJ, July 28, 1915, Cornell, Series IV Box 14; *DMW*, p. 99.
59 "Her thighs, fuller": JJ, *Portrait*, p. 171.
59 "we have decided": *DMW*, p. 99.
59 deleted two words: Ibid., p. 103.
59 "stupid censoring": Weaver to JJ, July 28, 1915, Cornell, Series IV Box 14.
60 sent the manuscript: JJ to Grant Richards, Nov. 27, 1905, *LII*, p. 128.
60 no advance: Richards to JJ, Feb. 17, 1906, Cornell, Series IV Box 13.
60 cut several passages: JJ to Richards, May 5, 1906, *LII*, p. 133.
60 "Two Gallants": Richards to JJ, April 23, 1906, Cornell, Series IV Box 13.
60 objected to the word *bloody*: Ibid.
60 "she did not wish": JJ, "Grace," *Dubliners* (New York: Viking Press, 1962), p. 157.
60 "if any fellow": JJ, "The Boarding House," ibid., p. 68. The Viking edition does not italicize *his*, but other editions do, and the word is italicized in Joyce's drafts and proofs.
60 the favor of listing: JJ to Richards, May 13, 1906, *LII*, p. 136.
60 "An Encounter": JJ to Richards, May 5, 1906, *LII*, p. 134.
60 "bottle-green eyes": JJ, "An Encounter," *Dubliners*, p. 27.
60 "beyond anything": Ell, p. 329.
60 nothing but the title: JJ to Richards, May 13, 1906, *LII*, p. 137.
60 advancement of Irish civilization: JJ to Richards, June 23, 1906, *LI*, p. 64.
60 "I cannot write": JJ to Richards, May 5, 1906, *LII*, p. 134.
61 "do no good": Richards to JJ, May 10, 1906, Cornell, Series IV Box 13.
61 "The appeal to my pocket": JJ to Richards, May 13, 1906, *LII*, p. 137.
61 "Remember" he wrote: Richards to JJ, May 10, 1906, Cornell, Series IV Box 13.
61 "the very careful": Ibid., Sept. 24, 1906.
61 several other publishers: *LII*, p. 109n; Ell, p. 231; Ell, p. 267.
61 George Roberts: Colum and Colum, *Our Friend Joyce*, pp. 88–90; David Gardiner, *The Maunsel Poets: 1905–1926* (Dublin: Maunsel & Co., 2004), pp. 2–6.
61 "Here's this fellow": JJ and Hans Walter Gabler, *Dubliners: A Facsimile of Drafts & Manuscripts* (New York: Garland, 1978), p. 215 (Yale 2.7–18). See also JJ to Richards, May 13, 1906, *LII*, p. 137.

61 "bloody old bitch": Ell, p. 311; P. J. Keating, *The Haunted Study: A Social History of the English Novel, 1875–1914* (London: Secker & Warburg, 1989), p. 271. The first version is in the 1906 draft sent to Richards. The second is in Joyce's 1909 draft. The version published in 1914 reads "his old mother."

61 a public letter: JJ, "A Curious History," reprinted in *Egoist* 1, no. 2 (Jan. 15, 1914), pp. 26–27.

61 threatened to sue: JJ to George Roberts, July 19, 1911, *LII*, p. 289.

61 wrote to King George: Ell, p. 315.

62 secure written authorization: Colum and Colum, *Our Friend Joyce*, p. 97.

62 hesitated and windows smashed: McCourt, *Years*, p. 189.

62 "the publication of the book" and "clearly libelous": Roberts to JJ, Aug. 23, 1912, Cornell, Series IV Box 13.

62 went to the printer's shop: Ell, p. 335.

62 ruddy-faced man: Colum and Colum, *Our Friend Joyce,* p. 92.

62 They were "guillotined": *LII*, p. 318n.

63 "a monotonous wilderness": Qtd. in Jonathon Green and Nicholas Karolides, *Encyclopedia of Censorship* (New York: Facts on File, 1990), pp. 464–5. For the influence of this case, see Weaver to JJ, March 25, 1916, Cornell, Series IV Box 14.

63 common law offense and Obscene Publications Act: M.J.O. Roberts, "Morals, Art, and the Law: The Passing of the Obscene Publicans Act," *Victorian Studies* 28, no. 4 (Summer 1985), pp. 609–29; Colin Manchester, "Lord Campbell's Act: England's First Obscenity Statute," *Journal of Legal History* 9, no. 2 (1988), pp. 223–41. Obscenity had been an offense since a 1727 proclamation by King George III. The Obscene Publications Act does not specify sentencing. It details law enforcement powers.

63 gambling dens: Manchester, "Lord Campbell's Act," p. 227.

63 ships carrying arms: Metropolitan Police Act of 1839, 2&3 Vict. c. 47.

63 citizen's complaint: Manchester, "Lord Campbell's Act," pp. 229–231.

64 "no artistic merit": Campbell qtd. in Roberts, "Morals, Art," p. 616.

64 Literary London didn't object: Ibid., p. 618.

64 nine hundred members: Manchester, "Lord Campbell's Act," p. 239n.

64 Thomas Paine: *Times*, (London), Dec. 25, 1820.

64 helped Lord Campbell: Roberts, "Moral Act," p. 621.

64 In 1817 the Society: Manchester, "Lord Campbell's Act," pp. 224–5.

65 "She had to reach": Émile Zola, *La Terre* (Vizetelly ed.) qtd. in Edward de Grazia, *Girls Lean Back Everywhere: The Law of Obscenity and the Assault on Genius* (New York: Random House, 1992), p. 42.

65 Henry Vizetelly: William Frierson, "The English Controversy in Realism in Fiction 1885–1895," *PMLA* 42 (1928), p. 534; de Grazia, *Girls Lean Back*, pp. 40–42.

65 two-shilling edition: See Vizetelly's advertisements in the 1888 printing of George Moore's *Spring Days. A Realistic Novel. A Prelude to "Don Juan"* (London: Vizetelly & Co., 1888).

65 Vizetelly boasted: De Grazia, *Girls Lean Back,* pp. 43–44.

65 "the troughs": Tennyson, *Locksley Hall, Sixty Years After* (1886) qtd. in Frierson, "The English Controversy," p. 536.

65 three months in prison: Ibid., pp. 540–2; de Grazia, *Girls Lean Back,* pp. 44–51.

66 "some critic will": JJ to Grant Richards, May 13, 1906, *LII*, p. 137.

66 Church of England family: *DMW*, pp. 4–32.

66 vegetables like asparagus: Ibid., p. 27.

66 *Adam Bede*: Ibid., p. 33.

66 The first thing: Ibid., p. 83.

66 "reputation for quarrelling": Marsden to Weaver, May 7, 1917, qtd. in *DMW*, p. 137.

67 "a searching, piercing": Monro Saw & Co to JJ, June 24, 1919, *LII*, pp. 444–5.

67 "to forge": JJ, *Portrait*, p. 253.

67 river Weaver: *DMW*, p. 23.

67 abandon the novel: Herbert Cape to James Pinker, Jan. 26, 1916, Yale Joyce, Box 2 Fold

67   without so much as commenting: *DMW*, p. 102.

67   called the manuscript "hopeless": Richards qtd. in Ell, p. 384n.

67   could tolerate frankness: EP to JJ, Nov. 27, 1915, *EP/JJ*, p. 60.

67   "quite impossible": Werner Laurie to James Pinker, Jan. 17, 1916, Yale Joyce, Box 2 Folder 69.

67   "It is too discursive": Duckworth reader qtd. in *EP/JJ*, p. 64. My ellipsis.

68   "These vermin crawl": EP to Pinker, Jan. 30, 1916, *EP/JJ*, pp. 65–66;

68   "the universal element": EP, "'Dubliners' and Mr. James Joyce," *Egoist*, July 15, 1914, reprinted in *EP/JJ*, p. 29.

68   "absolutely permanent": EP to JQ, Sept. 8, 1915, *EP/JQ*, p. 48.

68   "I have been wondering": Weaver to JJ, Nov. 30, 1915, Cornell, Series IV Box 14.

68   a pamphlet of poems: *DMW*, p. 104.

69   "We could not": Billing and Sons qtd. *DMW*, p. 117.

69   thirteen printers refused: Weaver to JJ, May 19, 1916, Cornell, Series IV Box 14.

69   "And damn": EP to Weaver, March 17, 1916, EP, *Selected Letters of Ezra Pound* (New York: New Directions, 1971), p. 122. See also EP to JJ, March 16, 1916, *EP/JJ*, p. 75.

69   Joyce implored Pound: JJ to James Pinker, Jan. 9, 1916, *LII*, p. 370.

69   "There is no editor": EP to JJ, Jan. 16, 1916, *EP/JJ*, p. 62.

6. LITTLE MODERNISMS

71   117 magazine contributions: Robert Scholes, *Magazine Modernisms: An Introduction* (New Haven, Conn.: Yale University Press, 2010), p. 6.

71   wouldn't publish: Thacker, "Marsden and *Egoist*," p. 187, citing EP, *Selected Letters*, p. 259.

72   *Dana* published three: See Ell, p. 165.

72   they rejected: William Magee to JJ, June 30, 1904, Cornell, Series IV Box 11.

72   "Feminism" and male turnout: See *LR* 1, no. 2 (April 1914), pp. 44, 30.

72   "tortured and crucified": MCA, "Mrs. Ellis's Failure," *LR* 2, no. 1 (March 1915), p. 19 (italics in original). Baggett claims that this is "the first known editorial by a lesbian in favor of gay rights." See Jane Heap and Florence Reynolds, *Dear Tiny Heart: The Letters of Jane Heap and Florence Reynolds*, ed. Holly Baggett (New York: New York University Press, 2000), p. 3.

72   "Aren't you": *TYW*, pp. 68–69.

72   "I feel as if": Letter from Will Levington Comfort, *LR* 2, no. 1 (March 1915), pp. 56–57.

72   "I demand that life": *TYW*, p. 35.

72   assistant for *The Dial:* Ibid., pp. 28–31.

73   "A New Day": See, e.g., *LR* 1, nos. 7–8 (Oct. and Nov. 1914).

73   "stood pouring out": Eunice Tietjens, *The World at My Shoulder* (New York: Macmillan, 1938), pp. 63–69.

73   enthusiast of Nietzsche: See DeWitt C. Wing, "Dr. Foster's Articles on Nietzsche," *LR* 1, no. 3 (May 1914), pp. 31–32.

73   bird watching: DeWitt C. Wing, "Robins Nests," *Auk* 32 (1915), pp. 106–7.

73   vellum label hand-pasted: Christine Stansell, *American Moderns: Bohemian New York and the Creation of a New Century* (New York: Metropolitan Books, 2000), p. 201.

73   "If you've ever": MCA, "Announcement," *LR* 1, no. 1 (March 1914).

73–74 an upstairs room: *TYW*, pp. 11–13.

74   smoking cigarettes: Ibid., p. 24.

74   "conquer the world": Ibid., p. 11.

74   "The State": Emma Goldman, "Socialism: Caught in the Political Trap," in *Red Emma Speaks: Selected Writings and Speeches,* ed. Alix Kates Shulman (New York: Random House, 1972), p. 102.

75   "living force": Emma Goldman, "Anarchism: What It Really Stands For," ibid., p. 74.

75   "a cosmos": Emma Goldman, "The Individual, Society and the State," ibid., p. 111.

75   "the salvation of man": Goldman, "Anarchism: What It Really Stands For," pp. 75–76.

75   two Goldman lectures: MCA, "The Challenge of Emma Goldman," *LR* 1, no. 3 (May 1914), p. 6.

75   just enough time: *TYW*, p. 55.

75 **Six months later:** Ibid., pp. 67–74.

75 **"Applied Anarchism":** MCA, "Editorials and Announcements," *LR* 2, no. 4 (June–July 1915), p. 36.

75 **highest human ideal:** MCA, "The Immutable," Ibid., p. 21.

75 **"We thought we were":** "Christmas Tree Traps 'Anarchy' on North Shore," *Chicago Daily Tribune*, Jan. 21, 1915, p. 1.

75 **"Why shouldn't women":** "This Chicago Girl at the Age of 24 Smokes, Wears Pants and in Short Is Real Society Rebel," *Washington Post*, Oct. 31, 1915, p. E12.

76 **"missing link":** "Fool Killer Needed," *Daily Herald* (Mississippi), Nov. 3, 1915, p. 4.

76 **"overthrow of both":** Emma Goldman, "Preparedness: The Road to Universal Slaughter," *LR* 2, no. 9 (Dec. 1915), p. 12.

76 **"why didn't someone":** MCA, "Toward Revolution," *LR* 2, no. 9 (Dec. 1915), p. 5.

76 **Detectives showed up:** *TYW*, p. 75.

76 **"Editors' Row":** "Christmas Tree Traps 'Anarchy' on North Shore," *Chicago Daily Tribune*, Jan. 21, 1915, p.1.

76 **set up camp** and **"the original cleansing":** *TYW*, pp. 86–91; "Ours Is the Life; Others Are Odd: Miss Anderson," *Chicago Daily Tribune*, Aug. 9, 1915, p. 13.

76 **Oscar Wilde:** Linda Lappin, "Jane Heap and Her Circle," *Prairie Schooner* 78, no. 4 (2004), p. 14.

77 **mental institution:** Ibid., p. 12.

77 **"I know that":** Jane Heap to Florence Reynolds, July 20, 1909, *Dear Tiny Heart*, p. 38. I have maintained Heap's inconsistent capitalization of "God."

77 **Jane never quoted:** *TYW*, p. 124.

77 **begged her to write:** Ibid, p. 110.

77 **magazine's design:** Susan Noyes Platt, "*The Little Review*: Early Years and Avant-Garde Ideas," in Sue Ann Prince, ed., *The Old Guard and the Avant-Garde: Modernism in Chicago, 1910–1940* (Chicago: University of Chicago Press, 1990), p. 152.

77 **"I felt as if"** and **"The Ballad":** *TYW*, pp. 126–7.

78 **"Our culture":** MCA, "To the Innermost," *LR* 1, no. 7 (Oct. 1914), pp. 3, 5.

78 **" 'People' has become":** MCA, "The Artist in Life," *LR* 2, no. 4 (June–July 1915), pp. 18–20. My italics.

78 **"The ultimate reason"** and **"Now we shall have":** MCA, "A Real Magazine," *LR* 3, no. 5 (Aug. 1916), pp. 1–2; *TYW*, p. 124.

79 **"All things are nothing":** Max Stirner (trans. Byington), *The Ego and His Own* (New York: Dover, 2005), pp. 3, 366.

79 **forty-nine printings:** Lawrence Stepelevich, "The Revival of Max Stirner," *Journal of the History of Ideas* 35 (April–June 1974), p. 324.

79 **Joyce read Stirner:** Ell, 142n.

79 **Ezra Pound:** Michael Levenson, *Genealogy of Modernism: A Study of English Literary Doctrine, 1908–1922* (Cambridge: Cambridge University Press, 1984), pp. 72–74.

79 **Margaret Anderson:** MCA, "The Challenge of Emma Goldman," *LR* 1, no. 3 (May 1914), p. 6.

79 **"most powerful work":** Dora Marsden, *New Freewoman*, Sept. 1, 1913, p. 104. See also Garner, *Spirit*, pp. 102–3.

79 **Nietzsche and Ibsen:** See, for example, James Huneker, *Egoists: A Book of Supermen: Stendahl, Baudelaire, Flaubert, Anatole France, Huysmans, Barrès, Nietzsche, Blake, Ibsen, Stirner, and Ernest Hello* (New York: C. Scribner's Sons, 1921).

7· THE MEDICI OF MODERNISM

81 **while Quinn dressed:** *MNY*, p. 165.

81 **above-market prices:** Ibid., p. 168.

81 **In 1912, Quinn:** Ibid., pp. 144–7.

82 **biggest single contributor:** Ibid., pp. 144–5.

82 **"epoch making":** Milton W. Brown et al., *Story of the Armory Show* (Greenwich, Conn.: New York Graphic Society, 1963), pp. 43–44; *MNY*, p. 147.

82 **an understatement:** See Bruce Altshuler, ed., *Salon to Biennial: Exhibitions that Made Art History,* vol. 1. With the exception of Paris's 1905 Salon d'Autumne, no other exhibition was nearly as large since 1863.

82 **fewer than 250:** Roger Fry and Desmond McCarthy, "Manet and the Post-Impressionists" Exhibition Catalogue (London: Grafton Galleries, 1910).

82 **about 1,300 artworks:** Altshuler, *Salon to Biennial,* p. 153.

82 **burned in effigy** and **three hundred thousand:** Milton Brown, "The Armory Show and Its Aftermath," in *1915, The Cultural Moment: The New Politics, the New Woman, the New Psychology, the New Art and the New Theatre in America*, ed. Adele Heller and Louis Rudnick (New Brunswick, N.J.: Rutgers University Press, 1991), pp. 166–7.

82 **"a lunatic fringe":** Theodore Roosevelt, "A Layman's Views of an Art Exhibition," *Outlook* 103 (March 29, 1913), pp. 718–20.

82 **rushed to New York:** Brown, *Story of the Armory Show*, pp. 121–3.

82 **more art than anyone:** *MNY*, p. 209.

83 **read an article:** EP, "Affirmations," *New Age,* Jan. 21, 1915, p. 312.

83 **"If there is a 'liver' ":** JQ to EP, Feb. 25, 1915, qtd. *MNY*, p. 198.

83 *wrote* **the new tariff:** *MNY*, pp. 157–9.

83 **"If there were":** EP to JQ, March 9, 1915, *EP/JQ*, p. 20.

83 **"Are there any damd "** and **"I don't want":** Ibid., May 21, 1915, pp. 27–28.

83 **"The rest are sheep."** Ibid., Sept. 8, 1915, p. 47.

84 **"a young chap":** Ibid., Aug. 11, 1915, p. 37. My ellipsis.

84 **"Joyce," Pound assured:** Ibid., Sept. 8, 1915, p. 48.

84 **remembered hearing:** JQ to JJ, April 11, 1917, NYPL; *MNY*, p. 30.

84 **ideas for a title:** EP to JQ, Aug. 26, 1915, *EP/JQ*, p. 40.

84 **"I think active America":** Ibid., p. 41.

84 **feminized objects:** See, e.g., Steven Lubar, "Men / Women / Production / Consumption," in Roger Horowitz and Arwen Mohun, eds., *His and Hers: Gender, Consumption, and Technology* (Charlottesville: University Press of Virginia, 1998), pp. 12–13.

84 **"No woman shall":** EP to JQ, Oct. 13, 1915, NYPL; *EP/JQ*, pp. 53–54.

85 **"the non-existence":** EP, "James Joyce—At Last the Novel Appears," *Egoist* 4, no. 2 (Feb. 1917), pp. 21–22 qtd. *EP/JJ*, p. 90. My ellipsis.

85 **aristocracy of taste:** EP to JQ, July 27, 1916, *EP/JQ*, p. 79.

85 **"the patron then":** Ibid., March 9, 1915, p. 23.

85 *"absolutely free":* JQ to EP, Feb. 9, 1916, NYPL.

86 **"Ten years teaching":** EP to JQ, April 8, 1916, NYPL.

86 **"We want a little":** JQ to EP, Aug. 26, 1916, NYPL.

86 **"seems to be looking up":** EP letter in *LR* 3, no. 2 (April 1916), p. 36.

86 **"I loathe compromise":** MCA, "A Real Magazine," *LR* 3, no. 5 (Aug. 1916), pp. 1–2.

87 **wanted the same things:** EP to MCA, Nov. 29, 1916, *EP/LR*, p. 4.

87 **two thousand subscribers:** *LR* 3, no. 2 (April 1916), p. 25.

87 **"official organ":** EP to MCA, Jan. 26, 1917, *EP/LR*, p. 6.

87 **peppered her:** Ibid., Nov. 29, 1916, and Jan. 26, 1917, pp. 4–7.

87 **£150 per year:** Ibid., Jan. 26, 1917, p. 6.

87 **"BOMM!":** Ibid., Feb. 8, 1917, p. 15.

87 **it had enthusiasm:** EP to JQ, Feb. 8, 1917, *EP/JQ*, pp. 95–96.

87 **nauseating "Washington Squareite":** JQ to EP, March 24, 1917, NYPL.

87 **"The thing I really":** Ibid., May 3, 1917.

88 **four-room apartment:** *TYW*, pp. 152–3.

88 **Hart Crane:** Ibid., p. 153.

88 **advertising manager:** Clive Fisher, *Hart Crane: A Life* (New Haven, Conn.: Yale University Press, 2002), p. 80.

88 "What shall I do": *TYW*, p. 154.

89 Joyce wrote: *LR* 4, no. 2 (June 1917), p. 26.

89 immigrant named Popovitch: *TYW*, p. 157.

89 price increases: *LR* 4, no. 6 (Oct. 1917), p. 42.

89 "the simple and beautiful": MCA, "What the Public Doesn't Want," *LR* 4, no. 4 (Aug. 1917), p. 20.

89 "I want to": EP to MCA, Nov. 5, 1917, *EP/LR*, p. 139.

89 "I don't want": Ibid., p. 141.

89 Press advertising: Gerald J. Baldasty, *The Commercialization of News in the Nineteenth Century* (Madison: University of Wisconsin Press, 1992), p. 59.

90 sixty-five million: Frank Mott, *A History of American Magazines* (Cambridge: Belknap Press of Harvard University Press, 1958–1968), pp. 1–17.

90 "sandwichmen": Morrisson, "Marketing British Modernism," p. 451–2.

90 two hundred copies: Ibid., p. 466n; Thacker, "Marsden and *Egoist*," p. 189.

90 seven thousand books: *MNY*, p. 111.

90 Manet's *L'Amazone:* Ibid., p. 91.

90 disorderly ranks: Sheldon Cheney, "An Adventurer Among Art Collectors," *NYT Magazine*, Jan. 3, 1926, pp. 10, 23, qtd. *MNY*, p. 651.

90 why she began: Platt, *"The Little Review,"* p. 139; Lappin, "Jane Heap and Her Circle," p. 7.

91 enjoyed Quinn's irascibility: MCA, "Collection of Memoires and Private Papers" ("My Collection"), Yale Anderson, Box 12 Folder 236.

91 "full of radium": JQ qtd. *MNY*, p. 290.

91 like piles of money: MCA to Solita Solano [n.d.], 1968, Yale Anderson, Box 12 Folder 236.

91 "a damned attractive": JQ to EP, Oct. 31, 1917, NYPL.

91 "a typical Washington Squareite": Ibid., June 2, 1917.

91 butcher's paper: "'Little' in Butcher Paper," *Chicago Daily Tribune*, Nov. 18, 1916, p. 5.

91 "could come in": JQ to EP, June 2, 1917, NYPL. My italics.

91 "go ahead": Ibid., June 6, 1917. See also *TYW*, pp. 207–8.

91 "a firm hand": JQ to EP, June 2, 1917, NYPL.

91 "he expresses approval": EP to MCA, May 17, 1917, *EP/LR*, p. 57.

91 "be a comfort": Ibid., May 25, 1917, p. 58.

91 "amiable spirit" and "She hadn't any": EP to JQ, June 18, 1917, NYPL.

91 secure advertisements: JQ to MCA, Sept. 21, 25 and 26, 1917, UWM, Box 4 Folder 2.

92 "I shall, of course" and "Will you": JQ to Jane Heap, Aug. 7, 1917, UWM, Box 4 Folder 2.

8. ZURICH

93 two months' salary and collateral to purchase: JJ to A. Llewelyn Roberts, July 30, 1915, *LII*, p. 357.

93 haven for smugglers: Budgen, *Joyce and Ulysses*, pp. 27–34.

93 In July 1916: Hugo Ball, *Flight Out of Time: A Dada Diary* (Berkeley: University of California Press, 1996), pp. xxiii, 56, 64, passim.

93 "How does one": Hugo Ball, "Dada Manifesto" (1916).

94 nearly half: Budgen, *Joyce and Ulysses*, p. 34.

94 "As a foreigner": Austrian government report (July 31, 1916) qtd. Stanzel, "Austria's Surveillance of Joyce," pp. 361–71.

94 "most undesirable people": Rumbold to Gaselee, July 18, 1918, BNA, F.O. 395/209/003–4.

94 "Professor Joice": July 9, 1916 report to the Imperial and Royal Defense Headquarters in Tyrol, qtd. in Stanzel, "Austria's Surveillance of Joyce," pp. 368–9. See also Stanzel, "Austrian Subtext of Joyce's *Ulysses*"; McCourt, *Years*, p. 249; Budgen, *Joyce and Ulysses*, p. 34.

94–95 "As an artist": Georges Borach, "Conversations with James Joyce," in Potts, *Portraits of the Artist in Exile*, p. 71.

95 "Herr Satan": Budgen, *Joyce and Ulysses,* p. 35.

95 surviving on the breadline: July 9, 1916, letter from k.u.k. Militärattaché to Imperial and Royal Defense Headquarters qtd. in Stanzel, "Austria's Surveillance of Joyce," p. 368.

95 institutional grants: Ell, pp. 392, 406.

95 had his reservations: Gordon Bowker, *James Joyce: A New Biography* (New York: Farrar, Straus and Giroux, 2012), p. 227.

95 "Club des Étrangers": Ell, p. 407.

95 home alone: Marilyn Reizbaum, "Swiss Customs," *JJQ* 27, no. 2 (Winter 1990), p. 213 qtd. in Carol Shloss, *Lucia Joyce: To Dance in the Wake* (New York: Farrar, Straus and Giroux, 2003), p. 66.

95 signature dance: Budgen, *Joyce and Ulysses,* p. 190; Carola Giedion-Welcker, "Meeting with Joyce," in Potts, *Portraits of the Artist in Exile,* p. 273; C. P. Curran, *James Joyce Remembered* (New York: Oxford University Press, 1968), p. 90; Ell, pp. 430, 433.

96 "Ther-r-r-re he goes": Victor Llona, "Mrs. James Joyce and Her Controversial Husband," *Cimarron Review* 70 no. 74 (Jan. 1986), pp. 55–60, p. 56.

96 spoke Triestino: Ell, p. 389.

96 writing on the floor: Lucia Joyce, "The Real Life of James Joyce," Lucia Joyce Papers, HRC, Box 1 Folder 3.

96 "I write and think": JJ to EP, July 24, 1917 (unpublished), qtd. in Ell, p. 416. I am eliding a sentence after "think."

96 in February 1917: Ell, p. 413.

96 going to burst: Casey Albert Wood, *A System of Ophthalmic Therapeutics; Being a Complete Work on the Non-Operative Treatment, Including the Prophylaxis, of Diseases of the Eye.* (Chicago: Cleveland Press, 1909), p. 807.

97 In 1907 and "disabled": SJ, Trieste Diary, May 23–July 4, 1907, Tulsa, Series 1 Box 142.

97 twelve more: Weaver to Brewerton, Aug. 30, 1922, BL; JJ to Weaver, Oct. 27 and 28, 1922, BL.

98 Joyce's condition: JJ to Forrest Reid, May 10, 1917, *LII,* p. 395; Weaver to Marsh, Sept. 11, 1917, *LII,* p. 407. Joyce describes both a synechia and secondary glaucoma from iritis.

98 sticky fluid: Wood, *System of Ophthalmic Therapeutics,* pp. 764–5.

98 right eye blind: Ibid., p. 765.

98 most appealing treatment: Ibid., pp. 766–7.

98 separate the synechia: Ibid., p. 430.

98 increased intraocular pressure: Ibid., pp. 62, 429; Francisco J. Ascaso and Jordi Bosch, "Uveitic Secondary Glaucoma: Influence in James Joyce's (1882–1941) Last Works," *Journal of Medical Biography* 18, no. 1 (Feb 2010), pp. 57–61, p. 60n19.

98 give Joyce atropine: JQ to EP (enclosure from Dr. Shannon), July 7, 1917, NYPL.

98 developed glaucoma: NB to JQ, April 30, 1917, *LII,* p. 395.

98 fainting, headaches, throat irritation: Wood, *System of Ophthalmic Therapeutics,* pp. 59, 429.

98 hallucinations: Jan Dirk Blom, *A Dictionary of Hallucinations* (New York: Springer, 2010), pp. 42–43; Manuchair S. Ebadi, *Desk Reference of Clinical Pharmacology* (Boca Raton, Fla.: CRC Press, 2008), p. 634.

98 irritated throat: JJ to Weaver, July 7, 1917, *LI,* p. 103.

98 began hallucinating: EP to JJ, March 17, 1917, *EP/JJ,* p. 103.

98 Quinn purchased: JQ to JJ, April 11, 1917, NYPL.

98 wrote to Nora: JQ to NB, May 25, 1917, NYPL.

99 "best eye expert" and "Poor fellow": JQ to EP, June 6, 1917, NYPL.

99 "Thanks for the photograph": EP to JJ, Dec. 20, 1916, *EP/JJ,* p. 85.

99 "by having a vertebra": Ibid., March 17, 1917, p. 101.

99 slips of paper: Ell, p. 420; JJ to Sykes, Dec. 22[?], 1917, *LII,* p. 415.

99 "Names and Places" and "tainted curds": Early Ulysses Subject Notebook for Drafts (1917) (II.i.1. Notebook), NLI, MS 36,639/3 (See online at http://catalogue.nli.ie/Record/vtls000357760#page/1/mode/1up); Myron Schwartzman, "*Ulysses* on the Rocks: The Evolution of the 'Nausikaa' Episode with a Suggested Addition to the Final Text," *Bulletin of the New York Public Library* 80, no. 4 (Summer 1977), p. 646.

100 was simply "We": Phillip Herring, *Joyce's Notes and Early Drafts for Ulysses* (Charlottesville: University Press of Virginia, 1977), p. 83.

100 known exactly where: Michael Groden, *Ulysses in Progress* (Princeton: Princeton University, 1977), p. 111.

100 note taking increased: Ibid., p. 43.

100 notes from his notes: See Luca Crispi, "A First Foray into the National Library of Ireland's Joyce Manuscripts: Bloomsday 2011," *Genetic Joyce Studies* 11 (Spring 2011).

100 small suitcase: JJ to JQ, Nov. 24, 1920, *LIII*, p. 30.

100 on both sides: See Proteus-Sirens Notebook (II.ii.1.a Notebook), NLI, MS 36,639/7A. http://catalogue.nli.ie/Record/vtls000357771#page/1/mode/1up.

100 manipulated conversations: August Suter, "Some Reminiscences of James Joyce," in Potts, *Portraits of the Artist in Exile*, p. 61.

100 Everything around him and small notebook: Budgen, *Joyce and Ulysses*, pp. 171–2.

100 talked to the cat: Maddox, *Nora: A Biography*, p. 150.

100 "Mrkgnao!": *Ulysses*, p. 45 (4: 25).

100 marketplace reminded her: NB to JJ, Aug. 4, 1917, *LII*, p. 401.

100 about the thunderstorms: Ibid., ca. Aug. 10, 1917, p. 402.

100 "I shall wait": Ibid., ca. Aug. 12, 1917, p. 403.

100 ashplant cane: Budgen, *Joyce and Ulysses*, p. 11.

100 Bahnhofstrasse: Ibid., 27.

101 the same colors: Liam Kelly, National Transport Museum of Ireland, May 18, 2011, email and photographs.

101 nearby bench: Gorman, *James Joyce*, p. 259; Ell, p. 417; JJ to EP, Aug. 20, 1917, *SL*, pp. 226–7.

101 halos around the: Arthur Lim, *Acute Glaucoma: Acute Primary Closed Angle Glaucoma, Major Global Blinding Problem* (Singapore: Singapore University Press, 2002), p. 13.

101 retinal arteries throbbing: Wood, *System of Ophthalmic Therapeutics*, p. 808.

101 his surgery: See Buffalo, Series XIX Folder 20. Joyce's 1921 drawing of his 1917 surgery indicates a peripheral iridectomy.

101 The surgeon held: Charles Beard, *Ophthalmic Surgery: A Treatise on Surgical Operations Pertaining to the Eye and Its Appendages, with Chapters on Para-Operative Technic and Management of Instruments* (Philadelphia: P. Blakiston's Son & Co., 1914), pp. 457–462; Josef Meller, *Ophthalmic Surgery: A Handbook of Surgical Operations on the Eyeball and its Appendages: As Practised at the Clinic of Prof. Hofrat Fuchs* (Philadelphia: Blakiston, 1912), pp. 180–6.

101 Exudate flowed over: JJ to Weaver, March 11, 1923, *LI*, p. 201.

101 nervous breakdown: NB to EP, Aug. 28, 1917, *LII*, p. 405; Weaver to JJ, Nov. 10, 1916, Cornell, Series IV Box 14.

101 flitting into corners: Blom, *Dictionary of Hallucinations*, pp. 42–43.

102 bled for two weeks: NB to Weaver, Sept. 8, 1917, *LII*, p. 406. See also EP to JQ, Sept. 10, 1917, NYPL.

102 ensconcing himself: Maddox, *Nora: A Biography*, p. 149.

102 asked Nora to cheat: Frank Budgen, *Myselves When Young* (London: Oxford University Press, 170), p. 188.

102 two and a half shillings: JJ to Pinker, July 8, 1917, *LII*, p. 399.

102 only 750 copies: Ell, p. 414.

102 "How many intelligent": EP to JJ, Aug. 15, 1917, *EP/JJ*, p. 123 (Pound's emphasis).

102 keeping his family warm: JJ to EP Aug. 20, 1917, *SL*, pp. 226.

103 "the bread of": *MBK*, p. 104.

103 "above all languages": JJ qtd. in Ell, p. 397.

103 advance all of civilization: JJ to Richards, June 23, 1906, *LI*, p. 64.

103 Scofield Thayer: Ell, p. 457.

103 Edith McCormick: Ibid., p. 423.

103 London law firm: Slack, Monro, Saw & Co. to JJ, Feb. 22, 1917, *LII*, p. 389. See also *DMW*, p. 134; Ell, p. 413.

103   annual salary: Ell, p. 313.
103   read portions and little to say: Ibid., pp. 421–2.
103   "wading like a heron": Budgen, *Joyce and Ulysses*, pp. 11–12.
104   "Why all this fuss": JJ qtd. in ibid., p. 320
104   doll's underwear: Suter, "Some Reminiscences of Joyce," p. 61.
104   "Among other things": Budgen, *Joyce and Ulysses*, p. 21.
104   all day on two sentences: Ibid., pp. 19–20.
104   graph paper: Philip Herring, "Ulysses' Notebook VIII.A.5 at Buffalo," *Studies in Bibliography* 22 (1969), p. 287–310.
104   "Can you read it?": Budgen, *Joyce and Ulysses*, p. 173.

9. POWER AND POSTAGE

105   "It was like a burning": *TYW*, p. 175.
107   "German agents": Christopher M. Finan, *From the Palmer Raids to the Patriot Act* (Boston: Beacon Press, 2007), p. 12.
107   "The only badge": *Albany Journal* ad qtd. in Christopher Capozzola, "The Only Badge Needed Is Your Patriotic Fervor: Vigilance, Coercion and the Law in World War I America," *Journal of American History* 88, no. 4 (March 2002), p. 1360.
107   "U.S. Secret Service" badges: Joan Jensen, *The Price of Vigilance* (Chicago: Rand McNally, 1968), pp. 41–42.
107   blackmail, wiretapping: Ibid., p.72; David Kennedy, *Over Here: The First World War and American Society* (New York: Oxford University Press, 1980), p. 82.
107   roughly three million: Jensen, *Vigilance,* p. 155. Not counting Justice Department cases.
108   Daniel Cohalan: see "Many Caught in the Web of Kaiser's Gold," *New York Tribune*, Sept. 23, 1917, p.1; "U.S. Exposes More German Plots," *San Francisco Chronicle*, Sept. 23, 1917, p. 1; *MNY*, p. 324.
108   a cargo ship: Jules Witcover, *Sabotage at Black Tom: Imperial Germany's Secret War in America, 1914–1917* (Chapel Hill, N.C.: Algonquin Books of Chapel Hill, 1989); Michael Warner, "The Kaiser Sows Destruction," *Studies in Intelligence: Journal of the American Intelligence Professional* 46, no. 1 (2002) pp.3–9.
108   "any disloyal, profane": Sedition Act of 1918, 40 Stat. 583.
108   highest government official: "Postal Officials Begin Wide Search," *NYT*, May 1, 1919, p. 3.
108   "embarrass or hamper": Donald Johnson, "Wilson, Burleson and Censorship in the First World War," *Journal of Southern History* 28 (Feb. 1962), p. 48.
108   only three hundred: Jensen, *Vigilance*, p. 15.
108   only eleven: Philip Melanson and Peter Steven, *The Secret Service: The Hidden History of an Enigmatic Agency* (New York: Carroll & Graf Publishers, 2002), p. 37.
108   It had 300,000 employees: United States Bureau of the Census; United States Civil Service Commission, *Official Register of the United States* (Washington, D.C.: Bureau of the Census, 1917), p. 11. (online)
108   422 inspectors: *Official Register*, p. 11.
108   56,000 postmasters: Louis Melius, *The American Postal Service: History of the Postal Service from the Earliest Times.* (Washington D.C.: National Capital Press, 1917), pp. 20, 97.
108   fourteen billion pieces: Ibid., p. 49.
109   "elevating our people" and half-century expansion: Gerald Cullinan, *The Post Office Department* (New York: F.A. Praeger, 1968), pp. 57–64.
109   volume increased one hundred times: Ibid., pp. 61, 104.
109   twenty-five cents: Jane Kennedy, "Development of Postal Rates: 1845–1955," *Land Economics* 33, no. 2 (1957), p. 95.
109   three cents: Ibid., p. 96.
110   two cents per pound: Ibid., p. 98; and Cullinan, *Post Office Department,* p. 250 (Appendix A).
110   one cent per pound: Kennedy, "Postal Rates," p. 99.

110 issue was $2.50: See Patten affidavit qtd. in JQ's memorandum for the "Cantleman" suppression, Case File 49537, 7E4, Box 142, 8/5/2. WWI Espionage Files, Post Office Records, NARA.

110 Joyce fan's subscription: The $2.50 annual rate was announced in 1917 but did not take effect until January 1918, two months later.

110 eight to fifteen times higher: See Brandeis dissent in *United States ex rel. Milwaukee Social Democratic Publishing Company v. Burleson*, 255 U.S. 407 (1921).

110 without court approval: Johnson, "Wilson, Burleson and Censorship," pp. 47–50.

110 Congress asked Burleson: Adrian Anderson, "President Wilson's Politician: Albert Sidney Burleson of Texas," *Southwestern Historical Quarterly* 77, no. 3 (Jan. 1974), pp. 345–47.

110 wore a black coat: Kennedy, p. 75.

110 "the most belligerent": Edward House, qtd. in Kennedy, "Postal Rates," p. 75.

110 "insidious attempt": Burleson to Wilson, Sept, 1920, qtd. in Johnson, "Wilson, Burleson and Censorship," p. 57.

111 a thousand people: Geoffrey R. Stone, "The Origins of the 'Bad Tendency' Test: Free Speech in Wartime," *Supreme Court Review* (2002), p. 444.

111 hundreds received prison: John Sayer, "Art and Politics, Dissent and Repression: *The Masses* Magazine versus the Government, 1917–1918," *American Journal of Legal History* 32, no. 1 (Jan. 1988), p. 74.

111 You knew it: cf. Justice Stewart's later opinion in *Jacobellis v. Ohio*, 378 U.S. 184 (1964).

111 beyond the authority: See Stone, "Origins of the 'Bad Tendency' Test."

111 train to Washington: Anna Louise Bates, *Weeder in the Garden of the Lord: Anthony Comstock's Life and Career* (Lanham, MD.: University Press of America, 1995), p. 82; Heywood Broun and Margaret Leech, *Anthony Comstock, Roundsman of the Lord* (New York: A&C Boni, 1927), pp. 129–32.

112 "The daily papers": Anthony Comstock, *Traps for the Young* (Cambridge, Mass.: Belknap Press of Harvard University Press, 1967), p. 13.

113 only a handful: United States Postal Service, *The United States Postal Service: An American History, 1775–2006* (Washington, D.C.: Government Relations, Postal Service, 2012), p. 62.

113 special agents collected debts: Ibid., p. 64.

113 one person per year: Donna Dennis, *Licentious Gotham: Erotic Publishing and Its Prosecution in Nineteenth-Century New York* (Cambridge, Mass.: Harvard University Press, 2009), p. 268.

113 prosecuted fifty-five: Broun and Leech, *Anthony Comstock*, p. 152.

114 protest rallies: Emma Goldman, *Living My Life* (New York: Penguin Group, 2006), p. 341.

114 eight policemen raided: Richard Drinnon, *Rebel in Paradise: A Bibliography of Emma Goldman* (New York: Harper & Row, 1976), p. 188; Goldman, *Living My Life*, p. 344.

114 "for the hideous crime" and officers were detailed: "Guard for Judge at Goldman Trial," *NYT*, June 27, 1917, p. 13.

114 press reprinted: See, e.g, "Emma Goldman and Alexander Berkman, Anarchists," *New York Tribune*, June 24, 1917, D2.

114 "The Star-Spangled Banner": "Anarchists Close Their Defense," *NYT*, July 7, 1917, p. 10; *Mother Earth*, July 1917, p. 134; Drinnon, *Rebel in Paradise*, p. 193.

114 defendant's table: Heap, *Dear Tiny Heart*, p. 47; Goldman, *Living My Life*, p. 350.

114 "Ezraized *Little Review*": "An Old Reader," *LR* 4, no. 5 (Sept. 1917), pp. 31–32.

114 "I wish you didn't": Letter from H.C.L., ibid., p. 33.

114 Subscriptions dwindled: *TYW*, p. 146.

115 the editors evicted: Heap to Reynolds, July 1917, *Dear Tiny Heart*, p. 47.

115 scrounged for money: Ibid., p. 50, *TYW*, p. 156.

115 potatoes: Yale Anderson, Box 14 Folder 251.

115 crepe de chine: *TYW*, p. 206.

115 "And when he beat": Wyndham Lewis, "Cantleman's Spring-Mate," *LR* 4, no. 6 (Oct. 1917), p. 14.

115 weighing room and The issue circulated: JQ's Brief in *Anderson v. Thomas G. Patten, Postmaster of the City of New York, Defendant* (Nov. 28, 1917) and accompanying documents, Case File 49537, 7E4, Box 142, 8/5/2, WWI Espionage Files, Post Office Records, NARA.

115 the final authority: Sedition Act of 1918, 40 Stat. 583.

115   "conclusive" and "clearly wrong": See *Masses Publishing Co. v. Patten*, 246 F. 24, 38 (2d. Circuit 1917) and Augustus Hand's decision in *Anderson v. Patten*.

115   "Words are the first": "Water, Salt and Sugar at $320 a Gallon," *Boston Globe*, Jan. 23, 1916, p. SM10.

115   "reading between the lines": William Lamar, "The Government's Attitude Toward the Press," *Forum* 59 (Feb. 1918), p. 139.

115   "You know I am not": Lamer qtd. in Sayer, "Art and Politics, Dissent and Repression," p. 53.

115–16   "The foreign editor" and "does not come within": JQ to Lamar, Nov. 5, 1917, Post Office Records, NARA.

116   planned to speak: JQ to MCA, Nov. 7, 1917, UWM, Box 4 Folder 2.

116   "because they come within": Augustus Hand decision, *Anderson v. Patten*, 247 p. 382, Nov. 30, 1917, Post Office Records, NARA.

116   out of the papers: JQ to EP, Dec. 2, 1917, NYPL.

116   "Alas!": Ibid.

117   a file on Margaret Anderson: Claire Culleton, *Joyce and the G-Men: J. Edgar Hoover's Manipulation of Modernism* (New York: Palgrave Macmillian, 2004), p. 80. Culleton notes that Anderson's file had been destroyed. That it was opened around the time the magazine was labeled anarchist is thus my speculation.

117   "Publication of Anarchist tendency" and Espionage Act: Case File 50839, Records Relating to the Espionage Act, WWI, 1917–1920, Office of the Solicitor, Records of the Post Office Department, Record Group 28, National Archives, Washington, D.C. See also Paul Vanderham, *James Joyce and Censorship: The Trials of Ulysses* (New York: New York University Press, 1998), pp. 18, 29–30 and p. 116 photo insert, Figure 1. Vanderham agrees that *LR* was singled out at least partly for its politics.

117   "I suppose": EP to JJ, Dec. 19, 1917 *EP/JJ*, p. 129. My ellipsis.

117   "Joyce has run wode": EP to MCA, Feb. 21, 1918, *EP/LR*, p. 189.

117   changed his mind: EP to JJ, June 7, 1918, *EP/JJ*, p. 143.

118   broke his glasses: See *Ulysses*, p. 456 (15: 3628).

118   *"By what touch"* and "the poignant": *TYW*, p. 155.

118   "This is the most beautiful thing": Ibid., p. 175.

118   three hundred: EP to MCA, Dec. 30, 1917, *EP/LR*, pp. 171–4.

118   if mentioning urination EP to JQ, Dec. 29–30, 1917, *EP/JQ*, p. 134.

118   "When dealing with religious": EP to JQ, Dec. 24, 1917, NYPL.

118   "For God's sake": EP to MCA, Dec. 30, 1917, *EP/LR*, p. 169.

119   "even if we go bust": EP to JQ, Dec. 29, 1917, NYPL.

119   "I think the statute": EP to JQ, Dec. 29 and 30, 1917, *EP/JQ*, p. 132.

119   "grotesque, barbarous": Ibid., Feb. 18, 1918, p. 142.

119   "man to man" and "I trust you are": EP to JQ, Jan. 18, 1918, NYPL.

119   "the inventions": EP, "The Classics 'Escape,'" *LR* 4, no. 11 (March 1918), pp. 32–34.

119–20   "might be the last straw" and make it stronger: JQ to EP, March 6, 1918, NYPL.

120   "There is nothing": Ibid., March 2, 1918.

120   "In the minds of": Ibid., May 20, 1918.

120   "one of the most sincere": JQ, "James Joyce, A New Irish Novelist," *Vanity Fair*, May 1917, pp. 49, 128.

120   "very nearly approaches genius": JQ to EP, Jan. 12, 1917, NYPL; *MNY*, pp. 273–4.

121   about thirty copies: JQ to JJ, April 11, 1917, NYPL.

121   "A new star": Ibid, p. 49.

121   copy portions: cf. EP to JQ, April 8, 1916, NYPL; EP to JQ, Feb. 26, 1916, NYPL.

121   visited Ireland: *MNY*, p. 16.

121   a malignant tumor: Ibid., pp. 334–6.

121   "I am still interested": JQ to EP, May 20, 1918, NYPL.

121 "snotgreen" and "the scrotumtightening sea": *Ulysses*, p. 4 (1: 78).
121 Jesus urinating: *LR* 4, no. 11 (March 1918), p. 19.
121–22 "That is what I call": JQ to EP, March 14, 1918, NYPL.
122 "He felt heavy": *Ulysses*, p. 55 (4: 460–1); cf. *LR* 5, no. 2 (June 1918), p. 50.
122 struck a line through: see Vanderham, *Joyce and Censorship*, p. 170; EP to JJ, March 29, 1918, *EP/JJ*, p. 131.
122 "I shall see": JJ to Forrest Reid, Aug. 1, 1918, *LI*, p. 117.
122 "Bad because you waste" and "I can't have": EP to JJ, March 29, 1918, *EP/JJ*, p. 131.
122 months without hearing: EP to JQ, Dec. 24, 1917, NYPL.
122 behind on rent: Heap to Reynolds, Oct. 21, 1918, *Dear Tiny Heart*, p. 63.
122 "It is so dirty": Ibid., pp. 61–62.
122 fever blisters: Ibid., Thanksgiving 1918, p. 70.
122 someone else: Ibid., Nov. 11, 1918, p. 67.
122 Spanish flu: *TYW*, p. 209.
123 avoid catching a glimpse: Heap to Reynolds, Oct. 21, 1918, *Dear Tiny Heart*, pp. 62–63.
123 Djuna Barnes: Linda Lappin, "Jane Heap and Her Circle," *Prairie Schooner* 78, no. 4 (2004), p. 18; Shari Benstock, *Women of the Left Bank: Paris, 1900–1940* (Austin: University of Texas Press, 1986), p. 239.
123 suicidal: Heap to Reynolds, Nov. 11, 1918, *Dear Tiny Heart*, p. 67.
123 "The Creature who writes": March 14, 1919, letter from an unidenitified Translation Bureau employee to an unidentified supervisor re: Feb–March *LR*. Case File 49537, 7E4, Box 142, 8/5/2,. WWI Espionage Files, Post Office Records, NARA.
123 "High on Ben Howth": *LR* 5, no. 9 (Jan. 1919), p. 47.
124 The Post Office notified: *LR* 6, no. 1 (May 1919), p. 21n. I am speculating that the belated ban on the January issue resulted from the employee's comments on the February–March issue. The January issue was apparently banned after the February–March issue went to press (Anderson's note appears in the May issue), and the Translation Bureau's comments happen in mid-March.
124 hour and a half: JQ to MCA, June 14, 1919, UWM, Box 4 Folder 3.
124 decision over the weekend: Ibid., June 17, 1919.
124 dismissed her: JQ to EP, June 18, 1919, NYPL.
124 "incests and bestialities": JJ, "Episode IX" ("Scylla and Charybdis"), *LR* 6, no. 1 (May 1919), pp. 17–35.
124 "The fact of s—t—g": JQ to EP, June 18, 1919, NYPL.
125 most brilliant defenses: EP to JQ, July 6, 1919, *EP/JQ*, pp. 176–77.
125 "a national scandal": Eliot to JQ, July 9, 1919, NYPL. My ellipsis.

10. THE WOOLFS

126 gray woolen gloves: VW, *The Diary of Virginia Woolf* (London: Hogarth Press, 1977), vol. 1, p. 140 (April 18, 1918).
126 tugged her collar: *DMW*, p. 119.
126 unseasonably cold: Daily Weather Report, April 14, 1918, National Meteorological Archive, Exeter, UK.
126 answered questions scrupulously: *DMW*, p. 40, and McAlmon, *Being Geniuses Together*, p. 42.
126 sudden prominence: Andrew McNeillie, "Bloomsbury," in *The Cambridge Companion to Virginia Woolf*, 2nd ed. (New York: Cambridge University Press, 2010), pp. 15–16.
126–27 "curiously disappointing": VW, "The Rights of Youth," in *The Essays of Virginia Woolf*, ed. Andrew McNeillie (London: Hogarth Press, 1987), vol. 2, p. 296.
127 "Every one": VW, "Charlotte Brontë," ibid., p. 29.
127 "on or about December 1910": VW, "Mr. Bennett and Mrs. Brown," *Essays*, vol. 3, p. 421.
127 "well-bred hen" and brown paper wrapping: VW, *Diary*, vol. 1, p. 140 (April 18, 1918).

127 refused to print it: Weaver to JJ, March 8, 1918, Cornell, Series IV Box 14.

127 "supplement" to *The Egoist*: *DMW*, p. 148.

127 first four episodes: Weaver to JJ, June 19, 1918, Cornell, Series IV Box 14.

127–28 incompetent and "How did she ever": VW, *Diary*, vol. 1, p. 140 (April 18, 1918).

128 back in a bun: *DMW*, p. 40.

128 spine keeping its distance: Ibid., p. 304.

128 A few days later and reading aloud: Ibid., p. 145 (April 28, 1918).

128 "Mr Leopold Bloom ate": *Ulysses*, p. 45 (4: 1–8).

128 "Mkgnao!" and "Mrkgnao!": Ibid., p. 46 (4: 16, 32).

128 quite satisfying: VW, *Diary*, vol. 1, p. 145 (April 28, 1918).

128 disgusting, unhealthy: Mansfield to Sydney Schiff, Dec. 28, 1921, in Vincent O'Sullivan and Margaret Scott, eds., *Collected Letters of Katherine Mansfield*, vol. 2 (Oxford: Oxford University Press, 1996), p. 432.

128 "I can't get over": Mansfield to Sydney Schiff, Jan. 15, 1922. Ibid., p. 434.

129 "But there's something in this": Mansfield qtd. in VW, *Diary* vol. 5, p. 353 (Jan. 15, 1941).

129 thirty-one pages and hour and fifteen minutes: VW, *Diary*, vol. 1, p. 136 (April 10, 1918).

129 "the only woman in England": VW, *Diary*, vol. 2, p. 43, qtd. in Celia Marshik, *British Modernism and Censorship* (Cambridge: Cambridge University Press, 2006), p. 11.

129 certain prosecution: Leonard Woolf, *Beginning Again: An Autobiography of the Years 1911–1918* (London: Hogarth Press, 1968), p. 247.

129 "We have read the chapters": VW to Weaver, May 17, 1918, in Nigel Nicolson and Joanne Trautman, eds., *The Letters of Virginia Woolf* (New York: Mariner, 1976), vol. 2, pp. 242–3.

129 "to reveal the flickerings": VW, "Modern Novels," in *Essays*, vol. 3, p. 34.

130 Eliot dined: VW, *Diary*, vol. 2, p. 67 (Sept. 20, 1920).

130 "what I'm doing": Ibid., p. 69 (Sept. 26, 1920).

130 spy code: EP to JJ, July[?] 1920, *EP/JJ*, p. 182.

130 "had bitched": EP to JJ, June 10, 1919, *EP/JJ*, p. 157.

130 "knockmedown cigar" and "broadshouldered": *Ulysses*, p. 251 (12: 502), p. 243 (12: 152–3).

130 burning pike that blinds: See JJ's schema reprinted in Hugh Kenner, *Dublin's Joyce* (New York: Columbia University Press, 1988), pp. 226–7.

131 Phoenician sailors: Groden, *Ulysses in Progress*, pp. 84–87.

131 "Bronze by gold": *Ulysses*, p. 210 (11: 1–16); *LR* 6, no. 4 (Aug. 1919), p. 41.

131 "I think I can see": Weaver to JJ, June 16, 1919, Cornell, Series IV Box 14.

132 "got knocked on the head" and "*Caro mio*": EP to JJ, June 10, 1919, *EP/JJ*, pp. 157–9.

132 as early as 1915: Proteus-Sirens Notebook (II.ii.1.a Notebook), NLI, MS 36,639/7A. See Luca Crispi, "A First Foray into the National Library of Ireland's Joyce Manuscripts: Bloomsday 2011," *Genetic Joyce Studies* 11 (Spring 2011).

132 eight-part structure: Daniel Ferrer, "What Song the Sirens Sang . . . Is No Longer Beyond All Conjecture: A Preliminary Description of the New 'Proteus' and 'Sirens' Manuscripts," *JJQ* 39, no. 1 (Fall 2001), p. 62–63.

132 changing radically: Groden, *Ulysses in Progress*, pp. 17, 37–52.

133 "darkbacked figure": *Ulysses*, p. 192 (520–1).

133 "Elijah is coming": Ibid., p. 186 (10: 284).

133 "perverted commas": JJ to Weaver, July 11, 1924, *LIII*, p. 99.

133 fall and winter: Schwartzman, "*Ulysses* on the Rocks," pp. 455–73.

133 purple notebooks bound with string: Cornell, Series I Box 2 Folder 23.

133 "Dearer than the whole": Joyce's process is reconstructed from the "Nausicaa" manuscript notebooks at Cornell as well as from transcriptions of the eight "Nausicaa" notesheets in Phillip Herring, *Joyce's Ulysses Notesheets in the British Museum* (Charlottesville: University Press of Virginia, 1972), pp. 125–61. For a published version of this manuscript passage, see James Joyce and Michael Groden, *Ulysses, "Wandering Rocks," "Sirens," "Cyclops," & "Nausicaa": A Facsimile of Manu-*

scripts & Typescripts for Episodes 10–13 (New York: Garland, 1977), p. 217. This volume is subsequently referred to as *JJA "Nausicaa" MS*.

134 **"in that novel that":** This phrase occurs in Joyce's notebook MS (see *JJA "Nausicaa" MS*, p. 216) but disappears in subsequent typescripts and published editions, including *The Little Review*, the 1922 Shakespeare and Company edition and the Gabler edition.

135 **"From everything in":** Cornell, Series I, Box 2 Folder 23; *JJA "Nausicaa" MS*, p. 216; *LR* 7, no. 1 (May-June 1920), p. 72.

135 **fifteen insertions and 879 more:** Herring, *Joyce's Ulysses Notesheets*, pp. 125–61.

11. BRUTAL MADNESS

136 **their favorite hero:** Gorman, *James Joyce*, p. 45.

136 **"inflamed with a desire":** Charles Lamb, *The Adventures of Ulysses* (Boston: Ginn & Co, 1894), p. 1.

136 **"Ulysses is not a hero":** Arthur Power, *The Joyce We Knew*, p. 104.

136 **"world-troubling seaman":** JJ to JQ, Nov. 17, 1920, NYPL.

136 **most complete human being:** Borach, "Conversations with James Joyce," p. 70, and Budgen, *Joyce and Ulysses*, pp. 15–17.

137 **"only a pretext":** Ell, p. 416.

137 **several nights a week and Ringsend:** JJ to NB, Aug. 7, 1909, *SL*, pp. 158–9.

137 **"Is Georgie my son?" and "Were you fucked":** Ibid.

137 **stop a man's beating heart:** JJ to NB, Dec. 3, 1909, *SL*, p. 182.

138 **fit of sobbing and slept at Eccles Street:** John Francis Byrne, *Silent Years: An Autobiography with Memoirs of James Joyce and Our Ireland* (New York: Farrar, Straus, and Young), pp. 156–7.

138 **"blasted lie":** John Byrne qtd. in JJ to NB, Aug. 19, 1909, *SL*, p. 159.

138 **"in her hand" and "Guide me" and curling up in her womb:** JJ to NB, Sept. 5, 1909, *SL*, p. 169.

138 **gloves and Donegal tweed:** Ibid., Nov. 1, 1909, pp. 176–7, and Oct. 27, 1909, pp. 173–6.

138 **ivory necklace and "Love Is Unhappy":** Ibid., Sept. 3, 1909, pp. 167–8.

138 **"great crimson bows":** Ibid., Dec. 6, 1909, p. 184.

138 **packages of cocoa and womanly:** JJ to SJ, Aug. 21, 1909, *SL*, p. 162; JJ to NB, Sept. 7 and Oct. 27, 1909, *SL*, pp. 170, 175.

139 **perfume and stains:** JJ to NB, Dec. 6, 1909, *SL*, p. 184.

139 **certain kind of letter:** Ibid., Aug. 22, 1909, p. 163.

139 **destroyed her letters:** Ell, p. 721. Maria Jolas told Ellmann that NB destroyed them on the eve of World War II.

139 **"Si":** Sotheby's "Catalogue Note," Lot 201, July 8, 2004, London auction, http://www.sothebys .com/en/auctions/ecatalogue/lot.pdf.f/201/L04407-201.pdf.

139 **"Inside this spiritual" and "your hot lips":** JJ to NB, Dec. 2, 1909, *SL*, p. 181.

139 **"of a young man":** Yeats to JJ, Dec. 18, 1902, *LII*, p. 23.

139 **"to fuck between":** JJ to NB, Dec. 6, 1909, *SL*, pp. 184.

139–40 **He listed and "Fuck me into you" and "grunting":** Ibid., Dec. 16, 1909, pp. 190–1.

140 **"Be careful":** JJ telegram qtd. in JJ to NB, Dec. 10, 1909, *SL*, p. 187. Italics in JJ's letter.

140 **"tore off" and "Fuck up":** Ibid., Dec. 3, 1909, p. 182.

140 **"disjointed":** Ibid., Dec. 16, 1909, p. 190.

140–41 **something she would do and she underlined it:** Ibid., Dec. 9, 1909, p. 186.

141 **thin arcs of the cursive:** Handwriting details from NB's letters at Cornell, Series IV Box 9.

141 **kissed the word:** JJ to NB, Dec. 10, 1909, SL, p. 187.

141 **"wild brutal madness":** Ibid., Dec. 11, 1909, p. 187.

141 **"hear and smell the dirty":** Ibid., Dec. 9, 1909, p. 186.

141 **"vulgar language":** Bruce Bradley, "'Something about Tullabeg': A Footnote on the Schooldays of James Joyce," *Studies: An Irish Quarterly Review* 93, no. 370 (Summer 2004), p. 164.

141 "half past six": Ell, p. 27.

142 "When you were with him" and "I love you": JJ to NB, Dec. 3, 1909, *SL*, p. 183.

142 "to feel you bending down": Ibid., Dec. 13[?], 1909, p. 189.

142 "Nora, Nora mia" and *"talking, talking"*: Ibid., Dec. 16, 1909, p. 191. My ellipsis (JJ includes an ellipsis shortly thereafter).

143 "ideal reader": JJ, *Finnegans Wake* (New York: Penguin, 2000), p. 120.

12. SHAKESPEARE AND COMPANY

144 candle flame: *SC*, p. 18; SBP, Box 168 Folder 4, and *SBLG*, p. 39.

144 "probably the best": Eugene Jolas qtd. in *SBLG*, p. 41.

144–45 collecting shrapnel and skeletons: SB to Cyprian Beach, March 11, 1919, *LSB*, pp. 55–56.

145 stagnant and "Please": SB to Slyvester Beach, Jan. 29, 1919, *LSB*, p. 46.

145 market vendors: Ibid., p. 63; Lenka Yovitchitch, *Pages from Here and There in Serbia* (Belgrade: S. B. Cvijanovich, 1926), pp. 75–80.

145 Gypsy women: *LSB*, pp. 54, 64.

145 She handed out: SB to Eleanor Beach, Feb. 2, 1919, *LSB*, p. 49.

145 pajamas and barefoot: SBP, Box 168 Folder 6, Box 169 Folder 3.

145 delousing plant: *LSB*, pp. 55, 58.

145 documenting inhabitants: SB to Slyvester Beach, Jan. 29, 1919, *LSB*, p. 47.

145 mimeograph: SBP, Box 168 Folder 6 and Box 169 Folder 3.

145 women controlled nothing: SB to Cyprian Beach, March 11, 1919, *LSB*, p. 56, March 11, 1919.

145 "The Red Cross has made": SB to Eleanor Beach, April 18, 1919, *LSB*, pp. 58–59.

146 nine generations: *SC*, p. 3.

146 changed her name: *SBLG*, pp. 21–22.

146 farm in Touraine: *SBLG*, p. 31.

146 khaki uniform: Ibid, p. 206.

146 villagers threw rocks: Ibid., p. 419.

146 deepened her perspective: SB to Eleanor Beach, Aug. 27, 1919, *LSB*, p. 76.

146 The low mountains: SB to Cyprian Beach, March 11, 1919, *LSB*, p. 55.

146 Black Sea wind: SB to Slyvester Beach, Jan. 29, 1919, *LSB*, p. 46.

146 crevices and low-roofed houses: Yovitchitch, *Pages from Here and There*, pp. 71–74.

146 muddy Sava River: SB to Eleanor Beach, Aug. 27, 1919, *LSB*, p. 50.

146 literary community: SBP, Box 166 Folders 2 and 5.

146 "I'm sure you would approve": SB qtd. in *SBLG*, p. 38.

146 "would be such hard": Eleanor Beach qtd. in *SBLG*, p. 32.

146 "Opening bookshop": *SC*, p. 17.

147 In March 1917: *SC*, p. 13; SBP, Box 168 Folder 1, and Box 166 Folder 2; and *SBLG*, pp. 33–34.

147 three thousand dollars: *SBLG*, pp. 38, 40.

147 flea market: SBP, Box 168 Folder 4.

147 purchased drawings: *SBLG*, p. 40.

147 Beige sackcloth and Serbian rugs: *SBLG*, p. 42.

147 first lending library: Cody qtd. in *LSB*, p. 312.

147 foreign books too expensive: Cody, Ibid., p. 313.

147 about fifty cents: Cody, Ibid., p. 310.

147 "running up and down": SBP, Box 166 Folder 1, and *SBLG*, p. 48.

148 Monday morning: *SBLG*, p. 40.

148 French literati: Ibid., p. 44.

148 Ezra Pound: SBP, Box 167 Folder 9 and Box 168 Folder 1.

148 nearly two-thirds: see http://www.measuringworth.com/datasets/exchangeglobal/result.php.

148 fifteen thousand Americans and four hundred thousand: Brooke Blower, *Becoming Americans in Paris: Transatlantic Politics and Culture Between the World Wars* (New York: Oxford University Press, 2011), p. 22.

148 American permanent residents: Ibid., p. 6.
148 One-way streets and "cocktails": Sisley Huddleston, *Paris Salons, Cafés, Studios* (Philadelphia: J.B. Lippincott Company, 1928), p. 20.
148 American churches and grocery stores: Ibid., pp. 6–7.
148 one hundred dollars: *SBLG*, p. 103.
149 Montparnasse: Nicholas Hewitt, "Shifting Cultural Centres in Twentieth-Century Paris," in *Parisian Fields*, ed. Michael Sheringham (London: Reaktion Books, 1996), pp. 38–40.
149 artist colony: William Wiser, *The Crazy Years: Paris in the Twenties* (New York: Atheneum, 1983), pp. 95–99.
149 more drinking establishments: W. Scott Haine, "Café Friend: Friendship and Fraternity in Parisian Working-Class Cafés, 1850–1914," *Journal of Contemporary History* 27, no. 4 (October 1992), p. 607.
150 assembly laws: Ibid., pp. 620–22.
150 pigeonhole box: *SC*, p. 102.
150 a hot Sunday afternoon and "The Irish writer": Ibid., pp. 34–35.
150 beneath the "cantankerous": *Letters of Ezra Pound*, p. 153 qtd. in Ell, p. 479.
150 nine-part structure: JJ to Budgen, March 20, 1920, *SL*, p. 251.
151 thousand hours: JJ to Budgen, May 18, 1920, *LII*, p. 464.
151 Beach saw: *SC*, p. 34, and SBP, Box 166 Folder 5.
151 cold cuts: SBP, Box 166 Folder 5.
151 ill-fitting suit: SBP, Box 168 Folder 7.
151 Joyce turned his glass: *SC*, p. 35, and *SBLG*, p. 63.
151 "Is this the great": *SC*, pp. 35–36, and SBP, Box 168 Folder 7.
152 "*Oolissays*": Nigel Nicolson, *Diaries and Letters, 1930–1939* (London: Faber Finds, 2004), p. 165.
152 a small notebook and "Is it coming in?": *SC*, pp. 36–37. My italics.
152 Joyce walked into: Ibid., p. 38; SBP, Box 166 Folder 5; SBP Box 168 Folder 1; and *SBLG*, p. 65.
152 horses, machinery: Ell, p. 25.
152 hid in the cupboard: *MBK*, p. 18.
152 cowering in his hallway: *SC*, p. 43.
152 radio: JJ to Weaver, May 12, 1927, *LI*, p. 252 (qtd. in Maddox, *Nora: A Biography*, p. 229).
152 fifth-floor servants' flat: Maddox, *Nora: A Biography,* p. 172.
153 borrowing a desk: *SBLG*, p. 68.
153 strain of writing: *SC*, p. 39.
153 Joyce sketched a picture: See drawing at University of Buffalo Archive, Series XIX Folder 20.
153 Nora groused: McAlmon, *Being Geniuses Together,* p. 182.
153 pencil and paper and "Look at him" and She wished: *SC*, p. 42.

13. HELL IN NEW YORK

154 cost of living doubled: Robert Murray, *Red Scare: A Study in National Hysteria, 1919–1920* (Westport, Conn.: Greenwood Press, 1980), p. 7.
154 thirty-six hundred strikes: Ibid., p. 9.
154 green boxes: "36 Were Marked as Victims by Bomb Conspirers," *NYT,* May 1, 1919, p.1.
154 prominent men: "22 Bombs Mailed in Plot to Slay Prominent Men," *Boston Daily Globe,* May 1, 1919, p. 1.
154 ten bombs went off: "See Reign of Terror as Aim of Plotters," *NYT,* June 4, 1919, p. 3.
154 man carrying a large suitcase and "We have been": "Palmer and Family Safe," *NYT,* June 3, 1919, p. 1.
155 bomber's head: "Activity in Washington," *NYT,* June 4, 1919, p. 1.
155 four times larger and "On a certain day": "Palmer Warns of Big Bomb Plot; Martens is Linked With Reds," *New York Tribune,* June 19, 1919, p. 1.
155 "more than twenty thousand": "See Reign of Terror," *NYT,* p. 3.

155 **ransacked offices:** National Popular Government League (R. G. Brown [et al.]), *To the American People: Report upon the Illegal Practices of the United States Department of Justice* (Washington, D.C.: National Popular Government League, 1920), pp. 16–21.

155 **deported on a ship:** "'Ark' with 300 Reds Sails Early Today for Unnamed Port," *NYT*, Dec. 21, 1919, p. 1.

155–56 **biggest Red Raid** and **authority of the Espionage Act:** "3,000 Arrested in Nation-Wide Round-Up of 'Reds,'" *New York Tribune,* Jan. 3, 1920, p. 1, and "Round-Up of 'Reds' Thwarts Big Revolutionary Plot," *New York Tribune,* Jan. 4, 1920, p. 1.

155 **manufactured confessions:** National Popular Government League, *To the American People,* pp. 32–36.

156 **a former YWCA:** "See Reign of Terror," *NYT*, p. 3.

156 **banned the January 1920 issue:** Jane Heap to JJ, ca. Feb. 1920, Cornell, Series IV Box 8.

156 **"the flatulent old"** and **"There's a bloody":** *LR* 6, no. 9 (Jan. 1920), p. 55.

156 **nearly half a million:** Ibid., p. 79.

156 **Ezra Pound would have a file:** Claire Culleton, *Joyce and the G-Men: J. Edgar Hoover's Manipulation of Modernism* (New York: Palgrave Macmillan, 2004).

156 **eve of the Red Raids:** Curt Gentry, *J. Edgar Hoover: The Man and the Secrets* (New York: Norton, 1991), p. 73.

156 **government librarian:** Ibid., p. 67.

156 **On September 16, 1920:** "Wall Street Night Turned into Day," *NYT*, Sept. 17, 1920, p. 9; "Trail of Bomb Plotters End with Explosion," *New York Tribune*, Sept. 24, 1920, p. 18; "Officials Convinced Time Bomb Caused Explosion in Wall Street," *Washington Post*, Sept. 18, 1920, p. 1; and "Havoc Wrought in Morgan Offices," *NYT*, Sept. 17, 1920, p. 1.

157 **in his Nassau Street office:** JQ to Walt Kuhn, Sept. 16, 1920, NYPL.

157 **greenish yellow smoke:** *MNY*, p. 475.

157 **toppling like tall grass:** JQ to Huneker, Sept. 18, 1920, NYPL.

157 **"a horrible price to pay":** JQ to Jacob Epstein, Oct. 11, 1920, NYPL.

157 **"seven or eight hundred thousand":** JQ to EP, Oct. 21, 1920, NYPL.

157 **"nothing but walking":** JQ to EP, June 10, 1918, NYPL.

157–58 **Ben Huebsch published:** see Kelly, *Our Joyce*, p. 80.

158 **"Militarism is not":** Max Eastman, "Editorial" and [Unsigned], "John S. Sumner, the New Censor, Takes Office," *Masses*, 8 (March 1916), p. 16.

158 **Sumner arrested:** C. M. Rogers, "Confiscate Issue of the Masses," *NYT*, Sept. 1, 1916, p. 20.

158 **"Copulation, or coitus":** Auguste Forel, *The Sexual Question: A Scientific, Psychological, Hygienic and Sociological Study* (New York: Rebman Company, 1908), p. 56.

158 **a thirty-nine-year-old lawyer:** "Comstock Rule in Vice Society Near Overthrow," *New York Tribune,* June 13, 1915, p. 1, and "Comstock's Work to Go On," *NYT,* Oct. 4, 1915, p. 18.

158 **had hardly been necessary:** See 1897 *NYSSV Annual Report*, p. 20.

159 **"They're all goddamn Jews!":** Tom Dardis, *Firebrand: The Life of Horace Liveright* (New York: Random House, 1995), p. 164.

159 **"Just as we have":** *NYSSV Annual Report (1919)* qtd. in Paul S. Boyer, *Purity in Print: Book Censorship in America from the Gilded Age to the Computer Age* (Madison: University of Wisconsin Press, 2002), p. 67.

159 **raided radical bookshops** and **now an anarchist text:** WHS, Monthly Reports Jan., Feb. and Aug. 1920.

159 **arrested 184:** See John Sumner, "Criticizing the Critic," *Bookman* 53, no. 5 (July 1921), p. 385.

159 **more than any in the vice society's history:** Based on *NYSSV Annual Reports.*

160 **"real American stock":** John Sumner, "Are American Morals Disintegrating?" *Current Opinion* 70, no. 5 (May 1921), pp. 610–11.

160 **German and Irish:** See *NYSSV Annual Report*, 1911, p. 18.

160 **"radical feminists":** Sumner, "Are American Morals Disintegrating?" pp. 608–9.

160 "And she saw": *LR* 7, no. 2 (July-Aug. 1920), p. 43. Here and elsewhere during the *Little Review* trial, I quote from the version of the "Nausicaa" episode as it was published in the July-August 1920 issue of the *LR*. Passages differ from the 1922 Shakespeare and Company edition and subsequent editions.

161 "And then a rocket": Ibid., pp. 43–44.

161 "a man of honour": Ibid., p. 42.

161 "Swell of her calf": Ibid., p. 48.

161 cut through their shared wall: Gilmer, *Horace Liveright*, p. 3, qtd. Jay Satterfield, *The World's Best Books* (Amherst: University of Massachusetts Press, 2002), p. 14.

161 indicted for wartime conspiracy: Sayer, "Art and Politics," p. 57.

162 homosexual rights: *Dear Tiny Heart*, p. 3. *Note*: Sumner's moment of realization is my speculation.

162 Irish Trotsky: I am indebted to Yale's Modernism Lab for this comparison. See http://modernism. research.yale.edu/

162 through the night and "The Star-Spangled Banner": "100,000 Observe Constitution Day at Scene of Explosion," *New York Tribune*, Sept. 18, 1920, p. 3. The date of John Sumner's purchase is deduced from MCA's January 12 deposition in Quinn's motion to transfer, SIU, Box 3 Folder 4; JQ to MCA, Feb. 5, 1921, SIU, Box 1 Folder 6, and WHS, Sumner Autobiography, Box 1 Folder 8, MS-26, p. 1.

162 while working on a case: *MNY*, pp. 459–60; JQ to Foster, Nov. 17, 1920, NYPL.

163 "editrix": JQ to Shane Leslie, June 21, 1922, NYPL.

163 "to urine and feces" and to promote themselves: JQ to EP, Oct. 16, 1920, SIU, Box 1 Folder 5.

163 "What did I tell you?": *TYW*, p. 215.

163 "An artist might paint" and "You'll be broadening": JQ to EP, Oct. 16, 1920, SIU, Box 1 Folder 5.

163 arguing with Sumner: *TYW*, p. 218.

163 "We glory in it": Sumner deposition, Oct. 21 1920, qtd. in Quinn's Motion to Transfer, SIU, Box 3 Folder 4; WHS, Monthly Reports, Box 2 Folder 7, Oct. 1920.

163–64 "This trial will" and lunch: JQ to EP Oct. 16, 1920, SIU, Box 1 Folder 5.

164 "I don't give a damn": WHS, Box 1 Folder 8, MS 26, p. 2.

164 Ogden Brower: WHS, Monthly Reports, Oct. 1920, Box 2 Folder 7.

164 "and she was trembling": *LR* 7, no. 2 (July-Aug. 1920), p. 43.

164 "If such indecencies": Sumner, "The Truth about 'Literary Lynching,' " *Dial* 71 (July 1921), p. 67.

165 "defiant" and "sheer self-exploiters" and "If Joyce wants": JQ to EP, Oct. 16, 1920, SIU, Box 1 Folder 5.

166 " 'Nausikaa' has been pinched": EP to JJ, ca. Oct. 30, 1920, *EP/JJ*, p. 185.

166 "Perhaps everything": EP to JQ, Feb. 21, 1920, *EP/JQ*, p. 185.

166 "overwrought nerves" and "He is not": EP to JQ, Oct. 31, 1920, *EP/JQ*, pp. 198–9.

166 Jefferson Market Courthouse: JQ to EP, Oct. 21, 1920; JQ to Shane Leslie, June 21, 1922, NYPL. "Negroes" is Quinn's word.

167 "so obscene, lewd, lascivious": Sumner deposition qtd. in JQ's Motion to Transfer, SIU, Box 3 Folder 4.

167 "who writes, prints": 145 N.Y. Supp. 492 § 1141.

167 "It is unnecessary": *Grimm v. United States*, 156 U.S. 604 (1895).

167 Quinn rushed: JQ to EP, Oct. 21, 1920, NYPL, and JQ to Foster, Oct. 22, 1920, postscript to August [sic for "October"] 20, 1920, NYPL.

168 "over-ripe": JQ to EP March 6, 1918, NYPL.

168 "I think the test": *Regina v. Hicklin* (1868) L.R. 3 Q.B.D. 360.

168 purview of the law shifted: Felice Flanery Lewis, *Literature, Obscenity and the Law* (Carbondale: Southern Illinois University Press, 1976), p. 7.

169 "You could not": JQ to Shane Leslie, June 21, 1922, NYPL.

169 "If a young man is in love" and Swift and Rabelais: JQ to EP, Oct. 21, 1920, SIU, Box 1 Folder 5.

169 "She leaned back far": *LR* 7, no. 2 (July-Aug. 1920), pp. 42–43. My ellipsis. Comma supplied after "heart."

170 he had a dirty mind: JQ to Shane Leslie, June 21, 1922, NYPL.

170 "There have been": JQ to JJ, Aug. 15, 1920, NYPL.

14. THE GHOST OF COMSTOCK

171 Sumner patrolled: See, e.g., WHS, Monthly Reports, Box 2 Folder 7, Aug. 1920, p. 3 and Jan. 1921, p. 3, passim.

171 unlocked and searched mailboxes: WHS, Box 1 Folder 7, pp. 64–65.

171 raids and stakeouts: E.g., Ibid., Sept. 20, p 3.

171 obtained warrants: E.g., Ibid., June 1921, p. 2.

171 complaining witness: Sumner, "Truth about 'Literary Lynching,'" p. 64.

171 supervised the burnings: See Boyer, *Purity in Print*, p. 98 photo insert, Figure 7.

171 threaten fourteen-year-olds: E.g., WHS, Box 2 Folder 7: Nov. 1920, p. 1; Dec. 1920, p. 3; March 1921, p. 2; April 1921, p. 3.

171 six male cross-dressers: WHS, Box 2 Folder 7, Oct. 1919, p. 6.

171 bathroom drawings: Ibid., March 1921, p. 1.

171 garden statuary: Ibid., May 1920, p. 2.

171 unfaithful spouses: E.g., ibid., Nov. 1920, p. 4, and July 1920, p. 2.

171 eloping teenagers: E.g., ibid., Dec. 1919, p. 2, and Dec. 1920, p. 2.

171–72 sailors on shore: Ibid., May 1920, p. 5.

172 plays, musicals: WHS, Box 2 Folder 7–8, passim.

172 conduit of information: WHS, Box 2 Folder 7: Aug. 1920, p. 3, and Sept. 1920, p. 2.

172 he lobbied senators: See, e.g., WHS, Box 2 Folder 7, Feb. 1921, p. 4.

172 "Years ago": "Comstock's Rule in Vice Society Near Overthrow," *New York Tribune*, June 13, 1915, p. 1.

172 breaking up fights and accountant: WHS, Sumner Autobiography, Box 1 Folder 7, p. 63.

172 barrel-chested: Charles Trumbull, *Anthony Comstock, Fighter; Some Impressions of a Lifetime Adventure in Conflict with the Powers of Evil* (New York: Fleming H. Revell Company, 1913), pp. 19, 21.

172 brought down New York's pornography industry: Bates, *Weeder in the Garden*, pp. 158–9.

172 hijacked a wagon: Trumbull, *Comstock,* p. 77; "A Large Seizure of Obscene Publications," *New York Tribune*, April 5, 1872, p. 8.

172 destroyed them with acid: Trumbull, *Comstock,* p. 66.

172 forty-five people: "Naughty Literature," *Atlanta Constitution*, Nov. 30, 1872, p. 4.

172 financial backers founded: Bates, *Weeder in the Garden*, p. 99.

173 "weeder in the garden": Comstock to Rainsford qtd. ibid., p. 3.

173 barely professionalized and mayoral despot: James Richardson, *Urban Police in the United States* (Port Washington, N.Y.: Kennikat Press, 1974), pp. 42–47. See also Eric Monkkonen, "History of Urban Police," *Crime Punishment* 15 (1992), pp. 547–80.

173 deputy sheriff: WHS, Box 1 Folder 7, p. 71.

173 565 years: *NYSSV Annual Report* (1913), p. 13.

173 2,948,168: *NYSSV Annual Report* (1912), p.16.

173 "obscene rubber articles": *NYSSV Annual Report* (1897).

173 Sixteen dead bodies: Broun and Leech, *Anthony Comstock*, p. 212.

173 Packages addressed: Trumbull, *Comstock*, pp. 137–141; Bates, *Weeder in the Garden,* p. 108.

173 Charles Conroy: "An Attempt to Kill A. J. Comstock," *New York Tribune*, Nov. 2, 1874, p. 12; Bates, *Weeder in the Garden,* p. 105; Anthony Comstock, *Frauds Exposed; or How the People Are Deceived and Robbed, and Youth Corrupted* (New York: J.H. Brown, 1880), pp. 258–9. Trumbull, *Comstock,* pp. 147–8.

174 "a pernicious tendency": William Blackstone, *Commentaries on the Laws of England* qtd. in Helen Lefkowitz Horowitz, *Rereading Sex: Battles Over Sexual Knowledge and Suppression in Nineteenth-Century America* (New York: Alfred A. Knopf, 2002), p. 40.

174 looks or filthy words: C.B., "The Confessional Unmasked," microfilm (The Protestant Electoral Union, 1867), pp. 51, 60–61.

175 "introduces his": Ibid., p. 64.

175 "It is asked": Ibid., p. 60.

175 a revelation: *Regina v. Hicklin* (1868) L.R. 3 Q.B.D. 360.

175 Cockburn and "notoriously bad": *Oxford Dictionary of National Biography*, http://www.oxforddnb.com.ezp-prod1.hul.harvard.edu/view/article/5765?docPos=1. See also "Chief Justice Cockburn Dead," *NYT*, Nov. 22, 1880.

175 defense attorney avoided: *Regina v. Hicklin* (1868) L.R. 3 Q.B.D. 360.

176 "maintain the Protestantism" and William Murphy and "every Popish priest": Walter Arnstein, "The Murphy Riots," *Victorian Studies* 19 (Sept. 1975), pp. 53, 56; Roger Swift, "Anti-Catholicism and Irish Disturbances: Public Order in Mid-Victorian Wolverhampton," *Midland History* 9 (1984), pp. 87–108; *Pall Mall Gazette*, Feb. 20, 1867 (n.p.); "The Riots at Birmingham," *London Review*, June 22, 1867, p. 692; and *Regina v. Hicklin* (1868) L.R. 3 Q.B.D. 360.

177 "There is," Comstock wrote and "*the boon*": Comstock, *Traps for the Young*, pp. 132–3.

178 "our tender infancies": Locke, "Some Thoughts Concerning Education," qtd. ibid., p. 8.

178 dying of pneumonia: "Comstock, Foe of Vice, Dies after Relapse," *New York Tribune*, Sept. 22, 1915, p. 1; "Anthony Comstock," *Boston Journal*, Sept. 23, 1915, p. 8; Bates, *Weeder in the Garden*, p. 200.

178 September 22: WHS, Box 1 Folder 7, p. 70.

179 Clarence Darrow: WHS, Box 1 Folder 6, MS-18, P-2.

15. ELIJAH IS COMING

180 "I am working like a galley-slave": JJ to Carlo Linati, Sept. 6, 1920, *LI*, p. 146.

180 gas stove and shawl: JJ to EP, Dec. 12, 1920, *LIII*, pp. 32–33.

180 fits of pain: Ibid., p. 34.

180 April 1920 and three months: Groden, *Ulysses in Progress*, p. 167.

180 ninth draft: JJ to JQ, Jan. 7, 1921, *LI*, p. 156.

180 late into the night: JJ to Larbaud, Feb. 23, 1921, *LIII*, p. 39.

181 *syphilis:* See JJ to Budgen, Michaelmas [Sept. 29], 1920, *LI*, p. 147.

181 "Dirty married man!": *Ulysses*, p. 361 (15: 385).

181 "I have a little private": Ibid., p. 461 (15: 3763–4).

181 "My more than": Ibid., p. 397 (15: 1600).

181 "Bronze by gold": Ibid., p. 460 (15: 3735).

181 "lazy idle": Ibid., p. 458 (15: 3671).

181 "vulture talons": Ibid., p. 357 (15: 259–60).

181 "No yapping": Ibid., p. 414 (15: 2189).

181 "Scotts tettoja" and "I have not received": JJ to JQ, Nov. 24, 1920, *LIII*, p. 30 (quoting JJ's Nov. 23, 1920, telegram). The telegram and translation are re-created as separate events.

182 Quinn cabled back and insisted: JQ to JJ telegram, Nov. 24, 1920, NYPL.

182 more counts: JQ to EP, Oct. 21, 1920, NYPL.

182 "Macilenza": JJ to JQ, Dec. 13, 1920, telegram qtd. in JQ to JJ, Dec. 19, 1920, NYPL.

182 "Private and reliable": JQ to JJ, Dec. 19, 1920, NYPL.

182 come up with a plan: JQ to EP, Oct. 16 and Oct. 21, 1920, SIU, Box 1 Folder 5.

182 overworked grand jury: JQ to MCA, Feb. 5, 1921, SIU, Box 1 Folder 6.

182 private edition: JQ to JJ, Aug. 15, 1920, NYPL.

183 "a showdown": Ibid., Dec. 19, 1920.

183 Joyce would never agree and "practical certainty": Ibid., Aug. 15, 1920.

183 escaped prosecution: JQ to Huebsch, Dec. 15, 1920, NYPL, and JQ to JJ, Dec. 19, 1920, NYPL.

183 different legal standards: JQ to Huebsch, Dec. 15, 1920, NYPL.

183 a *good* thing: JQ to EP, Oct. 16, 1920, SIU, Box 1 Folder 5.

183 fifteen hundred copies: JQ to MCA, Feb. 5, 1921, SIU, Box 1 Folder 6.

183–84 "serious financial loss": JQ's Motion to Transfer, SIU, Box 3 Folder 4.

184 demanded sexual favors: Yale Anderson, Box 2 Folder 22.

184 "We cannot apologize": Jane Heap to JJ, Jan. 9, 1920, Cornell, Series IV Box 8.

184 interrupted a performance: "Books and Authors," *NYT*, Dec. 26, 1920, p. 51; JQ to EP, Dec. 12, 1920, NYPL.

184 from $2.50 to $4.00: *LR* 7, no. 3 (Sept.-Dec. 1920), p. 2.

184 "Make following counter proposal": JJ to JQ, Jan. 8, 1921, telegram qtd. JQ to MCA, Feb. 5, 1921, SIU, Box 1 Folder 6. The order of the telegraph lines is speculation.

184 more than ten dollars: JJ to JQ, Jan. 7, 1921, *LI*, p. 155.

184–85 nobody made agreements: JQ to MCA, Feb. 5, 1921, SIU, Box 1 Folder 6.

185 "In financial difficulties": Watson(?) translation of JJ to JQ telegram, Jan. 13, 1921, NYPL.

185 "Cabling money requested": JQ to JJ telegram, Jan. 24, 1921, NYPL.

185 wholesale prices: See http://eh.net/encyclopedia/article/smiley.1920s.final.

185 National Bank of Commerce: *MNY*, p. 496; JQ to JJ, April 13, 1921, NYPL.

185 thirty thousand dollars: *MNY*, p. 496.

185–86 "Clients, banks": JQ to John Butler Yeats, May 2, 1921, NYPL.

186 "a financial reign": JQ to Walter Pach, May 5, 1921, qtd. *MNY*, p. 478.

186 partners quit: *MNY*, p. 458; Curtin breaks down, JQ to JJ, April 13, 1921.

186 iritis: JQ to Walt Kuhn, Sept. 16, 1920, NYPL.

186 Quinn worked and lost fees: JQ to JJ, April 13, 1921, NYPL.

186 "The trouble with me": JQ to John Butler Yeats, May 2, 1921, NYPL.

186 fifty pounds: Ell, p. 401.

186 magazine grossed: *DMW*, p. 459, Table 1.

186 several collapses: JJ to Weaver, Oct. 30, 1916, *LI*, p. 97.

186 first glimpse: Weaver to JJ, Nov. 10, 1916, Cornell, Series IV Box 14.

186 losing sleep: JJ to Weaver, Feb. 25, 1919, *LII*, p. 436.

186 314 copies: *DMW*, pp. 155–6.

186 multiple eye attacks: See Ell, pp. 441, 454; JJ to Weaver, Feb. 25, 1919, *LII*, pp. 436–7, 418n.

186 £5,000 war bond: *DMW*, pp. 157–60; Ell, p. 457.

187 danced a jig: *DMW*, pp. 157–8.

187 "delicacy and self-effacement": Weaver to JJ, July 6, 1919, Cornell, Series IV Box 14.

187 £2,000: Ell, p. 489, Maddox, *Nora: A Biography*, p. 177; *DMW*, p. 174.

187 several small gifts: E.g., *DMW*, p. 174, and JJ to Weaver, July 11, 1923, BL.

187 unfettered by marketplace: Monro, Saw & Co to JJ, June 24, 1919, *LII*, pp. 444–5 qtd. *DMW*, p. 158.

187 £300: Ell, p. 498.

187 fashionable clothes: See, e.g., Maddox, *Nora: A Biography*, pp. 138, 176, 271–2.

187 five-franc tips: Myron Nutting, "An Evening with James Joyce and Wyndham Lewis," Tulsa, Series 1 Box 176.

187 medical bills: JJ qtd. Ell, p. 541.

187 jury trial was denied: JQ to Shane Leslie, June 21, 1922, NYPL.

188 rushed to the DA's office and Sumner refused: JQ to MCA, Feb. 5, 1921, SIU, Box 1 Folder 6.

188 character witnesses and president of Harper & Brothers: JQ to MCA, Feb. 5 and 8, 1921, SIU, Box 1 Folder 6.

188 "There isn't the slightest": Ibid., Feb. 8, 1921.

188 "old and callous": JQ to EP, Oct. 16, 1920, SIU, Box 1 Folder 5.

189 woman in Chicago and "Damnable, hellish filth": *TYW*, pp. 221, 213–4.

189 "profound ignorance": *TYW*, p. 214.

190 *"First, the artist"* and **"Anything else"**: MCA, "An Obvious Statement (for the millionth time)," *LR* 7, no. 3 (Sept.-Dec. 1920), pp. 8, 10, italics in original.

190 **"the arranger of life"**: MCA to Reynolds, Aug. 14, 1922, Delaware, Box 4 Folder 34. MCA circled the phrase "the favorite enemy of the bourgeoisie."

16. THE PEOPLE OF THE STATE OF NEW YORK
V. MARGARET ANDERSON AND JANE HEAP

191 **"Greenwich Girl Editors"**: "Greenwich Girl Editors in Court," *Chicago Herald Examiner*, Feb. 15, 1921, p. 8, cited in Jackson Bryer, "James Joyce, Ulysses and the *Little Review*," *South Atlantic Quarterly* 66 (1967), p. 160, and Lawrence Rainey, *Institutions of Modernism: Literary Elites and Public Culture* (New Haven, Conn.: Yale University Press, 1998), p. 189.

191 **observation at Bellevue**: "Greenwich Village's Editoresses Fined," *New York Herald*, Feb. 22, 1921, p. 8, Yale Joyce, Box 17 Folder 321.

191 **"ultra-violet"**: "Magazines Are Published by Greenwich Artists," *Morning Oregonian*, March 26, 1922, p. 5.

191 **"window trimmings"**: *TYW*, p. 219.

191 **"Everyone stands up"** and **"Perhaps one can"**: MCA, "'Ulysses' in Court," *LR* 7, no. 4 (Jan.-March 1921), p. 22.

192 **Kernochan and two white-haired judges**: *TYW*, p. 219; JQ to Shane Leslie, June 21, 1922, NYPL.

192 **only one witness**: "Court Puzzled by Experts on Book's Morals," *New York Tribune*, Feb. 15, 1921, p. 5.

192 **"a one hundred and thirty"**: JQ to Shane Leslie, June 21, 1922, NYPL. See also JQ to JJ, April 13 and April 15, 1921, NYPL.

192 **caliber of Shakespeare**: "Court Puzzled by Experts on Book's Morals," p. 5.

192 **Broadway performances**: "Improper Novel Costs Women $100," *NYT*, Feb. 22, 1921, p. 12.

192 **wouldn't even bother**: JQ to MCA, Feb. 4, 1921, SIU, Box 1 Folder 6.

192 **mitigate sentencing**: Ibid., Feb. 8, 1921.

192 **find it repellant**: "Court Puzzled by Experts on Book's Morals," p. 5.

192 **"in no way capable"**: *TYW*, p. 220. MCA paraphrases Powys's argument.

192 **use technical terminology** and **"unveiling of the unconscious mind"**: MCA, "'Ulysses' in Court," *LR* 7, no. 4 (Jan.-March 1921), p. 24.

192-93 **"most emphatically"** and **"What's this!"**: "Court Puzzled by Experts on Book's Morals," p. 5.

193 **"We don't care"**: MCA, "'Ulysses' in Court," *LR* 7, no. 4 (Jan.-March 1921), p. 23. *Note:* The order of events, exchanges and particular arguments during the trial isn't always clear, and it varies from account to account. I've arranged it for narrative purposes.

193 **"When I wish to hear from you"**: "Judge Rebukes Comstock," *NYT*, May 17, 1914, p. 15. My exclamation point.

193 **suspicious of judicial hunts**: Geoffrey Stone, "Judge Learned Hand and the Espionage Act of 1917: A Mystery Unraveled," *University of Chicago Law Review* 70, no. 1 (2003), pp. 335-58, and Gerald Gunther, "Learned Hand and the Origins of Modern First Amendment Doctrine: Some Fragments of History," *Stanford Law Review* 27 (1975), pp. 719-73.

193 **"to reduce our treatment"**: *United States v. Kennerley*, 209 F. 119, 121 (D.C.S.D.N.Y. 1913).

194 **judges stopped him** and **"I am sure"**: *TYW*, p. 221.

194-95 **"I myself do not"** and **"Yes"** and **"Let me tell you"** and **"Don't try to talk"**: MCA, "'Ulysses' in Court," *LR* 7, no. 4 (Jan.-March 1921), pp. 24-25.

195 **cornerstone of his argument**: JQ to JJ, April 13, 1921, NYPL.

195 **"cubism in literature"**: "Ulysses Finds Court Hostile as Neptune," *New York World*, Feb. 22, 1921, p. 24.

195 **read a passage** and **"A monkey puzzle"**: "'Little Review,' Though It's Convicted, Refuses to Be Suppressed," *Jackson Citizen's Patriot*, March 6, 1921, p. 8; *LR* 7, no. 3 (Sept.-Dec. 1920), p. 48.

195 **poor eyesight**: "Improper Novel Costs Women $100," *NYT*, Feb. 22, 1921, p. 12.

195 **"This is my best exhibit!"**: JQ to JJ, April 13, 1921, NYPL. My ellipses.

195 "Does a reading": JQ to Shane Leslie, June 21, 1922, NYPL.
195 "experimental, tentative": Ibid. See also "Ulysses Adjudged Indecent; Review Editors Are Fined," *New York Tribune*, Feb. 22, 1921, p. 13.
196 "It's just the story": "Notes from New York," unidentified newspaper clipping, Yale Joyce, Box 17 Folder 321.
196 "He is an ass" and Quinn certified: JQ to JJ, April 13, 1921, NYPL.
196 gallantly pushed and "Not at all": *TYW*, p. 221.
196 "very lenient" and ten days in prison: WHS, Box 2 Folder 7, February 1921 Report.
196 Joanna Fortune: Jackson R. Bryer, "'A Trial-Track for Racers': Margaret Anderson and the *Little Review*" (PhD diss., University of Wisconsin, 1965), pp. 402–3. Bryer's source is a private letter to him from Fortune.
196 "That chapter": "Notes from New York," unidentified publication, Yale Joyce, Box 17 Folder 321.
196 "should be left": "Greenwich Girl Editors in Court," *Chicago Examiner*, Feb. 15, 1921, p. 8, qtd. in Bryer, "Trial-Track," p. 160.
197 examined the inkpad: *TYW*, p. 222.
197 "I thought of Joyce": JQ to MCA, Feb. 5, 1921, SIU, Box 1 Folder 6.
197 Salvation Army: "Tabloid Book Review," *Chicago Daily Tribune*, Feb. 6, 1921, p. A7.
197 girl's father: John Sumner, "The Truth about 'Literary Lynching,'" *Dial* 71 (1921), pp. 63–68.
197 "O sweety. All your": See Buffalo TS V.B.11.a and Cornell 57 in *JJA "Nausicaa" MS*, pp. 294, 257.
197 "O sweety all your little": *LR* 7, no. 2 (July-Aug. 1920), p. 57.
198 "every possible physical secretion": EP to JQ, Feb. 21, 1920, *EP/JQ*, p. 185.
198 "the episode where": JQ to EP, Oct. 21, 1920, SIU, Box 1 Folder 5.
198 "hoarse breathing" and "whitehot passion": Ibid., p. 42.
198 pretended not to: Jane Heap, "Art and the Law," *LR* 7, no. 3 (Sept.-Dec. 1920), pp. 5–9.
198 an innocent judge: JQ to Shane Leslie, June 21, 1922, NYPL.
198 added a new insert: Buffalo TS V.B.11.a, Joyce and Groden, *JJA "Nausicaa" MS*, p. 283.

17. CIRCE BURNING

199 ninth typist: *SC*, p. 63.
199 had thrown the manuscript and "threatened in despair" and wake up before dawn: *SC*, pp. 63–64; *SBLG*, p. 80.
199 arrows and inserts: Groden, *Ulysses in Progress*, p. 208.
199 Raymonde Linossier: *SC*, p. 152.
199 kept her copies hidden: Ibid., p. 106.
199 father's control and law school: SBP, Box 167 Folder 3.
199 five-page "novel": Les Soeurs X, "*Bibi-la-Bibiste*," *LR* 7, no. 3 (Sept.-Dec. 1920), pp. 24–29.
199 one of the only female barristers: Sidney Buckland and Myriam Chimènes, *Francis Poulenc: Music, Art and Literature* (Aldershot: Ashgate, 1999), pp. 101–2.
199 nearly one hundred pages: the extant fair copy, about half the text (from "the Virgins Nurse Callen" to "Gooood") is 144 pages long. The Rosenbach MS (in JJ's smaller hand) is 85 pages plus inserts. See *Ulysses: A Facsimile of the Manuscript*, ed. Clive Driver (New York: Octagon Books, 1975).
200 "A Whore": The "Circe" details Mr. Harrison presumably reads are gathered from the amanuensis retrieved fair copy (i.e., Buffalo TS V.B.13.b—the copy made from the text photocopied by Quinn). See Joyce and Michael Groden, *James Joyce Archive: Ulysses, "Oxen of the Sun" and "Circe" a Facsimile of Drafts, Manuscripts and Typescripts for Episodes 14 & 15 (Part 1)* (New York: Garland Pub, 1977), pp. 391–8. This volume is referred to as *JJA Circe* below. All formatting and textual details conform to the manuscript version.
200 "I'll wring the neck": *JJA Circe*, pp. 369, 403.
200 "*Introibo ad altare diaboli*": *JJA Circe*, p. 369. This is the final portion of amanuensis fair copy, which corresponds to "retrieved" version. See *JJA Circe*, p. 404.
200 "I'll do him in": *JJA Circe*, p. 370.

201 began tearing up: JJ to Weaver, April 9, 1921, *LIII*, p. 40; JJ to JQ, April 19, 1921, *LIII*, p. 41.

201 "Hysterical scenes": JJ to JQ, April 19, 1921, *LIII*, p. 41. The break elides the phrase "I believe."

201 Huebsch finally refused: JQ to JJ, June 5, 1921, NYPL.

201 "it is better to lose": JQ to Huebsch, April 13, 1921, qtd. in *MNY*, p. 486.

201 On April 21: *MNY*, p. 485.

201 squats over Bloom: *JJA Circe*, pp. 285–87; cf. *Ulysses*, pp. 435–36 (15: 2931–60).

201 "lap it up" and auctioned off: *JJA Circe*, pp. 295–96; cf. *Ulysses*, pp. 439–40 (15: 3075–96).

201 called Liveright back: JQ to JJ, June 5, 1921, NYPL.

201 "but I guess you're right": Liveright to JQ, May 15, 1922, NYPL.

202 "I rather admire": JQ to JJ, June 5, 1921, NYPL.

202 "My book will never": *SC*, p. 47.

202 "Would you like me": Sylvia Beach interview, http://www.youtube.com/watch?v=vm5QWjBOvPo. The wording of this exchange differs from SB's account in *SC*. *Note*: SB offered to publish a few days *before* the Circe burning.

203 about $400: See the Bureau of Labor Statistics' CPI inflation calculator: http://data.bls.govcgi-bin/cpicalc.pl.

203 66 percent of the profits: Ell, p. 505; *SBLG*, pp. 79–80.

204 come to his office and "used language unfit": *SC*, p 65.

204 nearly in tears and "He will get": JQ to Jeanne Robert Foster, May 25, 1921, NYPL.

204 took Quinn six weeks: JQ to JJ, June 5, 1921, NYPL.

204 "ULYSSES suppressed four times.": HRC, Lake Collection, Box 262 Folder 9.

204 drummed up buyers: SB to Holly Beach, April 23, 1921, *LSB*, pp. 85–86.

204 in Paris nightclubs: *SC*, p. 51.

204 names in a green notebook: Austin Archive, Box 262 Folder 10; *SBLG*, p. 88.

204 ordered twenty-five: *SBLG*, p. 87.

204 mobbed and doubled its normal revenue: SB to Holly Beach, April 23, 1921, *LSB*, pp. 84–85, 88.

205 "the most important book": SB to Eleanor Beach, April 1, 1921, qtd. in *SBLG*, p. 78. SB's ellipsis.

205 "American Girl Conducts" and "may mean that Miss Beach": Rosemary Carr, "American Girl Conducts Novel Bookstore Here," *Paris Tribune*, May 28, 1921, qtd. in *SBLG*, p. 84.

205 "It is a revolting": George Bernard Shaw to SB, June 11, 1921, qtd. in *SC*, p. 52.

205 "a ninth rate coward": EP, "Paris Letter," *Dial*, June 1922, reprinted *EP/JJ*, p. 198.

205 finish in 1918: JJ to C. P. Curran, March 15, 1917, *LII*, p. 392.

205 summer of 1919: JJ to Weaver, March 20, 1918, *LI*, p. 113.

205 early 1921: JJ to JQ, Nov. 24, 1920, *LIII*, p. 30.

205 April or May: JJ telegram to JQ, Jan. 8, 1921, qtd. in JQ to MCA, Feb. 5, 1921, SIU, Box 1 Folder 6.

205 three more weeks: JJ to Weaver, Oct. 7, 1921, *LI*, p. 172.

205 fifty or sixty more hours: JJ to Weaver, Nov. 25, 1921, BL.

206 "What act did Bloom": *Ulysses*, p. 546 (17: 70–82).

207 a series of letters: Ell, p. 501.

207 briefcase and contained the letters: JJ to Ettore Schmitz, Jan. 5, 1921, *SL*, p. 277n; Maddox, *Nora: A Biography*, p. 204.

207 red express stamp: Details of JJ's 1909 letters to Nora from Cornell, Series IV Box 4.

207 "fucked arseways" and told him to pull himself and "Yes," Joyce wrote back, "now I can remember" and "to fuck a farting woman": JJ to NB, Dec. 8, 1909, *SL*, pp. 184–5.

208 Christmas gift and imagined their grandchildren: Ibid., Dec. 22, 1909, p. 193.

208 "Write the dirty words big": Ibid., Dec. 9, 1909, p. 186.

208 Joyce thought of her: JJ to Budgen, Aug. 16, 1921, *SL*, p. 285.

208 more geological and earth: JJ to Weaver, Feb. 8, 1922, *LI*, p. 180.

208 "Id confuse him a little": *Ulysses*, p. 610 (18: 85–99).

209 Joyce's superstitions: *SC*, p. 43.

209 Greeks: JJ to Weaver, June 24, 1921, *SL*, p. 284; Myron Nutting, "An Evening with James Joye and Wyndham Lewis," Tulsa, Series 1 Box 176.

209 certain colors: JJ to Weaver, Sept. 20, 1928, *SL*, p. 338.

209   hosting dinner: Colum and Colum, *Our Friend James Joyce*, p. 133.

209   1+9+2+1: JJ to Weaver, April 3, 1921, *LI*, p. 161.

210   "I am raving": Larbaud qtd. in *SBLG*, p. 94, and *SC*, p. 57.

210   twenty-second address: Ell, p. 498.

210   leafy courtyard and polished floors and leather-bound books: *SC*, p. 69; SBP, Box 168 Folder 2;
       JJ to Francini Bruni, June 7, 1921, *LII*, p. 45.

210   thousands of soldiers: *SC*, p. 56, SBP, Box 168 Folder 2.

210   bars haunted by prostitutes: Nora Barnacle qtd. in McAlmon, *Being Geniuses Together,* p. 17.

210   thrown out: *SBLG*, p. 87.

210   "Jim, what is it": McAlmon, *Being Geniuses Together*, p. 171.

210   One night at a brasserie: Ibid., p. 23.

210   rolling on the floor: JJ to Weaver, Aug. 7, 1921, *LI*, p. 168.

210   skin stretched over: McAlmon, *Being Geniuses Together,* p. 25.

211   more than a month: Ell, p. 531 (from about July 3 to Aug. 7).

211   bandaged and "How is he": *SC*, p. 69.

211   cabinet edges: SBP, Box 168 Folder 1.

211   ten different episodes simultaneously: Luca Crispi and Ronan Crowley, "Proof^Finder: Proofs by
       Episode," *Genetic Joyce Studies* 8 (Spring 2008), http://www.antwerpjamesjoycecenter.com/GJS8/
       Proof%5Efinder/Proofs.Episode.jsp.

211   "Agenbite": Groden, *Ulysses in Progress*, p. 199.

211   twelve-hour days: JJ to Weaver, Aug. 7, 1921, *LI*, p. 168.

211   elaborate new scene: Ibid., p. 188.

211   "I'm a Bloomite": *Ulysses*, p. 401 (15: 1736); cf. "gloried in it," Sumner deposition dated Oct. 21,
       1920, quoted in Quinn's Motion to Transfer and JQ to EP, Oct. 16, 1920, SIU, Box 1 Folder 5. I am
       indebted to David Weir for this connection. See Weir, "What Did He Know and When Did He
       Know It?: *The Little Review*, Joyce and *Ulysses*" *JJQ* 37, no. 3/4 (2000), p. 402.

211   "stylish garters": *Ulysses*, p. 401 (15: 1750).

211   "passes through several": Ibid., p. 404 (15: 1842–3).

18. THE BIBLE OF THE OUTCASTS

213   "May I kiss": Richard Ellmann, "A Portrait of the Artist as Friend," *Kenyon Review* 18, no. 1 (Win-
       ter 1956), p. 67.

215   master printer and vine-covered: SBP, Box 168 Folder 8.

215   his father's days: *SC*, p. 47.

215   darned socks and afternoon meals: SBP, Box 168 Folders 2 and 5.

215   Darantière worked through: SBP, Box 166 Folder 5. He did not spell his name with an accent
       grave.

215–16 ran off the pages and illegible and repeatedly warned: Darantière to SB, June 9, 1921, Buffalo
       XIV.9, and Darantière to SB, June 16, 1921, Buffalo XIV.10.

216   time consuming: Darantière to SB, June 9, 1921, Buffalo XIV.9 ("*très onéreuses*").

216   all the galleys he wanted: *SC*, p. 58.

216   different additions to each and blank pieces: Luca Crispi and Ronan Crowley, "Proof^Finder:
       Placards," *Genetic Joyce Studies* 8 (Spring 2008). http://www.antwerpjamesjoycecenter.com/GJS8/
       Proof%5Efinder/Placards.jsp.

216   "*le* très grand": Darantière to SB, Sept. 30, 1921, Buffalo XIV.35, Darantière's emphasis.

216   could not even speak English: Maurice Hirchwald to SB, Oct. 11, 1921, Buffalo XIV.38.

216   five thousand francs: SB to Holly Beach, Sept. 22, 1921, *LSB*, p. 88.

216–17 help of Miss Weaver: JJ to Weaver, Nov. 25, 1921, BL. JJ asked Weaver for £75 for Darantière.

217   four galleys and five page proofs: Groden, *Ulysses in Progress*, pp. 188–9; Crispi and Crowley,
       "Proof^Finder: Proofs by Episode" and "Proof^Finder: Placards."

217 almost a third: *SC*, p. 58.

217 nearly half of "Penelope": James Van Dyck Card, *An Anatomy of "Penelope"* (Rutherford, N.J.: Fairleigh Dickinson University Press, 1984), p. 83.

217 about four thousand francs: Darantière to SB, Dec. 3, 1921, Buffalo.

217 "It's the great fanaticism is": NB qtd. in Djuna Barnes, "James Joyce," *Vanity Fair* (April 1922), p. 65.

217 match the Greek flag: *SC*, p. 63.

217 until January 31: Groden, *Ulysses in Progress*, p. 191.

217 telegram from Paris: SBP, Box 168 Folder 8; *SBLG*, p. 106.

217 Gare de Lyons: *SC*, p. 84; *SBLG*, p. 114; *LII*, p. 58n.

217 a crowd formed: *SC,* p. 85; SBP, Box 166 Folder 5.

217–18 nearly three and a half and "you never know": JJ to SB, Feb. 11, 1922, *JJ/SB*, pp. 10–11. This is its weight with its hard cover.

218 slather glue: *SC*, p. 86.

218 "Mr. James Joyce is a man": Sisley Huddleston, "*Ulysses*," London *Observer*, March 5, 1922, qtd. Robert Deming, ed., *James Joyce: The Critical Heritage* (London: Routledge & K. Paul, 1970), vol. 1, p. 214.

218 "a prodigious self-laceration": J. Middleton Murry, "Mr. Joyce's 'Ulysses,' " *Nation & Athenaeum*. April 22, 1922, pp. 124–5.

218 "dazzlingly original": Arnold Bennett, "James Joyce's *Ulysses*," *Outlook*, April 29, 1922, qtd. in Deming, *Joyce: Critical Heritage*, p. 221.

219 *Ulysses* was sold out: Ell, p. 531; *SBLG*, p. 120.

219 next two months: SB to Weaver, June 8, 1922, *LSB*, p. 93.

219 people would gawk: Ell, p. 532.

219 "the dirtiest, most indecent": Lawrence qtd. in Rachel Potter, "Obscene Modernism and the Trade in Salacious Books," *Modernism/Modernity* 16 (2009), p. 92.

219 Miss Beach's father: *SBLG*, p. 246.

219 "a freak production": *Liverpool Daily Courier*, qtd. in *DMW* endpapers.

219 "diabolic clairvoyance": *New York Herald* (Paris ed.), April 17, 1922, copied from Yale Joyce, Box 40 Folder 634.

219 "the maddest, muddiest": S.B.P. Mais, "An Irish Revel," *Daily Express*, March 25, 1922, qtd. *DMW* endpapers.

219 well-known editor: Robert Jackson, *Case for the Prosecution: A Biography of Sir Archibald Bodkin, Director of Public Prosecutions, 1920–1930* (London: A. Barker, 1962), p. 235.

219 "I say deliberately": James Douglas, "Beauty—and the Beast." *Sunday Express,* May 28, 1922, p. 5, in Yale Joyce, Box 17 Folder 327.

220 "literary Bolshevism": Shane Leslie, "*Ulysses*," *Quarterly Review*, Oct. 1922, reprinted in Deming, *Joyce: Critical Heritage*, p. 207, and Alfred Noyes, "Rottenness in Literature," *Sunday Chronicle*, Oct. 29, 1922, in Yale Joyce, Box 17 Folder 327.

220 "the man with the bomb": Mais, "An Irish Revel." My ellipsis.

220 "anarchical production": Edmund Gosse to Louis Gillet, June 7, 1924, SBP, Box 167 Folder 7; Ell, 528n.

221 "devilish drench": "Domini Canis" (Shane Leslie), *Dublin Review*, in Deming, *Joyce: Critical Heritage*, p. 201.

221 "the well-guarded": Shane Leslie, *Quarterly Review*, ccxxxviii (Oct. 1922), pp. 219–34, qtd. in Deming, *Joyce: Critical Heritage*, vol. 1, p. 211.

221 Josephine hid her copy: Ell, p. 530; *SBLG*, p. 124.

221 "I should think": SJ to JJ, Feb. 26, 1922, *LIII*, p. 58.

221 offered to sell it: Ell, p. 525.

221 "counting the cover": JJ to Josephine Murray, Nov. 10, 1922, *LI*, p. 193.

221 cut the pages: Ell, p. 526.

221   "I guess the man's": McAlmon, *Being Geniuses Together*, p. 182.

221   "You should approach": Faulkner qtd. in Philip Gourevitch, *The Paris Review: Interviews* (New York: Picador, 2009), p. 50.

222   drew a picture: *SC*, p. 116.

222   "That young man": JJ qtd. in *SBLG*, p. 275.

222   "I shall never write": Burton Rascoe, *A Bookman's Daybook* (New York: H. Liveright, 1929) p. 27.

222   "the Christian era" and calendar: *LR* 8, no. 2 (Spring 1922), p. 40.

222   told Margaret Anderson to reprint: EP to MCA (Jan.–April 1922 [n.d.]), *EP/LR*, p. 282.

222   "the whole boil": EP, "Monumental," qtd. in *EP/JJ*, p. 260.

222   barely started: *EP/JJ*, p. 11.

222   fake his own death: [Rodker?] to MCA, April 14, 1922, *EP/LR*, p. 283.

222   "a step toward making": T. S. Eliot, "Ulysses, Order, and Myth," *Selected Prose of T. S. Eliot* (New York: Harcourt Brace Jovanovich, 1975), p. 178.

223   "How could anyone write": T. S. Eliot qtd. in VW, *Diary of Virginia Woolf*, vol. 5, p. 353 (Jan. 15, 1941).

223   "It destroyed the whole": Ibid., vol. 2, p. 203 (Sept. 26, 1922).

223   "a book to which": Eliot, "Ulysses, Order, and Myth," p. 175.

223   "amused, stimulated" and "An illiterate, underbred": VW, *Diary of Virginia Woolf*, vol. 2, pp. 188–9 (Aug. 16, 1922).

223   ate with his fingers: VW, "Character in Fiction," *Essays of Virginia Woolf*, vol. 3, p. 434.

223   felt sorry for him: VW, *Diary of Virginia Woolf*, vol. 2, p. 199 (Sept. 6, 1922).

223   "I feel that myriads": Ibid., p. 200.

223–24   "as though one's mind": Mansfield to Sydney Schiff, Jan. 15, 1922, *Letters of Katherine Mansfield*, vol. 2, pp. 434–5.

224   "A mad book!" and "I have made": Yeats qtd. in Ell, p. 530. Ellmann's source is a 1947 interview with L.A.G. Strong.

224   Joyce was schizophrenic: Ell, p. 628.

224   "a new, universal": Carl Gustav Jung, "Ulysses: A Monologue," in *The Collected Works of CG Jung: The Spirit in Man, Art, and Literature* (London: Routledge and K. Paul, 1979), vol. 15, p. 132.

224   "I must read": VW, *Diary of Virginia Woolf*, vol. 2, p. 200 (Sept. 7, 1922).

224   "an incessant shower": VW, "Modern Novels," *Essays of Virginia Woolf*, vol. 3, p. 33.

224   returned to a short story and "cheapness" and "central things": VW, *Diary of Virginia Woolf*, vol. 2, pp. 247–49 (June 19, 1923); Quentin Bell, *Virginia Woolf: A Biography* (London: Hogarth, 1978), pp. 99–100, 105.

225   "fucked yes": *Ulysses*, p. 641 (18: 1511).

225   "I'll wring the bastard": Ibid., p. 490 (15: 4720–1).

225   "lick my shit": Ibid., p. 642 (15: 1531).

225   "the grey sunken": Ibid., p. 50 (4: 227–8).

225   "He says everything": Arnold Bennett, *Outlook*, April 29, 1922, copied from Yale Joyce Box 17 Folder 327.

226   "The lack of any conviction": Noyes qtd. in "Rottenness in Literature," *Sunday Chronicle*, Oct. 29, 1922, copied from Yale Joyce, Box 17 Folder 327.

19. THE BOOKLEGGER

229   Drake's and thirty-five dollars: JQ to SB, March 27, 1922, NYPL.

229   one hundred dollars: JQ to Weaver, Oct. 2, 1922, NYPL.

229   astonishing forty pounds: SB to Marion Peter, Sept. 19, 1922, *LSB*, p. 102.

229   NYSSV would soon discover: JQ to SB, March 27, 1922, NYPL.

229   full-page advertisement: JQ to SB, Feb. 4, 1922, qtd. in *MNY*, p. 531.

229   aggressive campaign and "high filth": "'Purity' War on Authors," *Weekly Dispatch*, Aug. 13, 1922, Yale Joyce, Box 9 Folder 194.

229   "She has tackled": JQ to JJ, April 4, 1922, NYPL.

229 contacted Mitchell Kennerley: JQ to SB, March 27 and March 30, 1922, NYPL.

230 "there wouldn't be a ghost": Ibid., March 27, 1922.

230 "about the same amount": Ibid., March 30, 1922, NYPL.

230 "the jaws of": SB to Marion Peter, Aug. 7, 1922, *LSB*, p. 101.

230 angry letters from New Yorkers: See Joseph Liepold to SB, April 15, 1922, and Sept. 1, 1922, Buffalo, Series XII.

230 seventeen copies: Mary Mowbray-Clark to SB, Jan. 11, 1923, Buffalo, Series XII. She received six in August.

230 The Sunwise Turn: Rainey, *Institutions of Modernism*, pp. 65–69.

231 "We are rather": Ruth McCall to Shakespeare and Company, May 3, 1922, Buffalo, Series XII.

231 "We cannot in any way": Mary Mowbray-Clarke to SB, July 22, 1922, Buffalo, Series XII.

231 There were rumors: Ibid., Jan. 11, 1923.

231 she entrusted ten: SB to Marion Peter, Aug. 7, 1922, *LSB*, p. 101.

231 "like telephone books": Mary Mowbray-Clark to SB, Jan. 11, 1923, Buffalo, Series XII.

231 customs agents seized two: SB to Marion Peter, Sept. 19, 1922, and May 29, 1923, *LSB*, pp. 102, 105.

231 didn't speak French and lessons: Michael S. Reynolds, *Hemingway: The Paris Years* (Oxford: Blackwell, 1989), p. 21; Jeffrey Meyers, *Hemingway: A Biography* (New York: Harper & Row, 1985), p. 59.

231 rabbit's foot: EH, *A Moveable Feast: The Restored Edition* (New York: Scribner, 2009), p. 91.

231 going to be a writer: Reynolds, *Paris Years*, p. 5.

231 added up the prices: EH, "Living on $1,000 a Year in Paris," *Toronto Star*, Feb. 4, 1922.

232 trust fund: Reynolds, *Paris Years*, p. 5, and Meyers, *Biography*, p. 58.

232 maid who cooked: Meyers, *Biography*, p. 63.

232 Cézanne on an empty: EH, *Moveable Feast*, pp. 69–70.

232 abstaining from sex: Meyers, *Biography*, p. 66.

232 letters of introduction: *SC*, pp. 77–78.

232 Hemingway walked: EH, *Moveable Feast*, pp. 69–70.

232 a music shop: *SBLG*, p. 91.

232 Walking into Shakespeare and Company: Hemingway, *Moveable Feast*, pp. 35–36.

232 talking about the war: *SC*, p. 78.

233 "Would you like" and barely healed: SBP, Box 166 Folder 4. Beach quotes Hemingway.

233 handing out chocolate and two hundred pieces: Meyers, *Biography*, pp. 31–32.

233 Stein, whom he met in February: EH to Grace Hall Hemingway, Feb. 14, 1922, *Letters of Ernest Hemingway* (Cambridge: Cambridge University Press, 2011), vol. 1, p. 328.

233 met Ezra Pound: Meyers, *Biography*, p. 73.

233 Pound was reading: Reynolds, *Paris Years*, p. 26.

233 Pound sent six: EH to Sherwood Anderson, March 9, 1922, *Letters of Ernest Hemingway*, vol. 1, p. 331.

233 Hemingway met Joyce and began drinking: Meyers, *Biography*, p. 82.

233 "Deal with him": JJ qtd. in "An American Storyteller," *Time*, July 7, 1999.

233 "Well, here comes James": Meyers, *Biography*, p. 83.

233 "Joyce has a most": EH to Sherwood Anderson, March 9, 1922, *Letters of Ernest Hemingway*, vol. 1, p. 331.

233 purchased *Dubliners*: *SBLG*, p. 115; Reynolds, *Paris Years*, p. 12.

234 *Dubliners* taught him: Meyers, *Biography*, p. 83.

234 gave Joyce a copy: See Wickser Collection, Buffalo, J69.23.8 TC141 H45 F37 1929.

234 "Jim Joyce": EH to Arthur Mizener, June 1, 1950, EH, Carlos Baker, and John Updike, *Ernest Hemingway, Selected Letters, 1917–1961* (New York: Scribner, 1981), p. 696.

234 His first selections: EH, *Moveable Feast*, pp. 35–36.

234 favorite authors had been: Reynolds, *Paris Years*, p. 6.

234 "Begin over": Gertrude Stein, *Autobiography of Alice B. Toklas* (New York: Vintage Books, 1961), p. 213.

234 "No one that I ever": EH, *Moveable Feast*, p. 35.

234 "He would live" and "He defends them": EH, "Homage to Ezra," *This Quarter* 1, no. 1 (Spring 1925), pp. 223–4.

234 like a saint: EH, *Moveable Feast*, p. 108.

234 distrust adjectives: Ibid., p. 135.

235 Hemingway stripped down: Wyndham Lewis, *Blasting and Bombardiering* (1937; Berkeley: University of California Press, 1967), p. 277.

235 Pound's left jabs and widen his stance: EH, *Moveable Feast*, pp. 108–9.

235 shadowbox between rounds: EH to Sherwood Anderson, March 9, 1922, *Letters of Ernest Hemingway*, vol. 1, p. 331.

235 on the sidewalks of Paris: McAlmon, *Being Geniuses Together*, p. 163.

235 a way to compensate: Reynolds, *Paris Years,* p. 64.

235 a boxing match: *SC*, p. 79; SBP, Box 166 Folder 4.

235 As a journalist: Meyers, *Biography*, pp. 91–100.

235 short stories in cafés and ribbons: Ibid., pp. 81–82.

235 his son's diapers: *SC*, p. 82.

235 gambled on horses: EH, *Moveable Feast*, pp. 61–62.

235 John Quinn mentioned: JQ to Harriet Weaver, Oct. 2, 1922, NYPL.

236 "Give me twenty-four hours": *SC*, p. 88.

236 his name kept out: Barnet Braverman to SB, Jan. 16, 1923, SBP, Box 123 Folder 13.

236 Knopf and Ben Huebsch: *SBLG*, p. 139.

236 twenty-five copies: Ibid., p. 125.

236 "Shoot books prepaid" and Canadian address: Braverman to SB, March 21, 1922 telegram, SBP, Box 123 Folder 13.

236 clarify his plans and "expedite": Braverman to SB, April 15, 1922, SBP, Box 123 Folder 13.

236–37 he was on his own and a room in Windsor and told the landlord: Ibid., Jan. 16, 1923. See also *SBLG*, p. 139; *SC*, p. 88.

237 break the law and five-thousand-dollar fine and five years: 35. Stat. 1129 § 245 (1909) and Michigan State Law Title 39 Chapter 406, 14787 § 1 (1912).

237 ban until 1949: "Ulysses Comes Out of Hiding," *Vancouver Sun*, April 13, 1950, p. 12.

237 books was 25 percent: Braverman to SB, Sept. 6, 1922, SBP, Box 123 Folder 13.

237 import duty of $6.50: Ibid., Jan. 16, 1923.

238 copywriter and salesman: *SBLG*, p. 119.

238 lectures and "Suffragists": Barnet Braverman, "Things in the Making," *Progressive Woman*, April 1913, p. 9.

238 six dollars a week: Barnet Braverman, "A Word about Moralists," *Progressive Woman*, Feb. 1913, p. 11.

238 "Womanhood," he wrote: Ibid., p. 7.

238 suffragist hunger strikers and wives and daughters faced: Braverman, "Things in the Making," *Progressive Woman*, April 1913, p. 7–8.

238 "The United States Constitution": Braverman, "Things in the Making," *Progressive Woman*, Nov. 1912, p. 9.

238 licensed prostitutes and "Behold the anti-vice": Ibid.

239 "the hideous U.S.": Braverman to SB, April 15, 1922, SBP, Box 123 Folder 13.

239 wooden dock and skyline: William Oxford, *The Ferry Steamers: The Story of the Detroit-Windsor Ferry Boats* (Toronto: Stoddart, 1992), pp. 54, 62 and 75.

239 ten-minute ferry: *SBLG*, p. 139.

239 unwrap the package: Braverman to SB, Jan. 16, 1923, SBP, Box 123 Folder 13.

239 beginning to eye him: *SC*, p. 88; SBP, Box 166 Folder 4.

239 the *La Salle*: Oxford, *Ferry Steamers*, p. 80.

240 built compartments: Philip P. Mason, *Rum Running and the Roaring Twenties: Prohibition on the Michigan-Ontario Waterway* (Detroit: Wayne State University Press, 1995), pp. 44–5.

240 recruited a friend and stuffed two copies: *SC*, p. 88. SBP, Box 166 Folder 4 (on two separate drafts).

240   shy: *SBLG*, p. 422.

240   boyish face: Barnet Braverman, "Social Service—Woman's Master Passion," *Progressive Woman*, April 1913, p. 12 (photograph).

20. THE KING'S CHIMNEY

241   Nora and the children were caught: JJ to Josephine Murray, Oct. 23, 1922, *LI*, pp. 189–90.

241   "O my dearest": JJ to NB, April 1922 (n.d.), *LIII*, p. 63. See also Maddox, *Nora: A Biography*, pp. 195–6.

241   fainted: JJ to NB, April 1922 [n.d.], *LII*, p. 63.

242   multiple tooth abscesses: EP to JQ, Aug. 10, 1922, NYPL.

242   wrapped in a blanket: Ell, pp. 535–6.

242   immediate iridectomy and the one he needed: SB to Weaver, June 11, 1922, *LSB*, pp. 95–96.

242   "Urgent reply": SB to Weaver, June 9, 1922 telegram, qtd. in *DMW*, p. 196.

242   cold compresses and "When the pain": NB qtd. in *SC*, p. 67.

242   inexpensive clinic: *SC*, p. 70, and SBP, Box 166 Folder 5.

242   "Too bad ye": *SC*, p. 71.

243   "by eliminating the poison" and he prescribed and "purify the blood": SB to Weaver, June 11, 1922, *LSB*, pp. 95–96.

243   apparently cocaine: JJ to SB, Sept. 5, 1922, *JJ/SB*, p. 13.

243   general health and "a more comfortable": SB to Weaver, June 8, 1922, *LSB*, p. 93.

243   relapse and fought off London doctors: SB to JJ, Aug. 29, 1922, *JJ/SB*, p. 12; JJ to Borsch, Aug. 24, 1922, BL.

243   "Mr. Joyce's mode": Weaver to SB, June 15, 1922, SBP, Box 35 Folder 18.

243   nights in pain, sweating: JJ to Richard Wallace, Aug. 15, 1922, *LII*, p. 65.

243   cold compresses: *DMW*, p. 201; SBP, Box 166 Folder 5.

243   stared at the brass knobs: JJ to Weaver, Sept. 20, 1922, *LI*, p. 186n.

243   perpetual darkness: Ell, p. 537.

243   afternoon arrival: JJ to Weaver telegrams, Aug. 18, 19 and 22, 1922, BL.

243   impeccable manners: *DMW*, p. 201.

243   had no pupil: JJ to Richard Wallace, Aug. 15, 1922, *LII*, p. 65; JJ to Louis Borsch, Aug. 24, 1922, BL. The condition—a complication of iritis—is called a pupillary membrane.

243   a fog and bluish green: Ernst Fuchs, *Text-Book Ophthalmology* (Philadelphia: Lippincott, 1917), p. 382; Sir John Parsons, *Diseases of the Eye: A Manual for Students and Practitioners* (London: J&A Churchill, 1918), p. 284.

244   blood seeped: Ell, p. 535.

244   dread of advancing blindness: *DMW*, p. 198.

244   receive 90 percent: Weaver to James Pinker, May 9, 1921, SBP, Box 123 Folder 14 (copy enclosed to SB). *Note:* Miss Weaver decided to publish the first U.K. edition of *Ulysses* a couple of months before meeting Joyce in August.

244   Pelican Press and changed their minds: *DMW*, p. 174.

244   solicitor informed her: Ibid., p. 199, and Weaver to SB, July 22, 1922, SBP, Box 35 Folder 18.

245   send it to the police: *DMW*, p. 200, and SB to Weaver, June 26, 1922, *LSB*, pp. 97–98.

245   "Bible of the Outcasts": Douglas, "Beauty—and the Beast."

245   Pound's dinner meetings: Iris Barry to Jane Lidderdale, 1966, UCL, Joyce/1/A/1.

245   Weaver asked Rodker: *DMW*, p. 203.

245   conscientious objector: *DMW*, pp. 173, 203–4, and Iris Barry, "The Ezra Pound Period," *Bookman* (October 1931), pp. 159–171.

245   his hunger strike: Iris Barry, Lidderdale Questionaire, UCL, Joyce/1/A/1.

245   two hundred pounds: Ibid., p. 204.

245   attracted literary pirates: Weaver to JQ, Nov. 15, 1922, NYPL.

245–46   Quinn heard the same and "a gang" and "It would be somewhat ironical": JQ to Weaver, Oct. 28, 1922, NYPL.

246   no longer had time: *DMW*, p. 203.

246   suffragette and *Egoist* reader and farm near Birmingham and weekly baths: Iris Barry to Joe Lidderdale, Dec. 1966, UCL Joyce/1/A/1; *DMW*, pp. 131, 203.

246   a friend's bookshop and rented a basement room: *DMW*, p. 204.

246–47   sold out in four days and table was covered with sheets: Ibid., p. 206. See also Ellmann's notes from John Rodker, Tulsa, Series 1 Box 182.

247   Miss Weaver refused and kept dozens: Ibid., p. 207. See also Lidderdale's questionnaire for Iris Barry, UCL, Joyce/1/A/1.

247   American middlemen: Weaver to JQ, Nov. 15, 1922, NYPL.

247   wholesaler unstitched the bindings and inside newspapers and first mate of an American merchant: *DMW*, p. 207. See also Ellmann notes on Rodker, Tulsa, Series 1 Box 182; Weaver to John Slocum, 1947, Yale Joyce, Box 29 Folder 555.

247   American shores duty-free: See Title II of Tariff Act of 1922, 42 Stat. 975.

247–48   mailing agency and hid behind the counter and Victorian wardrobe: Weaver to John Slocum, Feb. 25, 1947, Yale Joyce, Box 29 Folder 555.

248   bow on her hat: Iris Barry to Jane Lidderdale, Dec. 1966, UCL, Joyce/1/A/1.

248   stayed there for months and anxiety and "How could she?": *DMW*, p. 208.

248   slipped by New York customs agents: Weaver to JQ, Nov. 15, 1922, NYPL.

248   reports of missing copies: SB to Marion Peter, Sept. 19, 1922, *LSB*, pp. 102, 105; JQ to Rodker, Dec. 9, 1922, NYPL.

249   she noticed a detective: JJ to Weaver, Nov. 8, 1922, and Dec. 8, 1922, BL. See also *DMW*, 208n.

249   A raid in Boston: WHS, Box 2 Folder 8, November 1922 Secretary's Report.

249   General Post Office Building: JQ to Weaver, Dec. 9, 1922, NYPL.

249   customs officials forwarded the matter and "plainly obscene" and the furnace room: Edward C. Robinson to JQ, Aug. 27, 1923, NYPL. See Weaver to SB, May 24, 1923, SBP, Box 35 Folder 18. See also Weaver to John Slocum, Feb. 25, 1947, Yale Joyce, Box 29 Folder 555; Ell, pp. 505–6n.

249   black doors and a row of lower chambers: Description based on a photograph taken of John Sumner burning books in 1935 at an unidentified New York location. See Boyer, *Purity in Print*, p. 98 photo insert, Figure 7. The solicitor pausing over passages marked by customs is my speculation. Marking passages was a habit for books undergoing review.

249–50   Federal law required notification: Section 5 of the Comstock Act says that seized items "may be condemned and destroyed" following proceedings of municipal seizures "and with the same right of appeal or writ of error." See 17 Stat. 598 (1873).

250   "Obscenity?": Sisley Huddleston, "Ulysses," *London Observer*, March 5, 1922, qtd. in Deming, *Joyce: Critical Heritage*, p. 214.

250   The Home Office was the principal: Sir Charles Edward Troup, *The Home Office* (London: G. P. Putnam's Sons, 1925), p. 1.

250   carrying out the undersecretary's orders: BNA, H.O. 144/20071 (Old Ref. # 186.428/2).

250   undersecretary obtained the sixteen-page and "unreadable" and should be detained: Ibid. (Old Ref. # 186.428/1).

251   established precedent and prosecuted all capital crimes and twenty-three hundred cases: Robert Jackson, *Case for the Prosecution: A Biography of Sir Archibald Bodkin, Director of Public Prosecutions, 1920–1930* (London: A. Barker, 1962), pp. 170–171.

251   seized a single copy of *Ulysses* and page 704 and The owner objected and Bodkin's decision: BNA, H.O. 144/20071 (Old Ref. # 186.428/2).

251   "yes I think he made them": *Ulysses*, p. 620 (18: 535–44). Page 704 in 1922 edition.

252   "he made me spend": *Ulysses*, p. 621 (18: 586–89).

252   ruthless: Jackson, *Case for the Prosecution*, p. 168.

252   "He's a beast" and Suffragettes pelted him: Ibid., pp. 101–2.

252   cars were anathema: Ibid., pp. 243–5.

252   worked tirelessly and sallow and bags: Ibid., p. 17.

252 **disapproving glare:** Ibid., pp. 234–5.

252–53 **"As might be supposed" and "other morbid writers":** BNA, H.O. 144/20071 (Old Reference # 186.428/2).

253 **five hundred copies of** *Ulysses***:** Weaver to SB, May 24, 1923, SBP, Box 35 Folder 18; Weaver to John Slocum, Feb. 25, 1947, Yale Joyce, Box 29 Folder 555.

253 **prima facie obscene:** "R.J." to Jane Lidderdale, Dec. 7, 1966, UCL, Joyce/1/A/10.

253 **opportunity to appeal:** See Customs Consolidation Act 1876 c. 36, 39 and 40 Vict, Sections 207 and 208.

253 **couldn't bear the public scrutiny and advised against it:** *DMW*, pp. 216–7.

253 **customs officials burned them:** Weaver to SB May 24, 1923, SBP, Box 35 Folder 18.

253 **"King's Chimney":** *SC*, p. 96.

253 **burned the records:** BNA, H.O. 144/20071. Only ten of sixty-five files related to *Ulysses* survive in the National Archives. The rest are indicated "destroyed" on the covers of the surviving files. Three files following Bodkin's *Ulysses* decision are destroyed and may have contained details of the burnings. That the destruction happened by burning is my speculation.

21. THE PHARMACOPEIA

254 **warily eased himself into conversations:** See, e.g., Helen Nutting Diary, Tulsa Series, 1 Box 176.

255 **first eye patch:** JJ to Weaver, Nov. 17, 1922, *LI*, p. 197. See also Ell, p. 542.

255 **would pull his lower eyelid:** Wood, *System of Ophthalmic Therapeutics*, pp. 59, 430.

255 **douse it with cocaine:** JJ to Weaver, June 27, 1924, Yale Joyce, Box 1 Folder 27.

255 **a couple drops and a more potent relative:** Wood, *System of Ophthalmic Therapeutics,* p. 484.

255 **back-tooth iris forceps:** Beard, *Ophthalmic Surgery*, p. 93.

255 **With two snips, he cut away and Joyce's new pupil and separated the iris:** Lucia Joyce to Weaver, May 1, 1923, BL; Weaver to JQ, May 30, 1923, NYPL. Beard, *Ophthalmic Surgery,* pp. 437–9, 443. Reattachment of the iris is my speculation, though it is common in cases of synechia.

256 **most difficult:** Beard, *Ophthalmic Surgery,* p. 456.

256 **ninth attack and cataract extraction:** Edmund Sullivan, "Ocular History of James Joyce," *Survey Ophthalmology* 28 (1984), p. 414; see JJ to Weaver, Dec. 23, 1924, *LIII*, p. 111.

256 **complete iridectomy,** Lucia to Weaver, June 23, 1924, BL.

256 **twelfth surgery:** See June 1930 medical report, Berg Collection, NYPL (Reprinted in *LIII*, pp. 197–8).

256 **conjunctivitis, episcleritis and blepharitis:** See, e.g., JJ to Weaver, Sept. 20, 1928, *LI*, 266.

256 **retina atrophied:** Ell, p. 664 (Source: Joyce to Léon, July 12, 1932, *LIII*, p. 248).

256 **eyes hemorrhaged and lost vitreous fluid:** June 1930 medical report, Berg Collection, NYPL (Reprinted in *LIII*, pp. 197–8); Sullivan, "Ocular History," p. 414.

256 **"slowly nearing extinction":** JJ to SB, Aug. 26, 1924, *JJ/SB*, p. 47.

256 **prescription was +6.5:** EP to JJ, March 17, 1917, *EP/JJ*, pp. 101–2.

256 **it was +17:** Francisco J. Ascaso and Jan L. van Velze, "Was James Joyce Myopic or Hyperopic?" *British Medical Journal,* Dec. 15, 2011, p. 343. Ascaso and van Velze base their conclusion on Alfred Vogt's 1932 prescription for Joyce's glasses at the University of Buffalo (Series XIX Folder 27).

256 **reduced his vision in other ways:** Ibid., James Ravin, "The Multifaceted Career of Louis Borsch," *Archives of Ophthalmology* 127, no. 11 (2009); Ell, pp. 417, 568–9; JJ to Weaver, March 11, 1923, *LI*, p. 201; June 1930 medical report, Berg Collection, NYPL.

256 **1/30 and 1/800 to 1/1000:** June 1930 medical report, Berg Collection, NYPL.

256 **children's books:** JJ to Weaver, Dec. 2 and 15, 1928, BL.

256 **"mode of life":** Weaver qtd. in *DMW*, p. 198.

256 **good food:** SB to Weaver, July 9, 1922, *LSB*, p. 99.

256–57 **strain of writing** *Ulysses***:** "James Joyce Regains Sight," *Chicago Tribune*, May 10, 1923, copied from Yale Joyce, Box 9 Folder 195.

257 the weather: See, e.g., JJ to Weaver, April 22, 1917, *LI*, p. 102, and Aug. 20, 1917; JJ to James Pinker, Aug. 20, 1917, *LII*, p. 404.

257 steam baths, mud baths, sweating powders: SJ, Trieste Diary, May 23–July 4, 1907, Tulsa, Series 1 Box 142.

257 iodine injections: JJ to Weaver, May 28, 1929, *LI*, p. 280; Sylvia Beach, "James Joyce's Eyes," ca. 1929 (n.d.), Buffalo, Series XIX Folder 18.

257 tonic called synthol: JJ to Weaver, March 5, 1926, *LIII*, p. 138.

257 "endocrine treatment": *LSB*, p. 99; *EP/JJ*, p. 212.

257 electrotherapy: JJ to Weaver, Dec. 23, 1924, *LIII*, p. 112; SB to Weaver, June 11, 1922, *LSB*, pp. 95–96; SJ, Trieste Diary, May 23–July 4, 1907, Tulsa, Series 1 Box 142.

257 having electrodes attached: Wood, *System of Ophthalmic Therapeutics*, pp. 163–4.

257 put multiple leeches: See, e.g, JJ to Weaver, Aug. 29, 1922, BL; JJ to Weaver, Oct. 22, 1922, BL; NB to Weaver, Dec. 10, 1924, BL; and Helen Fleischman to Weaver, June 1, 1930, BL.

257 dionine to dissipate his nebulae: See, e.g., JJ to Weaver, Feb. 26, 1923, BL; JJ to Weaver, March 18, 1923, BL; Weaver to JQ, May 30, 1923, NYPL.

257 salicylic acid and boric acid: Ell, p. 538. See also Aug. 6, 1931, prescription, Yale Joyce, Box 24 Folder 515.

257 He took pilocarpine: See, e.g., JJ to Weaver, Dec. 2, 1928, BL; Ell, p. 607.

257 induced delirium and hallucinations over the years: EP to JJ, March 17, 1917, *EP/JJ*, p. 103; JJ to Weaver, Dec. 23, 1924, *LIII*, p. 112; Ell, p. 685; SBP, Box 166 Folder 5, and Box 168 Folder 2. For delirium and hallucinations in scopolamine, see Daniel Safer and Richard Allen, "Central Effects of Scopolamine in Man," *Biological Psychiatry* 3, no. 4 (1971), pp. 347–55.

257 room was haunted: JJ to Weaver, May 7, 1924, BL; June 1930 medical report, Berg Collection, NYPL (reprinted in *LIII*, pp. 197–8).

257 scopolamine orally: JJ to Weaver, Jan. 20, 1926, *LI*, p. 239.

257 "attack of giddiness": JJ to Weaver, Oct. 2, 1928, BL.

257 "No—I'm free, free!" and wildly handled puppet: Myron Nutting to Ellmann, Feb. 17, 1958, Tulsa, Series 1 Box 176.

257 panic attack and hallucinations and into the snowy street: JJ to Weaver, Jan. 18, 1933, BL.

257 sleeping pills: Ibid., Oct. 2, 1928, and Jan. 18, 1933. Joyce took as many as six per night.

257 his teeth: Weaver to JQ, May 30, 1923, NYPL; Brewerton to Weaver, Sept. 12, 1922, BL.

257 theory of infection: Thomas Pallasch and Michael Wahl, "Focal Infection: New Age or Ancient History?" *Endodontic Topics* 4, no. 1 (2003), pp. 32–45.

258 "a great many Irish": JQ to Weaver, Oct. 2, 1922, NYPL.

258 extracted ten of Joyce's teeth: NB to Weaver, April 5, 1923, BL.

258 seven more teeth: George Joyce to Weaver, April 21, 1923, BL; Weaver to JQ, May 30, 1923, NYPL.

258 shop fronts: Ell, p. 579.

258 "I dream about my eye": JJ to Weaver, May 22, 1923, BL.

258 charcoal pencil: JJ to Weaver, March 28, 1923, *LIII*, p. 73. JJ began *FW* ca. March 11, 1923.

258 stripes on wallpaper: JJ to Weaver, Sept. 28, 1922, *LI*, p. 186.

258 Place de la Concorde: Arthur Power, *From an Old Waterford House: Recollections of a Soldier and Artist* (Waterford: Ballylough Books, 2003), p. 129.

258 Sylvia Beach would bring: *SC*, p. 71.

258 holding on to himself: Budgen, *Joyce and Ulysses*, p. 321.

259 Cloves of garlic and small kitchen and Nora stayed: *SC*, pp. 70–71; SBP, Box 166 Folder 5.

259 rippled windows and warped walls: Myron Nutting, Tulsa, Series 1 Box 176.

259 helped put leeches: *SC*, pp. 71–72.

259 napkin and canthus: Beard, *Ophthalmic Surgery*, p. 51.

259 in the jar and "the creatures" and fell on the floor: SBP, Box 168 Folders 2 and 4.

259 lay awake screaming: SBP, Box 168 Folders 2, 4 and 5.

22. GLAMOUR OF THE CLANDESTINE

260 *The Great Gatsby*: Matthew Bruccoli, *Some Sort of Epic Grandeur: The Life of F. Scott Fitzgerald* (Columbia: University of South Carolina Press, 2002), p. 217.

260 **drunk young man**: *SBLG*, p. 159.

261 **filled orders from**: Ibid., p. 105, and SBP, Box 166 Folder 5.

261 **Officials who aided**: See Section 305(b) of the Tariff Act of 1922, 42 Stat. 975.

261 *Merry Tales for Little Folks*: SC, p. 98.

261 **biography**: Emails to me from SIU-Carbondale curator, Sept. 17, 2010.

261 **"Tell Mrs. Bullis"**: SB to Holly Beach, Nov. 27, 1926, qtd. *SBLG*, p. 254.

261 **"Madam"**: L. W. Schwaebe to Holly Beach, Dec. 16, 1926, qtd. *SBLG*, p. 254.

262 **A Paris art dealer and "14 books"**: JQ to SB (JQ to Charles Pottier enclosure), June 5, 1922, Buffalo, Series XII. See also JQ to SB, Sept. 20, 1922, NYPL.

262 **three Picassos**: JQ to Paul Rosenberg, May 30, 1922; Paul Rosenberg to JQ, June 12, 1922, NYPL; JQ to Charles Pottier, June 7, 1922, NYPL.

262 **a Cézanne**: *MNY*, p. 533.

262 **liver cancer**: Ibid., p. 627.

262 **prosecution, which it avoided they and Customs officials and The chief constables**: BNA, H.O. 144/20071 (Old Ref. # 186.428/2).

262 **issued warrants**: Ibid. (Old Ref. # 186.428/61).

262 **A 1908 law**: Post Office Act of 1908, 1908 c. 48, Section 18.

262 *The Clique*: Carmelo Medina Casado, "Sifting through Censorship: The British Home Office *Ulysses* Files (1922–1936)," *James Joyce Quarterly* 37, no. 3/4 (Spring/Summer 2000), p. 486.

262 **strike Joyce's *name***: Marshik, *British Modernism and Censorship*, pp. 161–2.

263 **town clerk of Stepney**: BNA, M.E.P.O. 3/930/021.

263 **"red hot Socialist"**: BNA, M.E.P.O. 3/930/015-7.

263 **a radio program and "I am not permitted"**: Harold Nicolson to SB, Dec. 2, 1931, Buffalo, Series XII.

263–64 **walked into Galloway & Porter and Leavis was certain**: F. R. Leavis, "Freedom to Read," *Times Literary Supplement*, issue 3192 (May 3, 1963), p. 325.

264 **"boy and girl undergraduates" and "take active steps" and "This is an amazing" and "If the last forty" and hoax**: BNA, H.O. 144/20071 (Old Ref. # 186.428/7).

264 **"as to who and what"**: Bodkin to Chief Constable Pearson, July 24, 1926, ibid.

264 **called Leavis into his office and The Home Office knew and "will be open"**: Leavis, "Freedom to Read" p. 325.

265 **"I don't pretend to be" and crossed out and "prompt criminal proceedings"**: Bodkin to Albert Charles Seward, July 31, 1926, BNA, H.O. 144/20071 (Old Ref. # 186.428/7).

265–66 **"I happen to know" and "the glamour of" and "I'm glad you didn't"**: Leavis, "Freedom to Read," p. 325.

266 **rumors spread and "disfavor" and "We don't like the books"**: Ibid., p. 325.

23. MODERN CLASSICS

267 **the first books of Hemingway**: Dardis, *Firebrand: Life of Horace Liveright*, p. xv.

267 **his ads had testimonials**: Satterfield, *World's Best Books*, p. 31.

267 **fonts that blared**: Bennett Cerf, *At Random: The Reminiscences of Bennett Cerf* (New York: Random House, 1977), pp. 40–41.

267 **book-launch party**: Satterfield, *World's Best Books*, p. 31.

267 **Dreiser and wild man Eugene O'Neill**: Cerf, *At Random*, pp. 33, 35.

267 **showmen and bootleggers**: Ibid., pp. 31, 41–42.

267 **knew everyone**, Dardis, *Firebrand*, pp. 68–70.

267 **mix Pernod**: Cerf, *At Random*, pp. 31–32.

268 false account statements: Ibid., p. 31.

268 wide-eyed: Ibid., p. 33.

268 left him $125,000: Ibid., p. 11.

268 royalty payments: Dardis, *Firebrand,* p. 217.

268 "If you'd like to start" and a $25,000 loan: Ibid., p. 27.

268 Boni's idea: Cerf, *At Random,* p. 40.

268 the first twelve: Dardis, *Firebrand,* p. 54.

268 prices soared: Cerf, *At Random,* p. 63.

269 ignoring the Modern Library: Ibid., p. 40.

269 Quinn balked: JQ to Horace Liveright, May 11, 1922, NYPL.

269 "a declension into the sunset": Ibid., May 17, 1922.

269 He reminded Quinn: Horace Liveright to JQ, May 15, 1922, NYPL.

269 "a trip I've dreamed of": Bennet Cerf, diary entry, May 20, 1925, Cerf Papers, Box 11.

269 midtown speakeasy and "Oh, how I'd like to" and Cerf had to fight: Cerf, *At Random*, pp. 44–46.

269–70 275,000 copies and highest price ever paid: Satterfield, *World's Best Books*, p. 36.

270 at one in the morning: Bennet Cerf, diary entry, May 20, 1925, Cerf Papers, Box 11.

270 "Where the hell": Cerf, *At Random,* p. 46.

270 office of six people: Ibid., p. 57.

270 "one of the nicest": Ibid., p. 62.

270 visiting booksellers and redesigning: Ibid., pp. 60–62.

270 every month: Modern Library descriptive catalogue, qtd. in Cerf, *At Random,* p. 62.

270 became substantially *older:* Satterfield, *World's Best Books*, p. 122.

270 "We just said": Cerf, *At Random*, p. 65.

271 expensive limited editions: Ibid., p. 77.

271 carried Random House: Ibid., p. 78.

271 a million books: Satterfield, *World's Best Books*, p. 2.

271 for forty million: Cerf, *At Random*, p. 62.

271 dominated the market: Satterfield, *World's Best Books*, pp. 2, 65–87.

271 "a collection of the most": Modern Library catalogue, qtd. in Cerf, *At Random*, p. 63.

271 College enrollment: Gerald Graff, *Professing Literature: An Institutional History* (Chicago: University of Chicago Press, 1987), p. 59.

271 "Reading of Masterpieces": *Columbia University Bulletin of Information, 1920–1921* (Morningside Heights, N.Y.: Columbia University), p. 35.

272 "treat the *Iliad*": John Erskine, *My Life as a Teacher* (Philadelphia: J.B. Lippincott Co., 1948), p. 166.

272 Masterpieces showed readers and "a comfortable chair": Erskine qtd. in Joan Shelley Rubin, *The Making of Middlebrow Culture* (Chapel Hill: University of North Carolina Press, 1992), pp. 168–9.

272 inspired by a freshman course: Cerf, *At Random*, p. 14.

273 tiny copy of *Romeo and Juliet*: Satterfield, *World's Best Books*, p. 17, and Dardis, *Firebrand*, p. 48.

273 they expanded the series: Dardis, *Firebrand*, p. 49, and Satterfield, *World's Best Books*, p. 18.

273 million books a year: Satterfield, *World's Best Books,* p. 17.

273 "Most of the books" Modern Library catalogue, qtd. in Cerf, *At Random*, p. 60.

273 "modern classics": See, e.g., *NYT Book Review*, April 25, 1937, p. 17, qtd. in Satterfield, *World's Best Books*, p. 53.

273–74 Knopf faced criminal charges: Dawn Sova, *Literature Suppressed on Sexual Grounds* (New York: Facts on File, 2011), pp. 108–9.

274 "You came here in a wagon": Samuel Roth, *Count Me among the Missing*, pp. 265–72; (unpublished autobiography) Roth Papers, Box 1 Folder 8.

274 *School Life in Paris*: Ibid., Box 1 Folder 7, p. 177.

274 ripped off everyone: Leo Hamalian, "Nobody Knows My Names: Samuel Roth and the Underside of American Letters," *Journal of Modern Literature* 3 (1974), pp. 908, 914.

274 *Wanna Go Home, Baby*?: Jay Gertzman, "Not Quite Honest: Samuel Roth's 'Unauthorized' *Ulysses* and the 1927 International Protest," *Joyce Studies Annual* 2009 (2009), p. 51.

275 "a portrait of the metamorphoses": Roth, *Count Me among the Missing*, Roth Papers, Box 1 Folder 8.

275 five different prisons: Roth, *Count Me among the Missing*, p. 297. Roth Papers, Box 1 Folder 8.

275 a small bookshop: Samuel Roth to Joseph Roth, March 27, 1919, Roth Papers, Box 37 Folder 10.

275 basement with a window: Roth, *Count Me among the Missing*, p. 128. Roth Papers, Box 1 Folder 10.

275–76 Roth visited the old man's shop and he made $130: Ibid., Box 1 Folder 7, pp. 176–9; Box 2 Folder 1, p. 161.

276 *Two Worlds Quarterly* and *Beau*: Gertzman, "Not Quite Honest," p. 39. In text, I use *Two Worlds* to refer to the monthly magazine, not the quaterly.

276 Lewis Carroll: *TWQ* 2, no. 5 (Sept. 1926).

276 Boccaccio: Ibid., no. 8 (June 1927).

276 Chekhov: Ibid., no. 2 (Dec. 1925).

276 Waugh: Ibid., no. 5 (Sept. 1926).

276 cartoonish drawings: E.g., ibid., no. 8 (June 1927).

276 three to five dollars: Roth Papers, Box 1, Folder 8. (Chapter 12).

276 first men's magazine and finance *Beau* for a year: Roth, *Count Me among the Missing*, pp. 264–66. Roth Papers, Box 1 Folder 8.

276 "Mr. Roth Is Building": Gertzman, "Not Quite Honest" p. 61 (fn. 23).

277 Post Office inspectors arrested and Four months after Roth's trial: Ibid.

277 "Among other things": Roth to JJ, May 10, 1922, SBP, Box 129 Folder 3.

277 "Every issue will contain": *Two Worlds* letterhead qtd. from Yale Pound, Box 49 Folder 1942.

277–78 politely declined: Weaver to Roth, June 8, 1922, Roth Papers, Box 38 Folder 12.

278 "the size of a needle's head": Weaver to SB, July 22, 1922, SBP, Box 35 Folder 18.

278 wrote to Ezra: Robert Spoo, *Without Copyrights: Privacy, Publishing, and the Public Domain* (New York: Oxford University Press, 2013), pp. 172–3

278 Pound burst forth: EP to Roth, July 4, 1922, Roth Papers, Box 36 Folder 31.

278 check and four promissory notes: Spoo, *Without Copyrights*, pp. 200–2.

278 fifty dollars per issue and "Make it as long": Roth to EP, Nov. 19, 1925, Box 45 Folder 1942, Yale Pound Papers.

278 "the grey sunken crater": Gertzman, "Not Quite Honest," pp. 53–54.

278 tried to persuade John Sumner: Adelaide Roth, Roth Papers, Box 16 Folder 5.

279 Roth met with Hemingway: Roth, *Count Me among the Missing*, Roth Papers, Box 1 Folder 8.

279 eight thousand subscribers and fifty thousand: Gertzman, "Not Quite Honest," p. 45.

279 Quinn told everyone: See, e.g., JQ to SB, Feb. 4, 1922, NYPL.

279 portions of a magazine and American-manufacutred plates: Spoo, *Without Copyrights*, pp. 67–9, 97–103, 156–60. Spoo clarifies that obscenity itself did not invalidate copyright.

279 "organize a gang": EP to JJ, Nov. 19, 1926, *EP/JJ*, p. 225.

279 $500,000 lawsuit: "Sylvia Beach Sues Mr. Roth for $500,000," *Chicago Tribune* (Paris Edition), March 27, 1927 in Yale Joyce, Box 18 Folder 333.

279 an injunction preventing: Gertzman, "Not Quite Honest," p. 40.

280 a formal protest: *SC*, p. 182.

280 nine hundred publications: Gertzman, "Not Quite Honest," p. 51.

280 "The thought of such an outrageous": Roscoe Ashworth to JJ, May 16, 1927, SBP, Box 129 Folder 2.

280 "If you are": Arthur Doyle to Roth, (n.d.), Roth Papers, Box 35 Folder 17.

280 "a forceful advisory capacity": Roth, *Count Me among the Missing*, p. 264, Roth Papers, Box 1 Folder 8.

281 ten bricks wide and toilet: Roth Papers, Box 1 Folder 8.

281 "My lovely and valiant": Samuel Roth to Richard and Adelaide Roth, Nov. 2, 1928, Roth Papers, Box 36 Folder 33.

281 "learn to love them": Samuel Roth to Richard Roth, Nov. 15, 1928, Roth Papers, Box 36 Folder 33.

281 sleeping in parks: Hamalian, "Nobody Knows My Names," p. 890.

281 a girl named Anna: Roth, *Count Me among the Missing*, p. 204, Roth Papers, Box 1 Folder 10, pp. 113–4.

281 *First Offering* and made him happy: Roth Papers, Box 1 Folder 8, p. 297.

281 acquainted with: Gertzman, "Not Quite Honest," p. 35.

282 "nut poet" and "either a fool or a wild man": JQ to Weaver, July 22, 1922, NYPL.

282 rejection letters: Roth Papers, Box 35 Folder 17.

282 "Of all the writers": Roth to JJ, Feb. 12, 1921, Buffalo, Series XI.

282 "DIJON.—DARANTIERE": My discussion of the physical details from a comparison of the 1927 Shakespeare and Company edition and Samuel Roth's pirated edition at the Harry Ransom Humanities Research Center, University of Texas at Austin. See also "Edition of 'Ulysses' to End Pirating Is Copy of Pirated Book," Yale Joyce, Box 17 Folder 321, unidentified newspaper clipping.

283 Loewinger Brothers: See John Slocum and Herbert Cahoon, *A Bibliography of James Joyce* (New Haven: Yale University Press, 1953).

283 "Sylvia Bitch": Adelaide Roth, *In a Plain Brown Wrapper* (unpublished), Roth Papers, Box 16 Folder 2, p. 28.

283 Roth's perspective: Roth, *Count Me Among the Missing*, Roth Papers, Box 1 Folder 8, pp. 297, 299.

283 in a plain truck: *SC*, pp. 180–81.

283 In October 1929: WHS, Box 1 Folder 8, MS 26, pp. 3–4; "Seize 3,000 Books As 'Indecent' Writing," *NYT*, Oct. 5, 1929, p. 22.

284 a detective was waiting and extradited to Pennsylvania: Roth, *Count Me Among the Missing*, p. 220, Roth Papers, Box 1, pp. 210–22.

284 "right to have": *TWQ* 1, no. 4 (June 1926).

284 *Two Worlds* title: Roth Papers, Box 1 Folder 10, p. 177.

284 one-year scholarship and never graduated: June 13, 2012, email to me from Columbia University's Office of the Registrar.

284 never received a high school degree and School of Journalism: Cerf, *At Random,* pp. 12–14.

285 "the only vehicle": *TWQ* 2, no. 8 (June 1927).

285 books as "Deals": See 1933 Cerf Diaries, Cerf Papers, Box 11.

285 "you heavenly" and telegrams to a woman named Marian: Bennet Cerf Telegrams, Cerf Papers, Box 3 (March-April 1933).

24. TREPONEMA

286 end of the English language: August Suter, "Some Remembrances of Joyce" in Potts, *Portraits of the Artist in Exile*, p. 64.

286 "All the world's in want": JJ, *Finnegans Wake*, p. 278.

286 "Jim is writing": Richard M. Kain, Carola Giedion-Welcker, and Maria Jolas, "An Interview with Carola Giedion-Welcker and Maria Jolas," *JJQ* 11, no. 2 (1974), p. 96.

286 "I make nothing": EP to JJ, Nov. 15, 1926, *EP/JJ*, p. 228.

287 "I do not care much": Weaver to JJ, Feb. 4, 1927, qtd. in Ell, p. 590.

287 "It is possible": JJ to Weaver, Feb. 1, 1927, *SL*, p. 319.

287 capital gift of £12,000: *DMW*, p. 217.

287 gave Joyce £850: Ibid., p. 224.

287 began to divest: Ibid., p. 274.

287 "The truth is that": SB to JJ, April 12, 1927, *LSB*, pp. 319–20.

288 Beach's mother: *SBLG*, p. 260.

288 threw a chair: Shloss, *Lucia Joyce*, pp. 215–6.

288 Beckett: Ibid., p. 189.

288 catatonic: Ibid., p. 219.

288 diagnosed: Ell, p. 651.

288 clairvoyant: JJ to Weaver, Oct. 21, 1934, *LI*, pp. 349–51.

288 "Whatever spark or gift": JJ qtd. in Shloss, p. 7.

288 fur coat: JJ to Weaver, Nov. 11, 1932, *LI*, p. 326.

288   seawater: Ell, p. 662.

288   smuggled her out: Ell, p. 657; Shloss, pp. 232, 235.

288   "Tell him I am": Lucia Joyce qtd. in Shloss, p. 8.

288   helping Nora pack: Stuart Gilbert, *Reflections on James Joyce: Stuart Gilbert's Paris Journal* (Austin: University of Texas Press, 1993), pp. 47–48.

289   Nora was hospitalized: Ell, p. 607; Kevin Sullivan, *Joyce Among the Jesuits* (Westport, Conn.: Greenwood Press, 1983), p. 58; Maddox, *Nora: A Biography*, pp. 246–7.

289   adjoining room: JJ to SJ, Dec. 15, 1928, *LIII*, p. 184.

289   bed next to hers: Ell, p 607.

289   nurses shouting: JJ to Weaver, Dec. 2, 1928, *LI*, 278.

289   bumped into furniture: Adolph Hoffmeister, "Portrait of Joyce" in Potts, *Portraits of the Artist in Exile,* pp. 128–9.

289   milk and sugar: Maddox, *Nora: A Biography*: p. 298.

289   held on to her arm: Jacques Mercanton, "The Hours of James Joyce," in Potts, *Portraits of an Artist in Exile*, p. 251.

289   "I deserve all this": JJ to Weaver, March 11, 1931, *LI*, p. 303.

289   The bacteria can inhabit: William Hinton, *Syphilis and Its Treatment* (New York: Macmillan, 1936), pp. 61–134.

290   *paralysis*: Hoffmeister, "Portrait of Joyce," p. 132. See also Joyce's short story, "The Sisters."

290   affinity for the eyes: T. C. Spoor et al., "Ocular Syphilis: Acute and Chronic," *Journal of Clinical Neuro-Ophthalmology* 3 (1983), pp. 197–203; Curtis Margo and Latif Hamid, "Ocular Syphilis," *Survey of Ophthalmology* 37, no. 3 (Nov.-Dec. 1992), pp. 203–20.

290   conjunctivitis, episcleritis, blepharatis: JJ to Weaver, Sept. 20, 1928, *LI*, p. 266.

290   the most common: Margo and Hamid, "Ocular Syphilis, p. 215.

290   vary dramatically and Only a third: Ibid., p. 205. See also Kathleen Ferris, *James Joyce and the Burden of Disease* (Lexington: University of Kentucky Press, 1995), p. 81.

290   twelve more attacks over the next fourteen years: Weaver to Brewerton, Aug. 30, 1922, BL; JJ to Weaver telegram, Oct. 28, 1922, BL.

290   best to appease Joyce: See, e.g., JJ to Weaver, Feb. 26, 1923, BL.

290   a minor procedure: JJ to Weaver, Oct. 4, 1922, *LII*, p. 67.

290   refused to take a drug called salvarsan: JJ to Weaver, March 18, 1930, *SL*, p. 348; Lucia Joyce to Weaver, April 18, 1930(?), BL. Borsch and his assistant, Dr. Collinson, discussed the possibility of a "cure" for syphilitic eye troubles but exclude "the drug in question" because it "had a bad effect on the optic nerve." That salvarsan is the drug in question is my inference. Lucia Joyce mentioned that the unnamed treatment has bad side effects for both the optic nerve and the retina. The date of her letter is Weaver's estimate.

291   salvarsan's side effects: John Hinchman Stokes, *Modern Clinical Syphilology* (Philadelphia: W. B. Saunders, 1936), p. 705–6; Hinton, *Syphilis,* p. 218. Stokes notes a case of "violent rapidly progressing neuroretinitis," and Hinton (citing Skirball and Thurman) notes optic neuritis in 2.7 percent of patients. See also Allen Brandt and J. W. Estes, *No Magic Bullet: A Social History of Venereal Disease in the United States Since 1880* (New York: Oxford University Press, 1987).

291   less than 125 pounds: JJ to Weaver, April 8, 1928, *LIII*, p. 175.

291   fatigue and "large boil": JJ to Weaver, Sept. 20, 1928, *LI*, p. 266.

291   drug called galyl: Arthur Foerster, "On Galyl, A Substitute for Salvarsan and Neosalvarsan," *Lancet* 186 (Sept. 18, 1915), pp. 645–7; JJ Abraham, "Arseno-Therapy in Syphilis, with More Particular Reference to 'Galyl'," *British Medical Journal* 1, no. 2776 (1914), pp. 582–3; Harold Spence, "Clinical Results of 1,000 Intravenous Injections of Galyl," *Lancet* 186, no. 4815 (Dec. 11, 1915), pp. 1292–4; W. Lee Lewis, "Recent Developments in the Organic Chemistry of Arsenic," *Industrial and Engineering Chemistry* 15, no. 1 (Jan. 1923), pp. 17–19.

291   shots to syphilitic soldiers: L. W. Harrison, "The Treatment of Syphilis," *Quarterly Journal of Medicine* 40 (July 1917), p. 339.

291   arsenic and phosphorus: JJ to Valery Larbaud, Oct. 7, 1928 [date uncertain], *LIII*, p. 182; JJ to Weaver, Oct. 23, 1928, BL; published in *LI*, p. 270. This letter is misdated as Oct. 28 in *LI*.

291 **several injections:** "An Experience of Galyl," *New York Medical Journal*, 104, no. 1–13 (1916), p. 328.

291 **improved a patient's appetite:** See Sir Gilbert Morgan, *Organic Compounds of Arsenic and Antimony* (London: Longmans, Green, and Co., 1918).

291 **greenish-gray powder:** Harrison, "Treatment," p. 339.

291 **every other day for three weeks:** JJ to Valery Larbaud, Oct. 7, 1928 [date uncertain], *LIII*, p. 182; JJ to Weaver, Oct. 23, 1928, BL; published in *LI*, p. 270. In both letters, Joyce indicates he was receiving injections of arsenic and phosphorus for three weeks. Identifying this as galyl is my deduction after consulting available French and American pharmacopeias, national formularies and pharmaceutical dispensaries from the late 1920s. No other medication matches the description of "arsenic and phosphorus" injections, and galyl was used exclusively to treat syphilis. At least two doctors suggest precisely three weeks of injections. See, for example, Emile Brunor, "Notes on a New Organic Arsenic Preparation," *American Medicine* 20 (July 1914), p. 476.

292 **became ravenous:** JJ to Weaver, Oct. 23, 1928, BL; reprinted in *LI*, p. 270.

292 **toffee, cream sweets and Turkish delight:** Maddox, *Nora: A Biography,* p. 243.

292 **Slim:** J. B. Lyons maintains that Joyce suffered from an autoimmune affliction called Reiter's disease. See J. B. Lyons, *James Joyce and Medicine* (Dublin: Dolmen Press, 1973), and his more vehement article, "James Joyce: Steps Towards a Diagnosis," *Journal of the History of Neurosciences* 9, no. 3 (2000), pp. 294–306. As I have written elsewhere, the symptoms, progression and duration of Reiter's simply do not match Joyce's medical history. See my *Harper's* article for a more detailed explanation. After ruling out Reiter's syndrome, the only other reasonable differential diagnosis for Joyce's recurrent anterior uveitis is a rare ailment called Behçet's disease. My rough estimate is that the chances that Joyce had Behçet's are three in a million. Behçet's disease appears to be caused by both genetic and environmental components. See A. Gül, "Behçet's Disease: An Update on the Pathogenesis," *Clinical and Experimental Rheumatology* 19, no. 24 (2001). It most commonly afflicts people from Turkey and countries along the ancient Silk Road to Japan. While the prevalence of Behçet's among Irish people in the early twentieth century is impossible to determine (the disease was first identified in 1937), the prevalence in the United Kingdom in the latter half of the twentieth century is roughly five in one million. See C. C. Zouboulis, "Epidemiological Features of Adamantiades-Behçet's Disease in Germany and in Europe," *Yonsei Medical Journal* 38 (1997), p. 414 (Table 2). The largest Scottish study suggests the prevalence in Scotland is 2.7 per million (fifteen cases in a population of over five million). See J. Jankowski, et al., "Behçet's Syndrome in Scotland," *Postgraduate Medical Journal* 68 (1992), p. 568. Zouboulis suggests that about half of U.K. patients develop ocular symptoms (p. 416), while Chamberlain and Jankowski put the numbers lower. Only one-third of the Scottish patients studied had severe ocular symptoms (exhibiting posterior uveitis, not anterior). See Jankowski, p. 567. Chamberlain's study recorded eight of thirty-two cases with eye problems and only four involving iridocyclitis. See M. A. Chamberlain, "Behçet's Syndrome in 32 Patients in Yorkshire," *Annals of the Rheumatic Diseases* 36 (1997), pp. 491–9, p. 495. Both Chamberlain and Jankowski find that the disease is more prevalent among British women than British men. Taking high numbers in all cases of Behçet's with ocular symptoms, we could roughly (and perhaps generously) estimate Joyce's chances of having Behçet's-indused iritis at three in a million. If Joyce did indeed have Behçet's, he may have been, statistically, the only person in Dublin to have had it (Co. Dublin's population in 1901 was 448,000). Suggesting that Joyce had Behçet's rather than syphilis is like suggesting that a man staggering out of a pub and slurring his speech is suffering from a traumatic brain injury rather than a few too many drinks. It's possible, but exceedingly unlikely.

292 **most common cause:** Parsons, *Diseased Eye*, p. 293.

292 **Quinn and Ezra Pound suspected:** JQ to EP, May 1, 1921 (May 7th addendum), NYPL.

292 **ten thousand cases:** Claude Quétel, *History of Syphilis* (London: Polity Press in Association with Basil Blackwell, 1990), p. 180.

292 **two medical degrees:** Ravin, "Multifaceted Career of Borsch," pp. 1534–7.

292 **medical records:** Ferris, *Joyce and Burden of Disease*, p. 2; Sullivan, "Ocular History of Joyce," p. 414.

293 looking up *glaucoma*: *DMW*, pp. 251, 307.

293 "A young French": JJ to Weaver, March 18, 1930, *SL*, p. 348.

293 both eyes bandaged: See, e.g., George Joyce to Weaver, May 6, 1923, BL; SJ., Trieste Diary, May 23-July 4, 1907, Tulsa, Series 1 Box 142; Nutting to Ellmann, April 26, 1955, Tulsa, Series 1 Box 176.

294 Syphillis "disabled": SJ, Trieste Diary, May 23-July 4, 1907, Tulsa, Series 1 Box 142; Erik Schneider, "A Grievous Distemper: Joyce, and the Rheumatic Fever Episode of 1907," *JJQ* 38, no. 3/4 (Spring-Summer 2001), pp. 456-7.

294 periodic fainting spells: Morgan, *Organic Compounds*, p. 291; Harrison, "Treatment of Syphilis," pp. 311, 314. Morgan notes that low blood pressure (for two to three days after injection) is a side effect of galyl, and Harrison cites low blood pressure and syncope as side effects of other arsenicals.

294 "venereal ill-luck": JJ to SJ, Oct. 4, 1906, *LII*, p. 171.

25. SEARCH AND SEIZURE

296 including a statement of fact: See *Patterson v. Colorado*, 205 U.S. 454 (1907).

296 until 1925: *Gitlow v. New York*, 268 U.S. 652 (1925).

296 "bad tendency": Michael Kent Curtis, *Free Speech, 'The People's Darling Privilege': Struggles for Freedom of Expression in American History* (Durham, N.C.: Duke University Press, 2000), pp. 386-90; Geoffrey Stone, "The Origins of the 'Bad Tendency' Test: Free Speech in Wartime," *Supreme Court Review* (2002), pp. 441-53; and David Rabban, *Free Speech in Its Forgotten Years* (Cambridge: Cambridge University Press, 1997), pp. 533-48.

296 "clear and present danger": *Schenck v. United States*, 249 U.S. 47 (1919).

297 "When men have realized": *Abrams v. United States*, 250 U.S. 616 (1919).

297 son of a Jewish Czech immigrant: Ernst Papers, Box 544.1

297 erratic fortunes: Morris Ernst, *The Best Is Yet* (New York: Harper & Brothers, 1945), pp. 3, 50-51.

297 kept the rejection letter: Ibid., Box 551.4.

298 Supreme Court lamp: Alden Whitman, "Morris Ernst, 'Ulysses' Case Lawyer, Dies," *NYT*, May 23, 1976; and Ernst, *Best Is Yet*, pp. 13-14.

298 American Bar Association: Fred Rodell, "Morris Ernst," *Life*, Feb. 21, 1944, p. 105.

298 the country's greatest asset: Morris Ernst, "The So-Called Marketplace of Thought," *Bill of Rights Review* 2 (1941-42), pp. 86-91.

298 used by entrenched powers: Ernst, *The Best Is Yet*, pp. 112-4.

298 "a pervading influence": Ernst, *To the Pure . . . A Study of Obscenity and the Censor* (New York: Viking Press, 1928), p. 283.

298 "six deadly adjectives": Ibid., pp. vii-x, 282.

299 In 1928, he defended: John M. Craig, "'The Sex Side of Life': The Obscenity Case of Mary Ware Dennett," *Frontiers: A Journal of Women Studies* 15, no. 3 (1995), pp. 145-66.

300 rejected his argument: See *United States v. Dennett*, 39 F. (2d) 564 (1930); *U.S. v. Married Love* 48 F. (2d) 821 (1931); and *U.S. v. Contraception* 51 F. (2d) 525 (1931).

300 approached Sylvia Beach's sister: *UvU*, p. 77.

300 Beach heard rumors: Boske Antheil to SB, June 9, 1931, SBP, Box 129 Folder 3; Adrienne Monnier to Paul Claudel, Dec. 16, 1931, Berg Collection, NYPL; *SBLG*, p. 320.

300 "This would be the grandest": Lindey to Ernst, Aug. 6, 1931, *UvU*, p. 77.

301 gave Beach world rights and free himself from legal fees: *SBLG*, pp. 308-9; Benjamin Howe Connor to JJ, Dec. 16, 1931, Yale Joyce, Box 2 Folder 70.

301 blithely ignored: SBP, Box 167 Folder 9, and *SBLG*, pp. 316-7. Huebsch offered a royalty at JJ's expense. See SBP, Box 166 Folder 3.

301 asking Hemingway: *SBLG*, p. 317.

301 She wanted Joyce: SB to Lawrence Pollinger, June 11, 1931, qtd. in *SBLG*, p. 317.

301 "a modest estimate": SB qtd. in *SBLG*, p. 318.

301 made a counteroffer: *SBLG*, p. 318.

301 a retainer: Ernst to Huebsch, Oct. 21, 1931, *UvU*, pp. 99-100.

301 **Huebsch gave up:** Huebsch to Cerf, Dec. 17, 1931, *UvU*, p. 100.

301 **"first really important":** Cerf, *At Random*, p. 94.

302 **"I don't know just":** Cerf to Ernst, Dec. 22, 1931, *UvU*, p. 101.

302 **"What right do ya":** SB qtd. in *SBLG*, p. 322. (Source: SBP, no box or folder cited)

302 **"But what about":** *SC*, pp. 204–5.

302 **called Joyce:** JJ to Weaver, Dec. 13 and 22, 1932, BL.

302 **signed a contract:** Robert Kastor to JJ telegram, qtd. in JJ to James Pinker, March 25, 1932, BL.

303 **unfriendly feelings:** Ernst to Cerf and Klopfer, April 20, 1960, Ernst Papers, Box 68.4.

303 **5 percent of all trade:** Cerf to Ernst, March 23, 1932, *UvU*, p. 108.

303 **Supreme Court repeatedly affirmed:** See, e.g., *Ex Parte Jackson* 96 U.S. 727 (1878); *Public Clearing House v. Coyne*, 194 U.S. 497 (1904).

303 **Tariff Act:** Tariff Act of 1930 19 USC § 1305 Section 305(a).

304 **classic couldn't be obscene:** Ernst Brief qtd. in *UvU*, p. 256. Ernst cites *U.S. v. Three Packages of Bound, Obscene Books* (1927), the case against John Herrmann's *What Happens*.

304 **judge had barred all:** "Bars Book Experts at Obscenity Trial," *NYT*, Oct. 4, 1927.

304 **tried again:** Craig, "'Sex Side of Life'," p. 152.

304–5 **detailed instructions:** Cerf to Paul Léon, April 19, 1932, *UvU*, p. 119.

305 **SS *Bremen*:** Léon to Cerf, April 27, 1932, *UvU*, p. 129.

305 **firm sent a letter:** Lindey to B. N. Handler (Acting Deputy, Collector of Customs), May 2, 1932, *UvU*, pp. 133–4.

305 **Lindey called:** Lindey to Handler, May 6, 1932, *UvU*, p. 135.

305 **stamping everything** and **"Get out":** Cerf, *At Random*, p. 92.

305 **arrived, safe and sound:** Morris Ernst, "Reflections on the *Ulysses* Trial and Censorship," *JJQ* 3, no. 1 (Fall 1965), pp. 3–11, reprinted in *UvU*, p. 47.

305 **Ernst went *back*:** Ibid., reprinted in *UvU*, p. 47; Morris Ernst and Alan Schwartz, "Four-Letter Words and the Unconscious," *Censorship: The Search for the Obscene* (New York: Macmillan, 1964), reprinted in *UvU*, p. 33.

305 **"I think there's something"** and **"Aha!"** and **"Oh, for God's sake"** and **"I *demand*":** Cerf, *At Random*, pp. 92–93. My italics on *"demand"* and exclamation after "book!"

305–6 **clearly listed the *Bremen*:** Cerf to Paul Léon, April 19, 1932, *UvU*, p. 119.

306 **bulging with papers:** The original seized copy is at the Columbia's Rare Books & Manuscripts library. For a list of enclosures, see *UvU*, p. 131.

306 **"Only a casual glance":** *Heymoolen v. United States*, T.D. 42907, qtd. in *UvU*, p. 144.

306 **"forfeiture, confiscation":** H. C. Stewart, Asst. Collector, to Lindey, May 24, 1932, *UvU*, p. 149.

307 **less than half** and **send scholarly books:** Lindey to Ernst, June 14, 1932, *UvU*, p. 154.

307 **"they want everything":** *Ulysses*, p. 621 (18: 582–95).

307 **"a literary masterpiece"** and **George Medalie:** Coleman paraphrased in Lindey to Ernst, July 23, 1932, *UvU*, p. 157.

307 **"the only way":** Coleman paraphrased in Lindey to Ernst, July 30, 1932, *UvU*, p. 157.

307 **Republican nominee:** "George Zerdin Medalie," *Encyclopaedia Judaica.*, ed. Michael Berenbaum and Fred Skolnik, 2nd ed. (Detroit: Macmillan Reference USA, 2007).

308 **foolish the previous year:** Medalie paraphrased in Ernst to Lindey, Aug. 12, 1932, *UvU*, p. 158.

308 **needed to see them all:** Ernst to Lindey, Sept. 27, 1932, *UvU*, p. 160. That Medalie is stalling is my speculation.

308 **taking *Ulysses* to court:** Ernst to Cerf, Nov. 11, 1932, *UvU*, p. 164.

308 **as soon as possible:** Cerf to Léon, April 19, 1932, *UvU*, p. 119.

308 **flooded with questions:** Lindey to Ernst, Sept. 20, 1932, *UvU*, p. 159.

308 **Warner Brothers:** Cerf to Léon, Oct. 11, 1932, *UvU*, pp. 161–2.

308 **that summer:** Ibid., April 19, 1932, p. 119.

308 **"some time between now and March":** Ernst to Cerf, Nov. 11, 1932, *UvU*, p. 164.

308 **interest would wane:** Cerf paraphrased in Lindey to Ernst, Sept. 20, 1932, *UvU*, p. 159.

308 **Coleman might insist:** Ernst to Cerf, Nov. 11, 1932, *UvU*, p. 164.

308 **performance of purity:** Ernst, *To the Pure*, pp. 5–9.

309 **a signed copy:** Ernst sent Woolsey a signed copy of *To the Pure* two days after the *Married Love* decision. See Ernst to Woolsey, April 8, 1931, Ernst Papers, Box 393.4.

309 *Oxford English Dictionary:* See *United States v. One Obscene Book Entitled "Married Love,"* 48 F. 2d 821, and *United States v. One Book, Entitled "Contraception,"* 51 F. 2d 525 (1931).

309 **"out of the question for months":** Ernst to Lindey, March 20, 1933, *UvU*, p. 175.

309 **generally unfavorable:** Lindey to Ernst, April 20, 1933, *UvU*, p. 177.

309 **"technical reasons":** Lindey to Cerf, May 24, 1933, *UvU*, p. 184.

309 **wasn't the first time:** Lindey to Ernst, June 14, 1932, *UvU*, p. 154.

310 **"It was learned yesterday":** "Ban Upon 'Ulysses' to Be Fought Again," *NYT*, June 24, 1933, qtd. in *UvU*, p. 204.

310 **written it himself:** Ernst, "Reflections on *Ulysses* Trial and Censorship," reprinted *UvU*, p. 47; Roger Baldwin to Ernst, Nov. 1 and Nov. 11, 1929, Ernst Papers, Box 143.16.

310 **Back in February:** Frances Steloff to SB, Feb. 11, 1933, SBP, Box 129 Folder 2.

310 **"We have come to realize":** Lindey to H. C. Stewart, June 1, 1933, *UvU*, p. 189, Lindey's italics.

310 **Coleman felt ambushed:** Lindey to Ernst, June 30, 1933, *UvU*, p. 207. That Coleman found out from the *NYT* article is my speculation.

310 **Three days later, Coleman's office:** Lindey to Ernst, June 27, 1933, *UvU*, p. 207.

310 **"strait-laced Catholic":** Lindey to Ernst, June 6, 1933, *UvU*, p. 202.

310–11 **impatient Judge Coleman** and **recovering from pneumonia** and **August 22:** Lindey to Ernst, July 25, 1933, *UvU*, p. 213.

311 **Pope had inadvertently blessed:** *SBLG*, p. 338.

311 **"a notorious pirate"** and **"Can we write him":** Cerf to Ernst, Oct. 20, 1932, *UvU*, p. 163. The pirate in question was Joseph Meyers, not Samuel Roth.

311 **"*Please send me*":** Black to Cerf, Sept. 26, 1933, Cerf Papers, Box 3.

312 **"*Dear Mr. Black*":** Cerf to Black, Sept. 29, 1933, Cerf Papers, Box 3.

312 **He wrote back:** Black to Cerf, Sept. 26, 1933, Cerf Papers, Box 3.

312 **"There is a growing":** Cerf to Black, Oct. 12, 1933, Cerf Papers, Box 3.

312 **"Also I can assure":** Black to Cerf Oct. 25, 1933, Cerf Papers, Box 3.

26. *THE UNITED STATES OF AMERICA V. ONE BOOK CALLED "ULYSSES"*

313 **lumber up and wore a tie:** Various Woolsey details are taken from Woolsey family photographs, home movies and unpublished documents provided by John Woolsey III. Library details are taken from my visit to Petersham, where the library still stands.

313 **picking blueberries** and **town hall of Prescott:** Forrest Davis, "Ulysses," *New York World-Telegram*, Dec. 13, 1933, qtd. *UvU*, p. 342.

313 **considered it hypocritical** and **bottle of sherry:** Jack Alexander, "Federal Judge," unpublished Woolsey profile, ca. 1938, p. 6.

314 **longest criminal court case:** "Press: A Welcome to *Ulysses*," *Time*, Dec. 18, 1933.

314 **ninety-eight witnesses** and **alumni association:** "109-Day Trial," *Time*, July 17, 1933.

314 **"just about the hardest":** John Woolsey qtd. in "Talk of the Town," *New Yorker*, Jan. 8, 1944.

314 **first few chapters:** Nicholas Atlas to Ernst, Oct. 6, 1933, *UvU*, p. 233.

314 **trove of supplementary** and **already owned:** Lindey to Woolsey, Sept. 12, 1933, *UvU*, p. 226.

314 **legal titles** and **poetry and fiction:** Observed at Woolsey's Petersham library.

314 **Samuel Johnson:** Davis, "Ulysses," reprinted in *UvU*, p. 343.

314 **read them all:** "Talk of the Town," *New Yorker*, Jan. 8, 1944.

314 **He collected:** "A Welcome to *Ulysses*," *Time*, Dec. 18, 1933.

315 **first New World ancestor:** Davis, "Ulysses," reprinted in *UvU*, p. 341; Alexander, "Federal Judge," p. 6.

315 **Yale since 1705:** Alexander, "Federal Judge," p. 7.

315 **He was the descendant:** John Woolsey II, "Family History: The Woolseys," n.d., unpublished; John M. Woolsey file, Yale College Alumni Records.

315 **"The God that holds you":** Jonathan Edwards, "Sinners at the Hands of an Angry God" (1741).

315 "seared his soul" and "the most precious": "Ulysses Case Reaches Court after Ten Years," *New York Herald-Tribune*, Nov. 26, 1933, reprinted in *UvU*, p. 286.

315 "it would be just those": *U.S. v. Kennerley*, 209 F. 119 (1913).

315 "Stately, plump": *Ulysses*, p. 3 (1: 1).

316 "What did each do": Ibid., p. 573 (15: 1032–9).

317 "yes when I lit": Ibid., p. 611 (18: 143–57). The 1922 edition mistakenly moved the first two lines of this quotation ("yes when I lit" until "was going to") to the following page. I quote the corrected Gabler edition.

318 "Ill put on my best": Ibid., p. 641 (18: 1508–16).

318 dark X's like targets: See the seized copy of *Ulysses*, Rare Book & Manuscript Library, Columbia Univ., p. 733.

318 several times: *United States v. One Book Called "Ulysses,"* 5 F.Supp. 182 (1933).

318 journalistic exposé: Alexander, "Federal Judge," p. 8.

319 filled to capacity: "Ulysses Case Reaches Court After 10 Years," reprinted in *UvU*, p. 284.

319 for weeks and suited his taste: *Annual Report of the House Committee, 1932–3*, qtd. in *Publication of the New York Bar Association* 40, no. 5 (Oct. 1985), p. 535.

319 was also Woolsey's chauffeur: John Woolsey, Jr. "Assorted Notes," n.d., unpublished.

319 gold ring: Davis, "Ulysses," reprinted in *UvU*, p. 342.

319–20 "The government can't" and Maggie and etymology: Ernst, "The Censor Marches On," *Best Is Yet*, qtd. in *UvU*, p. 22.

320 "Suppose that a girl" and "I don't think that": "Court Undecided on 'Ulysses' Ban," *NYT*, Nov. 26, 1933, p. 16. *Note:* The trial accounts (from Ernst, *NYT*, *Daily Boston Globe* and *New York Herald-Tribune*) vary slightly from one another, and the sequence of events is difficult to determine. I have combined accounts and coordinated the sequence of statements for narrative purposes.

320 "the present critical point": *U.S. v. Kennerley*, 209 Fed. 119 (1913), qtd. in Defense brief, *UvU*, p. 244.

320 so-called sunsuits: Defense Brief, *UvU*, p. 246.

320 modern classic and "of acknowledged excellence": Ibid., pp. 255–6.

320–21 "Mr. Coleman" and "I should say": "Ulysses Case Reaches Court After Ten Years," reprinted in *UvU*, pp. 286–7. See also "Ruling on 'Obscene' Holds Fate of Book," *Daily Boston Globe*, Nov. 26, 1933, p. A4.

321 "new and startling": Government Brief, qtd. in *UvU*, p. 295.

321 "almost perfect" and "majestic genius": *UvU*, p. 240. The quotations are from Paul Rosenfeld and Rebecca West.

321 "superb" and "classically exquisite": "Ulysses Case Reaches Court After Ten Years," ibid., reprinted in *UvU*, p. 286.

321 "THE FEDERAL": Defense brief, *UvU*, p. 255.

321 "No one would dare attack": "Court Undecided on 'Ulysses' Ban," *NYT*, Nov. 26, 1933, p. 16.

322 "An occasional word": Government brief, *UvU*, pp. 300–3.

322 Clement Wood's *Flesh:* Ibid., pp. 253, 304.

322 "endless blasphemy": Ibid., p. 299.

322 "Ill tighten my bottom well": *Ulysses*, p. 642 (18: 1530–2).

322 "I do not think": "Ulysses Case Reaches Court After Ten Years," ibid., reprinted in *UvU*, pp. 286–7.

322 disgusting: See *U.S. v. Married Love* 48 F. (2d) 821 (1931).

322 skillfully integrated: "Court Undecided on 'Ulysses' Ban," *NYT*, Nov. 26, 1933, p. 16; "Ruling on 'Obscene' Holds Fate of Book," *Daily Boston Globe*, Nov. 26, 1933, p. A4.

323 dragging its feet: Lindey to Ernst, Nov. 6, 1933, *UvU*, p. 279.

323 contact Woolsey personally: Ernst to Woolsey, Nov. 14, 1933, *UvU*, p. 280.

323 "Judge, as to" and didn't win him many friends: Ernst, "Censor Marches On," reprinted in *UvU*, p. 22.

323 "This, your honor": Ernst and Schwartz, "Four-Letter Words," Dec. 13, 1933, reprinted in *UvU*, p. 34.

323   "For example, Mr. Ernst?" and "Oh—": Ernst, "Censor Marches On," reprinted in *UvU*, p. 22.

323   "Counselor, that isn't": Ernst and Schwartz, "Four-Letter Words," Dec. 13, 1933, reprinted in *UvU*, p. 34.

323   nearly an hour: "Ulysses Case Reaches Court After Ten Years," reprinted in *UvU*, p. 284.

323   "led a monastic" and "an austere": Defense Brief, *UvU*, p. 239.

323–24   painstakingly structured and listed dozens and "It is axiomatic": Ibid., pp. 257–260.

323   Random House wasn't: *UvU*, p. 242.

324   "ineluctable modality": *Ulysses*, p. 31 (3: 1–4), qtd. in Defense Brief, *UvU*, p. 260.

324   "Some of it was": "Ruling on 'Obscene' Holds Fate of Book," *Daily Boston Globe*, Nov. 26, 1933, A4.

324   "This isn't an easy case" and lit a cigarette: "Ulysses Case Reaches Court After Ten Years," reprinted in *UvU*, p. 285.

324   ivory holder: Davis, "Ulysses," reprinted *UvU*, p. 342.

324   "Still" and He broke off and "Still, there is that": "Ulysses Case Reaches Court After Ten Years," reprinted in *UvU*, p. 285.

324   *Ill let him know*: *Ulysses*, p. 641.

324   "Did you really" and Ernst had tried: Ernst and Schwartz, "Four-Letter Words," reprinted in *UvU*, p. 34.

325   "Your honor, while arguing" and "I've been worried": Ernst, "Censor Marches On," reprinted in *UvU*, p. 23. I've changed "back of your bench" to "behind your bench."

325   "That, Judge": Ernst, "Reflections on the *Ulysses* Trial and Censorship," qtd. *UvU*, p. 49; "Ulysses Case Reaches Court After Ten Years," reprinted in, *UvU*, p. 285.

325   "a weird epitome": "Ulysses Case Reaches Court After Ten Years," reprinted in *UvU*, p. 286.

325   hornrimmed glasses: *Ulysses*, p. 594 (17.1878).

325   pickers' shacks and suicide: John Woolsey, Jr., "Family History: The Woolseys," n.d., unpublished.

325   from a window: Interview with John Woolsey III, June 15, 2010.

325   "bothered, stirred": "Ulysses Case Reaches Court After Ten Years," reprinted in *UvU*, p. 286.

325   "O that awful deepdown torrent": *Ulysses*, pp. 643–4 (18: 1597–609).

326   "There are passages": "Ulysses Case Reaches Court After Ten Years," reprinted in *UvU*, p. 286. See also Woolsey qtd. in "Talk of the Town," *New Yorker*, Jan. 8, 1944.

326   customary Saturday lunch: John Woolsey, Jr., "Judge John M. Woolsey," *JJQ* 37, no. 3/4 (Spring/Summer 2000), p. 368.

327   Literature Committee: Century Association, *The Century Association Yearbook* (New York: Century Association, 1933), p. 99.

327   Canby and Merrill, Jr.: Lindey to Ernst, Dec. 7, 1933, *UvU*, p. 317.

327   a publisher: John Woolsey, Jr., "Assorted Notes" n.d., unpublished.

327   "puritanic censorship": Henry Canby, "Crazy Literature," *Definitions: Essays in Contemporary Criticism* (New York York: Harcourt, Brace and Company, 1924), p. 111.

327   "obsession with": Henry Canby, "Sex in Fiction," in *Definitions*, p. 87.

327   "somewhat tragic" and "powerful commentary": *United States v. One Book Called "Ulysses,"* 5 F.Supp. 182 (S.D.N.Y 1933).

327   vanity: Interview with Peggy Brooks, Nov. 11, 2009. Brooks may be the last surviving person to have known the judge personally.

327   longhand and revised: Woolsey, Jr., "Judge John M. Woolsey," p. 368.

327   didn't get along: See Gerald Gunther, *Learned Hand: The Man and the Judge* (New York: Oxford University Press, 2011), p. 289. Hand later said Woolsey was "a bit of a show-off" but said he later "came to like [Woolsey]."

328   chimed on the hour and rugs and upholstery: Alexander, "Federal Judge," p. 4; Woolsey family photographs; John Woolsey, Jr., "My Early Life (1916–1930)," n.d., unpublished.

328   a dreary Thanksgiving and "I fear, Sir": Alexander, "Federal Judge," pp. 15–16.

328   an eighteenth-century poem: Woolsey to Ernst, April 4, 1935, Ernst Papers, Box 36.3.

328   dripping razor: "Talk of the Town," *New Yorker*, Jan. 8, 1944. Note: The connection between the two Thanksgivings and their bearing on the passage in the decision cited here is my speculation.

328–29   "Joyce has attempted" and "has been loyal": *United States v. One Book Called "Ulysses*," 5 F.Supp. 182 (S.D.N.Y 1933).

329   a half-blind artist: *UvU*, p. 239.

330   "historic for its authority": "The Press: A Welcome to Ulysses," *Time*, Dec. 18, 1933.

330   "Watchers of the U.S. skies": "Books: *Ulysses* Lands," *Time*, Jan. 29, 1934. Joyce was on the cover of this issue.

330   "Thus one half": JJ to Constantine Curran, Dec. 20, 1933, *LI*, p. 338. JJ's ellipsis.

330   Lucia cut: Ell, p. 667.

330   10:15 and "Go ahead": Harry Hansen, "The First Reader," *New York World-Telegram*, Jan. 25, 1934, qtd. *UvU*, pp. 11–12.

330   Reichl, a PhD: See Martha Scotford, "Ulysses: Fast Track to 1934 Bestseller," *Design Observer*, Dec. 2, 2009 http://observatory.designobserver.com/entry.html?entry=12067.

330   most widely read: Gunther, *Learned Hand*, p. 285. See also Irving Younger, "Ulysses in Court: A Speech," *Classics of the Courtroom: The Litigation Surrounding the First Publication of James Joyce's Novel in the United States*, ed. James McElhaney (Minnetonka: Professional Education Group, 1989).

331   initial printing of ten thousand: Lewis Gannett, "Books and Things," *New York Herald-Tribune*, Dec. 9, 1933, qtd. *UvU*, p. 330.

331   "a really phenomenal figure": Cerf to Léon, Jan. 17, 1934, *UvU*, p. 357.

331   thirty-three thousand: JJ to Weaver, April 24, 1934, *LI*, p. 340.

331   check for $7,500: Cerf, *At Random*, p. 101.

331   fifth highest-selling: Satterfield, *World's Best Books*, p. 140.

331   Roth's edition: "Edition of 'Ulysses' to End Pirating Is Copy of Pirated Book," unidentified newspaper clipping, Yale Joyce, Box 17 Folder 321.

27. THE TABLES OF THE LAW

332   "to arrest developments": BNA, H.O. 144/20071 (Old Ref. # 186.428/60).

332   MacCarthy and "whether we regarded": Ibid. (Old Ref. # 186.428/41).

332   examined Woolsey's decision: Ibid. (Old Ref. # 186.428/43).

333   Martin Conboy, a close friend and St. Gregory: "Conboy Is Named Federal Attorney; Succeeds Medalie," *NYT*, Nov. 26, 1933.

333   regent: "Georgetown Hears Roosevelt Praised," *NYT*, June 13, 1933.

333   Catholic Club: "Conboy Denounces Religion in Politics," *NYT*, April 28, 1924.

333   former lawyer: *UvU*, p. 12.

333   "This is an obscene": "Conboy Recites from Ulysses and Girl Flees," *New York Daily News*, May 18, 1934, reprinted in *UvU*, p. 449.

333   didn't even *exist*: Ernst, *To the Pure*, qtd. in *UvU*, p. 376.

333   Hicklin Rule: Government Brief, *UvU*, p. 374. Conboy cites *Bennett, Rosen* and *Dunlop*, among others.

333   all irrelevant and "A book that is obscene": Government Brief, *UvU*, p. 376.

333   "No reasonable man": Ibid.

333   list of fifty-three: Ibid., p. 374.

333   "unchaste and lustful" and "Are you going": "Ulysses, 'Unchaste and Lustful,' No Lunchtime Story for 3 Judges," *New York World-Telegram*, May 16, 1934, reprinted in *UvU*, p. 444.

333   gasped and walked out: "Conboy Opens U.S. Appeal to Bar *Ulysses*," *New York Herald-Tribune*, May 17, 1934, and "Conboy Recites from *Ulysses* and Girl Flees," *New York Daily News*, May 18, 1934, reprinted in. *UvU*, pp. 447, 449.

334   most publicized obscenity case: Gunther, *Learned Hand*, p. 284.

334   annoyed and "that's a very dangerous" and "give the book" and "could excite": Ibid, pp. 288–9.

334 "Who can doubt": *United States v. One Book Entitled Ulysses by James Joyce*, 72 F.2d 705 (2d Cir. 1934), Manton dissent. The title of the case changed slightly at the Circuit Court.

334 "I cannot say": Augustus Hand qtd. in Gunther, *Learned Hand*, p. 288.

334 "course, blasphemous": *United States v. One Book Entitled Ulysses by James Joyce*, 72 F.2d 705 (2d Cir. 1934).

335 "the admirable way": BNA, H.O. 144/20071 (Old Ref. # 186.428/49).

335 Winkworth and "whether you are able" and "If I can purchase a copy" and "if this limited edition": Ibid. (Old Ref. # 186.428/60).

336 "inadequate" and intent and context and "to take no further action": Ibid. (Old Ref. # 186.428/61).

336 cataracts and an artificial pupil: June 1930 medical report, Berg Collection (reprinted in *LIII*, pp. 197–8); Vogt to JJ, Dec. 1, 1930, *LIII*, p. 208.

336 could not fully see: JJ to SJ, Aug. 3, 1930, *LIII*, p. 48; JJ to Herbert Gorman, Oct. 5, 1930, *LIII*, p. 203.

336 "You would do better": JJ qtd. in Paul Léon, "In Memory of Joyce," in Potts, *Portraits of the Artist in Exile*, p. 289.

EPILOGUE

338 "Say! What was the most": *Ulysses*, p. 438 (15: 3042–3).

338 "utterly without": *Roth v. United States* 354 U.S. 476 (1957).

339 "turgid welter": Edith Wharton to Bernard Berenson, Jan. 6, 1923, in *Letters of Edith Wharton* (New York: Scribner, 1988), p. 461.

339 "a dogged attempt": E. M. Forster, "Fantasy," in *Aspects of the Novel* (New York: Harcourt, Brace, 1927), p. 177.

339 "I feel like shouting": Hart Crane qtd. in Deming, *Joyce Critical Heritage*, p. 284.

339 "some fanatic": Hart Crane, letter, July 27, 1992, in Brom Weber, ed., *The Letter of Hart Crane* (New York: Hermitage House, 1952), p. 95.

339 "Oh, yes": Vladimir Nabokov, *Strong Opinions* (New York: McGraw-Hill, 1973), p. 56.

339 "And there shall be": Henry Miller, *The Henry Miller Reader* (New York: New Directions, 1969), p. 227.

340 two Joyceans: See Danis Rose and John O'Hanlon, *The Lost Notebook: New Evidence on the Genesis of Ulysses/James Joyce* (Edinburgh: Split Pea Press, 1989).

340 missing accent marks: See John Kidd, "Gaelic in the New *Ulysses*," *Irish Literary Supplement* 4, no. 2 (Fall 1985), pp. 41–42.

340 "a divine work of art": Nabokov, *Strong Opinions*, p. 56.

340 one hundred thousand: Julie Brannon, *Who Reads Ulysses?: A Rhetoric of the Joyce Wars and the Common Reader* (New York: Routledge, 2003), p. 11.

341 mock trial: Nola Tully, ed., *Yes I Said Yes I Will Yes* (New York: Vintage Books, 2004), p. 83.

341 Two hundred cities: Ibid., p. 129.

341 "Yo, Bloom": Aaron Beall qtd. in Tully, *Yes I Said Yes*, p. 78.

341 sixteen hours and warns the audience and cab drivers, travel agents: Isaiah Sheffer in Tully, *Yes I Said Yes*, pp. 15, 81; "Bloomsday Marathon on West Side," *NYT*, June 17, 1983.

341 first Bloomsday: Peter Costello and Peter Van de Kamp, *Flann O'Brien: An Illustrated Biography* (London: Bloomsbury, 1987).

341 stop traffic: "Bloomsday in Dublin, a Time for Rejoycing," *NYT*, June 19, 1977.

341 breakfast to ten thousand: Tully, *Yes I Said Yes*, p. 73.

341 crowded onto the stairs: Robert Nicholson, in Tully, *Yes I Said Yes*, p. 75.

341 hats and striped blazers: "They May Not Have Read 'Ulysses,' but It's a Good Excuse for a Highbrow Party," *NYT*, June 17, 2004, p. E3.

341 Dignam's funeral: Nicholson, in Tully, *Yes I Said Yes*, p. 75.

342 "Here's me!": JJ qtd. in *MBK*, p. 7.

SELECTED BIBLIOGRAPHY

Anderson, Margaret C. *My Thirty Years' War: An Autobiography*. New York: Covici, Friede, 1930.

Arstein, W. L. "The Murphy Riots: A Victorian Dilemma." *Victorian Studies* 19 (1975), pp. 51–71.

Bates, Anna Louise. *Weeder in the Garden of the Lord: Anthony Comstock's Life and Career*. Lanham, Md.: University Press of America, 1995.

Beach, Sylvia. *Shakespeare and Company*. Lincoln: University of Nebraska Press, 1991.

—— and Keri Walsh. *The Letters of Sylvia Beach*. New York: Columbia University Press, 2010.

Beard, Charles Heady. *Ophthalmic Surgery: A Treatise on Surgical Operations Pertaining to the Eye and Its Appendages, with Chapters on Para-Operative Technic and Management of Instruments*. Philadelphia: P. Blakiston's Son & Co., 1914.

Broun, Heywood, and Margaret Leech. *Anthony Comstock, Roundsman of the Lord*. New York: A. & C. Boni, 1927.

Budgen, Frank. *James Joyce and the Making of Ulysses*. Bloomington: Indiana University Press, 1960.

C.B. *The Confessional Unmasked: Showing the Depravity of the Roman Priesthood, the Iniquity of the Confessional and the Questions Put to Females in Confession*. Microfilm. Protestant Electoral Union, 1867.

Cerf, Bennett. *At Random: The Reminiscences of Bennett Cerf*. New York: Random House, 1977.

Clarke, Bruce. "Dora Marsden and Ezra Pound: *The New Freewoman* and 'the Serious Artist.'" *Contemporary Literature* 33, no. 1 (Spring 1992), pp. 91–112.

Colum, Mary Maguire, and Padraic Colum. *Our Friend James Joyce*. Garden City, N.Y.: Doubleday, 1958.

Cullinan, Gerald. *The Post Office Department*. New York: F. A. Praeger, 1968.

Dardis, Tom. *Firebrand: The Life of Horace Liveright*. New York: Random House, 1995.

Deming, Robert H. *James Joyce: The Critical Heritage*. 2 vols. London: Routledge & K. Paul, 1970.

Eliot, T. S. *Selected Prose of T. S. Eliot*. New York: Harcourt Brace Jovanovich, 1975.

Ellmann, Richard. *James Joyce*. Rev. ed. New York: Oxford University Press, 1982.

Fitch, Noël Riley. *Sylvia Beach and the Lost Generation: A History of Literary Paris in the Twenties and Thirties.* New York: Norton, 1983.

Fuchs, Ernst. *Text-Book of Ophthalmology.* Philadelphia: Lippincott, 1917.

Garner, Les. *A Brave and Beautiful Spirit: Dora Marsden, 1882–1960.* Aldershot: Avebury, 1990.

Gertzman, Jay. "Not Quite Honest: Samuel Roth's 'Unauthorized' *Ulysses* and the 1927 International Protest." *Joyce Studies Annual* 2009 (2009), pp. 34–66.

Groden, Michael. *Ulysses in Progress.* Princeton: Princeton University Press, 1977.

Hamalian, Leo. "Nobody Knows My Names: Samuel Roth and the Underside of American Letters." *Journal of Modern Literature* 3 (1974), pp. 889–921.

Heap, Jane, and Florence Reynolds. *Dear New York: Tiny Heart: The Letters of Jane Heap and Florence Reynolds.* Edited by Holly A. Baggett. New York University Press, 2000.

Hemingway, Ernest. *A Moveable Feast.* New York: Scribner, 1992.

Jackson, Robert, and Sir Archibald Bodkin. *Case for the Prosecution: A Biography of Sir Archibald Bodkin, Director of Public Prosecutions, 1920–1930.* London: A. Barker, 1962.

Joyce, James. *Critical Writings.* Edited by Ellsworth Mason and Richard Ellmann. London: Faber and Faber, 1959.

——. *Dubliners.* New York: Viking Press, 1962.

——. *James Joyce's Letters to Sylvia Beach, 1921–1940.* Edited by Melissa Banta and Oscar A. Silverman. Bloomington: Indiana University Press, 1987.

——. *Letters of James Joyce.* 3 vols. London: Faber and Faber, 1957–1966.

——. *Poems and Shorter Writings: Including Epiphanies, Giacomo Joyce, and 'A Portrait of the Artist.'* Edited by Richard Ellmann, A. Walton Litz, and John Whittier-Ferguson. New York: Faber and Faber, 1991.

——. *A Portrait of the Artist as a Young Man: Text, Criticism, and Notes.* Edited by Chester G. Anderson. New York: Viking, 1968.

——. *Selected Letters of James Joyce.* Edited by Richard Ellmann. New York: Viking Press, 1975.

——. *Stephen Hero.* New York: New Directions, 1963.

——. *Ulysses.* Edited by Hans Walter Gabler, with Wolfhard Steppe, Claus Melchior, and Michael Groden. New York: Vintage Books, 1993.

Joyce, Stanislaus. *My Brother's Keeper.* Cambridge: Da Capo Press, 2003.

—— and George Harris Healey. *The Complete Dublin Diary of Stanislaus Joyce.* Dublin: Anna Livia Press, 1994.

Leavis, F. R. "Freedom to Read." *Times Literary Supplement*, May 3, 1963, p. 325.

Lidderdale, Jane, and Mary Nicholson. *Dear Miss Weaver: Harriet Shaw Weaver, 1876–1961.* London: Faber and Faber, 1970.

Maddox, Brenda. *Nora: A Biography of Nora Joyce.* Boston: Houghton Mifflin, 1988.

McAlmon, Robert. *Being Geniuses Together, 1920–1930.* Baltimore: Johns Hopkins University Press, 1997.

McCourt, John. *The Years of Bloom: James Joyce in Trieste, 1904–1920.* Madison: University of Wisconsin Press, 2000.

Morrison, Mark. "Marketing British Modernism: *The Egoist* and Counter-Public Spheres." *Twentieth Century Literature* 43, no. 4 (Winter 1997), pp. 439–69.

Moscato, Michael, and Leslie LeBlanc. *The United States of America v. One Book Entitled "Ulysses" by James Joyce: Documents and Commentary: A 50-Year Retrospective.* Frederick, Md.: University Publications of America, 1984.

O'Connor, Ulick, ed. *The Joyce We Knew.* Cork: Mercier Press, 1967.

Potts, Willard, ed. *Portraits of the Artist in Exile: Recollections of James Joyce by Europeans.* Seattle: University of Washington Press, 1979.

Pound, Ezra. *Early Writings: Poems and Prose.* Edited by Ira B. Nadel. New York: Penguin Books, 2005.

——. *Pound/The Little Review: The Letters of Ezra Pound to Margaret Anderson: The Little Review Correspondence.* Edited by Thomas L. Scott, Melvin J. Friedman, and Jackson R. Bryer. New York: New Directions, 1988.

——. *Pound/Joyce: The Letters of Ezra Pound to James Joyce, with Pound's Essays on Joyce.* Edited by Forrest Read. New York: New Directions, 1967.

——. *The Selected Letters of Ezra Pound to John Quinn, 1915–1924.* Edited by Timothy Materer. Durham: Duke University Press, 1991.

Reid, B. L. *The Man from New York: John Quinn and His Friends.* New York: Oxford University Press, 1968.

Reynolds, Michael S. *Hemingway: The Paris Years.* Oxford: Blackwell, 1989.

Roberts, M.J.D. "Morals, Art, and the Law: The Passing of the Obscene Publicans Act, 1857." *Victorian Studies* 28, no. 4 (Summer 1985), pp. 609–29.

Satterfield, Jay. *The World's Best Books: Taste, Culture, and the Modern Library.* Amherst: University of Massachusetts Press, 2002.

Spoo, Robert. *Without Copyrights: Piracy, Publishing and the Public Doman.* New York: Oxford University Press, 2013.

Sumner, John. "The Truth about 'Literary Lynching.'" *Dial* 71 (July 1921), pp. 63–68.

Thacker, Andrew. "Dora Marsden and *The Egoist*: 'Our War Is with Words'." *Twentieth Century Literature* 36, no. 2 (1993), pp. 179–96.

Tully, Nola, ed. *Yes I Said Yes I Will Yes: A Celebration of James Joyce, Ulysses, and 100 Years of Bloomsday.* New York: Vintage Books, 2004.

Vanderham, Paul. *James Joyce and Censorship: The Trials of Ulysses.* New York: New York University Press, 1998.

Wees, William C. *Vorticism and the English Avant-Garde.* Toronto: University of Toronto Press, 1972.

Wood, Casey A. *A System of Ophthalmic Therapeutics; Being a Complete Work on the Non-Operative Treatment, Including the Prophylaxis, of Diseases of the Eye.* Chicago: Cleveland Press, 1909.

Woolf, Virginia. *The Diary of Virginia Woolf.* Vols. 1–5. Edited by Anne Olivier Bell and Andrew McNeillie. London: Hogarth Press, 1977–84.

——. *The Essays of Virginia Woolf.* Edited by Andrew McNeillie. London: Hogarth Press, 1988.

——. *The Letters of Virginia Woolf,* Vol. 2, *1912–1922.* Edited by Nigel Nicolson and Joanne Trautmann. London: Hogarth Press, 1976.

INDEX

CREDITS

———

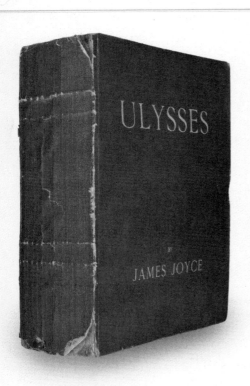